ANITBEET PRODUCTIONS PRESENTS

A Thug's

Redemption

By Yani

When Jamal decides to take matters into his own hands by avenging his best friend's murder, he is forced into the street life, forever in debt to his cousin Samir, one of Philadelphia's biggest drug lords. After finding love, separating himself from the game and turning his life around, fate comes into play when a desperate act by his younger brother Shawn, brings back the haunting night from Jamal's past. Secrets are revealed and Jamal is forced back into the street life to save his brother, as well as himself. In this story about friendship, love and the dangers of North Philly streets, Jamal will soon learn that mistakes are hard to clean up and will cost him dearly in the end.

A Thug's Redemption

By Yani

Published by Anitbeet Productions

Copyright © 2011 by Yani

This book is a work of fiction. Names, characters, places and incidents are products of the author's imagination or are used Fictitiously. Any resemblance to actual events or locales or persons, living or dead, is entirely coincidental

All rights reserved, including the right to reproduce this book or portions thereof in any form whatsoever.

ISBN **978-0-615-64058-7**

Printed in the U.S.A.

DEDICATION

This book is dedicated to the memory of friends and family who were lost to the many Jamals, Khalils and Samirs in the world: Rodney Brown, Raheem Solomon, Saleem Dunmore, Jamil Dunmore, Raheem Dunmore, Faheem Thomas-Childs, Michael Blackshear, Bashir Shackleford, Paris Grant, Garrick Sanders, Tovoyia Owens, Linwood Bowser, Chris Spence, Donnie Skipworth, Andre Cain, Renaldo Jackson (Scooter), Juanita Martinez, Damien Batson. R.I.P to all of you. You're gone but surely never forgotten

ACKNOWLEDGMENTS

Thank you to all of my friends who stayed on top of me as I created this story. If any names are left out, I apologize as it was not intentional. Taherrah Prophet, Shekia Ceaser, Dana Banks, Ernestine Lambert, Krystal Garvin, Jasmine Anosika, Brione Manson, Tyisha Quattlebaum, Jaszmine James-Banks, Ezekiel Goodwin and Christopher Goodwin. A special thank you goes to my mother Betty Bunn, who almost threw this book in the trash when I was hand writing it because of the profanity that was in it. Thanks for giving me a chance to express myself. This story definitely needed to be told. And a special thank you to those who thought I would not complete it or see it through to publication.

i

PROLOGUE
TRAGEDY STRIKES

It began on one of July's hottest days during the summer of 1998 in North Philadelphia. Jamal, who was 15 at the time, and his 13 year old brother Shawn, were with their best friend Raheem, waiting for the fourth member of their battling crew on the corner of their usual hang out, 26th and Bailey Streets. Maurice was always late, and even though it was agreed amongst the four of them to meet, that day was no exception because he was late again.

"Damn, where is this nigga?" Jamal asked as he looked up the street to see if Maurice was coming.

"I know, man. He talked all of that trash about how he was gonna drop some crazy bars on me and he ain't even here," Shawn added as he leaned into the wall.

"He's probably with Ashley getting it in," Raheem laughed as he popped some cheese curls into his mouth. "I heard that she gives crazy brain to Mar." He and his friends burst out laughing.

"Here he comes now," Shawn said after spotting Maurice coming across the street.

Maurice greeted his friends with handshakes and pounds. "What's up, y'all?"

"You're late, little nigga," Jamal scolded him.

"I know, Mar. Where were you?" Raheem asked with a slight grin on his face. He was the jokester of the group; a medium height kid with thick and curly hair, golden brown skin and dark eyes. No matter what was going on, he always had a joke and kept the people surrounding him laughing.

Maurice returned the same look. "None of your business, youngin." He then turned to Shawn. "You ready for me to bust your ass again?"

Shawn sucked his teeth and frowned at Maurice. "You stay talking shit. It's cool though. I have something for your ass."

Their friends became hype and gathered around as they knew it was about to go down. It was known throughout the neighborhood that this was their corner to battle on. Most days, it was like being in Bed Stuy when Biggie Smalls free-styled. When Jamal and company came through the spot, the excitement was soon to follow.

"Okay, let me see what you got," Maurice replied.

"Do the beat from Busta Rhymes' *Dangerous*," Shawn told Raheem.

Yani

Raheem balled up his bag of cheese curls and took a drink from his bottle of Hawaiian Punch to rinse his mouth out. He started the beat as they huddled around with Shawn and Maurice bobbing their heads.

The battle started and immediately everyone became hype over Shawn's hot lyrics. Lyrically, Shawn was the bomb and everyone knew it. The metaphors he used and the way his rhymes flowed together, everyone just knew that it would only be a matter of time before somebody signed him. If basketball wasn't his heart and soul, he might have taken his skill more seriously.

Though he was the younger brother of Jamal, he stood slightly taller and was light-skinned. His hair was extremely dark and wavy, almost appearing jet black when the sun hit it. His eyes were small and made him appear sleepy at times but the neighborhood girls adored him despite the slight gap between his front two teeth. Shawn had an athletic build and was slightly muscular. He was the quiet one of the bunch. He and his older brother Jamal were like night and day.

At the end of his rap, everyone gave Shawn handshakes and pounds. Before Maurice had a chance to get his freestyle in, an unknown bystander stepped over to Shawn.

"Yo, that shit was hot. I'm trying to battle you, so what's up?" the guy asked. He appeared rough and rugged; a tall and skinny individual with a rusty brown skin complexion which resembled an old penny in need of some shining. His attire consisted of worn down, dirty Timberland boots, faded, black Guess jean shorts that almost appeared gray, and a knock off Polo shirt. He was also over-due for a hair-cut.

Shawn and his friends looked at each other and then looked at this clown as if he had lost his mind.

"Who are you?" Jamal retorted as he stared at the individual in disgust after peeping the way he looked.

"I'm Khalil, who the fuck is you?" Khalil replied back in the same tone once he detected Jamal's hostility.

Jamal made a move towards Khalil as if he was going to break his neck. "Nigga, I will put you on your fucking back...!"

Shawn and his friends grabbed Jamal before anything could jump off. He then cut his eyes at Khalil. "It's cool. It's kinda like a private thing anyway."

Khalil looked him over as if he were trash. "What the fuck are you talking about? This ain't your corner. Don't let that mediocre shit you spit get your head big. I just wanted to battle you right quick."

Maurice and Raheem looked at each other and then looked at Shawn. They wanted to see how he was going to react. He had definitely been challenged.

"Yo, you're not going to talk to my baby brother like that. If you wanna battle, then that's what's up. But don't let your mouth get you fucked up out here, for real." Jamal had a hot temper and was ready to throw hands whenever and with whomever. He was the total opposite of Shawn personality wise; loud, rowdy and fearless. Jamal was a little darker than Shawn with a honey brown complexion and also had a medium build. He had a scar on his left cheek from an accident as a child when he fell from a tree. His eyes held the same sleepy appearance as Shawn's did, and he kept his hair close cut and wavy also. He was slightly bow legged and always walked with a lean, which gave him the look of a miniature pimp. No matter what was going on, Jamal stayed with a straight face not wanting to give anyone the impression that they could ever catch him "slipping". To this day, he had yet to lose a fight and was waiting for Khalil to give him a reason to run up in his mouth.

"Whatever," Khalil replied slightly rattled by Jamal's demeanor. "Are you battling or what? What's up?"

"Alright, you can go first," Shawn replied.

Raheem started another beat and everyone began bobbing their heads again. Khalil started off pretty good, but then towards the middle of his free-style and all the way through to the end, it turned into a complete joke. When it was finally over, Shawn gave him his props anyway. He then told Raheem to do the beat to DMX's *Ruff Ryder's Anthem*. Already having the most of his free-style in order from the moment that Khalil opened his mouth, Shawn began to drop bombs on him from start to finish. He embarrassed the hell out of him; clowning him from his needs of a haircut, all the way down to his "butt naked" Timberland boots.

The crowd was ecstatic once again. Jamal was laughing extra hard in Khalil's face making him look even more stupid.

"That was hot," Khalil painfully admitted. "You wanna go again?" he asked hoping to redeem himself.

"Naw, it's cool. I'll catch you another time," Shawn replied not really in the mood to embarrass him again. He turned back to his brother and friends.

Khalil felt slighted. "Oh, so now you're bitching up on me? Oh you're corny as shit, nigga. That shit was lame anyway."

Jamal stepped to Khalil and got all the way in his face. "Yo dawg, what the fuck did I just tell you? You're about to get your ass whipped out this camp."

"You better get the fuck out my face with that tough Tony shit, nigga you don't know me like that." Khalil made the biggest mistake of pushing Jamal. Jamal reacted on instinct and punched Khalil square in his mouth, busting his lip. Khalil touched the blood that poured from his lip and then threw his hands up. Jamal was ready. He hadn't given out a good ass whipping in a while. They began fighting with Jamal whipping Khalil's ass like he stole something causing an even bigger crowd to come around.

The owner of the store heard the commotion and came outside waving his .40 caliber pistol in the air.

"Get your little asses from in front of my damn store making all of this ruckus. I told y'all before about the dumb shit!!" Old man Bob hollered. The bystanders, including Shawn and Jamal and their friends, scattered like roaches.

Once they were safely around the corner, Jamal and his friends stopped to catch their breath. They began to cut through the Johnson Homes Projects.

Maurice burst out laughing. "Yo, you played the shit outta that nigga, Shawn."

His friends laughed with him. "I know, right? That shit was comical," Raheem chimed in.

"That's what his little bitch-ass gets for coming to our corner talking shit," Jamal replied as he rubbed his knuckles which were sore from punching so hard. Just as they were getting ready to cut through the heart of the projects, they heard a young girl screaming that somebody had a gun. They all turned to see what the fuss was about and saw Khalil coming towards them holding a 9mm with murder in his eyes. Basic instinct told them to run like hell, and they all did.

"Split up!" Jamal yelled as he pushed his brother in one direction and ran in another. Maurice ran with Shawn, and Raheem ran with Jamal. Coming to what seemed like a dead end, Jamal and Raheem began to scale a fence to get out, not wanting to back track.

Jamal jumped over first, landing on his feet before falling to the ground. Raheem was getting ready to jump over when his pants leg got caught on the fence.

"Come on!" Jamal yelled, not wanting to leave his friend behind.

"I'm stuck!" Raheem yelled back. "My fucking leg is stuck." Raheem panicked as he tried to free himself. Jamal was about to climb back onto the fence to help Raheem when Khalil appeared from around the corner. He aimed his gun at Raheem.

"NO!!!" Jamal screamed as the gun went off. The bullet hit Raheem in his chest and knocked him from the fence and onto Jamal. Scared, Khalil fled the scene.

Jamal tried to sit up from under the weight of Raheem and saw blood on his hands. "Raheem! Raheem!" he yelled.

He pulled his friend into his lap and held him. Raheem looked up at him with wide eyes. Jamal rocked him, telling him to hold on before screaming for help. Tears poured out of his eyes with the taste of salt from them getting into his mouth as he talked to Raheem telling him to hold on because help was on the way. Even if the ambulance had made it in time, Raheem didn't have a chance. He was losing blood too fast. He frowned in pain as he touched the gold chain around his neck that displayed his name.

A THUG'S REDEMPTION

Jamal heard him mumble something and leaned closer. He faintly heard Raheem murmur Deisha's name, his girlfriend at the time whom he cared about more than anything in the world.

"I got you, homie. I got you. Don't worry it's gonna be alright." He looked up in the sky and screamed for help again as loud as he could as he rocked Raheem in his arms. But when he looked back down at Raheem, he knew he was looking into his best friend's dead eyes.

Shawn and Maurice along with others ran around the corner and stopped on the other side of the fence. They both looked down at Raheem and Jamal not wanting to believe what their eyes were seeing. A crowd had gathered by the time the ambulance finally arrived and they had to push through to get to Jamal and Raheem. Jamal laid Raheem on the ground and pulled the chain from around his friend's neck and clenched his fist around it. A sheet was placed over Raheem just as his girlfriend Deisha ran around the corner. She also pushed through the crowd.

"Where is he? Where's Raheem?" she shrieked, not wanting to believe the story that had spread so quickly. Shawn and Maurice tried to grab her to calm her down. Jamal put his fists to his face praying that this was a bad dream. He leaned over with his hands on his knees trying to get in air as it felt as though all of the oxygen in the world had been taken away. Deisha came over to him and he stood up. His shirt and his jeans had Raheem's blood on them and she looked horrified. How could he tell her that her boyfriend was killed because of him?

"Jamal, where is Raheem?" Deisha asked again. "What happened?!"

Jamal grabbed her hand and put Raheem's chain in it. The blood from it got onto her hands. Deisha looked down at it and shook her head.

"No Jamal. No!" she whined and sobbed. He put his arm around her and briefly told her what happened through his own sobs.

"He was stuck to the gate and I was trying to get him off and the dude came out of nowhere and shot him. It happened so fast."

Deisha snatched away from him and looked at Jamal with fire in her eyes. "Are you kidding me? ARE YOU KIDDING ME?? He was looking for you! He was coming after you and now my boyfriend is dead because of you! Because you can't walk away from a fucking fight!" Deisha started swinging on Jamal, hitting him in his chest, screaming and yelling before Maurice was able to get her off of him and pull her away. Jamal closed his eyes still hearing her screams and still seeing Raheem falling from the fence and into him after being shot, and then seeing his lifeless eyes looking up at him. Those images flooded his vision all at once. Jamal swore the shit wasn't over. There was going to be hell to pay. He promised that no later than a week after they buried Raheem, Khalil's family would be burying him too.

Jamal went to his cousin and told him everything that happened. Samir was one of the biggest drug dealers in Philadelphia and had connections with Russians, drug territories in North Philly, Germantown, Nicetown, Olney, West Oak Lane and even parts of West Philly. He stood a little over six feet tall with skin color matching a smooth, Hershey candy bar. His eye brows were thick and bushy with eye lashes that accentuated his pearly, dark eyes. He wore his hair in dreads pulled back into a pony-tail that hung just above his shoulders. Samir had a striking presence and was feared by every other nickel and dime dealer in the city. Either you worked for Samir or your ass got worked and with the police connections that he had, he was damn near untouchable. Nobody dared to fuck with him.

Fucking with Samir was bad for your health.

Jamal told Samir what his intentions were and was adamant in his need for revenge for his friend Raheem. He was willing to do whatever he had to do to make sure Khalil didn't live to see another day, even if it meant losing his own life. Raheem wasn't just his best friend, but like another brother to him as well and every night that passed after his death, Jamal was haunted by the events that transpired that day.

Samir was happy to oblige Jamal. He always knew Jamal was a rider and had the perfect mentality to run the city beside him with just a little grooming and schooling about the drug game. Samir knew having a soldier like Jamal by his side they would be unstoppable once Jamal was old enough. There was no need to bargain or reason with him. He had already decided on a sentence for Khalil. Death: Street Justice Style. So Samir agreed to help Jamal carry out his revenge knowing that would be a way to initiate Jamal into the drug game. He had enough police connections to make sure that Jamal didn't get caught.

The date was set for the night before Raheem's funeral. During the day, Samir's cronies threw bricks and rocks at the street lights to cause a black-out once the sun set. Not realizing what was going on, the neighborhood kids began to join in thinking it was all fun and games.

Once the sun set, everything was in order. Samir had two .44 caliber Smiths and Wessons, a .44 Magnum, a sawed off shot gun, two Glock 9s and a Desert Eagle. If Khalil wasn't alone, whoever was with him was about to catch a bad one.

They had already staked out Khalil's hangout. They weren't surprised that he was sitting outside with some of his homies, smoking blunts, getting high out of their minds, and talking about getting money.

"They're going to have a closed casket for all of those pussies," one of the guys said as he loaded a clip into his gun.

"Mark-ass niggas think this shit is a game. Getting money? Oh you niggas won't be getting shit after tonight. Believe that," another guy replied as he tossed a gun and a clip to Jamal. Jamal had been silent the entire night. He put a pair of black gloves on and held the gun in one hand and the clip in the other. He looked at them both feeling unsure about what he was getting ready to do.

A THUG'S REDEMPTION

Samir noticed the look on his face. "Jamal, are you cool?" he asked his little cousin. Jamal nodded his head slowly. "Are you sure? Because if you're having second thoughts about this, just say the word and we'll take you home and do this without you."

Jamal thought for a second. The images of Raheem falling from the gate and dying in his arms sealed Khalil's fate. He slammed the clip into the gun and cocked it. "No. I want this muthafucka."

"Let's do this shit," the driver of the car said. He started the engine and they slowly crept down the street towards Khalil and his crew. They were still smoking, talking and laughing, unaware of the untimely demise they were about to meet.

One of the guys noticed the black squatter creeping up on them. "Yo Lil, who's that?" he asked, letting his eyes do the pointing to the car.

Khalil squinted, his vision impaired by his high. When he noticed the Black Death Mobile, he dropped his blunt and yelled for his friends to run.

They darted up the street as the car screeched and then sped after them. Jamal shot at Khalil a few times but missed. After hitting Khalil's two friends and seeing them down but not moving, Samir aimed at Khalil and shot him in his back, putting him down.

"Stop the car!" Jamal said, wanting to finish it.

"What?" the driver of the car asked. He was ready to get the hell out of dodge before someone called the cops.

"Stop the fucking car!" Jamal yelled, almost in tears.

"Stop the car," Samir instructed.

The driver stopped the car and Jamal jumped out, cocking his gun. He walked back to Khalil and kicked him in his ribs, causing him to yelp like a puppy. He then used his foot to turn him over on his back.

"Turn the fuck over, pussy!" Jamal seethed through clenched teeth, shaking tremendously from adrenaline and anger.

"This shit ain't even cool! I don't even know you, nigga! What the fuck are you doing?" Khalil piped after he turned over, not recognizing Jamal.

"You killed my fucking homie and now you're acting like you don't know me, bitch!" Jamal growled. He aimed the gun at Khalil's face. Khalil looked at Jamal wide eyed, finally recognizing him. Before getting the chance to plead his case, Jamal silenced him forever with four shots to his face and neck. He looked at his dismembered victim and then up at the sky, silently telling Raheem that he could rest now.

Samir and company sped up to Jamal. "Jamal, come on nigga. Come the fuck on! Get in the fucking car nigga, let's go!!" His cousin yelled at him.

Jamal jumped inside of the car and they sped off into the darkness. He had his revenge and now it was over, or so he thought. Little did Jamal know, this was just the beginning and would be one mistake that would come back to bite him in his ass, costing him more than he was willing to spend.

CHAPTER 1
GETTING HOOKED UP

Over two years have passed since the murders of Raheem and Khalil. Although the streets were talking, there wasn't enough concrete evidence to put Jamal away for the murder of Khalil. Samir saw to that, thanks to his police connections. Jamal also tucked the gun away safely never to really look at it again.

Jamal did his best to keep up on his end of the bargain. He began selling drugs for Samir, only to get busted less than a year later. His case was thrown out due to a technicality, thanks to Samir and his friends at the Round House. Trouble still seemed to follow him no matter where he went, and he ended up being arrested several times for being a passenger in a stolen car, fighting, and just being at the wrong place at the wrong time. His popularity grew with the police who weren't on the take. Sometimes they would see him on the street and speak to him as if he were one of their old war buddies. As a precaution and due to Jamal's probation officer, Samir removed Jamal from the drug game until the heat died down.

Somehow, Deisha and Maurice began dating. She still showed her loyalty to Raheem by wearing his chain, but at the time, Maurice had her heart. She was walking down the street one breezy October afternoon with her two best friends, Chanda and Tamera. She was trying to talk Tamera out of making what she felt as though would be the biggest mistake of her life, which was hooking up with Jamal. Deisha was like a leader when it came to her best friends, stepping in as a mother figure and in some cases, over stepping her boundaries. She felt as though with all of the horrible things she had witnessed with her mother being a drug addict and her boyfriend being killed so young, that she could be their voice of reason.

"Come on, Tammy. You can't be serious. Of all people, Jamal?" Deisha cringed at the thought of her best friend hooking up with her worst enemy. After two years, Deisha was still blaming Jamal for Raheem's murder.

"Would you get off of it? Let me do me and mind your business," Tamera replied, becoming utterly annoyed.

"What could you possibly see in him?" Deisha asked.

"He's smart, funny, cute, and cool to talk to," Tamera explained.

"He's a fucking thug!" Deisha exclaimed.

Chanda burst out laughing. "Deisha, stop."

"She needs to." Tamera rolled her eyes.

"I'm serious," Deisha continued. "Every time you turn around, he has his ass in something."

"Something like what?" Tamera asked, giving Deisha the screw face.

"Hmm, let's see. He's forever getting locked up. I'm surprised his ass ain't in jail right now." Chanda snickered. She covered her mouth when she saw Tamera giving her the evil eye. "Plus, I heard that he shot at Lucky not that long ago."

"Yeah, I heard about that shit, too." Chanda chimed in.

"That's because Lucky tried to rob their damn house," Tamera explained.

"Tammy, Jamal has changed. He is really bad news," Chanda told her.

"Bad news ain't the word. Every time you turn around, his ass is in something. And he has a funny way of dragging others down with him," Deisha stated.

"Yeah, like Maurice," Tamera giggled.

Deisha glared at her. "Maurice does not get caught up in the shit that Jamal gets into," she replied defensively.

"Whatever. Y'all really do need to mind y'all own business."

"We're just looking out for you, Tammy. I mean, Deisha does have a point. Look at all the things that he's been getting into. And let's not forget what he did to Khalil," Chanda stated.

Deisha swallowed back her soda and said as she waved her hand in the air, "Now that's one thing that I would personally thank him for."

"That was just a rumor. I am sick of y'all always telling me who I can and cannot talk to like y'all are my mother or something. Y'all track record ain't that hot either. Deisha, you can barely keep up with your man because he's forever sniffing around Jamal. And Chanda…" Tamera said as she looked her friend up and down distastefully. "You don't even have a man."

Chanda was laughing until her name was put into it. She rolled her eyes at Tamera and said, "Whatever. I'm working on that now."

"Yeah, leave Chanda alone, because from what I hear, Shawn likes her." Deisha said, teasing.

"Shawn!" Chanda piped.

"Shawn Williams? Basketball Shawn?" Tamera asked in disbelief.

"Yup," Deisha smiled as she nodded her head.

"That can't be right." Chanda replied. "Myisha told me during the summertime that Shawn wasn't worried about any girls because all he was worried about was basketball and getting into Temple." Chanda replied, running down the information that she pumped from one of the cheerleaders.

"Yeah well, that ain't what he told me," Deisha replied.

"What did he tell you?" Chanda asked hesitantly. She was afraid to ask. Chanda had a crush on Shawn for the longest time but could never bring herself to tell him because they had been friends for so long.

"I asked him if he knew that you liked him and he said yeah."

Chanda groaned. "Why did you do that, Deisha?"

"Because I got tired of hearing about him all of the time. You were always about to drool on yourself whenever he came around."

Chanda covered her face. "Oh my God! What else did he say? How come he never said anything to me?"

"I don't know. He just said he figured you liked him but wanted you to say something." Deisha turned her attention back to Tamera. "Now back to you, Ms. Harrison. You think you're grown now. I hope you know what the hell you're getting into."

"Oh stop it. I know what I'm doing. Jamal just needs a good influence. Maybe I can be that for him."

"He needs more than a damn influence," Deisha mumbled.

"Whatever. You just worry about your own man. Speaking of which, here comes your estranged boyfriend now, Ms. Know-it-all," Tamera laughed. "Hey, Maurice."

"What's up, Tammy? What's up, Chanda?" He gave Deisha a kiss.

"What's good, Mar-Mar?" Chanda spoke back.

"Hey, have you seen Jamal around?" Tamera asked, getting ready to put her plan into action.

"Yeah, he's around 23rd and Turner Street shooting craps with Man-Man and some other dudes," Maurice told her.

"Why am I not surprised?" Deisha mumbled.

Tamera gave her the evil eye and then tore a piece of paper out of her notebook. She quickly scribbled her number down on the paper and gave it to Maurice. "Well when you see him, can you give this to him and tell him to call me?"

Maurice took the paper and looked at it strangely. "Oh-kay."

"Thanks. See y'all." Tamera and Chanda left Deisha and Maurice alone so they could head to Chanda's house.

"What was that about?" Maurice asked Deisha once they were out of ear shot.

"Tammy has a very scary crush on Jamal," Deisha told Maurice as they walked to her house.

"Yeah, that shit is scary. So what's up with us tonight?"

"I got a lot of homework and a Physics Lab that I need to get cracking on."

"On a Friday, Deisha? Damn. I was hoping you would come to my house and chill. We can bust a grub..."

"Or a nut?" Deisha smartly remarked. She was tired of Maurice constantly hinting on sex when she had already made it clear that she wasn't ready.

"Damn, all that? Look at you. I wasn't even talking about that. I just wanted to spend some time with you since I barely get to see you. We go to the same school but hardly have any classes together. Then after school, you always got your face in a damn book."

"You should do the same because your grades are slipping."

Maurice sucked his teeth and ignored her. They continued to her house and sat on her steps in silence watching the little kids play up and down the street.

Maurice cleared his throat and decided to ask Deisha a question that had been on his mind for quite some time. "Boo, are you still a virgin?"

Deisha looked at him crossly. "What do you mean, *still*?"

"I mean, are you a virgin?" Maurice corrected himself.

"You make it seem like I should have given it up already," Deisha snapped still not answering the question.

"Okay, can you just answer the question?"

Deisha let out a deep sigh. "Raheem was my first. But since it only happened once and I never did anything with anybody after that, I still consider myself a virgin."

"Well I want to be your first," Maurice said, nudging her playfully.

"And why is that?" Deisha asked doubtfully.

"Because I want to make sure that you don't get hurt, again."

Deisha cut her eyes at Maurice. "And what makes you think that Raheem hurt me?"

Maurice got up from her steps ready to leave to avoid another argument. "You need to stop getting so defensive all the time." Deisha began to play with the earring in her ear. Maurice stared down at her. "You think I'm just trying to smash and bounce afterwards, don't you?"

"No," Deisha mumbled.

"Good, because I'm not." He took hold of Deisha's hands and pulled her up from the steps. "If I was one of these lil knuckle heads out here that just wanted you for some ass and you ain't give it to me after the first couple of dates, I would've been rolled out. It's no rush. Just remember that a nigga do have needs." And with those final words, he gave her a kiss. "I'll call you later on. I gotta go meet Shawn and Jamal over 23rd and Turner Street. I just wanted to see you real quick."

"Okay." Deisha replied. Maurice waited for her to go in the house before leaving.

Chanda and Tamera were sitting in Chanda's bedroom. Chanda was supposed to be helping Tamera with her Physics Lab, but they were too busy chit-chatting.

"Seriously Tammy, what is the deal with this crush on Jamal?"

Tamera sat her notebook down and looked over at Chanda. "If you and Deisha don't leave me alone about this. I know what I'm doing."

A THUG'S REDEMPTION

"We're just looking out for you, Tammy. Jamal is bad news. I knew him longer than all of y'all and he really did change. Not for the good either."

Before Tamera could make a comment, Chanda's doorbell rang. "Go get the door. Maybe it's somebody trying to be your man so you can keep your nosey ass out of my business."

"Shut up," Chanda giggled as she made her way down the steps. Not thinking of whom it could be, Chanda opened the door and came face to face with her crush, Shawn Williams. She was startled at first and then began to blush.

"Hey Shawn," she smiled.

"Didn't your mom ever teach you not to answer the door before asking who it is first?"

Chanda laughed nervously. "What are you doing here?"

"I just came by to holla at you real quick." They both stood there in silence and Chanda began to feel silly. She was normally an assertive girl unafraid to speak her mind and very confident. She never had a problem approaching a guy that she was interested in, but it was something about Shawn that made her nervous. She knew she was an attractive girl standing at 5 foot 6 with a curvy frame. Her hips were wide with long shapely legs, thick thighs and toned calves. She had a pretty brown complexion with eyes that resembled a China doll. She also had dimples when she smiled. Chanda wore her hair like most teenaged girls in long individual braids with a few of them pulled back into a ponytail. Guys were very much attracted to her and were always in her face. But she only had eyes for one guy and he was standing in front of her. Shawn cleared his throat, snapping her out of her thoughts. "Can I come in?"

"Oh, I'm sorry," Chanda said as she opened the door wider. Shawn came in and Chanda stared at him before closing the door behind him. He was much taller than she remembered, standing almost at 6 foot 3. His lean, muscular build resembled that of a shooting guard, the position that he played on University City High School's Basketball team. He still had a baby face, but his deep voice could cause confusion if one were to try to guess his age. His hair was freshly cut with dark waves moving about his head and he wore one diamond studded ear ring in his left ear. Shawn was fine as hell and just being that close to him nearly took Chanda's breath away. He sat on the couch and she sat across from him in a one seated chair.

"Damn girl, I don't bite. You can sit next to me."

Chanda giggled nervously and joined Shawn on the sofa. She slung her long individual braids over her shoulder. Shawn nudged her playfully. "So what's up?" "Nothing really." Chanda blushed again.

"I heard you were into me," Shawn teased. When Chanda didn't say anything, he nudged her again. "Don't get all quiet on me, now. Why you ain't say anything?"

Yani

"Because you were trying to do your basketball thing and we've been cool for so long that I ain't think you wanted to mess up our friendship. How come you didn't say anything?" Chanda asked back.

Shawn took a couple of her braids in his hand and started playing with them. "Because I was waiting for you, but you were taking too long. So if you don't have a dude, pass me your number so I can call you."

Chanda giggled like a giddy school girl. Shawn unclipped his cell phone from his jeans and Chanda was about to spit her phone number to him when her mother and younger brother came in.

Chanda's mother looked down at her as if she had lost her mind. "Chanda, you know better than to have a boy in my house when I'm not home."

"I'm sorry, Mom. We were just talking."

"I don't care," her mother scolded.

"How are you doing?" Shawn spoke, rising from the couch.

"I'm fine and yourself?" Chanda's mother spoke back. "Chanda, take some of these bags into the kitchen. Did you mop the floor and clean the bathroom like I told you to?"

Chanda winced knowing that a tongue lashing was sure to follow. "No, I forgot."

"See what I mean? How do you think you're going to have company and you can't even do what the hell I tell you to do? You don't bring anybody in my house when it's not clean. I shouldn't have to come home after working all day, cook dinner and clean the house. This shit doesn't make any damn sense." Chanda sat the bags in the kitchen and then came back into the living room with Shawn. He could tell that she was embarrassed.

"Don't feel bad. I go through the same shit at home with my mom," he whispered with a smile.

"Yeah, but my mom is worse. Some of the shit she be doing don't even make any sense," Chanda replied.

Shawn fell silent knowing it was too soon to talk about her home life. "So what's up with the number?" he asked instead. Chanda gave him her number and then walked him to the door. "Alright, I'll let you go so you can mop those floors and I'll call you tonight."

"Okay." Chanda replied, super excited. She closed the door behind him and then bolted upstairs to her bedroom. Tamera was flipping through her CDs.

"I'm thinking I don't have to ask who was downstairs," Tamera said as she looked at the CD booklet to the *Dynasty* album.

"It was Shawn," Chanda replied, grinning from one ear to the other. "He's going to call me tonight."

"That's what's up. Maybe we can double date with him and Jamal," Tamera smirked.

A THUG'S REDEMPTION

Chanda frowned. "I'm not even gonna go there with you." They giggled. Chanda sighed as she slipped on her slippers. "Come downstairs with me while I clean the kitchen."

Tamera followed Chanda downstairs as asked and they began to talk about Shawn and Jamal endlessly while Chanda did her chores.

Shawn headed over to 23rd and Turner Street to meet up with his brother and Maurice. He wasn't planning on staying long. He was anxious to get home so he could call Chanda and they could hook up.

As usual, Jamal was shooting craps with some of the local drug dealers. He was taking their money of course, and enjoying every minute of it. One of the guys was beginning to turn into a sore loser. Jamal was taking all of his money and the round they were playing was no exception.

"That's right, niggas. Put up and shut the fuck up. Stop bitching. Time to pay the piper." Jamal was talking shit. It was almost a routine thing whenever he came on the block to gamble with his friends. The guys emptied their wallets to him but the sore loser decided he was going to be slick and short change Jamal convincing himself that he wouldn't notice with all of the cash flow coming his way.

Jamal looked at the money that the sore loser gave him and could immediately tell without counting it that it wasn't the right amount. "Hold up, hold up, hold the fuck up. What the fuck are you doing, yo?" Jamal spat.

The sore loser looked at Jamal as if he didn't know what he was talking about. "What?"

"You know what nigga, don't try to play me. Where is the rest of my money?"

"Yo I gave you your money, son. You better count that shit," the sore loser retorted. Before the guy could get any other words out of his mouth, Jamal punched him in it and began whipping his ass. "That's for trying to play me like I can't count, pussy! Don't ever in your fucking life disrespect me like that again!" Jamal scowled as he kicked the guy. His short temper was a lot worse than it was a couple years prior. Catching his first body had made him cocky, and knowing the reputation his cousin Samir had also made him feel that he was untouchable.

Shawn shook his head. "Here we go," he mumbled as he put his hands to his head.

Jamal stopped kicking the guy and began to walk away. "Look at this shit. He got blood on my new damn sneakers. I should kick his ass again for that shit." He opened a bottle of spring water that he had with him, and poured it on his new Air Jordan sneakers. Jamal had shot up in height and also stood at 6 foot 3. He had a more muscular build than Shawn with broad shoulders and a broad chest. His presence was intimidating as he did not appear to be 17. The mustache and neatly trimmed goatee that stretched from his chin and around his jaw line to connect with his side burns, made him appear to be old enough to drink. His eyes were dark and looking into them could make a person feel as though he was staring *through* them.

"Damn Mal, was it really that serious?" Maurice asked as he looked at the sore loser as he gathered himself and tried to get up off of the ground.

"Fucking right it was. You don't fuck with my money. It's consequences and repercussions for that shit. It's the principle of the whole thing." Jamal slapped his brother a handshake. "Where are you coming from?"

"Oh, I had to make a stop real quick. Nothing serious." Shawn replied not wanting to tell his brother of his plans to hook up with Chanda.

Jamal looked at him suspiciously. "Oh okay. So what's up, niggas? What's popping tonight?"

Maurice reached in his back pocket. "Yo, I ran into Tammy and she said to give this to you."

"What's this?" Jamal asked as he opened the paper. Shawn peeped over his shoulders. "What did she give me this for?"

Maurice shrugged his shoulders. "She just told me to tell you to call her. Deisha said that she has a very scary crush on you."

"Yeah, that shit is scary. Good girls who like bad boys." Shawn and Maurice laughed.

"Both of y'all can suck my nuts." They all laughed as Jamal tucked the paper in his pocket. "I'll holla at her later to see what's up. She does have a nice frame."

"I ain't trying to be around here tonight, man. Let's go down South Street or something." Maurice suggested.

"I thought you were chilling with what's her name," Jamal said. The blood was obviously still bad between him and Deisha.

"Come on yo, you know what her name is. Y'all need to cut that shit out," Maurice replied.

"She still won't give you any cuddy?" Jamal joked.

"Man, fuck outta here," Maurice retorted. Jamal laughed. "She had stuff to do with her aunt," he lied.

"Whatever, nigga." Jamal looked at his brother. "Why are you so quiet?"

"I've got a game coming up soon. I'm just going over some plays in my head," Shawn lied. He was really thinking about Chanda and couldn't wait to get home so he could call her.

"South Street, y'all?" Maurice asked.

"Yeah, it's Friday so it's gonna be a ho-asis down there," Jamal said as he rubbed his hands together. They laughed as they walked towards Broad and Cecil B. Moore to catch the subway train.

The next morning, Tamera was heading to the store to pick up a half gallon of milk. Chanda was supposed to walk with her, but she was too busy on the phone boo loving with Shawn. She was humming a tune to herself when a guy fell into stride with her.

"How're you doing?" the guy asked. He appeared scruffy and raggedy which completely turned Tamera off.

Tamera was the tallest among her friends; a slender girl with slight curves. She stood just less than six feet tall with a skin complexion that matched the color of beach sand. Her eyes were a chocolate brown and were also round with long eye lashes and thick, neatly arched eye brows that gave her a look of innocence. She had long, thick, dark brown hair that fell just past her shoulders. She was dressed in a pair of gray Old Navy sweat pants and a matching hooded jacket. Her hair was neatly swept into a ponytail, which blew slightly in the autumn breeze. Tamera's crisp, white Adidas shell-top sneakers polished off her early morning jogger look and the scruffy young man was immediately attracted to her. Though the feeling was not mutual, Tamera remained polite and spoke back. "Hello."

"Can I walk with you?" Mr. Scruffy asked.

"Naw, that's okay. I kinda just want to walk and think and enjoy the morning air."

"Well damn, I can't talk to you?" Mr. Scruffy's attitude definitely matched his appearance, which turned Tamera off even more.

"No it's cool, I have a boyfriend," Tamera lied.

"Well fuck you then, bitch. You're lucky I even spoke to your yellow, stuck up ass. Boney-ass bitch."

Tamera stopped dead in her tracks and looked at the guy as if he had lost the last of his damn mind. "Don't be calling me a bitch because I didn't want to talk to your dirty looking ass. Go home and take a fucking shower and brush your teeth before you call yourself getting in a girl's face!"

"Shut up, bitch before I smack the shit outta you," the guy said as he walked closer to her.

Before Tamera had a chance to say anything else, Jamal was walking towards them. "Yo dude, do we have a problem here?"

The guy took a couple of cautious steps back from Tamera when he saw Jamal. "Oh naw, I ain't know this was you," Mr. Scruffy said as he looked at Tamera, nervously.

"That's beside the fucking point, Skip. You don't talk to a female like that. You better keep it moving homie before I put foot to ass out here!" Jamal threatened.

The guy began to walk away mumbling under his breath. That was the last time that he was going to let Jamal get away with that shit.

"Are you alright?" Jamal asked Tamera.

"Yeah I'm cool. He was tripping hard," Tamera replied still shaken up from her early morning confrontation.

"What are you doing out here this time of morning anyway?" Jamal asked. He zipped his black hooded sweat shirt up after a strong breeze blew around them. He was wearing a loose fitting pair of Girbaud jeans and another pair of Jordan sneakers. Though he was wearing a fitted baseball cap, he still pulled his hood up onto his head out of habit.

"I was on my way to the store to pick up some milk. Chanda was supposed to walk me, but she's too busy on the phone boo loving with your brother."

Jamal frowned unaware of his brother's recent hook up. He decided not to say anything. "I was just about to ask you what you were doing around here because I know this ain't your neck of the 'hood."

Tamera giggled. "Well what about you? What are you doing out so early? You don't seem like the early bird type."

"Oh I got into some shit with my mom and I rolled out. I ain't feel like dealing with her shit early in the morning."

"Oh," Tamera replied quietly. They fell silent as they continued walking to the store.

"Mar gave me your message," Jamal said.

"What message?" Tamera asked as she played dumb. She wanted to see if Jamal ever considered her for a potential girlfriend.

"Oh so you're going to play dumb on me now. I see how you do."

"You're talking about my phone number?"

"Yeah, what was that about?" Jamal asked.

"I wanted you to call me," Tamera said bashfully.

"Ha, let me find out that Tammy likes bad boys." Tamera laughed as they walked into the food market. "So what, are you trying to holla at me or something?"

"I wouldn't have given you my number if that weren't the case."

"Okay," Jamal smiled. He fell back a couple steps so he could take a look at her. He shook his head smiling, as he liked what he was seeing. He silently wondered to himself why he never came at her before.

Once inside of the store, Jamal ran into a guy that he was cool with from the neighborhood. Tamera let them catch up while she purchased a few things. When she finished, Jamal took the bags from her so they could walk back to Chanda's house.

"So are you sure about this? I mean I know that you heard that I get into some crazy stuff sometimes."

"Yeah, Deisha has been relentless in trying to talk me out of this," Tamera replied.

"Hmm, Deisha. I wish she'd learn to mind her fucking business sometimes," Jamal said coolly.

Tamera fell silent not wanting to discuss her best friend. "So what she said is true? As far as the hustling and trouble that you've been into?" she asked innocently.

Jamal hesitated for a moment wanting to pick his words carefully before answering. "I've done things that I'm not exactly proud of. Everybody has their reasons for why they do the things that they do. I wouldn't have done some of the things that I've done if I didn't have a good reason for doing it. And for now, I'll leave it at that. If you still want to talk to me not knowing what those things are, that's what's up. If not, I'll understand," Jamal replied.

"Like you said; everybody has their reasons for doing some of the things that they do. I have my reasons for still wanting to talk to you." Tamera smiled at him.

"And why is that?" Jamal asked curiously.

"Because there's something about you that attracts me to you," Tamera replied as she glanced away. They reached Chanda's house and Tamera retrieved her bags from him.

"Are you going to be home later?" Jamal asked her.

"Yeah, my dad wants me to come home early. I'm surprised he let me stay out last night."

"Damn, your pops is strict like that?" Jamal joked.

Tamera hesitated for a moment. "Yeah… my mom was killed a few years ago and ever since then, he's just been really protective over me."

"Damn, I'm sorry to hear that. He ain't gonna have that shit with me and you. He's gonna take one look at me and be like oh hell no. You probably can't have phone calls after nine, can you?" Jamal joked. Tamera laughed out loud. "Shut up!"

"I'm fucking with you. What time do you have to be home?"

"Around 2 o'clock."

"Alright, well I'll holla at you around then," Jamal said backing away from the steps.

"Okay," Tamera blushed. She went into the house and closed the door behind her.

While Tamera was putting the milk away, Chanda was upstairs boo loving on the phone with Shawn. They were having a deep discussion about the Sixers' stunning record.

"That game against the Heat was hot!" Chanda said, excited.

"I know. I thought they were going to lose until Eric Snow got that steal at the end of the game," Shawn replied, also excited.

"How do you beat the Heat? With just a little bit of Snow." Chanda joked. They laughed together. "A lot of people hate on Snow, but that nigga is the one you want on the floor when it's time for a game winning shot."

Shawn was impressed. He was surprised that Chanda held that kind of passion for basketball. He was beginning to like her even more. "So what's up with us? I want you on the floor after I hit a game winning shot," Shawn said changing the subject.

Yani

Chanda was speechless. She smiled and said, "I always come to the games."

"Yeah, but still, what's up with us? Do you wanna do something about this crush or what?"

"Yeah," Chanda replied bashfully.

Shawn cracked a grin. "So what are you doing tonight?"

"I'm hanging out with my younger brother. I was going to order some pizza for us while we watched the game. You can come chill with us too, if you want to."

"Well, I have to make some runs. I'll call you when I'm done, alright?" Shawn replied.

"Okay," Chanda smiled. She hung up and then skipped down the hall to her mother's room.

"Yeah," her mother answered with the sound of sleep distorting her voice.

Chanda cracked her door open. "Mom, is it okay if I have company tonight?"

"Damn, ain't Tamera here already? What are you trying to do, have a house party up in here or something?"

Chanda laughed. "No, Ma. Tammy has to leave soon. Shawn wanted to know if he could come keep me company later and watch the game."

"What the hell is wrong with his momma's TV?" Ms. Johnson joked.

"Mom…" Chanda groaned.

Chanda's mother looked at her suspiciously. "Is he supposed to be your boyfriend or something?"

Chanda hesitated. "Not really. We're just cool. So can he?"

"I don't care. You just make sure this house is clean; the bathroom, the steps, kitchen, living room and dining room."

"Yes ma'am." Chanda grinned. She closed her mother's door and skipped back to her bedroom anxiously awaiting Shawn's arrival.

Deisha was sitting in her bedroom on her bed propped up on her pillows. She was talking on the phone with Maurice.

"What are you doing today? Or should I even bother to ask?" Maurice asked sarcastically.

"What's that supposed to mean?" Deisha asked in return.

"Every time I turn around, you got your nose in a book. You act like you don't even have time for me."

"It's not that. I just wanna make sure that my grades are straight so I can get into Penn State," Deisha explained.

"Well, when am I gonna fit into your equation?" Maurice moped.

Deisha sighed. She really hadn't spent that much time with Maurice since the new school year had started. She definitely didn't want him to feel like he needed to go elsewhere for attention. She had already noticed how other girls flirted with him openly regardless of the fact that everyone knew they were together. Maurice had grown to be extremely handsome. He was shorter than his two best friends, Jamal and Shawn, standing at 5 foot 10. He had a slim build with broad shoulders. His tiny, chestnut colored eyes, curly hair, medium brown skin with dimples almost made him look Dominican. The girls in school thought he looked exotic. He was sexual eye candy to most of them as well as the girls from the neighborhood. His humble and humorous nature made him even more appealing because he was not cocky or conceited about his gorgeous looks. And though he could have any girl in the school or neighborhood that he wanted, Deisha's sassy attitude, smart mouth and intelligence appealed to him more than anyone else.

"What are you doing today?" Deisha asked giving in.

Maurice smiled knowing that he had her exactly where he wanted her.

"Nothing really; Mal is chilling with Tammy. Shawn is chilling with Chanda. I'm the only one that got a girl and don't hardly see her." Maurice was laying it on thick.

"Tammy seriously hooked up with Jamal!" Deisha exclaimed. "You gotta be fucking kidding me. I don't believe this shit. See, nobody listens to me."

Maurice felt as though he was losing her. "Um, we're losing focus over here. That's Tammy's business, not yours. Can we get back to the matter at hand?"

"Oh yeah, right; what were we saying?" Deisha asked, shaking her head.

"I was saying you should come spend the night with me."

"Boy, I can't come spend no night with you! What tip are you on?"

"You need to come spend something. You act like you gotta avoid me or something because you think all I want to do is fuck you. I don't want to just fuck you like that. I just want you here with me."

Deisha was quiet for a moment. Finally, she gave in. "Who's there with you?"

Maurice grinned. "My mom went to A.C for the weekend with her boyfriend and my sister is at my cousin's house for the weekend."

Why am I not surprised? Deisha thought to herself. "Alright," she sighed. "Let me get showered and dressed and I'll come chill with you today."

"The whole day?" Maurice asked in disbelief.

"Yes, the whole day," Deisha assured him.

"Alright, bet. See you when you get here." They hung up with each other. Deisha remained on her bed looking at the *Raheem* chain that was around her neck. She got up and grabbed some clothes. She then wrapped her hair and took a shower.

Yani

Deisha plotted on a way to spend the day and night with Maurice without making her aunt suspicious. She had a best friend type relationship with her aunt and could talk to her about anything, but she didn't want to risk being caught trying to spend the night with Maurice. Her aunt was like a mother to her; taking custody of her when she was 12 years old due to her real mother being strung out on drugs and being deemed unfit to care for Deisha. Under her aunt's care, guidance and love, she had developed into a well-rounded young lady, an honor roll student, track star and hopeful college student at Penn State. She was also extremely beautiful, yet she would never admit that she is the splitting image of her mother. They both had the same smooth, flawless skin that was the color of a coconut shell, shoulder length medium brown hair, and dark brown almond-shaped eyes that held a look of sadness to them. Her lips were full and pouty and she had a beautiful smile. Being a track star, her body had an athletic build; toned thighs and calves, a flat stomach, slim waist and wide hips. She was beautiful from head to toe but always reminded herself that her beauty was only skin deep and her brains would get her much further than her "booty", which was one of the reasons she pushed herself so hard academically. She promised herself that she would never end up like her mother.

As Deisha washed herself, she began to wonder why she waited so long to consummate her and Maurice's relationship. Although she hadn't told him yet, she loved him and was grateful for the role he was playing in her life since Raheem's passing. She got out of the shower and began to get dressed. She then called Tamera hoping she had gotten home from Chanda's house already.

"Hello," a deep, intimidating voice answered.

"Damn!" Deisha cursed herself. "How are you, Mr. Harrison? It's Deisha, Is Tammy around?" Deisha asked sweetly.

"She just walked in. Hold on...Tammy! Deisha is on the phone." A few seconds later, Tamera answered on another extension.

"I got it, Daddy." They waited for her father to hang up the phone before they engaged in conversation. When he did, Deisha burst out laughing. "What?" Tamera asked.

"Ya pop is a trip. I see he's still in uniform. Serge doesn't play any games, does he?"

"Shut up, Deisha. What do you want?" Tamera asked, obviously annoyed.

"I can't believe you actually hooked up with that mofo," Deisha said as she shook her head.

"I really don't feel like hearing it, so if that's what you're calling for, you might as well hang up."

"Whatever. It's your life." Deisha mumbled.

"Yup, and I got enough people trying to run it. I don't need you up in the mix, too." Tamera said as she cradled the phone between her ear and her shoulder.

"Anyway, I was calling because I need a huge favor."

"What else is new?" Tamera rolled her eyes.

"Ew, what's up with the attitude today? Damn girl, get the bug out of your ass." When Tamera didn't say anything in return, Deisha became serious. "Tammy, are you okay?"

"I'm okay," Tamera mumbled.

"Are you sure? Is it Serge again? Damn it Tammy, is he still trying to make you run five laps around the block?"

Tamera giggled. "You need to stop."

"On the really real though, if you need to talk, I'm here for you." Deisha told her.

Tamera sighed wanting to change the subject. "So what do you need?"

"Alright, if my aunt asks in the near future, me and you hung out tonight and I stayed the night at your crib."

"Huh?" Tamera asked, confused.

"I'm spending the night with Maurice. Just cover for me."

"Well, what if she calls here?" Tamera asked.

"She won't, trust me. My aunt doesn't check behind me like that. She trusts me. You know how tight we are," Deisha assured her.

"Yeah well, if she finds out about tonight…"

"She won't because you're my best friend and I know you'll do me this one solid."

"Alright, alright, damn. But you owe me. And I want all of the juicy details too," Tamera giggled.

Deisha squealed. "Thanks girl. I love you. You're the best."

"I'm so sure. Look, I gotta go. Serge is barking about the Saturday chores."

"Okay. I'll call you tomorrow. Thanks again."

"You're welcome." They hung up. Deisha packed up the rest of her personals and went to join her aunt in the kitchen.

"Hey Aunt 'Chelle."

"Hey Deisha," her aunt spoke back.

"I'm on my way over to Maurice's house because he's been complaining about me spending more time in the library than I do with him."

"I was beginning to wonder what was going on between you two. I barely see him anymore," her aunt replied.

"We're still together. I've just been on my P's and Q's because my heart is set on going to Penn State."

"I know sweetie, but when you're in a relationship that has to balance out. I'm making Chicken Marsala tonight. Are you and Maurice coming back here for dinner?"

"Actually, can you save me some? Tammy's pop is on another power trip and she wanted to know if I could spend the night."

Michelle knew her niece was running a game on her but she didn't say anything. Instead, she smiled and said, "Sure, honey."

"Thanks Aunt 'Chelle," Deisha said before she turned to head for the front door.

"Um Deisha, one thing before you go."

"Yes Aunt 'Chelle," Deisha said as she turned back around.

"Make sure Maurice uses a condom." She smiled and winked at her niece before turning back to finish washing off the chicken breast for dinner.

Deisha flinched. "Aunt 'Chelle, we're not…"

"Girl please," Michelle interrupted her. "I was 17 once myself. Game recognizes game."

Deisha laughed nervously. "Okay Aunt 'Chelle."

"Have fun!" Michelle yelled out as Deisha was closing the door behind her.

Deisha decided to make a pit-stop at Chanda's house on her way to see Maurice.

Chanda dropped what she was doing when she heard the doorbell. "Coming!" she shouted as she bolted down the stairs. She looked out the window and frowned when she saw Deisha. She opened the door. "Damn, I thought you were Shawn." Chanda sucked her teeth.

"Well, you thought wrong," Deisha said as she came in. "I see your mom still has you playing the role of the Black Cinderella."

Chanda laughed out loud. "You're such an ass, shut up." She closed the door behind Deisha and plopped down on the couch beside her. "So what brings you here today? Maurice ditched you for Jamal, again?" Chanda snickered.

"You know you can go straight to hell, right? Do not pass go, do not collect $200. Just go straight to hell." They both laughed. "For your information, I'm on my way over there now. I'm spending the night with him."

Chanda looked at Deisha wide eyed. "What?! And where the hell are his mom and little sister going to be?"

"His mom is somewhere staying with her own man for the weekend, and his little sister is staying with some cousins."

"Well, I know Ms. Niecie is slipping or something. How is she going to let you stay out all night with Mar all willy-nilly like that and not say anything?" Chanda piped.

Deisha started biting her nails. "Actually, she doesn't know."

"Are you serious?!" Chanda screeched.

"Shush!" Deisha squealed, pinching her. "Tammy is covering for me."

"Oh HELL no! You know Serge will deep fry her muthafucking ass like catfish if he finds out about that shit. I don't know why you got that poor girl involved."

Deisha burst out laughing. "You ain't shit for that one."

"Whatever. I know you're scared aren't you?" Chanda inquired.

"Girl, I'm just as nervous as ever."

"Well shit, you should be. It's been so long it's like you're losing your virginity all over again. And Mar, we know that nigga ain't had pussy since pussy had he." This time Chanda was laughing by herself as Deisha gave her the evil eye. When Chanda realized that Deisha wasn't laughing with her, she stopped and cleared her throat. "Sorry."

"Yeah I bet. I'm serious though, Chanda. Do you think I should do it?"

"Do you think you should do it?" Chanda asked back.

"I want to. I just don't want him to start acting funny towards me afterwards."

"I doubt that he will. Besides, he stayed this long after it took you so long to give it up. Why would he leave now? You know that boy loves him some Deisha. But one thing is for certain, and two things are for sure. Your ass has to go." Deisha and Chanda both got up from the couch with Chanda showing Deisha to the door. "You ain't got to go home but you got to get the hell out of here," Chanda laughed.

Deisha laughed with her. "Alright already. You don't have to be like that. I'm going."

"Let me know how everything goes tonight," Chanda said as Deisha was leaving.

"I will. And I want the dirt from you too, Miss Thang."

"Oh no doubt. See you, Deisha."

Deisha waved and Chanda closed the door behind her. She then ran upstairs to finish getting herself ready for her night with Shawn.

"Hello, can I speak to Tammy?" Jamal asked as he was walking down the street talking on his cell phone.

"This is she. May I ask whose calling?"

"Damn, you don't recognize your man's voice when he calls?" Jamal asked jokingly.

Tamera smiled as she twirled the phone cord around her finger. "My man, huh? Well the fact that I don't have a man yet and this is the first time that you've called me Jamal, no I didn't. But only you would be that bold."

"Damn girl it's like that? I'm not your man now?"

"I said, yet. We never agreed to anything. You haven't even taken me out, yet."

"Well that's what I'm calling you for. Maybe we can work something out when I get there. You're not busy are you?"

"No not really," Tamera replied.

"Can I come through so we can talk about us?" Jamal asked sweetly.

Tamera couldn't resist his charm. "Okay," she agreed.

"Alright, where do you live at again?" Jamal asked, stopping in the middle of a sidewalk.

"I'm over on 27th and Sharswood Street." Tamera replied and then gave him the address.

Jamal looked around and then doubled back. "Okay. I'll be there in like fifteen minutes." Jamal told her as he glanced at his watch.

They hung up and Tamera rushed to her room to change her clothes. She didn't want Jamal to see her in the same thing that she had on earlier when she went to the store. It had warmed up outside so she put on a short sleeved, pale blue shirt, and a pair of dark blue, form fitting, Lady Enyce jeans. She grabbed her low top Air force Ones and brushed her long hair back into a ponytail. Just as she was putting on her earrings, she heard the doorbell ring. She took one last glance at herself. Satisfied with her appearance, she ran down to answer the door.

"Hey beautiful," Jamal said when she opened the door for him. She blushed.

"Hi," Tamera replied remaining behind the glass storm door.

"Why are you standing in the doorway? Come outside. I know your pops don't have you on lock like that," Jamal teased.

"No he doesn't." Tamera smirked. To prove Jamal wrong, she stepped from behind the storm door and closed it behind her. "There, is that better?"

Jamal gave Tamera the once over, making no bones about it. It made her a little uncomfortable, but she asserted herself. Jamal smiled at her, liking what he saw.

"So what were you doing?" Jamal asked, trying to keep his mind out of the gutter.

"The usual Saturday cleaning."

"Damn girl, do you ever go out?" Jamal asked as he leaned onto her gate.

"Go out where?" Tamera asked.

"Like to the movies, the club Dancers… anywhere?"

Tamera thought for a moment. "I went to Dancers like twice but my dad said I couldn't go back because I didn't get home until like four in the morning and he found out I was fighting."

Jamal looked at her with his eyebrows raised, surprised. "You… were fighting?"

Tamera grinned. "Shut up. You make it seem like its taboo. It was Deisha's fight, but some of the other girls got hype like they just had a batch of gangsta cookies and thought they were going to swing on me too, but I wasn't trying to hear that." Jamal burst out laughing. "What? What's so funny?" Tamera asked laughing with him.

"Gangsta cookies though?" Jamal chuckled some more. Tamera giggled with him. "I can't even picture you fighting."

"And why is that?"

"Because, you're the good girl and you're so quiet."

Tamera became serious. "I am a good girl. But don't think you can just do whatever just because I'm quiet. I'm cool as long as you don't cross me." Their eyes locked and at that moment Tamera gained more respect from Jamal than any other female that he had dealt with. He knew she was real from that statement alone and decided at that point she was going to be his girl.

Jamal cleared his throat. "Well, just don't be getting into any more fights. You're too pretty for that."

Tamera smiled again. She was about to pry into his personal life to get to know more about him but was interrupted when her father came to the door.

"Why didn't you tell me you were stepping outside? I'm calling you all over the house and you're nowhere to be found. Next time, let somebody know where you are," her father scolded her. He was an intimidating man; standing an inch taller than Tamera, but was heavy set with a thick beard, bald head and mahogany skin. His face held slight scars from an off and on battle with eczema and his eyes were a deep brown. Though he was normally a mild tempered man at his place of work, when it came to his only daughter, his temper was that of a short fuse easily set off by the smallest offense.

"Sorry daddy," Tamera replied as she looked at the ground. Jamal noticed how frightened she had become.

Mr. Harrison looked Jamal over and immediately decided that he didn't like him. "Who the hell is this?"

Normally Jamal would have had something smart to say or would've been ready to kick the old man in his teeth. But out of respect for Tamera, he tried a different approach. He stuck out his hand to be shaken. "How are you doing, sir? My name is Jamal."

"He goes to school with me, daddy. He just stopped by to say hello," Tamera said quickly when she saw her father ignore Jamal's attempt to shake his hand.

Mr. Harrison got a closer look at Jamal and recognized him as one of the guys he saw all the time on 23rd and Turner Street, shooting craps when he passed through to go to work. He even thought that he saw him getting handcuffed and taken away a few times. Knowing Jamal, he probably did.

"Oh, hell no! Get your juvenile delinquent ass off of my damn porch right now," Mr. Harrison scowled.

Yani

Jamal looked at Tamera confused.

"Daddy, what are you talking about?" Tamera asked.

"No, I know who he is. Every time I come through that neighborhood I see him hanging with those little thugs and hoodlums over by Ridge Avenue. You better get from in front of my house right now before I call the cops."

"Dad, it's not that serious," Tamera tried to explain.

"It's cool, yo. I'll just holla at you in school on Monday," Jamal said as he was leaving the porch.

"I'd think twice about that if I were you!" Mr. Harrison hollered from behind. Jamal ignored him as he headed back to his house.

"That wasn't necessary daddy," Tamera told her father. She was embarrassed.

"If you know like I know, you better shut the hell up and get your ass in the house. Since when do you start bringing these trifling niggas in front of my damn door…?" Mr. Harrison slammed his front door and continued scolding Tamera.

Deisha was at Maurice's house. They were sitting in his bedroom on the floor with Deisha sitting between his legs getting a good head massage from him. She had her eyes closed and felt like she was in a trance as his fingers moved methodically through her scalp.

Maurice was enjoying his alone time with Deisha. He slid his fingers from the roots of her dark, thick, shoulder length hair to the tips. He then slid his hands over her neck and rubbed it as he slid his tongue in her ear before pulling her lobe into his mouth. The kisses he planted on her neck made her shiver. She turned to the side, forcing his hands to wander to her breast. She found his mouth and their kiss began with their tongues exploring each other's mouths. Maurice laid Deisha back and kissed over her neck as he unbuttoned her shirt. He kissed down her neck to her stomach and began to unbutton her jeans. Deisha began to lose her nerve.

"Wait!" Deisha said quickly moving away.

"What's wrong?" Maurice asked as he looked up at her.

"Do you have a condom?" she asked innocently.

"You know it," Maurice said as he nibbled on one of her nipples through her bra.

Deisha tried not to let her fears show but Maurice could already detect them.

"Are you sure about this?" he asked as he gently stroked between her legs with his fingers.

Deisha was breathless. "Yes," she answered as she closed her eyes. She put her hands to her face trying to control herself.

Maurice undid her jeans and pulled them down. He then threw her legs open and put them over his shoulders before humming on her vagina through her black, laced panties. Deisha felt like she was going to lose it and bit down one her hands to keep from screaming. He then eased her panties down with his teeth and stuck two fingers inside of her to explore her wetness. Deisha shrieked cumming immediately. Maurice smiled, loving her reaction. He felt like a kid in a candy store. He licked his lips and put his face between her legs, munching away like Deisha was an entrée at the Old Country Buffet.

Deisha felt like she was in Heaven and was ready to throw a tantrum when he stopped. But the ride was far from over. He pulled her up and laid her on his bed. And the passion began as they explored every possible position known to man including the ones Maurice remembered seeing in his Hustler magazines and any extras that he could twist Deisha's body into. When it ended, Deisha kept her arms and legs wrapped around him and they cuddled their sweaty bodies together falling asleep.

Meanwhile back at Chanda's house, Chanda was moussing her long, individual braids, making sure that she was absolutely gorgeous for her night with Shawn. She was looking dapper in a pair of faded blue Express jeans and a midnight blue, long sleeved, layering tee that was form fitting and accentuated her voluptuous bust. She polished her casual attire off with a silver, charmed necklace from Juicy Couture, medium sized, silver bangle earrings, and a matching silver charmed bracelet. She turned to the left and then to the right to check out her appearance. When she was satisfied, she called her brother downstairs.

"Huh?" her brother asked once he reached the middle of the steps.

"I'm ordering out some pizza and drinks. I'm having company, so once you get your food don't come back down here for anything. I'm not playing, Kareem."

"Alright," Kareem whined, wanting to hurry back upstairs and finish playing Tekken Tag.

"Alright my ass. Go back upstairs and I'll call you when the pizza gets here."

Kareem scurried back up to his room just as the doorbell rang. Chanda took one last look in the mirror and then out of bad habit, she opened the door before checking to see who it was.

"What did I tell you about opening the door for people before finding out who it is first?" Shawn joked as he smiled at her.

Chanda laughed. Shawn opened his arms to hug her and she obliged feeling like she belonged there once they were around her. She let him in and marveled over his appearance before she closed the door behind him. Shawn was dressed in a gray hooded sweat shirt with a short sleeve, dark blue and white striped Polo shirt and dark blue Guess jeans. His tanned, hiking Timberland boots and fitted baseball cap completed his *hip-hop* appearance.

"The Sixers are getting ready to play on UPN. You wanna watch it?" Shawn asked as Chanda went into the kitchen to get the pizza menu.

"Hell yeah. What time does it come on?" Chanda replied.

Shawn looked at his watch. "We have some time. It doesn't start until 9:30pm."

"Who's playing?" Chanda asked as she picked up the cordless phone. "They're playing the Lakers," Shawn replied with a huge grin on his face.

"Oh, hell yeah. I'm on that shit." Chanda laughed and Shawn laughed with her. "Who do you think is going to win?"

"I'm a Sixers fan no doubt but um… the Shaq and Kobe combo is too much for the Sixers. Defensively, they don't have anyone to go up against Shaq. Ratliff is good but he ain't that good."

"Yeah and the hack-a-Shaq technique shit isn't going to fly tonight because big boy has been hitting his free throws lately," Chanda replied. "Sausage and pepperoni?"

"That's cool. Not just that though, you got niggas on the floor that can hit inside the paint and are deadly from the outside," Shawn added.

"Yeah like Robert Horry, Derek Fisher, and let's not forget Kobe Bryant and Rick Fox with his pretty ass," Chanda laughed again. "Sprite or Pepsi?" she asked.

"Sprite of course," Shawn smiled at her. "And if Shaq starts banging on niggas all crazy like he did against Toronto the other night, the Sixers can forget about it."

"Basically, they might as well sit back and take this "L". It's gonna be a hot game though," Chanda concluded after hanging up the phone from ordering their food. She grabbed her purse and pulled out a ten and a twenty.

"Chanda gets money," Shawn joked. "You want me to pitch in?"

"Naw it's cool, I got it. You can treat next time," Chanda replied as she sat next to him on the couch.

"So it's going to be a next time?" Shawn asked sweetly as he began to play with her braids again. Chanda smiled bashfully. "You got something on the side of your face."

"Where?" Chanda asked almost panicking.

"I got it, chill." Shawn told her. He was lying his ass off and was using that as a way to kiss her. He used his thumb to wipe the corner of her mouth. He then traced over her bottom lip with his thumb and tilted her chin to kiss her slowly slipping his tongue in her mouth. Chanda felt like she was going to melt. They were starting to get more into it when the doorbell rang.

Shawn stopped and used his thumb to wipe out the corner of her mouth again. Chanda got up from the couch to answer the door. This time she remembered to look to see who it was before she answered. The pizza had arrived. She paid for it, leaving the man a nice tip and then closed and locked the door.

"Kareem, come downstairs and get your food!" she yelled up the steps. Shawn changed their television to UPN just as the game was coming on.

Kareem shot down the steps and grabbed a glass out of the kitchen cabinet.

"Did you wash your hands?" Chanda asked him, giving him the evil eye.

"Yup," Kareem said as he grabbed three slices of the piping hot pizza and tossed it onto his plate. He pulled some of the cheese off and popped it into his mouth, cooling it and chewing it at the same time. Chanda watched him with a frown on her face as her brother smacked his lips and poured himself a glass of soda.

"You act like a scavenger sometimes, you know that? Why don't you slow down?" Chanda chastised him.

"The game is about to come on," Kareem explained as he grabbed some napkins.

"You like basketball young bol?" Shawn asked as he came into the dining room to get some pizza.

Kareem looked up at Shawn astonished. He had seen him numerous times playing basketball at The Recreation Center and was mesmerized by how quick he was on the court and how slick his ball handling skills were.

Shawn was his hero and he couldn't believe that he was in his home.

Shawn noticed the stare. He had seen Kareem on the courts also and admired the kind of game he had to be so young. Though Kareem was shorter than some of the other players, he used that as an advantage to maneuver around them. He was quick and also had a slick ball handling skill with the ability to do cross-overs like some of his favorite street-ball players from the *And-1* videos he watched such as A-O and Hot Sauce. While Chanda resembled their father more, Kareem looked just like their mother with big, round dreamy brown eyes and thick lips. He had a cinnamon colored skin complexion with slight acne on his forehead. He kept his hair in a close fade haircut since his mother would not allow him to wear braids, and had a lean and fit frame.

Shawn held his hand out to shake Kareem's. "What's up, Lil Man?"

"What's up?" Kareem replied trying to sound cool.

Chanda cleared her throat to snap Kareem out of his trance and remind him of what she told him earlier. Kareem grabbed his plate of pizza and his glass of soda and sulked towards the stairs.

Shawn noticed his sadness. "Young bol, when's the next time you're going to be at the Rec?"

"Monday after school," Kareem replied.

"Alright, I'll be in the gym like around four, four-thirty. I'll show you some moves okay?"

"Okay," Kareem replied. He almost couldn't contain his excitement. He rushed upstairs to his room to eat his pizza and watch the game.

"I didn't know that was your brother. He's nice as shit on the courts at The Rec," Shawn said as he grabbed a slice of pizza and poured himself a glass of soda.

"Yeah, he's a pain in my ass, too. Now that he's been running with these little dudes from Blumberg, I find myself having to check his ass because of his smart mouth," Chanda replied as she made her way over to the couch.

Shawn sat down next to her. "He just needs some positive guys to be around and he'll be cool. Don't worry about it. I'll keep an eye on lil man when he's at The Rec. I'll make sure that he stays out of trouble."

Chanda smiled at him as butterflies filled her stomach. Shawn Williams was sitting in her living room. She had to be dreaming.

The game came on and Chanda became extra hype each time a good play was made or there was a bad call or no call on a foul. Shawn watched her, enjoying every minute of it. They stole moments away, kissing each other. After the game ended, they talked for a moment while Shawn helped her clean up.

"What time is it?" he asked her as he tied up a trash bag for her.

"Almost 12:30am." Chanda replied as she stretched.

"Alright, I'm about to roll out. Let me take my light-skinned ass home before Keys starts bitching."

Chanda chuckled. "Who's Keys?"

"That's my mom," Shawn said sucking his teeth. "Knowing her ass, she's probably still breaking her neck at that nut-ass job."

Chanda walked him to the door. "Oh. Well, call me when you get in the house so I know that you got home okay."

"I will," Shawn agreed. He leaned over and gave her a long wet kiss before going. Chanda closed the door behind him and leaned up against it smiling as more butterflies invaded her stomach. She floated up to her bedroom and fell out on her bed. Shawn Williams was her boyfriend finally, and everything was all good.

That next Monday morning, Deisha was on the school's balcony after coming from her locker. She spotted Maurice in the commons area by the Multi Media Charter talking to Shawn and Jamal. Although she couldn't hear what he was saying, she could tell by his body language that he was talking about what happened between the two of them Saturday night and Sunday morning. She thought for a moment and it dawned on her that he hadn't called her since she left his house. Her face flushed. Just as she was turning away so she could go to advisory, Maurice looked up and saw her.

"Shit! I hope she didn't just see what I was doing," he thought to himself.

Deisha sat next to Chanda and Tamera in advisory.

"What is wrong with you?" Chanda asked, detecting an attitude from Deisha.

"Nothing," Deisha replied in a snappy tone.

"Oh Lord, what did Maurice do this time?" Tamera asked.

Deisha was getting ready to tell them what was on her mind when the infamous trio came into the classroom. "I'll tell y'all later," she told her friends as she looked at Maurice distastefully.

"Tammy, come here real quick," Jamal called out. Tamera got out of her seat and walked over to Jamal to see what he wanted.

Shawn came over to Chanda and whispered in her ear. Chanda burst out laughing. He then kissed her and went to his desk. Deisha whipped her head around to Chanda damn near getting whip lash.

"Did he just kiss you?" Deisha gawked.

Chanda blushed as some of the other girls in the class stared at her enviously.

Maurice had a few words with the advisor and then went over to Deisha. He tried to give her a peck on her lips but she turned her face from him. Maurice looked at her for a space of heart beats.

"You know what? I'm not for your theatrics shit today. I'll deal with you later."

Deisha cut her eyes at him and then rolled them. "Whatever," she mumbled. Maurice went over to his seat near Shawn and sat down.

"Why are you acting like that towards him?" Chanda whispered.

"I said I'll tell you about it later," Deisha hissed.

Chanda backed off. "Okay."

Out in the hall, Jamal was talking to Tamera about his confrontation with her father.

"What's up with your pops? Dude was tripping hard on Saturday."

"He's just real protective over me. He's been like that since my mom died," Tamera replied as she looked at the floor.

Jamal studied her for a second. "He shook the shit out of you, yo. It looked like he put the fear of God in you when he came to the door," Jamal half way joked. When Tamera didn't say anything, Jamal became serious. He could tell it was more to the situation than he could see. He figured what's done in the dark will eventually come to the light. He put his arms around her and squeezed. Tamera buried her face in his chest, smelling his cologne. She closed her eyes and hugged him back.

"Damn girl, you're so soft," Jamal squealed playfully.

Tamera giggled. Although she was trembling, it felt good being in his arms.

Jamal kissed her ear when he heard the bell ring. "Come on so we can go to class."

Their elective period was the only free time that Deisha had to tell her two best friends about her explosive night with Maurice. She was giving them every single detail, blow for blow, lick for lick. Her friends were shocked that Maurice did so much.

When Deisha finished her story, Chanda fanned herself with her worksheet and Tamera jerked on her collar to get some air.

"Damn," was all that Chanda could say.

"Too hot for me," Tamera added. "I don't even know why you dropped so many bombs on me like that when you know that my ears are sensitive." They all shared a laugh.

"I don't get it, though. If Maurice was hitting it that good, what's the problem?" Chanda asked. She was waiting for the other shoe to drop. "Because after I left, it was like he ain't had two words to say to me. He ain't even call me yesterday."

"Well he tried to talk to you this morning, but you gave him your ass to kiss," Chanda replied.

"And he was with Jamal yesterday. That's probably why he didn't call you," Tamera added.

"Whose side are you on?" Deisha asked sucking her teeth.

"I'm not on anybody's side. I'm just kicking the actual factuals," Chanda replied as she started her worksheet.

"Actual factuals my ass. I'm tired of him putting Jamal before me."

"Here we go again," Tamera huffed.

"Why don't you just talk to him later on and see what he has to say? I bet he chew your ass out for how you acted earlier," Chanda giggled.

"Yeah, and it won't be nothing like Saturday night either," Tamera laughed with her.

"Shut up!" Deisha found herself laughing with them. "No, he's going to be the one that gets the ass chewing if he doesn't have a good got-damn explanation for not calling me."

"Oh please. It's not that serious," Chanda told Deisha.

"Yeah, we'll see."

After school, Deisha didn't wait for Maurice to call her when she got home. She called him and it was as Chanda and Tamera said it would be. The only thing that bothered Deisha about their conversation was how short Maurice was with her. He wasn't trying to deal with her because of how she was acting. He felt like she was being paranoid and was beginning to wish that he didn't have sex with her. To avoid any arguments with her, he decided to give her a little time to cool off and then he would talk to her. Deisha didn't see it that way. She thought Maurice was trying to avoid her purposely and she didn't like that shit at all.

Things were going great for Shawn and Chanda. She was learning more about him every day. She used to wonder how he always had so much money and hoped that he wasn't selling drugs like Jamal. Shawn had his own hustle which was basketball. Chanda had no idea how big Shawn aka Shizz's name was. He almost had legendary status at The Recreation Center where he was known for crossing over his opponents, making them fall to their knees, his speed, his ball handling skills as well as the way he would dunk on any opponent, big or small. He also had a mean jump shot and could hit half court jump shots at will. Hustlers and ballers from all over Philly came to bet on Shawn and watch him play. He was the younger generation's hero, his name being on the lips and hearts of them as well as some of the groupies who hung around trying to get his attention. Their dreams were all shattered whenever he won a game and would give Chanda a hug and a kiss before introducing her to his friends as his "wifey".

Jamal and Tamera were taking things slow. They stole moments away whenever her father worked late. They'd stay up late at night talking on the phone until the early hours of the morning. When her father was working the graveyard shift at the hospital, Jamal would call her from his cell phone while standing in her backyard. It frightened Tamera at first, but she thought it was so romantic. She would let him in and they would stay up all night talking and watching television.

Deisha on the other hand, was still suspicious about Maurice's behavior. He was spending less time with her and more time with Jamal. The truth of the matter was, that's how it's always been since she became such a study freak. To Deisha, it became more noticeable after they had sex.

On a brisk November morning, Deisha ran into Maurice at the bus stop while on her way to school. She had a million and one thoughts running through her mind but didn't know what to say.

"Hey," she said hesitantly.

"What's up?" Maurice spoke back. They became quiet. The 61 bus pulled up and they got on, making their way to the back to sit in their usual seats.

"What are you doing after school?" Deisha asked breaking the silence.

"I'm going downtown with Jamal for a little while to grab some sneaks from the Gallery," Maurice told her.

Deisha sucked her teeth and sighed. She was irate. She wasn't going to hold her tongue any longer. "You know what? I'm so sick and tired of you always putting that trifling mofo before me," she blurted out.

Maurice looked at her as if she were crazy. "What are you talking about now?"

"You know what I'm talking about. You're always bitching about me not spending time with you but whenever I try to, you're forever dissing me for Jamal."

"Yo, I ain't in the mood for your shit. It's not like I ain't already have plans. I ain't putting him before you, he just asked first. You're always talking that dumb shit."

"No the dumb shit is how you've been acting lately," Deisha retorted.

"How I've been acting?" Maurice asked back. "Deisha, you better go ahead with that shit. You're the one acting funny. Always thinking I'm supposed to bow down and kiss your ass. Fuck out of here with that shit."

"I never said I wanted you to kiss my ass. But you better watch how the hell you're talking to me," Deisha snapped back.

"Oh I guess I'm supposed to just sit here and let you disrespect me like that. You must don't know my name."

"Whatever Maurice," Deisha flagged him and looked out of the window. Other passengers were eaves dropping enjoying the early morning drama. It was waking them up better than Dunkin Donuts coffee.

"I know it's whatever. You need to accept the fact that Jamal is my homie. He's been my boy since kindergarten. How you think I'm just going to drop him because you got old-ass beef with him. You need to grill that shit up and eat it. Raheem is dead. Stop blaming Jamal for that shit and move the fuck on. It wasn't his fault."

Deisha sucked her teeth and looked at Maurice as if he were crazy. "Yes the fuck it was!"

"Like I said, Jamal was my boy before you and he's going to be my boy after you." Maurice stopped and shook his head. He didn't mean to say the last part and he knew he had hurt Deisha with those words.

Deisha moved to the front of the bus when she spotted an available seat and then got off a stop earlier to catch the train to school. Maurice decided to let her cool her heels before making amends with her.

At school, Deisha spotted Tamera at her locker and stormed over to her.

"You need to do something with your little hood-rat boyfriend because I'm sick of him being in the way of my relationship," Deisha hissed. She had no real reason to drag Tamera into her problems. But she was seething and was looking to throw the blame on somebody.

Tamera was already in a bad mood from the never ending drama in her house. She looked at Deisha as if she were crazy. "Deisha, don't start that dumb stuff this morning because I am not in the mood. I got enough drama in my life. I don't need yours all up in the mix, too."

"Whatever. I am sick and tired of having to go through the motions with my dude because yours is causing a conflict with my relationship," Deisha continued to rant. She couldn't see that she was the real cause of her and Maurice's problems.

Tamera decided to set her straight. "Deisha, please. You are the damn conflict. Your own insecurities is gonna cause your relationship to tank not Jamal. You need to just accept the fact that Jamal and Maurice are best friends. I'm tired of you running around blaming Jamal for stuff. It's not him it's you, so get out of my face." Tamera pushed past Deisha and went to advisory. Deisha stood on the balcony hurt and angry.

A THUG'S REDEMPTION

The tension from Deisha's argument with Maurice and Tamera could be felt all day. It was annoying the hell out of Chanda and she was anxious as hell to get one of them alone so she could get the dirt.

After taking the L train together, instead of Maurice going to the Gallery with Jamal, he decided to talk to Deisha and patch things up with her. Tamera hung with Jamal in the Gallery instead and they rode home together. Jamal cracked endless jokes making Tamera laugh until they got to the corner of her block. After the confrontation with her father, he never walked her to her front door. She turned to hug him but Jamal stopped her. Up until that day they had never really kissed. He gave her pecks on the lips, cheek or forehead but that day he wasn't going to hold back any longer. He kissed her longingly, slowly sliding his tongue in and out of her mouth. Tamera responded positively. He stopped and gave her a huge hug, squeezing her tightly.

"Does your pop have to work tonight?" he asked her.

"Yes," Tamera replied shyly.

"Call me when he leaves so I can come chill with you."

"Okay," Tamera agreed. She turned away and walked to her house.

After closing and locking the front door, she called out to her father. "Daddy, I'm home!" She dropped her book bag on the floor and started taking her coat off. Her father startled her as she was hanging it up.

"Your report card came today," her father said to her as he approached her slowly, almost looking as if he was stalking her. Tamera started backing up, hating the look that he was giving her. She knew that something had to be wrong with her report card for him to look the way that he did. "You want to explain to me how the hell you failed Physics?"

Tamera was speechless. She didn't know what to say and definitely didn't like the look in his eyes or the way that he was stalking her in the corner. Before she could say anything, her father had advanced to her and slapped her in her face. He grabbed her by her hair and yanked her head back.

"Understand something," her father started as he got all the way in her face. "You ain't been getting no failing grades and you're not about to start that shit now. So whatever's going on, you better fix it and fix it quick. Do you understand me?!"

"Yes," Tamera whimpered with fear in her eyes as they swelled up with tears. Her father let her hair go but stayed in her face as she continued to whimper.

"Until your grades improve, no hanging out with those little fast ass girls you've been hanging with and unless you're getting tutoring, you bring your ass straight home, you got that?!" her father piped.

"Yes sir."

"Go on upstairs and get your homework done. I'll see you in the morning before you leave for school."

Yani

Tamera wiped her eyes with her sleeve and grabbed her book bag before making her way upstairs. When she heard the front door slam shut and lock, she burst out in tears and ran up to her bedroom. She managed to get herself under control and called Jamal.

"Yo!" Jamal answered.

Tamera cleared her throat. "Hey."

"What's up girl? Your pop left?" Tamera didn't answer because the tears had started to come again and she was quickly trying to get it together not wanting to break down. "Boo, you heard me?" Jamal asked after turning the volume up on his phone. "Babe, talk to me. What's wrong?"

Tamera couldn't hold it in any longer and she broke down in tears.

"Talk to me Ma, what's wrong?"

"My dad," Tamera managed to say through her sobs. "My report card came today and he saw that I failed Physics. He gripped me up by my hair and slapped me in my face." She sniffed and wiped her eyes.

Jamal knew that something was going on with her father but he was hoping that it wasn't on a physical abuse level. He shook his head angrily wanting to fuck her father up. "Did he leave?" he asked her.

"Yes," Tamera replied, gaining her composure.

"I'm on my way," Jamal said as he grabbed his coat.

"No, don't. He said that I couldn't have company or anything."

"Yo, I'm not leaving you in that house by yourself like that. Your pop is on some other time, for real. He was out of order for that shit, real rap. You need me there with you. Otherwise you wouldn't have called."

Tamera was quiet for a moment but then gave in. He was absolutely right. She called him because she wanted to feel protected with his arms around her.

"I'll be there in 20 minutes," Jamal told her before hanging up his phone and leaving out. When Tamera answered the door, Jamal gave her a huge bear hug. She let him in and closed the door behind him. They sat on the couch and Tamera laid her head in his lap. He ran his fingers through her long dark hair, soothing her. After moments of silence, Tamera began telling Jamal things that she never told Deisha or Chanda. That night, Jamal would find out shocking truths about Tamera's home life and her past.

Apologies, promises and forgiveness were what was going on between Maurice and Deisha. Maurice promised to spend as much time with Deisha as he did with Jamal and Deisha promised to accept Jamal as his best friend. She also silently promised to herself that it would be a long time before she had sex with him again.

That weekend, Deisha and her friends were planning on hanging out in Center City together. The only person missing from their posse was Tamera. She hadn't been hanging out with them after school like she normally did. Deisha decided to give her a call and find out what was up.

"Hello," Tamera answered on the second ring.

"Hey girl, what's up?" Deisha perked.

"Nothing. I'm just working on this Newton's Law of Motion Lab," Tamera said plainly.

"Why don't you take a break and hang out with us?" Deisha suggested.

"Hang out with who?" Tamera asked

"It's me, Maurice, Chanda, Shizz and Jamal."

Tamera jumped out of her bed and looked out of the window. "It must be some flying pigs or something for you to be hanging out with Jamal."

Deisha burst out laughing. "Shut up. I promised Maurice that I would be more civil with Jamal."

"Right…" Tamera said doubtfully. She had a feeling that Deisha had some kind of hidden agenda. "As much as I would love to see you and Jamal hang out, Jamal already asked me and I can't. My dad put me on punishment."

"For what?" Deisha asked.

"I failed Physics and he wasn't too pleased with it so now I'm on house arrest."

"Doesn't Serge work today?"

"Yeah, why?" Tamera asked suspiciously.

"Well, we can hang out downtown at the movies before they close down that theatre and have you back home before your dad gets back in from work."

"No I don't think I should do that, Deisha." Tamera protested.

"Come on, Tammy. You know you want to. You know you want to see Jamal. I don't know why you're fronting. Come on. Please? Pretty, pretty please?" Deisha begged.

"Alright, shut up! Just shut up." They giggled together. "Let me comb my hair and change my clothes."

"Meet us on 22nd and Ridge Avenue. We're going to go down to the Gallery and maybe over to the movies."

"Okay. I'll see y'all in 20 minutes." They hung their phones up and Tamera rushed to get ready. The entire time she had a feeling that she should keep her ass in the house. But she was tired of staying home, tired of her father ridiculing and criticizing her for every little thing she did. Most of all, she was tired of her father putting his hands on her and slapping her around.

Tamera bolted out of the house and locked the door behind her. She high tailed it over to 22nd and Ridge Avenue where her gang of friends were patiently waiting for her.

"Oh shit! Serge is gonna whip that ass if he finds out you snuck out of the house!" Chanda yelled. Her friends laughed. Jamal threw his arm around her neck and kissed her on the cheek.

Yani

The 33 bus pulled up in no time and they all climbed aboard elated that the bus wasn't crowded. They sat in the very back of the bus talking loudly and cracking jokes. Instead of going to the Gallery, they decided to just go to the movies. Just as Tamera was coming through the doors, a guy bumped into her almost knocking her backwards.

"Watch where the fuck you're going," the guy hissed at her.

"You bumped into me," Tamera replied looking at him crossly.

Jamal stepped in between Tamera and the guy. "Nigga, you better watch where the fuck you're going and watch how you're talking to my girl real rap before I run up in your mouth."

Another guy, short and stocky, stepped over to them causing Shawn and Maurice to step in making it look like a good old fashioned Mexican stand off without the guns.

"You better keep that shit moving, yo. You don't want any work," Shawn said to the short and stocky guy.

Short and Stocky grabbed his friend. "Come on yo, fuck those niggas." He pulled his friend along and they headed over to buy their snacks.

"You cool?" Jamal asked Tamera as they got in a separate line to buy popcorn.

"Yeah." Tamera shook her head. "Niggas are so ignorant these days."

"Don't worry about it. He knew what was good for him." They stood in the line with Deisha and the rest of their friends, buying snacks and drinks for the movies. Once inside of the theatre, Tamera stood on the outside of an aisle waiting for Jamal when the same guy came past her and bumped her again, causing her to spill her drink over the front of her shirt.

Chanda and the others turned around when they heard her shriek.

"Yo, what the fuck are you doing?" Jamal piped.

"You got a fucking problem then, what?" the guy who bumped Tamera snapped back. Jamal slid Tamera to the side and took his hoody off.

"We got the whole fucking aisle," Short and Stocky chimed in as his friend threw his hands up.

Jamal and the guy began fighting with Jamal whipping his ass so badly it was sad. Whenever his opponent tried to dodge a left, Jamal hit him with a right. It almost looked like he was bobbing and weaving into the punches.

"Maurice, Shawn! Y'all not going to break that up?" Tamera asked, becoming frightened.

"Hell naw, shit let them fight," Shawn said as he stood in a chair to get a closer look.

"No," Tamera said, pushing past so she could try to stop Jamal. She grabbed his arm just as the guy was throwing a punch. He missed Jamal but caught Tamera on the side of her face. Jamal reacted in an instinct and hit the guy with a three piece, knocking him on his ass.

"Oh shit!" Maurice exclaimed. "Hit that nigga, Jamal! Hit him!"

Shawn grabbed Jamal and Short and Stocky grabbed his friend, helping him get up from off of the ground. Security came in after hearing the commotion and escorted them out. Jamal and his friends left the movie theatre and began walking to the Gallery not ready to return home.

"Let me see your face," Jamal gestured to Tamera. She stood in front of him and he looked her over. He didn't say anything. He just nodded his head as if he were satisfied with what he saw.

"He mangled my face?" Tamera asked him.

"No. But you can tell that he hit you." Jamal answered as they continued walking down the street. "We gotta get you to a store to get another shirt. I'm ready to whip dude ass again." Jamal shook his head. They headed over to The Gallery and Jamal stopped in the Gap to buy Tamera another shirt. They walked around talking, laughing and bussing on people as time quickly passed by.

"What time is it?" Tamera finally asked.

Jamal looked at his watch. "Almost six-thirty. Why?"

"Oh my God, I was supposed to have been home. My dad gets off at six and will be home any minute," Tamera panicked.

"Just tell him that you went to the library and lost track of time." Jamal suggested.

Tamera nodded deciding to go along with the plan. They rode the 48 bus home and Jamal walked her to the corner of her block.

"I'll call you if anything goes wrong," Tamera said quickly.

"Alright," Jamal said as he gave her a kiss.

Tamera rushed home hoping that things didn't go wrong. She was also hoping that her father, by some miracle, worked over-time and hadn't gotten home yet. She cracked the front door open and silently slipped inside. She didn't see any sign of her father so she crept up to her room. Just as she was about to open her door, her father came out of his room.

"Where the hell were you?" he asked in a loud and intimidating voice.

"Oh, I was at the library looking up some information and I lost track of the time," Tamera stammered, hoping that her father bought the story.

"Five hours?" Mr. Harrison asked, knowing that his daughter was lying. "The library closed at two. It's past seven. Now I'm going to ask you again and you better not stand here in my face and tell me another bold faced lie. Where were you?"

Tamera opened her mouth to speak but nothing came out. She lowered her eyes and looked at the floor.

"I'm waiting," her father said, having a good idea what she was going to tell him.

"I was with Jamal," Tamera mumbled.

"You were with who?" he asked, making her repeat herself.

"I said, I was with Jamal," she replied louder. "I wanted to see him."

Yani

"What did I tell you? I said that I didn't want you around him and you go behind my back. Plus you leave this house when I specifically told you not to. Then you purposely lied in my face." Tamera tried to speak but he cut her off. "Not one damn word. And what happened to your face?"

"I fell off of a bike," Tamera lied again.

"Are you lying to me again?" her father hounded.

"No," Tamera panicked.

He grabbed her by her collar and pushed her into the wall. "Did he put his hands on you?!" he yelled, scaring her.

"No he didn't touch me. I swear he didn't touch me," she cried. "Why are you doing this to me?"

"Call him," Tamera's father demanded as he let her go.

"What?" she asked confused.

"I said call him and tell him that you can and will never see him again as long as you live in my house. Do you understand me?" Her father grabbed the cordless phone and gave it to her. Tamera took the phone and wiped her face. She dialed Jamal's number and waited for him to answer. Shawn answered instead.

"Who's this?" Shawn asked, not recognizing Tamera's voice.

"It's Tamera. Can I speak to Jamal?"

"What's up Tammy?" Shawn replied before handing the phone to Jamal.

"Yo!" Jamal answered.

"Jamal I can't see you anymore," she wasted no time telling him.

"Wait a minute. Why not?" Jamal asked.

"Don't ask me why. You already know why." Tamera's father snatched the phone from her and hung it up.

"Don't make me break your ass up in here. Now try that shit again!" her father threatened.

Tamera went up to her bedroom and plopped onto her bed burying her face into her pillow. She started to think of her mother, wishing she were there.

Jamal hung up the phone and looked at it.

"What happened?" Shawn asked.

"Tamera just broke up with me." He shrugged his shoulders. "I'll find out what the deal is on Monday." The phone rang again and Jamal answered it. "What's up Sa? What's going on...?" Shawn looked at Jamal and watched him as he left the living room. When Jamal lowered his voice, he knew that their cousin Samir must have been calling to have Jamal do something for him that would lead to more trouble. He shook his head and flipped the channel to ESPN. It was no point in him even saying anything to Jamal. He never listened. When Jamal hung up and ran up to his room, Shawn decided to be a little nosey.

A THUG'S REDEMPTION

Jamal went into his bedroom and reached into the top of his closet pulling out his shoe box. He sat it on his bed and pulled out the gun that he used to kill Khalil with. He held the gun in his hands and then aimed it at the wall. Shawn walked into his room and stopped dead in his tracks.

"Jamal," he said breathlessly. That was the first time that he was that close to a real gun. Jamal looked at him and sat the gun to the side. "Where did you get that from?"

"Samir gave it to me a while back," Jamal replied.

"Why do you still have it?"

"Just for a rainy day," he put the gun back in the shoe box and sat it back in the top of his closet. "I haven't pulled the trigger in more than two years," Jamal mentioned.

"So you did kill him," Shawn concluded before he could get the full story for himself.

"Killed who?" Jamal asked playing dumb. He knew who Shawn was referring to.

"Come on, don't act stupid Jamal. You know who I'm talking about; Khalil."

Jamal didn't answer him at first. "You know I did. So why are you asking?"

"But why?" Shawn asked him.

"Because he killed my young bol and was going around bragging about that shit. That's why." Jamal was beginning to grow tired of Shawn's questions.

"What do you need the gun for now?"

"Samir needs me to do something for him. Don't go running your mouth to mommy or anybody else. Don't worry about me. I can handle mine."

Shawn left the room realizing at that moment that something terrible was about to go down.

Tamera managed to avoid Jamal at school until they were sitting in the gym room one day. She was on the bleachers reading a book when Jamal purposely sat behind her next to Maurice.

"Are you and Deisha going on the Junior Prom?" Jamal asked Maurice.

"Naw. I told her I wasn't going. It's a waste of time and a waste of money. What about you? Are you going to that trash?" Maurice chuckled.

"I was going to take this girl that I had started to like. But her old man started tripping and all of a sudden she doesn't want to be with me no more. She doesn't call me, ignores me in school. I gets no holla from her anymore," Jamal replied as he looked at Tamera.

Tamera caught on to who he was referring to and got off of the bleachers and walked over to the water fountain to get a drink of water.

Yani

Jamal followed behind her. "Why won't you talk to me?" he asked her.

"I told you why already," Tamera replied before sipping some more water.

"No you didn't."

"Well, all you need to know is that I can't see you anymore," she answered.

"No. I want to know why?" Jamal insisted.

"Because my dad said so, that's why."

"When are you going to start thinking for yourself instead of always letting what your dad say stop you from having what you want. Pretty soon, you're not going to know what you want yourself. That shit ain't cool."

"I want you," Tamera whispered.

"Then stop letting your dad come between us." Jamal hugged Tamera and she laid her head on his chest. She knew what he said was right. She liked Jamal a lot but didn't want to disobey her father. But she was tired of him treating her like everything she did was wrong. It was time to start living for herself.

Deisha and Chanda were in their elective class talking about Jamal again. "I thought he changed but he's going right back to his old shitty ways. I saw him on the corner of 23rd and Turner Street the other day and I could've sworn I saw him selling drugs," Deisha whispered.

"Shawn is starting to get new on me, too. He used to talk to me all the time. Now it's like every time we talk about something, he either gets distant or he changes the subject to sex or something."

"He tried you before?" Deisha inquired.

"Yeah but I always had an excuse," Chanda replied.

"Y'all only been talking since October and he's already pushing up on you. I thought I knew Shawn better than that," Deisha said, being too quick with her judgment.

"Deisha, you don't know shit. You're always assuming shit about somebody and don't ever be right," Chanda snapped.

"Don't talk to me like that, Chanda," Deisha said, looking at her best friend as if she had lost her mind.

"No because you swear you know everything. Everybody's not like you waiting forever in a damn day to have sex with their dude." Chanda straightened her papers out on her desk and got back to her work clearly annoyed. Deisha rolled her eyes and then got back to her own school work. After calming down and realizing that she was a bit quick with her words, she decided to lighten the mood with a few jokes to make her friend laugh. And as usual, all was forgiven and they went back to their giggling, gossiping ways.

Jamal and Tamera began talking again on the low. They had little codes that Tamera would put in his cell phone so they would be able to talk without her father hassling them. If there were any emergencies or she wanted to meet him anywhere or just wanted to let him know that she was home after they were done hanging out, she would leave a three digit number in his cell phone and they would let things flow from there.

Shawn was coming in the house from basketball practice when he overheard Jamal talking on the phone. He could tell by the hostility in his brother's voice that some drama was about to go down.

"Yeah, that nigga was talking some real shit but I got something for him…" Shawn heard Jamal saying on the phone. "…Yeah he think I won't bust a cap in his ass… It's in my closet, nigga… alright bet… Tomorrow." Jamal hung up his phone and Shawn walked the rest of the way upstairs as if he didn't hear anything.

The next day while Jamal was in the shower, Shawn snuck into his room and looked in the top of the closet. He took out the shoe box and looked inside. As soon as he saw the gun, the back of his throat dried as fear knotted his stomach. He took the gun out and sat the shoe box back in the top of the closet just like the way he found it. Then he crept back out of Jamal's room and went into his own.

Jamal got out of the shower and went into his room to get dressed. While he was putting on his clothes, Shawn knocked on the door.

"What?" Jamal asked as he was putting his jeans on.

"I'm about to run to the store, you want something?" Shawn asked.

"Naw, I'm cool. I might not be here when you get back. If you need anything, I'll be around Redner Street."

"Alright," Shawn replied. He left the house. Jamal put his sneakers on and then went to the closet to get the gun out. The guy Shawn heard him talking on the phone with was their cousin, Samir. Jamal had started selling drugs for him again and had already run into some beef. There were some new heads on the block trying to sell for someone else. That was a no-no in Samir's book. If you didn't work for him, there was no way you were going to sell on his turf and live to talk about it. Jamal looked inside of the shoe box and was surprised to see the gun wasn't in there. He checked his dresser drawer, under the bed, and under his mattress, all which turned up empty. He stood in the middle of his room puzzled as he looked around trying to figure out where he put his gun. It then dawned on him that his younger brother Shawn had it.

"Shawn… DAMN!" Jamal snatched his jacket from off the back of his door and ran out of the house, leaving his cell phone behind on top of his dresser.

Tamera was at a corner store buying some snacks to have while she did her homework. Right before she paid for her things, she overheard two guys talking about Jamal.

Yani

"Yeah, Jamal thinks he's the shit, trying to tell somebody where they can't sell like that's his block or something. He better get the fuck outta here. I'm trying to make this paper. I ain't got him or his punk-ass cousin to think about," the first guy said as he paid for his blunt and Pepsi.

"Yeah Chaz, but you know that nigga's crazy. Him and his cousin. You better chill with that shit," his friend warned him.

"Naw, fuck him. Everybody else around there can be scared of them but fuck that pussy. Wait until I see him." They left the store. Tamera was startled. She had to hurry up and get home so she could warn Jamal. As soon as she got in the house, she picked up the phone and left a message on his cell phone, leaving 357 in it. That was one of the codes Jamal told her to use if anything was seriously wrong. During normal circumstances, Jamal would answer her right back. But since he didn't have his phone, he couldn't. She called him a few more times but still got no answer. She came up with the same results when she called his house.

Tamera paced back and forth in her living room as she held the cordless phone in her hand. She tried desperately to remember Shawn's number. When she finally thought of it, she dialed it and left the emergency code in his phone with her phone number. When Shawn saw it, he called the number back, familiar with the code because it was one that his brother gave him as well.

"What's the deal?" Shawn asked when Tamera answered the phone.

"Shawn, where is Jamal?" Tamera panicked.

"Why? What's wrong?"

"I just heard these guys in the Papi store talking about Jamal and Samir and one of the guys said he was going to do something to Jamal the next time he saw him. Where is he?!" Tamera practically screamed in his ear.

"He told me he would be on Redner Street." Shawn replied feeling sick to his stomach knowing that his brother could be in trouble and wouldn't be able to defend himself because he took his gun.

"Get him and bring him home, now!" Tamera ordered him.

"I just took his gun..." Shawn said out loud.

"What the hell is he doing with a gun?! Is he selling again? You know what, just get him home!" Tamera said before hanging up.

Shawn hung up the phone and headed over to Redner Street. Just as he was coming close to the block, he could hear Jamal arguing with another guy. Shawn ran around the corner just as the guy was pulling out his gun. Some of the people who were watching, scattered like roaches. Others backed up, but continued watching.

Shawn pulled out the gun that he had. "Yo, what the fuck is going on?" he asked, thinking that he had arrived just in time.

Jamal stood between Chaz and his brother. "Shawn, stay out of this and go home," Jamal said keeping an eye on the guy with the gun.

"Aw shit! Your brother is here, too? That's even better," Chaz said as he aimed his gun at Shawn. Shawn aimed the gun that he had at Chaz.

"Ain't shit jumping off. Just go ahead, dude," Shawn replied. His heart was racing from fear and adrenaline, but he was not going to back down.

"Nigga, you're hard. Just pull the fucking trigger, bitch," Chaz taunted him with a grin on his face. He knew Shawn didn't have it in him to pull the trigger. He could tell by the look in his eyes.

"Shawn!" Jamal hollered, trying to get his younger brother's attention. Shawn aimed the gun with both of his hands.

"Do it, bitch!" Chaz continued to taunt.

"Shawn, don't do it, man. Just run," Jamal pleaded to his younger brother shifting his eye contact back to Chaz. Shawn looked at the guy also and then looked at Jamal as if he didn't know what to do. He closed his eyes and squeezed the trigger. When nothing happened, his eyes widened and he looked at Jamal. Jamal reacted quickly by pushing Shawn to the ground just as Chaz shot at them. One of the bullets hit Jamal in his back and went through his side. Chaz ran from the scene.

Shawn felt something warm dripping on his hand. He rolled his brother over and saw the blood seeping through his hooded jacket. He frowned and hollered out for someone to call the cops. Tears streamed out of his eyes as he held his brother tighter, listening to him wheezing.

"Breathe Jamal. Just breathe. Please don't leave me here," Shawn begged.

Tamera had also called Maurice just in case Shawn couldn't find Jamal. They heard the gun shots and then heard Shawn screaming and ran in that direction. Maurice got a glimpse of Jamal on the ground and grabbed Tamera. She tried to jerk away from him.

"No Maurice let me go," she insisted trying to get away from him.

"No, Tammy you don't need to see this," Maurice said hugging her and keeping her back turned to Jamal. Tamera cried, fearing the worst. Maurice shook his head having flash backs from when Raheem was on the ground bleeding to death in Jamal's arms. His eyes became teary as he feared history was repeating itself.

It seemed like forever for the cops to show up. An oxygen mask was placed over Jamal's face after he was placed onto the stretcher and the ambulance took him away. Maurice saw the cops talking to Shawn and then he was placed in the back of a cop car and taken away.

"What hospital are they taking him to?" Tamera asked one of the detectives that were still on the scene.

The police officer flipped through his tablet. "They're taking him to Temple University. Do you know the victim?"

"Yes. He's my boyfriend. His name is Jamal Williams and he's 17 years old. I have to go." Maurice grabbed her after he flagged down one of his friends and got him to agree to take them to the hospital. As Tamera was running to the car, her father snatched her by her arm.

"Where the hell do you think you're going?" he fumed at her.

"To the hospital, let me go," she answered, trying to pull away.

"Who the hell do you think you're talking to? Bring your ass home right damn it NOW!" Mr. Harrison yelled at Tamera.

Tamera snatched away from him and screamed as loud as she could, "GET OFF OF ME!"

Her father recoiled and took a step back. Tamera climbed in the back of the car with Maurice and they sped off.

They sat in the waiting room for what seemed like hours waiting to hear how Jamal was doing. Finally, a doctor came over to them.

"He'll pull through. The bullet exited from his left side and thankfully no major arteries and no organs were damaged. He did lose a great deal of blood and we needed to do a blood transfusion. Right now he's been sedated and is completely out of it but he will be just fine. He was very, very lucky."

Tamera let out a sigh of relief and Maurice hugged her. "Can I see him?" she asked the doctor.

"Yes, but make it brief. Some tests needs to be run and then we're going to move him to his room." Tamera followed the doctor down the hallway while Maurice stayed behind waiting for Shawn and his mother to arrive. When Tamera saw Jamal lying in the hospital bed with tubes going in and out of his arms she wanted to break down and cry. She decided to hold it in until she got home.

"I swear I never thought I would be crying over you," she said as she sat next to him. "But then again, I never saw myself in this situation before." She began telling Jamal everything that happened while she was at the store and how she tried to call him but couldn't get a response. "I was finally able to catch up with Shawn. I guess if I would've done that sooner, this wouldn't have happened to you. Then again, maybe this happened for a reason." Tamera looked at him in silence and then stood up to leave. "I know you think I'm probably just saying this now because of the situation that you're in but, I love you. And I'm so glad I followed my heart instead of listening to Deisha and my father." She kissed Jamal on the forehead. Then she walked over to the door and took one last look at Jamal before leaving out.

Tamera went over to a pay phone and called Deisha. Ms. Niecie answered the phone instead.

"Hi Ms. Niecie, can I speak to Deisha, please?" Tamera asked in a shaky voice.

"What's wrong sweetheart?" Ms. Niecie asked.

"My boyfriend was shot earlier and I rode to the hospital with Maurice and one of his friends but I don't have car fare to get home." She sniffed and wiped the tears from her eyes.

"Jamal?" Ms. Niecie asked.

"Yes."

"Well Deisha is sleeping right now. But if you want me to, I can pick you up and take you home. Oh my God, I heard they were shooting around there earlier, but I didn't know it was your boyfriend. I'm so sorry, Tamera. Is he okay?"

"Yes, he's sedated right now but they said he was going to be okay. Thank you Ms. Niecie. Can you please come get me?"

"Sure sweetheart. What hospital are you in?"

"Temple University."

"Okay. I'm on my way." They hung up with each other. Tamera sat on the bench and put her hands to her face as she leaned on her knees. She knew she was going to be in a world of trouble once she got home.

Ms. Niecie drove Tamera to her house. Knowing that it was about to be some trouble with her father, Tamera asked Ms. Niecie if she would come inside with her. As soon as Tamera got inside, her father began yelling and cursing at her.

"How do you think I could just leave my friend bleeding to death in the street like that because you think that you know what's best for me? You don't know anything!" Tamera was finally standing up to her father.

"You think that you're that grown that you can stand in here and talk to me anyway you want to?! I told you I didn't want you around him and that's what the hell I meant!" her father yelled.

"I don't care what you want!" Tamera yelled back. Her father back slapped her in her mouth making her fall into the dining room chair. Ms. Niecie ran into the room and grabbed him trying to calm him down.

"Come on Darnell, this is your only daughter. Why would you want to push her away like that? All she wants is a little freedom to be who she is," she tried to reason with him.

"Well if she wants freedom, then she can get the hell out of here!" Mr. Harrison yelled.

"Well then, that's what I will do," Tamera said as she rushed past her father and ran up to her bedroom. She started packing her things, having no idea where she was going to go.

"Tammy?" Ms. Niecie knocked on her bedroom door. "Do you wanna stay with me?" she asked, saddened that such a nice young lady like Tamera would be going through something like this at home.

"Could I, please? I can't stay here anymore. I'm tired of him slapping me around and he's about to make me do something in here that'll land me in jail," Tamera said through her bedroom door as she threw more clothes inside of her duffle bag.

Yani

"I understand what you're going through," Ms. Niecie sympathized.

Tamera snatched her bedroom door open and said in a very low voice, "You couldn't possible understand what I am going through."

Ms. Niecie looked at Tamera and for the first time she saw hate in her eyes. "Let me help you with that." She took one of the duffle bags from Tamera and they walked down the stairs together.

Tamera stood in front of her father as he sat in his recliner reading a book. "I'll be back for the rest of my things."

"Make sure you leave your key," he replied not even looking up from his book. Tamera and Ms. Niecie left the house and headed to her new home.

The police were interrogating Shawn. Unfortunately for him, the gun that he had was dropped when Jamal pushed him to the ground. His finger prints were all over it and what made the situation even more unfortunate is not only was the gun stolen, but it was one that only police officers were supposed to have. Shawn was about to be in some deep shit.

"So whose gun was it?" one of the officers asked as he sipped on his mug of coffee.

"I found it," Shawn lied with a straight face. No way was he going to snitch on his brother and tell about Khalil. He would rather go down for his brother's shooting than to let something like that happen.

"Oh, you just happened to find a gun when your brother was in trouble as you said earlier," the other cop mocked as he sat in front of Shawn on the other side of the table.

"No. I found it a couple of weeks ago. I ain't know what to do with it, so I kept it."

"So if we do a trace on the gun, it wouldn't come back in your name would it?"

Shawn laughed at the cop. "Not a smart question for a cop to ask. I'm 16 years old. The last time I checked, you have to be 21 to get a license to carry and buy a gun." Shawn shook his head at their stupidity.

"Oh you're a little smart-ass, huh?" the first cop smirked. "So where did you find this gun?"

"I found it in a lot on my way home," Shawn told them.

"I'm going to get straight to the point. Did you shoot your brother?" the second cop asked. To Shawn, he looked like one of the crooked detectives from the movie *Rapid Fire*.

"What type of shit is that? You can look at the gun and see that I didn't pull the trigger because for one, the gun didn't have any bullets. For two: ain't no gun powder on my hands or on the gun."

"Then if you didn't do it, who did?" the questionable cop asked.

"I don't fucking know him. All I know is he was pointing a gun at me and my brother and I was pointing mine at him," Shawn said defensively.

"Yours?" the questionable cop asked with a smirk on his face.

"The one I found man, you know what I meant." Shawn shook his head and leaned back in his chair.

"We want you to look at some photos that we have," the second cop said as he moved towards the door.

"Hell no," Shawn refused. "I'm not fingering anybody. Y'all say that y'all are going to protect me and then the next thing you know, I mysteriously turn up dead in a lot somewhere." Shawn got up from his seat and grabbed his coat. "I need to go see my brother."

The cops stopped him. "You're not going anywhere, son. Your finger prints are on that gun. We can easily get you for possession of a weapon."

Knowing that he was a minor, Shawn looked at both of the cops and said, "I want my phone call." It was time for him to reach out to Samir.

The next day, Chanda found out what happened to Jamal. She was highly upset that Shawn didn't call her to let her know what happened or that he was okay. She was even more pissed when she found out he was held by the cops and questioned in the shooting. She immediately called Shawn to find out how both he and Jamal were doing.

"Hey Shawn, I just heard what happened to Jamal and I called to see if he was alright," Chanda said when Shawn answered the phone.

After all of the drama that he had endured at the police station and then all of the madness that he had to hear from his mother along with all of the fake people that were calling and stopping by, people who in his eyes never gave a damn about him or Jamal, he was in a sour mood. He didn't like that his brother had to get shot before people showed some concern.

"How'd you find out?" he asked instead of answering the question.

"I got a phone call from Deisha." Shawn became quiet, still refusing to answer her question. "Shawn?"

"Why the fuck is everybody all concerned about Jamal now when before he wasn't nothing to y'all but another nigga on the street? And Deisha… oh I bet that bitch was real happy to hear Jamal got shot. She's a fucking trip." Shawn was fuming.

Chanda was already in a pissed mood herself. Shawn's comment just made it worse. "I just called to see if you and your brother were okay. Don't get me confused with these other niggas out here because I ain't them. You got locked up and almost got shot and you didn't even bother to let me know you were okay and I'm supposed to be your girl! So what the fuck kinda shit is that, Shawn?!" She slammed the phone down and pushed it to the side. Her anger quickly worked her up an appetite so she decided to go to the store. While she was on her way, she spotted a girl who repeatedly gave her dirty looks whenever she came to The Recreation Center to watch Shawn play basketball. Chanda referred to her as the Bold and Fugly because in her words, "the bitch was fucking ugly". Miss Bold spotted Chanda also and decided to approach her.

"Aye girl, is your name Chanda?" Miss Bold asked as she stopped close to Chanda.

Chanda looked at her ready for her to say or do something she didn't have any business saying or doing so she could punch her in the mouth.

"Yeah, why?"

"I heard that you wanted to fight me," the girl lied. She just wanted an excuse to say something to Chanda, jealous that Shawn wouldn't give her the time of day.

"If I wanted to fight you, I would've fought you already," Chanda retorted.

Miss Bold tried to swing on Chanda while she was talking but Chanda slapped it out of the way and punched her in the face. She started pounding the girl in her face with a fury after anxiously awaiting this day to finally come. One of Chanda's neighbors grabbed her, trying to break it up after seeing how badly her opponent was getting beat up.

"Get off of me!" Chanda practically growled as she kept a good grip on the girl's braids. "I wanted a piece of this trick-bitch's ass for two months. Let me whip her ass for two good minutes." Miss Bold managed to hit Chanda in the face and they started fighting wildly in the middle of the street. Chanda wrestled the girl on top of someone's car setting off the car alarm and then got her in a head lock and started tearing her ass up. Her mother spotted her fighting from up the street and ran over to break it up just as Chanda was about to stomp her. The girl scrambled to her feet and was grabbed by someone who pitied her. She cursed at Chanda, telling her how she was going to get hers.

As Chanda and her mother reached the house, her mother yelled, "What the hell are you doing out here fighting in the damn streets like you've lost your damn mind? I raised you better than that!"

"She started with me," Chanda huffed. "She came up to me talking about she heard that I wanted to fight her and while I was talking, she tried to swing on me," she explained as she tried to catch her breath.

"You never had a problem with any of these girls around here before, so why now?"

"She's been trying to start with me ever since me and Shawn started going together," Chanda replied.

"Don't you ever let me catch you out there fighting like that again," her mother warned.

"Can I run to Deisha's house real quick?" Chanda asked as she grabbed her jacket.

"For what?" her mother asked.

"Shawn's brother was shot yesterday."

"Oh, was that the guy that was shot on Redner Street yesterday?" her mother asked.

"I don't know. That's what I'm trying to find out."

"Go ahead. But don't stay out there too long because these fools are getting crazy and you have school tomorrow," her mother told her.

"I won't," Chanda replied as she left the house. When she arrived at Deisha's house, Tamera was lying across a bed crying. It appeared as though she had been crying for a long time. Deisha saw Chanda standing in her door way and motioned for her to come into the room.

"How's Tammy?" Chanda asked.

"She's been crying all night," Deisha responded as she moved hair out of Tamera's face.

"All night?" Chanda repeated. "She stayed the night or something?"

"She lives here now. But that's another story for later." Deisha ran her fingers through Tamera's long, thick hair trying to soothe her. "Tammy, he's not dead," she whispered. "Go see him."

"I can't," Tamera mumbled.

"He won't forgive you if you don't," Chanda told her as she sat on the bed next to her. The tears began to flow down Tamera's cheeks even more. "Shawn's pissed off because everybody's been calling about Jamal. He should be glad that people are even concerned about his punk ass."

"I'm sorry it had to happen but with everything that he's into, it was only a matter of time," Deisha said.

Tamera sat up and looked at Deisha angrily. "Don't start Deisha, because you weren't there and you don't even know what happened. He pushed Shawn out the way so he didn't get shot."

"Oh my God, are you serious?" Chanda replied with her mouth gaped open. "What the hell did Shawn have to do with anything?"

"Damn," was all that Deisha could think to say.

Tamera ignored the question and got off of the bed. "I guess I will go to the hospital," she said as she leaned close to the mirror and wiped her eyes. She ran a comb through her head and then left out without saying anything else. She went straight to the hospital and up to Jamal's room. She peeked inside and motioned for Shawn to come to the door.

"How is he?" she whispered.

"He was awake earlier. He asked for you but when he saw that you weren't there, he went back to sleep."

"How's your mom?" Tamera asked.

"Man, she went fucking crazy when my cousin called her. They had me down at the police station trying to say that I shot Jamal." Shawn shook his head.

"Yeah I heard that he pushed you out of the way. What was Jamal doing with a gun anyway? Is he selling again?" Tamera asked.

Shawn didn't respond. He figured that was Jamal's story to tell because he wasn't sure what was going on himself. He just knew that their cousin had some kind of pull with the cops because their tone changed drastically and they let him go without any other problems. "You should go in and see him. He's been wanting you here for a while now."

Tamera walked into the room and sat in a chair beside Jamal's bed. He opened his eyes and looked at her.

"What took you so long?" he asked weakly.

"I needed to take care of some things at home," she answered, trying to maintain her usual tone.

"I told you those streets were going to get you killed or land you up in a hospital somewhere. And now look what happened. You're laid up in the hospital, got your brother pulling out guns," Shawn and Jamal's mother said angrily.

Jamal looked at Shawn. "You shouldn't have been there. I don't care what was going on. Don't ever put yourself in a situation like that. Not even for me," Jamal scolded.

"Tamera called me because she couldn't get to you and knew you were in trouble. I was only trying to…"

Jamal interrupted him. "I don't care. You shouldn't have been there. Next time just let me handle things. I don't want you caught up in anything because of me."

"If I didn't come, he would've killed you," Shawn said quietly. The pain was present in his voice when he spoke those words. He got up and left the room. His mother followed him out to make sure he was okay.

Jamal looked at Tamera. "Why did you say that last night?" he asked her.

"Say what?" Tamera asked innocently.

"You said you loved me," Jamal reminded her.

Tamera blushed with embarrassment. "I thought you were sleeping."

"Just because my eyes were closed, that doesn't mean I was asleep. I was hiding from the doctors because I was tired of them poking me and shit." He sighed and looked her over for a moment. "Did you mean it? Or was it like one of those heat of the moment things because I got a cap busted in my ass?" he half way joked.

"I wouldn't have said it if I didn't mean it." Tamera looked at her watch and then got out of the chair she was sitting in. "I have to go back home so I can finish packing."

"Finish packing?" Jamal repeated. "For what? Where are you going?"

"I moved out of my dad's house and Deisha's aunt is letting me stay with her."

"Damn. I know Deisha was probably happy like shit when she found out that I was shot." Jamal assumed.

Tamera lied, "Actually she felt really bad and said that she would be up to see you."

"It's amazing that something bad had to happen to me in order for people to show me some love," Jamal said mostly to himself.

"Well don't include me in that category because that's not the case with me at all." She leaned over and gave Jamal a kiss. "I have to go, alright?" Tamera left and went to her house to pack up some more of her things.

Chanda was heading back to her house after leaving Deisha and ran into Shawn. She was still angry about what he said to her on the phone earlier.

Shawn stopped in front of her. "Hey."

"Don't 'hey' me," Chanda retorted. She walked around him.

"What's wrong with you?" Shawn asked as he followed behind her.

"Why did you catch an attitude with me earlier when all I wanted to know is how your brother was doing?" Chanda asked as she stopped and turned to face him.

"Because man. I was just in a bad mood with the way people were acting. The cops were trying to make it seem like I was the one who shot Jamal and then my mom snapping out. Jamal mad at me and I was only trying to help. It's just been rough. But I didn't mean to take it out on you and I'm sorry," Shawn apologized as he grabbed her hand.

Chanda pulled her hand from his grip and frowned at him. "Don't try that sorry shit now."

Shawn looked at Chanda for a moment and then nodded his head. "Okay, forget it then." He turned and started walking towards his house.

"Alright, alright I was joking, damn," Chanda said as she wrapped her arms around one of his.

"Naw, it's cool. Go ahead with that shit now," he said playing along with her but sounding serious.

Chanda laid her head on his shoulder as they were walking down the street. "I said I was joking." Shawn wrapped his arm around her waist and they turned back towards her house. "I was fighting earlier," Chanda told him.

"Who were you fighting?" Shawn asked.

"You know Tyrone's sister with the big-ass frog eyes? She's always at The Rec loud and shit with her pigeon-head girlfriends. Pete and Khaleef said she looks like Kermit the Frog's twin sister."

Shawn burst out laughing when he realized who Chanda was talking about. "Yeah, I know who you're talking about. She tried to talk to me before."

"Yeah, well I beat her ass today. Fucked that bitch up something lovely! Poppy-eyed bitch. I can't stand jealous bitches. I bet it will be a minute and a half before she shows up at The Rec." Chanda said laughing at the situation.

"Damn, all of that though?" Shawn said referring to her excessive use of profanity. "You curse like a grown-ass man."

"I can't help it," Chanda said and then giggled. They walked on some more in silence. When they got to her house, there was a note left on the dining room table letting her know that her mother and younger brother went to the movies. "Damn, my mom rolled out on me with Kareem and went to the movies." Her and Shawn sat on the couch and talked about what happened with him and Jamal the day before. Out of nowhere, Shawn kissed Chanda. They made out on the couch, caressing each other. At first Chanda wanted more, but when Shawn went for the buttons on her blouse, she stopped him. Shawn backed off and Chanda scooted away from him. After a few moments of awkward silence, Shawn stood up to leave. "I'm about to head back to the hospital to see Jamal before I get ready for school tomorrow. I'll call you later on, okay?"

Chanda nodded, avoiding eye contact. Shawn gave her a peck on the lips and then left the house.

Maurice was at the hospital with Jamal listening to what happened that led up to him being shot. They talked quietly as Jamal told him about the new guys trying to sell on Samir's turf. Maurice didn't know that his best friend had started selling drugs again. Listening to the things that Jamal told him about the life style and all of the connections that Samir had gave him chills and made him feel like he was listening to the plot of some movie.

"Damn man. That's crazy. You should've seen the expression on Shawn's face after you got shot."

Jamal shook his head. "I never wanted Shawn to go through what I went through with Raheem."

"What about the gun that Shawn had? Is it going to trace back to you?" Maurice asked.

"I don't know who the hell that gun is going to trace back to. Samir gave it to me. The only reason the cops traced it back to Shawn is because of his finger prints from when he dropped it."

"What did he tell the cops?"

"He just told them that he found the gun a couple of weeks ago on his way home from school."

Deisha opened the door and came in. Maurice purposely told her to meet him there before they went to the movies, hoping that would squash the beef between her and Jamal when she saw him for herself.

"Hey Jamal," Deisha spoke after closing the door behind her.

"What's up?" Jamal spoke back, looking at Deisha crossly. She was the last person he expected to walk through his door. "I guess your wish came true."

Deisha was quiet as she thought of what to say. She didn't want to sound hateful, but she didn't want to sound like she was full of shit either. "I guess the saying *be careful what you wish for* is true." Deisha shrugged her shoulders not knowing what else to say.

"Alright Jamal, we're out. I'll holla at you one day this week after school. Do you know when you're coming home?" Maurice asked as he stood up to leave.

"Naw, I'm guessing no sooner than the end of the week." Maurice slapped Jamal a hand shake and he and Deisha left out to go to the movies.

Tamera and Chanda were at Tamera's house the next day after school. Chanda was helping Tamera pack up the rest of her things so she could take them back to Deisha's house. They were trying to get done before her father came in from work. Chanda saw a trophy on Tamera's dresser and picked it up.

"What was this for?" she asked before putting it in a bag.

"A singing contest back in the ninth grade," Tamera replied blandly as if it didn't mean anything.

"Aw snap! You won first place."

"Yeah, but it doesn't matter because right after that I had to say goodbye to my mom." Tamera replied sadly.

"What happened to her?" Chanda asked.

"She was killed in a car accident."

Chanda stared at Tamera for a moment as she continued to pack. She never knew her mother was dead. She picked up a Gold medal. "Damn, what was this for?"

"That was from a double-dutch tournament the summer before that."

"Dag girl, you're just rolling in the prizes." Chanda chuckled trying to lighten the mood. Tamera continued to move about as though nothing fazed her at that moment.

"None of it means anything to me anymore. My dad never came to any of my shows to see me perform. He was always putting me down, especially if I didn't do things the way he felt as though I should do them. He was never satisfied with me just being me." They finished packing the rest of Tamera's things and then she called Ms. Niecie to come pick her up. Chanda and Tamera sat on the couch talking while they waited. Moments later, Mr. Harrison came through the door.

"Is that everything?" her father asked as he looked at all of her bags.

"Yes," Tamera replied quietly.

"Good. Give me your key."

Tamera reached in her book bag and gave the key up without hesitation. After Mr. Harrison went up to his bedroom and closed his door, Ms. Niecie knocked on the front door and they began to load all of Tamera's belongings into her jeep.

Yani

"Is that the last one?" Ms. Niecie asked as Chanda carried out a big, black duffle bag.

"Yes," Chanda replied as she placed it in the trunk.

"Do you want to say good-bye to your dad before you go?" Ms. Niecie asked Tamera.

Tamera thought for a moment. "No, I just want to leave." They got into Ms. Niecie's jeep and drove away.

Everyone was wondering when Jamal was going to return to school. A week after Tamera moved in with Deisha and her aunt, Jamal was out of the hospital and back home. Tamera sat at his house keeping him company his first day home. Even though they were talking, Jamal was barely saying anything to her. He was busy watching her, thankful that he had Tamera in his life.

"What?" Tamera asked, finally noticing his stare. "Why do you keep staring at me? Do I have crust in my eye or something?" she joked.

"No," Jamal smiled. "I'm just thinking."

"About what?" she asked.

"How come you're still with me? I almost got me and my brother killed. My brother could've gotten locked up because of me. How can you stand me?"

"I don't know," Tamera said after thinking for a moment. "Like I said before; there is something about you that draws me to you." She stood up and stretched. "I have to go home. Are you coming to school tomorrow?"

"No," Jamal replied as he motioned for her to come over to him. He gave her a hug and squeezed her tightly. Tamera kissed him but he wouldn't release his hold on her so she stayed there, enjoying it. When he finally stopped, she laid her forehead against his and closed her eyes. She truly loved Jamal and had never felt this way about anyone before. She kissed his forehead, said goodnight and left.

CHAPTER 2
TOO MUCH PRESSURE

Things seemed to be getting back to normal. Jamal started going back to school a few days after he got out of the hospital. People treated him the same and that's what made him feel good. He didn't want a lot of fake people in his face giving him special treatment because he took a bullet and lived.

Shawn and Chanda were becoming hot and heavy. Chanda wanted so badly to take things further with Shawn, but she didn't want to be seen as a fast ass who gave it up quickly. Meanwhile Maurice and Deisha were having more sex than they were going out. It was as if they couldn't get enough of each other. One day, Tamera and Deisha were in Tamera's room decorating when Tamera accused her of being addicted to sex.

Deisha laughed out loud. "I'm not addicted."

"Yes the hell you are," Tamera accused her friend as she hung up a Destiny's Child poster. "Anytime he wants that hit, all he has to do is call you over and you come on the run. You're his little booty call," Tamera teased.

Deisha laughed some more. "Shut up, Tammy. You know it's only a matter of time before Jamal has your head smacking up against a headboard somewhere."

"No he won't because he knows that I am a virgin and he told me whenever I was ready," Tamera said proudly.

"Stop beating me in the head with the bullshit. Jamal ain't told you no shit like that," Deisha replied as she looked at Tamera sideways.

"Yes he did. So it ain't going to be nothing running up in me, yet."

"Yet?" Deisha repeated. "What do you mean, yet?"

"I'm just saying, it might be soon."

"Let me find out," Deisha smiled as she placed stuffed animals on Tamera's dresser. "You know, I will admit that you and Jamal do make a cute couple. He comes to school more and doesn't hang out with his little cronies on 23rd and Turner Street as much. You've really been a good influence on him, Tammy. I think y'all are going to make it."

"Aww thanks, Deisha. That means a lot. And I'm glad that y'all are getting along now. He told me y'all used to be real cool in Elementary school and in Vaux."

"Yeah, we were tight back then..." Deisha said as she thought back to their childhood days of playing tag in the school yard and talking about

Street Fighter 2. She smiled to herself as she remembered the crush she had on him in the second grade. They continued their girl talk as they finished decorating Tamera's room.

    Shawn was hanging out with Chanda at her house after school. They were in the living room playing cards and watching a basketball game. Shawn leaned over to kiss her but tried to peek at her cards instead.

    "Stop playing," Chanda giggled as she pushed his face away. "Sike, naw." Shawn leaned over and kissed her for real but jumped back when he heard her mother coming downstairs. They smiled at each other.

    "Chanda, walk Shawn to the corner because it's getting late and you still have school tomorrow. Take Kareem with you so you don't have to walk back by yourself," Chanda's mother told her as she went into the kitchen.

    "Hi Ms. Johnson," Shawn waved.

    "How are you, Shawn?" Ms. Johnson replied back.

    Chanda got up and gave Shawn a helping hand almost falling into the sofa. They laughed together. "Kareem!" Chanda shouted up the steps. "Come downstairs and walk me to the corner."

    "Aww man. For what?" Kareem whined with an attitude as he came down the stairs.

    "Because I said so. Now come on," Chanda replied as she passed him his coat.

    "What's up, Lil Man?" Shawn said as he gave Kareem a handshake.

    "What's up?" Kareem replied, still believing that Shawn was one of the coolest people he had ever met.

    "Are you still working on those moves that I showed you?" Shawn asked as he put his own coat on.

    "Yeah."

    "That's what's up." They walked out of the house towards the corner.

    On their way there, Shawn stood behind Chanda. He held her hands and whispered explicit thoughts as to what he wanted to do to her in her ear, making her laugh.

    "You better stop before my brother hears you," Chanda whispered as they continued down the street.

    "When are you going to come to my house?" Shawn asked her.

    "I'm always around there," Chanda replied, trying to dodge what he was really referring to.

    "You know what I'm talking about," Shawn said, squeezing her hands.

    "Ouch Shawn," Chanda giggled.

    "Yeah that's exactly what I'm going to make you say," Shawn whispered back to her.

"Whatever," Chanda said as she smiled and rolled her eyes. "I'll think about it."

They reached the corner and Shawn gave her a kiss. "I'll call you when I get in the house."

Chanda watched him walk away for a moment. "Come on," she said to her brother. They started walking back towards the house. "Kareem, I saw you take money out of mommy's wallet. You've been acting real funny lately since you've been hanging with them little niggas from Blumberg Projects. I don't want you hanging with those little dudes because they're ignorant and I don't like them. If you're not going to The Rec after school, you bring your ass straight home or I'm telling mommy, you hear me?" Chanda scolded her brother.

"Man, I didn't take any money out of mommy's purse. And those are my friends. We just be chilling after school. We don't do anything," Kareem replied smartly.

"Kareem, I'm not playing with you and you better watch your mouth. Stay out those damn projects. You keep acting all crazy and I'll tell Daddy so he can snatch your little ass up and send you down South Philly. And you know Daddy don't play that tough Tony shit."

"Whatever man," Kareem mumbled. He pretended to be bouncing a ball, dribbling it between his legs and doing a cross over that Shawn taught him. He jumped in the air as if he were shooting a jump shot at the buzzer. Chanda watched him and smiled. Kareem had shot up in height and was almost as tall as she was. His voice had deepened and he was even beginning to lose his baby face appearance. Her younger brother was her world and she was willing to break her foot off in anybody's ass if they did anything to him.

The next day, Maurice and Jamal were in front of the school waiting for the doors to open up. Of course Maurice was telling Jamal that he could have Deisha whenever he wanted her.

"That girl addicted to my shit. Anytime I want it, I get it," Maurice said to Jamal as he leaned into the wall.

"Yeah, it's about to go down with me and Tamera. And she's a virgin, too. You know if you hit a virgin just right, they're never going to leave," Jamal laughed. "I can train her and mold her just right."

Maurice started laughing. "Man, Tammy is a good girl. She ain't giving you shit, Jamal. You might as well hang that shit up, now."

"I bet I hit that by Saturday," Jamal said to Maurice.

"Alright bet." They shook hands. "Saturday, and if not, fifty dollars."

"Aw shit. You might as well give me the money now. You know I don't play when it comes to money."

"Saturday, and I don't mean Sunday afternoon."

"Alright, Saturday," Jamal agreed.

"We should put Shawn in this bet because he's been trying to fuck Chanda for the longest," Maurice suggested.

"I know, right. He knows Chanda ain't even trying to give up no draws for his ass." Maurice and Jamal chuckled as Shawn walked over to them.

"What's up, niggas?" Shawn spoke as he gave his brother and his friend a handshake.

"Speak of the devil," Maurice grinned.

"What, y'all were talking shit about me or something?" Shawn asked.

"Yeah because you know Chanda ain't giving those panties up yet," Maurice joked.

"Nigga, I know you ain't talking when it took you more than a year to pop Deisha. And why you all worried about what I'm doing? I'm handling mine so chill with that shit," Shawn replied smartly.

"Yeah, nigga you're handling yours alright." Jamal pretended he was Shawn jerking off. "You know if Chanda ain't handling it for him if this nigga comes in with a cast on and shit." Jamal and Maurice burst out laughing.

"Professional jack off shit," Maurice laughed harder. Shawn looked at them both crossly but didn't say anything.

"You know we're only fucking with you, Shizz," Jamal said to his brother as he punched him in the shoulder.

"Whatever." Shawn replied blandly.

"I take it he wants a part of the bet," Maurice assumed.

"What bet?" Shawn asked.

"I bet you fifty dollars that you cannot and will not fuck Chanda by Saturday," Maurice challenged.

"Alright bet," Shawn agreed. "You might as well hand me your check, now. Oh my bad, you don't have a job."

"Nigga just make sure you have my money," Maurice replied.

The doors opened just as Tamera walked up. Jamal slung his arm over her shoulder. "You need some help studying?" he asked her sweetly.

"You're going to help me?" Tamera asked doubtfully.

"Yeah, you can come to my house after school and we can order out," Jamal suggested, trying to set his plan into motion early.

Tamera saw where the conversation was headed and slid from under his arm. "Damn, I completely forgot I said I was going to help Deisha with her English paper. Can I take a rain check?" Before Jamal could answer her, she kissed him on the cheek. "Thanks babe." She walked ahead of him to catch up with another girl from their class.

"Cross today off of your calendar." Shawn laughed from behind him.

Deisha saw Shawn in the hallway by his locker and tugged on his shirt. "What were you, Maurice and Jamal betting on outside?"

"How did you know we were betting on something?" he asked.

"You just told me," Deisha joked. "Plus I heard Maurice when he said he thought you wanted in on the bet."

"Oh, we were betting on a Sixers' game outside," Shawn lied quickly.

"No y'all weren't," Deisha said frowning at him.

"Yes we were. See ask Maurice. Yo Mar! Tell your girl we were betting on a Sixers game outside."

Maurice looked at Shawn and then looked at Deisha. "Oh yeah, because they were talking shit like my man A.I is not going to take us to the chip. I got money that says he will. Why do you wanna know?" Maurice replied.

"I don't know. Maybe I want in on this bet too," Deisha smiled, looking at the both of them.

"Naw, shorty. I don't think you want in on this one," Shawn said putting his arm over Deisha's shoulder.

"Yeah, maybe the next one," Maurice chimed in.

Deisha shrugged her shoulders and they went to class. When Shawn saw Chanda, he sat next to her and kissed the side of her mouth. Normally that would make her smile. Today, she continued to sit with her hands folded beneath her nose with an extremely serious look on her face.

"What's wrong?" Shawn asked her.

"My brother has been hanging with these little dudes around Blumberg Projects lately. Those little niggas look like nothing but trouble. He's been acting so differently lately, like he needs to be tough to fit in with those project hood-rats." Chanda shook her head. "He's about to get his ass into something, I can feel it."

"Alright, just calm down. I'll talk to your little brother and let him know those dudes ain't safe and neither is that block. He'll be okay. Nothing is going to happen to him." Shawn rubbed Chanda's neck.

After school, they caught the L train and then got on the 61 bus. Shawn was going to walk Chanda home and hang with her since she didn't have her keys but noticed there were police and ambulance not too far from her block.

"What happened?" Shawn asked one of the guys standing near a corner store.

"Somebody just shot up the block. These niggas around here crazy," the guy replied as he took a puff on his cigarette before plucking it onto the ground.

"I think I'ma just chill at your house for a little while until this dies down," Chanda said. They doubled back to Shawn's house. When they got there, Shawn made them some hot chocolate and heated up left over Salisbury steak, mashed potatoes and string beans for them to eat and they went up to his bedroom. Chanda began looking through his CDs.

Shawn stood behind her and then leaned in closer, pressing up against her backside. He kissed her neck and then asked her, "Are you still cold?"

"Not really," she replied blandly as she moved away from him. She lay across his bed with her hands folded behind her head, staring up at the ceiling. "What time is it?" she asked.

"Almost 4 o'clock," Shawn replied as he lay next to her. "You're torturing me."

Chanda laughed and then looked at him. "How am I torturing you?"

"It's like you're teasing me. And you're laughing at me like this shit is funny. I'm about to go beat my dick or something."

Chanda laughed harder. "I'm sorry." She scooted closer to Shawn and kissed him. They kissed for a moment and then Chanda stopped. She lay her head on his shoulder and closed her eyes. She didn't intend to but she fell asleep. Moments later, Shawn went to sleep right along with her.

Hours later, Shawn woke up first. He looked at his watch and saw that it was almost 7 o'clock. He didn't mean for them to sleep that long. He woke Chanda up so he could walk her home.

"Get up," he said to Chanda as he tapped her on her shoulder. "Get up girl, it's almost 7 o'clock."

Chanda jumped up and shrieked, "What!?"

"It's almost 7 o'clock. Come on so I can walk you home before you get into trouble. Your mom probably wondering where the hell you are," Shawn said as he grabbed his coat and put it on. They rushed to her house and Shawn gave her a brief kiss when they got to her door step. Chanda's mother opened the door causing the both of them to jump.

"Chanda, I've been calling all over looking for you. Where the hell were you?" her mother asked.

"Somebody was shooting around here and I didn't have my keys so I went to Shawn's house until things calmed down. We didn't mean to, but we fell asleep," Chanda said quickly.

"Why didn't you call me? If it weren't for Deisha, I would've been checking the hospitals to see if you were one of the ones that were shot! You could've come to my job if you didn't have your keys and I would've given you mine!" Ms. Johnson was furious. "Shawn, she will see you in school tomorrow. Chanda, get your ass in this damn house!" Chanda came in the house and Ms. Johnson slammed the door behind her and stood in front of Chanda with her hand on her hip. "You have no idea how worried I was trying to find out where you were when I found out what happened around here. What made you think that you could just go on about your day when something like that happened?"

"I'm sorry, Mom. I didn't mean to fall asleep. I was just going to hang out until you got home from work. I wasn't thinking about letting you know I was okay... I was just thinking about not being locked out in the cold," Chanda replied.

Ms. Johnson shook her head and took a deep breath. "Now, I know that you are sexually active because I saw the birth control in your dresser drawer."

"Mom!" Chanda yelped embarrassed by her mother's remarks. "Just because you found birth control in my room doesn't mean I'm doing anything."

"So you're going to stand in my face and tell me that you're not having sex when we both know that you are. Did you do something today?" her mother asked.

"Mom…" Chanda groaned.

"Don't mom me. Did you and Shawn have sex today or any other day?"

"No mom. He wanted to but I told him to wait because I wasn't ready."

Chanda's mother let out a sigh of relief. "Good. I know that you're 17 now but still, don't slip up. Go around the King Center and tell Kareem I said to bring his narrow ass home right now. I want both of y'all in this house where I can see y'all. Today was too much," Ms. Johnson said as she headed into the kitchen to start dinner.

When Shawn got back to the house from walking Chanda home, he saw Jamal sitting on the couch watching television.

"Did anything come on the news about the shooting?" Shawn asked as he hung up his coat.

"Naw, nothing came on yet. Maybe tonight, though. Mommy called all frantic wanting to make sure we were in the house and not running the streets. She cracks me up acting like she gives a damn when she wouldn't know if we were in the house or not since she's hardly the hell here anyway." Jamal hissed. He changed the channel and then looked over at his younger brother. "Why did you take my gun, Shawn?" Jamal asked out of nowhere.

"Because I didn't want you to get caught doing any dumb shit," Shawn answered. He had hoped that Jamal never asked him about that.

"But why? You didn't even know that the gun didn't have any bullets."

"Yeah well, it's a little too late to worry about that now, isn't it?" Shawn replied sarcastically. "I'm still waiting for you to tell me what the hell you needed a gun for in the first place. What, you were about to start selling for Samir again?"

"Why don't you stop worrying about me? Your worrying almost got both of us killed," Jamal snapped back. He shook his head regretting the way he said that. He took a deep breath. "I'm about to order some pizza for dinner, are you hungry?" Jamal asked his younger brother.

"Naw, I'm good," Shawn mumbled as he walked up to his room.

Jamal stood in front of the mirror and lifted his shirt up, looking at the bullet wound that almost cost him his life. He was tired of the hustling and selling drugs, fighting and getting into trouble. It seemed like he would never get from underneath Samir's heel. But that was all that he knew since he was 15 years old.

The next day after school, Chanda ended up back at Shawn's house in his bedroom. They were listening to CD's again when Shawn stood behind her and kissed her neck. She didn't say anything or try to stop him, so Shawn took it as his queue to take things further. He turned her around and kissed her. When she kissed him back, he began to move her over to his bed. Chanda stopped him and stepped away. She folded her arms over her chest and shook her head at him, smiling.

"Why do you keep trying?" Chanda asked him.

"Because I want to show you another way of saying I love you." Shawn replied honestly. Chanda was speechless. The moment that she had dreamed of since she was in the 9th grade: Shawn Williams had told her that he loved her. Her heart was about to jump into her hands. Shawn kissed her and she responded positively. He laid her on his bed and started to undress her. Not wanting to reveal her body to him completely, Chanda kept her shirt on. Shawn took things slow to make sure that she didn't think that he was just trying to screw her. He wanted to make sure he had a second chance with her.

When it was over, Chanda couldn't wipe the smile off of her face. Shawn slid from under the covers to get dressed knowing he had to walk her home soon. Chanda decided to do the same.

After putting her clothes on, she playfully threw her book bag at him. But as Shawn gave Chanda back her book bag, he accidentally said aloud, "I told Jamal and Maurice that they should've just given me the money up front."

Chanda was getting ready to put her book bag on when it dawned on her what he had just said. "What do you mean they should've just given you the money up front?" she hissed.

"That's not what I meant," Shawn tried to explain.

"No fuck that!" Chanda yelled, becoming irate as well as embarrassed. "You fucked me on a bet?" Chanda punched him in his chest. "How could you do this to me?"

Shawn tried to stop her, but she yanked away and hit him with her book bag.

"Get your fucking hands off of me!" She snatched her coat from off of the back of his chair knocking it down and rushed out of his room before storming down the steps.

Shawn followed behind her. "Chanda, it's not like that!" he continued after her.

"Get out of my face, Shawn!" She yanked open the door just as Jamal was walking up. She pushed past him and rushed home.

Jamal looked at her as though she was crazy. "What the hell? Did I just miss something?"

"Yeah, Chanda just found out about the bet," Shawn replied as if it were Jamal's fault that Chanda was as angry as she was.

"You hit that?" Jamal asked with a huge grin on his face. Shawn looked at his brother angrily before grabbing his coat and leaving out the house behind Chanda.

Chanda burst into her house and ran up to her room. She grabbed a change of clothes and a bath robe and got into the shower. She cried as she washed herself, thinking the absolute worst of Shawn. Her crush, the guy she had given her heart to, turned out to be no different than the rest and only wanted her for sex. And to make matters worse, her friends made a bet with him as to whether or not he would actually get to have sex with her. Chanda felt dirty and used. She got out of the shower and toweled off before going into her mother's bedroom to get the cordless phone so she could call her two best friends and councilors, Deisha and Tamera.

"Hello," Deisha replied after the third ring.

"Hey Deisha, it's Chanda."

"Well I'll be damned. It must be snowing or something. This girl spoke before starting a conversation. Something must be wrong." Chanda chuckled. "What's up, girl? Why do you sound so down?"

"I had sex with Shawn," Chanda replied as though she had just committed a mortal sin.

Deisha became excited. "Oh my God girl, you did!" She then calmed down. "Damn, was it that bad?"

"No, it was off the hook. It was what happened afterwards that pissed me off."

"What happened?" Deisha asked.

"I really don't feel like talking about it over the phone. Can you and Tammy come stay the night since we don't have school tomorrow?" Chanda asked her.

"Alright, give us twenty minutes," Deisha told her.

They hung up the phone and Chanda went back to her mother's room to put the cordless back on the receiver. She went back into her room and began watching television when she heard the doorbell ring.

"Damn, that was quick," Chanda mumbled to herself. She went downstairs and opened the door. It wasn't Deisha and Tamera however; it was Shawn.

"What did I tell you about opening the door for someone before asking who it is first?" Shawn asked trying to lighten the mood.

"Go to hell," Chanda replied as she tried to close the door in his face.

Shawn held the door open with his arm. "I need to talk to you," Shawn pleaded.

"No you don't. Go collect your money," Chanda said to him with disdain in her voice.

"Can you just listen, please?"

"No, can you leave me alone, please?" Chanda replied.

"So you're actually going to stand here and tell me that you don't have feelings for me anymore?" Shawn asked.

"No I don't," Chanda stated before she closed and locked the door in his face. She turned to go back upstairs when her doorbell rang again.

"Leave me the hell alone, Shawn!" Chanda yelled through the door.

"It's not Shawn!" Deisha and Tamera yelled back in unison.

Chanda went back to the door and opened it for her friends. "I'm sorry, y'all."

"We just saw Shawn walking down the street. He looked mad as hell. What happened to y'all?" Tamera asked.

"Come upstairs because I don't want my mom to come in while we're talking." They went up to Chanda's room. Deisha sat on the floor, Tamera sat on Chanda's beanbag chair and Chanda sat on her bed with a pillow in her lap.

"Now what happened?" Deisha asked.

Chanda ran down the story to her friends of her sexual encounter with Shawn up to the aftermath and finding out that Shawn made a bet that he would have sex with her.

"He fucked you on a bet?" Tamera asked. Deisha and Chanda looked at her shocked. They weren't used to her using profanity that strong.

"Yeah, that's what it seems like," Chanda giggled at Tamera's foul language. "And then he tried to explain that shit. I tried to knock the hell out of him and then I left."

"So that's what they were talking about outside the building yesterday," Deisha realized.

"Who?" Tamera asked.

"Who else? The trio: Jamal, Shawn and of course Maurice. I asked Shawn what they were betting on and he said a damn Sixers game. No wonder they wouldn't let me in on the bet."

"Do you think they were betting on me, too?" Tamera asked innocently.

"Most likely," Deisha smirked as if Tamera should've known better than to ask a question like that.

"I feel dirty. Seriously, like I thought that Shawn was different from the rest of these ass-holes out here," Chanda said as she crossed her arms over her chest.

"Girl, you should've known better. That's Jamal's brother," Deisha said once again blaming someone's screw ups on Jamal. To her, if you hung around Jamal or were related to him, you were guilty by association.

"But you can't judge a person based on how their brother, sister or whoever acts," Chanda said, coming to Shawn's defense.

Deisha crossed her fingers. "Shawn and Jamal go like this. Jamal has all kinds of influences on Shawn."

"Well if that were the case, Shawn would've been out there selling drugs, hustling and fighting just like Jamal," Tamera said, bringing up a good point.

"Exactly, because Shawn knows right from wrong," Chanda chimed in.

"And so does Jamal. But all he thinks about is making money and apparently, so does Shawn because he just fucked you for $100."

Chanda became silent. Ms. Johnson called upstairs. "Chanda, come downstairs for a minute!"

"Damn, I didn't even hear her come in," Chanda got up and went downstairs. "Hi Mom."

"How come you have your pajamas on? And who's upstairs?" Ms. Johnson asked.

"Deisha and Tamera. I was going to ask if they could stay the night since we don't have school tomorrow."

Ms. Johnson looked at her suspiciously. "Yeah okay. Somebody is on the porch for you."

"Who?" Chanda asked.

"They told me not to tell you who it was so y'all must've had a fight," Ms. Johnson said smiling.

Chanda looked at her mother and younger brother suspiciously. She went to the front door and opened it. She wasn't surprised to see Shawn waiting for her on the porch.

She closed the door behind her. "Why are you doing this?" she asked.

"Because I don't believe for one second that you don't have feelings for me anymore. If I was just talking to you so I could get the hit, do you honestly think I would be standing out here in the freezing cold trying to get you to forgive me. I'm really, truly sorry Chanda." He grabbed both of her hands and pulled her close to him so he could hug her. Chanda gave in and hugged him back.

"You get on my nerves boy," Chanda said.

"No I don't," Shawn said as he squeezed her before letting her go. I'll call you later on so we can talk about this. It's cold as shit out here," he said before giving her a big, wet, kiss. He took a step back to see what she was wearing. "Girl, you just don't know!" He laughed and Chanda slapped his arm.

"Go home Shawn, before I change my mind!" After Shawn left the porch, Chanda went back into the house and up to her bedroom. She plopped onto her bed and smiled.

"So what's the deal?' Deisha asked.

"We're still talking," Chanda said happily.

"That's good," Deisha said before she turned her attention to Tamera. "You better find out if Jamal was betting on you, too."

"Oh I will," Tamera said as if she were in deep thought. "You better believe that."

The next day, the girls decided to go to the Gallery to hang out and do a little shopping. They walked past a group of guys where one was bold enough to stop Tamera in hopes of getting her phone number.

"Girl, I have a fetish for your smile," the guy said sweetly, smiling at Tamera. "What's your name?"

"Tammy," Tamera said as she stopped in front of him.

"Do you have a boyfriend?"

"Sorta." Tamera answered.

"What does sorta mean? Either you do or you don't," the guy said to her.

"Well then, he's my boyfriend," Tamera said after laughing.

"Look, my name is Nafis. Let me get your number so I can hit you up sometime?" he asked. He took out his cell phone as if he knew Tamera would give the number to him. She gave the phone number to him but changed a digit to make it the wrong number. Nafis stored it into his phone and smiled.

"Okay bet, I'm going to call you tonight," he replied. Tamera nodded her head and they watched Nafis walk away.

"Damn, thank God for making creatures like that," Deisha whispered as she stared at his backside. "Maurice better be glad that I'm not the type of female to cheat."

"And you better be glad I didn't grab dude and start beating the shit out of him," Jamal said from behind them. Tamera jumped when she heard his voice. They turned around to see Maurice, Jamal and Shawn walking up behind them.

"See Deisha, you just never know when I'm going to show up," Maurice smirked.

Jamal grabbed Tamera by her arm and started pulling her towards the exit doors. "Come here, I want to talk to you." Tamera stumbled out behind him. "Who the fuck was that?"

"Just some guy that was trying to talk to me," Tamera said almost scared that he was going to hit her.

"Why you didn't tell him that you had a boyfriend?" The base in his voice made him sound more like her father.

"I did," Tamera replied.

"Then what the fuck did you give him?"

Tamera was too scared to answer. She was positive that in a couple of seconds, he was going to punch her in the mouth. Since she didn't answer him fast enough, he grabbed her arm and jerked her closer to him.

"What the fuck did you give him?!" he yelled again.

"I didn't give him shit!" Tamera yelled back trying to yank away. People stopped and watched. Tamera noticed them and that frightened her even more. "Let me go Jamal, you're hurting my arm." When he didn't release his grip she yelled, "Get off of me!"

Deisha walked out of the Gallery and went over to them. "Why don't you let her arm go, Jamal? Damn, what the hell is wrong with you?"

"Mind your business Deisha," Tamera warned.

"No, he doesn't have any business gripping you up like you're a fucking man!" Deisha snapped.

Jamal released his hold on Tamera's arm and glared at Deisha. "You need to mind your business and shut the fuck up," he snapped at her.

"No, you shut the fuck up! Ain't nobody scared of your bitch-ass! You swear you're tough when you really ain't shit without your nut-ass cousin at your back!"

Jamal smacked Deisha in her mouth, knocking her into a car.

"Oh shit!" Chanda exclaimed. She had followed Deisha outside with Maurice and Shawn having a feeling that something was going to jump off.

Maurice ran over to Jamal and threw him on top of the car that Deisha fell into. "What the fuck are you doing?" Maurice sneered.

Shawn pulled Maurice off of Jamal. "Get the fuck off of my brother!"

Maurice stepped back and snatched his hooded sweatshirt and shirt from over his head. "What then, Shawn! What! You can get some of the same," Maurice challenged.

Chanda pushed Shawn back. "No Maurice, y'all not fighting!"

"No let them fight, Chanda. He's always so quick to stick up for her when he knows somebody should've been smacked that bitch in her fucking mouth," Jamal retorted.

"Well step your bitch-ass in the street so I can smack you in your fucking mouth. You wanna smack somebody, nigga hit me!" Maurice continued to provoke Jamal. Jamal slid Chanda out of the way.

"No Jamal! I said y'all aren't fighting and that's what the hell I meant. Y'all are too cool for this. Squash this shit. Y'all about to let one nigga come between y'all and have y'all out here fighting. She didn't even give him the right damn number!"

Deisha was being held in a corner so she would calm down. She was cursing about how she was going to get her cousin Darrell, to shoot Jamal and his cousin.

"And Tamera, you're stupid because he's sitting up here betting on when he's going to fuck you and what, not but has the nerve to get mad because another nigga tried to talk to you. Get the fuck outta here with all of that!" Deisha spilled the goods since she was pissed off. Not only did she get her pride hurt, but she got smacked in front of her friends as well as in front of people that she did not know.

Yani

"Shut up, Deisha. You don't even know if it's true or not!" Tamera shot back at her.

Maurice picked up his shirt and hooded sweatshirt from off of the ground and put it back on. He then left with Deisha and they went to catch the bus home.

Tamera turned around and looked Jamal in the eye. "Did you?" she asked him.

"Did I what?" Jamal asked back.

"Did you bet on when you would have sex with me?" Jamal didn't respond. Tamera looked at him for a moment before she spoke again. "You're getting all bent out of shape about me giving a fake number to a guy and you're betting on when you're going to fuck me." Chanda and Shawn looked at Tamera not believing what she said. "Wow, that just made me feel about that important to you," she continued as she emphasized her point by holding her fingers up with two centimeters worth of space between them.

"But I'm not the one out here talking to other jawns though, am I?" Jamal argued.

"Oh I don't even want to hear that. You might as well be!"

"Well it's over now," Jamal said, shrugging his shoulders as if he didn't care.

"Why, because Shawn beat you to the hit?" Chanda was tempted to say something but stopped herself. "You asked me why I was with you and right about now, I really don't know. I tried to prove to Deisha that you weren't such a bad person and it's as if I have *idiot* written across my forehead. I don't want anything to do with you, Jamal." Tamera walked away to the bus stop so she could go home alone.

"I ain't sweating that shit, man. She's snapping about that dumb shit, man fuck her." Jamal snapped angrily, meaning the exact opposite.

Chanda frowned at him and then rolled her eyes. "Shawn I'm about to go home because I'm getting the worst chest pains and I need a re-fill on my inhaler. Too much excitement out here and I don't need the drama."

"Oh wow, I was about to ask you to come chill with me. But I don't want you to get sick out here." He gave her a kiss and then Chanda left to catch the 33 bus home.

When Tamera got home, she didn't say anything to Deisha at first. But then she thought about how foolish the day's events were and decided to go make amends with her friend.

"Yes," Deisha said when she heard a knock on her bedroom door.

"Did Jamal call?" Tamera asked without opening the door.

"Sure didn't," Deisha said blandly.

"Can I come in?" Tamera asked.

"Sure."

Tamera came in the room and sat on Deisha's dresser. They were silent at first not knowing what to say to each other.

"Are you mad at me, Tammy?" Deisha asked, breaking the silence.

"No… you tried to warn me about Jamal and I didn't listen."

"I only said something because he didn't have any business gripping you up the way that he did," Deisha said defensively.

"It's okay. I probably would have done the same for you." Tamera sighed and looked at Deisha. "He smacked you in your mouth. I can't believe he hit you."

Deisha felt her lip but didn't let it get her angry. "True. But from now on, I'm not coming in between you and Jamal anymore. That's the person that you decided to be with, so I'm keeping my mouth shut."

"Do you think I should call him?" Tamera asked.

"Do you think that you should?" Deisha asked back.

"Not really because he was wrong for that bet. I had a right to be mad at him," Tamera said. She didn't sound sure of herself and was hoping that Deisha would give her some advice.

"If you think so," Deisha said with a smile.

"Aww Deisha, come on. Help a sista out," Tamera pleaded.

"Not this time, Tammy. You need to decide whether or not you want to be with Jamal on your own because at the end of the day, it's your relationship and no one else's."

"Alright, I guess I'll just see him in school tomorrow and we'll talk then. If he wants to talk sooner, then he can call. After all, he was dead wrong." Tamera left the room and Deisha smiled. That was exactly what she would have told Tamera to do.

The next day at school, Maurice caught up to Shawn and Jamal in front of the building. "My bad about yesterday y'all," he apologized. "I guess I just got caught up in the moment."

"It's cool," Jamal said, giving Maurice a pound and accepting his apology. "I didn't want to fight you anyway because we're too cool for that."

"Yeah, it's all good," Shawn chimed in.

"Cool. We're still down for after school at the King Center, right?" Maurice asked.

"Yeah," Jamal replied, becoming distracted when he saw Tamera coming up the stairs to the building. Shawn elbowed him as if to remind him that he needed to fix their situation. Jamal already had it made up in his mind that he would talk to her as soon as they got to advisory.

Deisha was walking down the hallway with Chanda. Chanda's complexion was pale and she was wheezing slightly. "Girl, you need to go to the nurse or go home or something. You don't sound or look good at all."

Yani

"That nurse don't do shit. All she's going to do is stick a thermometer in my mouth and give me some Tylenol." Chanda laughed and then let out a dry cough. They went into their class and Chanda slid into her chair next to Shawn. Shawn looked at her when she laid her head on the desk.

"What's wrong?" he asked her.

"My chest hurts when I breathe and my mom didn't get my inhaler refilled last night," Chanda whispered as if it hurt to talk.

"It's probably from all the pollen in the air from the rain we just had," Deisha replied as she looked down at her friend. Chanda nodded in agreement. She raised her hand and asked their teacher for a drink of water. When she was given permission, Chanda stood up slowly and took a couple steps forward. It suddenly felt as if all of the air had been sucked out of the room. She fell to her knees and put her hand to her chest wheezing hard. Deisha and Shawn jumped from their seats and rushed over to her. With the teacher following behind.

"Class, I need you to back up so this girl can get some air! Deisha, call the main office and tell them I have a medical emergency up here and then knock on Mr. Jacobs's door and tell him to get in here, NOW!"

Deisha ran over to the phone to do as she was told. Chanda strained to get in enough air to breathe but that only made her chest feel tighter and she blacked out. Shawn was trying to remain calm but his heart was racing wildly. Their teacher laid Chanda on her back and listened to see if she could hear her breathing. When she didn't hear anything, she gave her two rescue breaths and then checked her pulse. She felt one and let out a sigh of relief.

"Please don't let this girl die in my class. I don't need something like this happening and I'm about to retire in the next few years." She breathed air in Chanda's mouth and then listened. She still didn't hear anything so she started again just as Mr. Jacobs came into the room.

"She stopped breathing?" he asked as he took off his jacket.

"Yes and I'm doing the best that I can, but I still can't get her breathing."

Mr. Jacobs looked around. "Does anybody have a paper bag that they may have brought some snacks in or something?" A student dumped out their Chinese food and passed the bag to Mr. Jacobs just as Chanda began coughing. Mr. Jacobs turned her over on her side and told her to take slow breaths "The ambulance is on their way," he told Chanda. She looked up at Shawn and he gave her a nod and a wink.

Five minutes later, the medics were coming down the hallway. They helped Chanda onto the stretcher and put an oxygen mask over her face. They took her pulse and blood pressure before they made their way out of the classroom. Right after the elevator doors closed, Jamal, Maurice and Tamera ran up the hallway to find out who was just taken away.

"Who did they just wheel off?" Jamal asked.

"Chanda had an asthma attack. She stopped breathing and they took her to the hospital. That shit was crazy," Deisha told them.

"Damn, that shit is crazy," Jamal repeated. "Are you all right?" he asked his younger brother.

"I'm cool." Shawn replied as he nodded his head.

A few hours later, Chanda's mother was notified at work of Chanda's admittance to University of Pennsylvania Hospital. She immediately dropped what she was doing and drove straight there.

"Excuse me, my daughter was just admitted here not too long ago for an asthma attack." She stated hastily once she got to the receptionist desk.

The receptionist appeared to have an attitude as if she didn't want to be bothered. "What's the child's name?" she asked.

"Chanda Johnson," Ms. Johnson told the receptionist.

"I'm sorry, I don't have a listing here for a Chanda Johnson," the receptionist replied after she briefly checked her computer.

"Her name has to be there," Ms. Johnson pleaded. "She was just admitted an hour ago."

"I'm sorry but we have no listing for a Chanda Johnson here," the receptionist told her again.

Ms. Johnson spelled her name out. "Would you look again? Please. That is all that I'm asking is that you look again."

The receptionist let out an annoyed sigh and checked her computer once more. When she didn't see anything she called over to another desk. "Yes, do you have a Chanda Johnson? First name spelled C-H-A-N-D-A last name Johnson. She was brought here an hour ago for an asthma attack?" She waited a couple of seconds. "Okay thank you." She hung up and turned back to Ms. Johnson. "We have your daughter. She's in room 615. Just take the elevator up to the 6th floor. When you get off, walk to your right down the hallway and hang a left. Her room is about two doors down."

"Thank you so much," Ms. Johnson replied as she let out a sigh of relief. She went up to her daughter's room and stood in the doorway. Chanda looked so peaceful lying on the bed with her long, thick hair falling over her shoulders. She made her way into the room when Chanda turned to face her. Ms. Johnson smiled but Chanda didn't smile back.

"Hi, sweetheart. How are you?" she asked her daughter. Chanda turned her back to her. "What's wrong?" she asked her.

"Mom, I told you that my inhaler was empty and you kept putting it off. Last night, I asked you if we could go to the hospital because it hurt when I breathed and all you told me was to open a window because my room was probably stuffy. This all could've been avoided if you would just listen instead of thinking you know everything because you don't," Chanda said angrily with a hoarse voice.

"I didn't think it was that serious," Ms. Johnson reasoned.

"Mom, I have asthma. The shit is pretty serious. Especially if your inhaler is empty," Chanda slipped but didn't apologize. She couldn't find any better way to get her point across.

"Who the hell do you think you're talking to? You better be damned glad that you're sick or else I'd slap your whole damned face off! I better not ever catch you using that kind of language around me, and you better not say anything like that to me again. Do you understand me?" her mother threatened. She was extremely upset at the way that Chanda had spoken to her. She decided to make her visit short lived.

"I'll bring Kareem up to see you later on. I just wanted to make sure that you were okay. Call me if you need anything and I'll pick up your prescriptions." When Chanda's mother left the room, tears pricked at her eyes but she refused to let them fall. Her mother never did come back with her younger brother. But that didn't surprise Chanda one bit. Shawn showed up after school with flowers and a get well card that her friends signed.

"Are you okay?" he asked her as she was reading the card.

"Yeah, it's just this damn hospital food that is pissing me off among other things. I wouldn't even be in here if my mom would just listen instead of thinking that she's medicine woman or some shit," Chanda hissed. She took a deep breath and decided to change the subject. "What happened to me today?"

"Well, you asked Mrs. Phillips for some water but when you got up, you fell to the floor and started wheezing. You passed out and Mrs. Phillips had to give you CPR. Deisha called the office so they could send the ambulance and Mr. Jacobs came in to help you, too."

"Ill, I know Mrs. Phillips did not put her crusty lips on me." Chanda said with a frown on her face.

"Would you rather it had been Mr. Jacobs?" Shawn asked her. Chanda thought about it and cringed. "I didn't think so. Anyway, they got you breathing again and then the ambulance came."

"Wow," Chanda said faintly. "Were you scared for me?" she asked him.

"A little. But I knew you were going to be alright," he said confidently. "I gotta go home though. I just wanted to check on you and make sure you were okay." He leaned over and kissed her.

"Okay. Tell everybody that I'm fine. And tell them to send me something good to eat because this hospital food is the worst."

Shawn laughed. "Alright." He left and closed the door behind himself.

The next day, Deisha was in a meeting with her track and field coach. For the past couple of weeks, the coach had been urging her to change her diet because she had been putting on weight. Deisha didn't think the weight issue was an issue at all. She was still one of the top long distance and sprinting runners in Philadelphia. Sometimes the coach made her feel uncomfortable with the way he moved in close to her and the way he would place his hand in the small of her back. She figured she would ignore it because she enjoyed being on the track team and didn't want to make a big deal out of nothing.

"It really wouldn't be much, Deisha. You're a terrific track star and you have some great colleges that are looking at you. You could get a scholarship that would pay your way all the way through. But you really need to watch your weight," her coach told her.

"I know. I'll try to watch all of the greasy foods that I've been eating: cheeseburgers, pizza and all that stuff." Deisha laughed a little.

The coach reached into his desk drawer. "If you want, I could call my dietician. They have some great supplemental pills that would probably help you out a lot. That way you don't have to tire yourself out with those sweaty exercises." The coach smiled at her and that made Deisha feel even more uncomfortable. He handed her a slip of paper. She looked at the paper cautiously.

"It's perfectly healthy. I take it all of the time and haven't had one problem."

"I don't know, Coach. I mean my weight gain isn't all that serious," Deisha replied as she handed the paper back to him.

"But it can get serious." The coach went over to his duffle bag. He pulled a bottle out and gave it to Deisha. "Here, I just got a refill on mine a couple of days ago. Just take two a day with a glass of milk."

Deisha took the bottle and looked at it. The coach gave her a reassuring smile and rubbed her back. Deisha returned a nervous smile and put the pills in her book bag.

"See you at practice tomorrow," her coach said as she left his office.

Deisha ran straight into Maurice as she left the gym room.

"Hey beautiful," he said to her, giving her a kiss.

"Hey Maurice, are you still coming to my house tonight?" she asked him.

"Damn girl, you gotta be so blunt about it?" Maurice joked.

"I wasn't talking about that," Deisha said as she smacked his arm. "I wanted you to keep me company."

"Oh, alright. What are y'all eating?" he smiled knowing that Deisha's aunt cooked.

"You're greedy. All we have are leftovers: ham, collard greens, ribs, macaroni and cheese and some cherry cheesecake."

"Damn! All of that! I'm definitely coming to your house tonight. Your aunt keeps a nigga well fed." Maurice chuckled as he rubbed his stomach to drive his point home.

Deisha laughed with him. "What class do you have next?"

"I have trig and I got a bad feeling that bitch about to spring a test on us."

"I just came from there and she didn't give us a test. Wait for me after your last period class," Deisha said as she turned to walk away.

"Alright." Maurice went to his class. Deisha went inside of the lunchroom and got a carton of milk. She went into the girl's bathroom and made sure nobody was nearby. She looked inside of her bag and took out the bottle of pills that the coach gave her. She was still apprehensive about taking the pills, but she figured it would be better than doing some sweaty exercises.

"Here goes nothing," she mumbled before popping the pills into her mouth. The taste made her a little queasy but she shook it off and threw the rest of the milk into the trash can. Just as she was putting the pills back into her bag, two girls came into the bathroom. She looked at herself in the mirror and then left for her next class.

At lunch, Deisha, Maurice and their friends sat at their usual table in the lunchroom.

"Chanda said to bring her something to eat if y'all come to see her because that hospital food is the worst," Shawn laughed.

"Man, you ain't never lied," Jamal chimed in. "Simple Temple got some of the nastiest food I ever had at a hospital."

"Are you going up there after school?" Maurice asked Deisha.

"Yeah but I can't stay long because I have a lot of homework to do," she replied.

"Deisha, do you have a mirror?" Tamera asked.

"It's in my book bag. Check the side pocket." Deisha replied absent mindedly. When Tamera got up to go into her book bag, she then remembered the pills that were in there. "No!" she yelled, making Tamera jump. She calmed down hoping that no one would get suspicious. "I mean, no. I'll get it." Her friends were looking at her as if she were crazy.

"Why did you get like that?" Tamera asked her.
Deisha waved her off. "I have some personal things in there, that's all. I didn't mean to yell."

"Duck y'all, she's packing!" Jamal joked as he ducked under the table. His friends as well as Deisha laughed.

"Boy shut up, I don't have anything."

Tamera handed her the mirror still looking at her crossly. "Lay off of the junk food. You're tripping."

Maurice put his hands around her waist. "Yeah, she's getting a little plump around here, too," he said with a smile.

"Uh oh," Shawn and Jamal said at the same time, chuckling.

Deisha smacked his arms away. "I'm not pregnant so shut up." She stood up and posed in front of them. "But for real y'all, do I look like I'm getting thick?" she asked her friends.

"You look like the same girl to me," Jamal said as he poured Doritos into his mouth straight from the bag.

"You look the same to me too," Tamera replied.

"Why? Who told you that you were getting thick?" Maurice asked her.

Deisha plopped back into her seat. "Nobody," she mumbled.

"Then what's the big deal?" he asked. "How come you didn't eat lunch?"

"I ate all that food that my aunt cooked last night and I wasn't all that hungry. Plus lunch is almost over anyway." She got up and grabbed her book bag. "See y'all." She waved to her friends before leaving out of the lunchroom.

"Something ain't right," Maurice said to no one in particular.

"Deisha's aunt cooks like that all the time and I've yet to see her miss a meal," Shawn replied.

"And since when was she worried about gaining weight?" Maurice added.

"She's on the track team. Maybe she's trying to stay fit for the Penn Relays," Jamal suggested.

"Naw, girlfriend almost lost the color in her face when I was getting ready to go into her book bag. It's something in there that she's not supposed to have," Tamera concluded. They all sat quietly thinking on Tamera's last comment.

"We graduate next year. She better not do some stupid shit," Maurice said as they began to head out of the lunchroom and go to their last period classes.

Maurice went to Deisha's house after school like they planned. While they were eating dinner, Maurice noticed that there was barely any food on her plate. He decided not to comment right away.

They sat on the floor working on their trigonometry homework joking around until Maurice finally decided to question Deisha on her recent behavior.

"What's up with this weight issue?" he asked her.

"Nothing. I just thought I was getting a little thick, that's all," Deisha replied.

"Really? So what, you're on a diet now or something? You didn't eat lunch and you barely ate anything for dinner."

Deisha snapped. "I wasn't hungry. Damn, get off of it."

"Okay, so why did you get loud when Tamera was about to go into your book bag?" he continued to question her.

"Because I felt like it," Deisha didn't like the way he was questioning her and was ready for him to leave early.

Maurice knew that there was a weight issue with Deisha because of how aggravated she was becoming. "Starving yourself is not going to make you lose the weight any faster," Maurice told her.

"Ain't nobody starving themselves," Deisha argued.

"You know if you have a problem, you can come to me, right?"

Deisha got up and started packing her book bag. "It's getting late, Maurice."

Maurice stood up smiling, taking the hint. He put his books in his book bag and Deisha walked him to the door. He kissed her and left. She locked the door and then looked at her book bag. She grabbed it and went into the kitchen, poured herself a glass of milk and placed two of the pills into her mouth. Just as she finished taking them, she heard Tamera coming down the steps singing, so she put the pills back in her book bag and continued to drink her milk.

"Maurice left already?" Tamera asked as she reached in the refrigerator for a snack.

"Yeah, he was getting on my nerves," Deisha told her as she placed her glass in the dishwasher.

"Oh." Tamera looked Deisha over carefully. "Are you okay?" she asked her.

"Yeah," Deisha sighed. Suddenly she caught a sharp pain in her stomach. She placed her hand on her stomach and then leaned forward, breathing heavy.

"Deisha, what is wrong with you?" Tamera asked as she went over to her to make sure that she was alright.

"I'm okay," Deisha assured her. "I'm just tired." She shook her head to clear it before grabbing her book bag. She gave Tamera a smile and went up to her room.

Shawn and Jamal were at home being lectured by their mother. Apparently, she was going to be working the night shift for the next two months and was laying down some rules for the house in her absence.

"I know that y'all are going to be home by yourselves a little more often than usual but the rules stay the same. I don't want any girls in here all hours of the night. Now, I can't stop y'all from having sex and I know that y'all already are. No partying, smoking cigarettes, weed or whatever the hell kids are smoking now-a-days. And I don't want people coming in here destroying my house and carrying on. All I ask is that you keep the house clean, and don't let the laundry pile up."

Jamal leaned back on the couch and put his hands behind his head. Shawn was sitting on the steps only half listening.

"No problem mom," Jamal said.

"Am I expecting too much from you two?" she asked her sons.

"It's gonna be the same except you won't be here when we get home from school. Same as usual," Shawn said flatly.

"Yes I will, but only for a short time though," she sighed. "I'm sorry things turned out this way. But it'll only be for a few more months, maybe just until the end of the school year, I promise."

"It really don't make me no never mind. It's been like this since as far back as I can remember," Jamal said smartly.

"Jamal, now don't start that shit," their mother said loudly. Jamal huffed and closed his eyes, tuning her out. "I'm doing this for us. I hate to see you act that way. You're so damn arrogant." Jamal stared up at the ceiling. "And while I'm gone, you stay out of those damn streets. I almost lost you once now I don't want to lose you."

"You ain't gonna lose me. And I'm not in the streets like that anymore," he answered back in the same tone as his mother.

"I love y'all, you both know that," she told her two sons. She looked down at Shawn. "Shawn, you haven't said two words since we've been talking. What's wrong?"

"Ain't nothing to say," Shawn continued to keep his low flat tone. Ms. Keyona saw that the situation was pointless so she decided to leave her sons alone and get dinner started.

The next day, Deisha was at track practice with one of the other girls on the track and field team that she had become friends with. They were getting changed in the locker room when Marissa noticed that Deisha didn't look well.

"What's wrong, Deisha? Why do you look so sick?" she asked.

Deisha lied. "It's my period. I didn't want my cramps to stop me from running so I took a couple of Motrin."

"Shit, that wouldn't have been me. I would've kept my ass home until time to go to class. You practice enough for both of us."

Deisha smiled. "I'm alright. Let's get started." They left the locker room and sat on the gym floor doing stretches with each other. After stretching and loosening up, they began doing laps around the gym room, jogging down one side and then sprinting down another. After the third sprint, Deisha began feeling dizzy and stopped by the coach's office. She bent over, leaning on her knees for support so she didn't lose her balance and tried to collect herself. Marissa jogged over to her.

"Girl, are you okay?" she asked Deisha as she placed a hand on her back.

"Yeah," Deisha replied as she tried to catch her breath. She stumbled over to the water fountain and took a few sips of water. The coach came to his doorway to see what was going on and then called Deisha into his office.

Yani

"I think those pills are messing me up," Deisha said as she leaned into his wall.

"Well, have you been eating regularly?" the coach asked her.

"No, not really," she replied.

"Well, you can't just stop eating all together. That's what the problem is."

"I don't know coach. I mean, I'd rather just work it out the regular way," Deisha said, shaking her head.

The coach put his arm around her. "It's nothing wrong. Just keep eating." Deisha sighed and the coach gave her a half hug, rubbing her arms. Deisha felt uncomfortable with him invading her personal space and moved away.

When she came out of the office, Marissa walked her back to the locker room. "Are you okay now?" she asked her friend.

"Yeah, I just need to put something on my stomach. I didn't really eat much this morning so I'm going to skip practice and grab something from the cafeteria real quick." Deisha replied as she began to change back into her school clothes.

"Okay girl, see you tomorrow!" Marissa waved and then jogged back to the gym room. Deisha thought about the way the coach always found reasons to hug her or rub her back. It gave her the creeps so she decided not to think about it as she continued to get dressed.

Maurice and Jamal were in their elective class bussing on one of their other classmates.

"Look at my man's Polo shirt," Maurice said with a chuckle. "That shit so old his sign looks like a man on top of a Rottweiler with a baseball bat." Maurice and Jamal roared with laughter.

"That shit looks like Tiger Woods on a pony with a golf club." They laughed some more. "And this nigga got the nerve to have on a Coochie Sweater. Not Coogie, *Coochie*. And he ain't got no neck. He's all head and shoulders," Jamal laughed, barely able to get the words out as they moved onto another classmate to make fun of. Maurice was balled up in his chair laughing so hard that he could barely breathe.

Tamera looked over at them. "What are y'all laughing at?"

"Look at my man's Tree sign. That shit looks like a marijuana plant," Jamal told her. They looked at their classmate's Timberland boots and started cracking up. Other students laughed quietly at their amateur Comedy View show. "Those bitches are on their last sole."

"Aw that's a shame. Why y'all talking about him like that? So what the strings in his boots so tight that they look like stitches," Tamera chimed in. She was trying to suppress her laughter but was unsuccessful.

"Aw, my baby got jokes. She got jokes," Jamal said as he slapped her a handshake.

"Ms. Harrison, Mr. Brown and Mr. Williams, There's an awful lot of noise back there. I hope you find your grades as funny as your jokes," their teacher said.

"I'm doing my work," Tamera said holding up her worksheet. She then mumbled to Maurice and Jamal. "She needs to mind her own business and shut the hell up. Dumb-ass. I thought she was supposed to be an English teacher. 'An awful lot of noise.' No, it's a whole lotta noise."

"That's right because my baby is edu-macated," Jamal replied. They started giggling again.

"Be quiet y'all, I'm trying to do my work," Maurice smirked loudly.

Tamera cut her eyes at him and then coughed into her hand. "Snitch." She and Jamal laughed out loud. "Okay, okay, okay. We have to finish our work y'all, come on." They sat quietly and got down to business. Moments later, Jamal looked up at the clock and sucked his teeth.

"Damn, it's only 11 o'clock."

"Time will pass, but will you? Back to work, Mr. Williams."

"She better go ahead with that nut-shit. Fucking bottle cap wearing bitch," Jamal mumbled. He and his friends started laughing again.

At lunch, Deisha had two plates of chicken, a pack of chocolate chip cookies, cheese fries, a cheese pretzel and flavored water. Maurice and the rest of their friends came over to the table and looked at the food that she had sitting in front of her.

"Got-damn, what are you feeding for two or something?" Shawn asked.

"No," Deisha answered as she bit into a piece of chicken. "The coach worked the hell out of me this morning and I'm hungry."

Maurice sat next to her. "Are you making up for yesterday?" He reached into her plate for a piece of chicken and Deisha smacked his hand away. "Ouch."

"No, I'm just hungry from track practice, that's all."

"So the weight issue is over?" Jamal asked her.

"There was never an issue," Deisha glared at him.

"Weight issue?" Chanda repeated. "What weight issue? What I miss?"

Shawn peered at Deisha, "It was nothing." Deisha and her friends ate in silence.

"Let me get a cookie, Deisha?" Jamal asked.

"I don't have anymore," she told him.

"Damn, it ain't shit else left in your plate. Did you eat the bones too?" Maurice joked.

Jamal began telling his friends about a fight that broke out on Turner Street the day before. They started laughing as he told the story when suddenly, Deisha felt sick. She jumped up, thinking she was going to make it to the trashcan in time but vomited on the floor instead.

Maurice got up and started walking over to her. "Are you alright?" he asked her.

"Don't touch me," Deisha said hoarsely. She began coughing and then leaned over a trashcan, vomiting again. She was breathing heavy with tears in her eyes when Maurice grabbed her by her arm and pulled her out of the lunchroom.

"I'm not even going to ask you what's up. Start talking," he demanded.

"I ate too much too fast," Deisha said as she leaned into the wall trying to collect herself.

"Get the fuck outta here," Maurice replied, not buying her story. He looked her over. "Are you pregnant?"

"No!" Deisha answered.

"If you are, you don't have to lie about it. I'm not going to leave you."

"I'm not pregnant. And if I were..." Deisha trailed off and slid down the wall. Maurice grabbed onto her. "I'm dizzy."

Maurice held her up. "Come on. I'm taking you to the nurse."

Back in the lunchroom, while the janitor was cleaning up Deisha's accident and while Tamera's friends weren't paying attention to her, she went into Deisha's book bag and found the bottle of pills.

"That damn girl lied," Tamera mumbled. She put the pills back into her book bag the way that she found them and sat next to Jamal. She leaned back on his chest and he kissed her neck.

"Do you think Deisha is pregnant?" Jamal asked as Tamera played with his fingers.

"She's not," Tamera replied with confidence.

"How do you know?"

"Believe me, I know."

"Come to my house after school," Jamal said to her.

"Why?" she asked, thinking she had a good idea.

"Because I want to show you something." Tamera looked up at him suspiciously. "Get your mind out of the gutter. I wasn't talking about that. I want you to hear a mixed tape that I made."

Tamera thought it over. "Yeah, I'll come." Jamal rest his chin on top of her head. "Are you glad to be out of the hospital?" she asked Chanda.

"Hell yeah! I hated being in the hospital doing those damn breathing treatments," Chanda replied.

"How come you didn't stay home?" Jamal asked her.

"Because it's too much going on in there. Between my mom acting like a complete bitch and trying to keep my brother from hanging with those little dudes in Blumberg, I figured I better just come to school before I hurt one of them."

"You know what I just realized?" Jamal asked no one in particular. "We all have some kind of problem at home where it's gotten to the point that we don't even want to be there anymore. Deisha and Maurice are the only ones that don't go through shit."

"Deisha had problems at home and that's why her aunt took custody of her when she was twelve," Tamera told him.

"I didn't know that," Jamal replied.

"We don't have any problems at home either," Shawn said.

"You're crazy. Where the fuck is our dad, Shawn?" Jamal snapped.

"Man, it's so many people out here that don't know where their fathers are that it's becoming normal," Shawn said defensively.

"No, that shit ain't normal. We practically raised ourselves since Mommy was never around. She never shows any interests in the things that we do. It's amazing we even turned out this good."

"Well, I don't see what the problem is," Shawn shrugged.

"Then nigga you need to open your eyes 'cause you might as well say we ain't got any parents. Mommy could've been found a better job where she could at least have the time to stop and see what we were up to instead of always leaving us with a sappy-ass 'Hi, blah-blah blah, see you when I get home." Jamal was becoming pissed off at how oblivious his younger brother was to their home life.

"When was the last time she came to one of your games, or did you just give up because you were tired of her being a no-show? She ain't ever show interest in anything I've done unless I was handing her money from the very shit she claimed to hate hearing about me doing. So if you asked me, yes it's a fucking problem," Jamal spat.

They sat quietly not knowing how to respond to Jamal's rant. The more each of them thought about it, the more they realized he was right. They all had issues at home. Maybe that common factor was what held their friendship together.

When it was time to leave, Tamera grabbed Deisha's book bag. She planned on having a talk with her friend.

Deisha was in her last period class sipping from a bottle of ginger-ale that the nurse gave to her. Tamera was in class with her. She wanted to ask Deisha about the pills that were in her bag but was a little scared to. She swallowed her pride and decided to ask her once their class was about to end.

"What's wrong with you?" she decided to ask.

"Nothing, why'd you ask?" Deisha replied as she read the handout that the teacher gave them.

"I found the pills," Tamera said in a whisper.

Deisha looked at the handout and then sat it on her desk. "Why the hell were you in my bag?" she hissed.

Tamera lied. "I needed a mirror."

"So what. You should've gone to the bathroom. Don't be going through my shit. I don't need you checking up on me." Deisha was pissed, as well as embarrassed.

"I wasn't checking up on you. But why are you taking diet pills?"

"You just answered your own question."

"What for? You're like one of the prettiest girls that I know. I used to envy you because you look the way you do and because I always thought you had a great personality. Until I learned to accept myself for who I am. You need to do the same because there is nothing wrong with the way you look." Tamera stared at Deisha as she played with her nails and shook her head. "You need to think for yourself instead of listening to whoever put that shit into your head."

The bell rang and Tamera packed up her things and left the class. When she caught up to Jamal, he was talking to a few of his friends.

"Are you ready?" he asked.

"Yeah," Tamera replied as she adjusted the straps to her book bag.

"What's wrong?"

"Nothing, I just need to hurry up and get outta here before I snap," she replied quickly.

"Snap on who?" Jamal asked, confused.

"Don't worry about it. You'll find out in due time. Come on because I'm ready to leave."

Jamal said bye to his friends and they left.

Chanda caught up to Deisha on the balcony by her locker. "What's up, girl? You alright now?" she asked her.

Deisha sighed. "Yeah I'm fine. When I go home I'm going to sleep."

"You're sure you're not pregnant?" Chanda asked in a whisper.

Deisha slammed her locker shut. "I'm not pregnant. I wish people would stop asking me that shit. If I was, you would be the first to know." She put the strap to her bag over her shoulder and walked towards stairway 3, running straight into Maurice. "What's up?" he asked her.

"Nothing," she said.

"Are you cool now?" Maurice asked.

"Yeah, the nurse gave me a ginger-ale. I'm just tired now."

"So you're not going to track practice today?" he asked her.

"No, I just want to go home and chill."

"Alright," Maurice said. "Let me get my jacket. I'll come with you." Deisha waited for Maurice and they rode home together. They sat in her house talking for a while. Deisha's book bag was partially opened and Maurice could see part of the pill bottle. He was curious as to what kind of pills his girlfriend would be taking.

"Deisha, do you have any frosty beverages, my throat is kinda dry?" Maurice asked with a charming smile.

Deisha giggled and went into the kitchen to pour him a glass of iced-tea. Maurice made sure that she wasn't looking when he went into her book bag. He took the bottle out and looked the pills over trying to understand why his girlfriend would be taking diet pills. Anger took over him.

Deisha came back into the living room but stopped when she noticed the look on Maurice's face. "Maurice, why are you looking at me like that?"

"Why did you lie to me? And what the hell are these?" he asked as he held up the bottle.

Deisha stood in front of him shocked. She didn't know what to say so she sat his cup of iced-tea on the coffee table and snatched the bottle of pills out of his hand. She put them back in her book bag and then sat on the couch in silence.

"Oh, so you're going to ignore me now?"

"You shouldn't have gone in my bag!" Deisha yelled.

"Don't even go there, Deisha. Why the hell would you be taking diet pills? No, skip that. Who put the idea in your head that you needed to lose weight?" Deisha still refused to say anything. "Yo, you can ignore me all you want. But until I find out what the deal is, I'm sitting right here. And I know you don't want your aunt to find out about this."

Deisha rubbed her hands through her hair and leaned back on the couch. "A couple of days ago, my coach called me into his office. He started telling me how proud of me he was because I broke three records. He noticed that I had put on some weight since the last few times that he weighed me." She sighed again. "To make a long story short, he told me about these diet pills, assured me that I would stay healthy and…"

"You took them," Maurice finished for her.

Deisha looked down at her hands. Maurice grabbed them and pulled her over to the mirrors that were hanging on her living room wall.

"Now, you look at yourself in this mirror and tell me if you think you need to lose weight."

Deisha looked at herself. "I don't know what to think anymore," she said in a low voice.

"For as long as I knew you, you never let what other people thought of you change what you thought of yourself. Looking at you right now, I can't tell if you lost weight or if you gained it." Deisha couldn't take him staring at her so she looked away. "Was it the pills that were making you throw up?" he asked her.

"I think so," Deisha replied.

Maurice shook his head. "Don't take them anymore."

"I won't."

Maurice put his arms around her waist. "You have a banging ass body. Don't mess it up over any damn drugs."

Deisha smiled as her aunt came in the house. "Y'all trying to see how much of a cute couple y'all make?" she asked them as she locked the door behind herself.

Deisha laughed and moved Maurice's arms. "Hi Aunt 'Chelle."

"Hey. How are you doing, Maurice?"

Maurice smiled. "I'm alright."

Ms. Niecie fixed her eyes on Deisha. "I saw Tamera and Jamal when I was on my way home. She said you were sick earlier. Are you alright?"

"Yeah I just ate too much too fast," Deisha replied. She glanced at Maurice.

"Do you know where they're going?" she asked. Deisha shook her head. "Oh well." Ms. Niecie made her way into the kitchen. "I'm making lasagna for dinner Maurice, are you staying?"

"Oh, most definitely," Maurice grinned as he rubbed his greedy palms together. He seldom ever turned down an opportunity to eat one of Ms. Niecie's home cooked meals. Deisha smacked his arm for being so greedy.

Ms. Niecie saw her and said, "Girl, you better leave that boy alone." Deisha smiled as her and Maurice sat on the couch together.

"Why did you get like that when your aunt said that she saw Tamera and Jamal?" Maurice asked Deisha.

"Because Tamera found the pills, too. But I know she won't snitch. She's not like that."

Tamera was in Jamal's basement listening to some beats and DJ'ing mix-tapes that he put together. She was nodding her head and moving to the beat, enjoying what she was listening to. Jamal watched her, smiling. Tamera looked around the basement in awe at the different kinds of equipment that Jamal had. She could tell that it was expensive and had a good idea where he got the money from. But she shrugged it off figuring at least he was putting it towards his talents.

Jamal came over to her and turned the volume down a little. "So what do you think?" he asked her.

"That was banging," she told him. "It looks like a mini studio down here. Where'd you get the money from to buy all of this stuff?"

Jamal hesitated for a moment and then said, "Hustling has its advantages. I would love to build a sound proof booth. I know some guys that want to lay some tracks and a couple other guys that want to buy beats from me."

"That's what's up. How come you don't try to DJ at clubs and stuff?"

"Well, for one I'm not old enough. But maybe in a few years, who knows?" His CD stopped so he turned the radio on. *Differences* by Genuine was playing on the radio. Tamera leaned into the table and began playing with her nails.

Jamal stood in front of her. "What's wrong?" he asked.

Tamera shook her head. She wanted him to kiss her, or perhaps more. He put his hands on her waist and kissed her neck. Tamera closed her eyes and Jamal stopped. They stared at each other for a space of heartbeats.

"Why'd you stop?" she asked.

"Do you want me to stop?" Jamal asked in return.

"Did I ask you to stop?"

Jamal chuckled before pulling her close to him and kissing her. He started unbuttoning her shirt. Tamera stopped kissing him to watch what he was doing. He started kissing her again and moved her over to the futon. Jamal lay on top of her and Tamera pulled his shirt over his head. He took her pants off and kissed over her neck and chest.

"Are you sure about this?" he asked her.

Tamera looked at him and thought for a moment. She nodded and whispered. "Don't hurt me."

Jamal kissed her again gently and pulled down her underwear and his boxers. Tamera felt him bumping against her leg and scooted away from him.

"Use a condom please?" she asked innocently.

Jamal leaned up. "Why?"

"Please," Tamera pleaded with him as she placed a hand on his bare chest. "I don't want to get pregnant."

Jamal looked around for his *special occasion box*. When he saw it sitting on another box next to them, he grabbed it and pulled a magnum Trojan out and put it on. They began kissing again as Jamal played with her body until he felt that she was ready. He then spread her legs and tried to enter her, but because of the pain, Tamera resisted.

"Ouch, Jamal it hurts," she whined.

Jamal kissed her again, holding onto her as he pushed his way inside of her. She shrieked and gritted her teeth as she scraped her nails across his back. Jamal moved slowly and gentle at first until he felt himself all the way inside of her. He ran his fingers through her hair as she gently bit his shoulder. Jamal increased his speed unable to control himself. The noises Tamera was making went from soft moans to loud pants. They climaxed and Jamal collapsed on top of her breathing heavy. Tamera couldn't believe that she had *done it*. She pulled the blanket up over her chest and Jamal wrapped his arms around her waist and pulled her close to him. They stared at each other in silence.

"Are you okay?" Jamal asked quietly.

"Yes," Tamera responded innocently. They laid there for a few more moments in silence before Tamera decided to get up and get dressed. She put her sneakers back on and pulled her hair into a pony tail. Jamal watched her, thinking about how much he had really began to care about her before he got up to get dressed too.

Yani

They left his house and walked to hers, hand in hand. When they got there Tamera looked at Jamal and couldn't stop blushing.

"What?" Jamal asked her as he grinned.

"Nothing," Tamera replied, shaking her head.

Jamal gave her a hug and squeezed her tightly before kissing her. "I'll call you as soon as I get in."

"Okay," Tamera replied. She unlocked the door and Jamal watched her walk inside.

Ms. Niecie came from out of the kitchen. "Tammy, where were you?"

"I was hanging out with Jamal just talking about some things like my dad and stuff. I'm sorry. I didn't mean to come home late."

"It's no problem. You can heat up the lasagna if you're hungry," Ms. Niecie told her.

"I'll probably come back down. I'm not really all that hungry yet." She went upstairs and knocked on Deisha's door.

"Yo!" Deisha replied through the door.

"Can I come in?" Tamera asked.

"Sure," Deisha replied.

Tamera opened the door and came in. She closed it and stood by Deisha's bed. "I didn't mean to go through your bag earlier," Tamera said apologetically.

"Don't worry about it. Maurice found them, too. I'm not going to take them anymore. The nurse thought I was pregnant."

Tamera giggled. Deisha looked at her curiously. It was something different about her friend that she couldn't quite put her finger on. She turned the TV off and stared at Tamera.

"What?" Tamera asked, nervously.

Deisha peered at her. "Where were you?"

Tamera looked away and lied. "I was at the Gallery."

Deisha sat up. "You're lying. Spill it."

"What?" Tamera asked, repeating herself.

"You heard me."

Tamera sighed and closed her eyes. "I lost my virginity today," she said after a moment.

"Aw sooky-sooky now!!" Deisha howled. "Give me the details!"

"Shhh!" Tamera hushed Deisha. She took a deep breath and then gave a detailed account of what happened between her and Jamal.

"Aww, my little girl is growing up," Deisha gushed.

"Shut up!" Tamera grinned.

"Was it good?" Deisha asked.

"Oh my God! I can't believe you just asked me that! It was worth waiting for," she replied.

"I ain't asked you that shit. I asked you if it was good." Tamera covered her face and fell onto her bed laughing. "He was putting it on you!

Oh shit, Jamal was putting it on you!" Deisha teased as she laughed. She gave Tamera a handshake. "Welcome to the club. I know y'all used something."

"Absolutely, I'm not trying to get pregnant."

Deisha got up and went over to her dresser drawer. She took out a box of condoms and then tossed them over to Tamera. "I'm going to give you the number to my gynecologist so she can set you up on some birth control. But still use condoms. I know you love Jamal and everything, but getting pregnant is the least of your worries. AIDS is killing niggas every day and you can't abort that shit." The telephone rang and Deisha answered it. "Hi Jamal," she said with a smile. "Yeah, hold on." She covered the mouth piece to the phone and whispered, "Aw, it's your first love, Tammy."

Tamera hopped off of Deisha's bed. "I'm going to get the phone out of Ms. Niecie's room. Hang it up when I do." She ran into the other room and answered on the cordless. "Hang the phone up, Deisha!" Tamera yelled down the hall when she heard her making kissing noises. Deisha laughed out loud and hung the phone up leaving Tamera to chat with her first love.

Chanda was at home helping her younger brother Kareem with his math work.

"If $3X + 4X = 28$, what is X, Kareem?" she asked her brother.

Her brother looked at the two numbers for a moment and then wrote down four. He looked at Chanda to see if he was right.

"There you go, Kareem. I told you, Algebra is easy." She rubbed his back.

"I asked mommy if she would help me but she said that she was too busy," Kareem told his sister.

"Don't worry about it. I'll help you out." She stood over her brother and continued helping him with his math homework when their mother came into her room.

"Chanda, didn't I tell you to wash those dishes?" their mother asked.

"I didn't forget. I was going to wash them when I finished helping Kareem with his homework."

"That's not what I said. I told you to go do those damned dishes, now. You can help Kareem when you're done," her mother snapped.

"Mom, his homework shouldn't be put off to do dishes when he needs help," Chanda mouthed off.

"I didn't ask you for your feedback. Take your ass downstairs and do those damned dishes!"

"Why can't I do them after I help Kareem with his homework? How is he supposed to do well in school if every time he comes to me for help, you find some reason for me to stop helping him," Chanda continued to argue.

"Don't start this shit, Chanda. I'm telling you to go do those damned dishes and you're giving me lip? If you had done the dishes when I first told you to, you wouldn't have to worry about me stopping you from helping Kareem with his homework."

"Yes you would because you always stop us from doing what we need to do as far as school goes. It's almost like you want us to fail. You stop us when we're doing our homework to go to the store. When was the last time you stopped to see what we were up to? Or showed the slightest interest in what we are doing?" Chanda was thinking back to what Jamal said in the school's cafeteria and it was starting to weigh on her.

"I'm not going to debate with you on this shit. Let me have to tell you one more time to go do those dishes and I'LL KICK YOUR ASS!!"

Chanda glared at her mother. She realized at that moment that what Jamal said was indeed true. She turned to her brother and said, "Kareem, if you have any more problems doing your homework, you come to me. You hear me?"

Kareem nodded his head. Chanda looked at her mother and went downstairs to the kitchen. She was washing the dishes when her mother came downstairs still running her mouth.

"The next time I tell you to do something I don't care what you're doing. You stop and do what I said to do. You don't question my authority. This is my damn house and you do what the hell I tell you to do when I tell you to do it."

Chanda didn't comment. She continued to do the dishes with sealed lips thinking that if she kept quiet, the conversation would end faster. She thought wrong. Her mother gripped her up by her arm thinking Chanda was trying to ignore her. When she tried to turn Chanda around, she jerked away, cutting herself deeply with a knife that she was washing. She screamed, dropping the knife and held her arm. Her mother took a step back and looked at her. Chanda pushed past her and ran upstairs to the bathroom, slamming the door behind her. She turned on the water and put her arm under it, wincing at the pain. When she didn't see any more blood coming out, she turned the water off and looked in the medicine cabinet just as her mother knocked on the door.

"Leave me alone!" she yelled through the door.

"Chanda, you know that was an accident," her mother tried to explain.

"There wouldn't have been an accident if you would've left well enough alone. The conversation was over when I came downstairs to do the dishes, but you just had to say something else. GET OUT OF MY FACE!!!" she screamed as she kicked the door. Ms. Johnson stood there for a moment and then went to her own room and shut her door.

Chanda looked at the alcohol and took it out of the medicine cabinet. She poured some onto a gauze pad and took a deep breath to brace herself. She placed it onto her wound and clenched her teeth together to suppress her scream after feeling the burning sensation. When she finished cleaning the wound, she wrapped it with another gauze pad and went to her room.

She waited for her mother to go to sleep before she packed up her clothes for school the next day inside of her book bag. She went to her brother's room and knocked on his door. When he answered, she went in and closed the door behind her.

"If mommy wakes up and asks where I'm at, just tell her that I went to bed. She can't get into my room because it's locked from the inside."

"Where are you going?" her younger brother asked her.

"Nowhere far. If I'm not back by twelve, just go to bed and I'll see you before you go to school."

Kareem nodded and she kissed him on the top of his head and left. Chanda walked over to Shawn's house and knocked on the door.

Shawn opened up the door, surprised to see her standing there. "Chanda, what are you doing here?"

She held up her arm. "Take a wild guess."

Shawn looked at her arm. "What happened?" he asked as he let her inside of the house.

Chanda sat on the couch and told him everything. "She keeps doing this. Constantly, every day and I can't take it anymore. I'm straight about to fucking lose it, man, I swear. And I know she's doing this shit on purpose." Chanda began tapping her foot and shaking her leg, trying not to cry, but she couldn't hold it in any longer. She leaned onto the arm of the couch and covered her eyes. "Why does she keep doing this to me?" she asked in a shaky voice. She broke down in tears as she sobbed. Shawn watched, not knowing what to say to make her feel better. He sat next to her and rubbed her back.

"Are you alright?" he asked her once she calmed down and they were sitting in silence. Chanda shook her head and lay in his lap. "What are you going to do?"

Chanda wiped her face. "I don't know. Can I stay with you tonight because if I go to Deisha's aunt's house, she's going to call my mom?"

"What are you going to change into for school tomorrow?" he asked her.

"I have some clothes in my book bag." Chanda replied.

"Alright, I'm not supposed to have anybody here but I'll let this slide." Shawn said half way joking.

Chanda smiled and sat up. "Thank you."

"Hold up, I'll be back." Shawn went upstairs to his brother's room and knocked on the door.

"Yo!" Jamal answered.

Shawn opened his door. "Chanda got into an argument with her mom and got this big-ass cut on her arm. Can she stay here tonight?"

"I don't care. What are you asking me for?" Jamal replied as he changed his television channel to ESPN.

"Alright." Shawn went back downstairs to get Chanda. "Come on." He led her back up to his room, which he had rearranged since the last time she had been in there.

"Why'd you change your room around? I liked it the other way."

"Yeah, me too," Shawn replied as he moved books and magazines from his chair and sat them in the corner on the floor. "But I needed more space. Do you want to play *Perfect Dark?*"

"Hell yeah! My brother has that game and it's fun as hell!" Chanda smiled as she plopped down on his bed.

They started playing the video game. Jamal came in and played a few rounds with them before he went to bed. When he left, Shawn turned the game off and then lay on the bed next to Chanda. He put his arm around her when she laid on his chest.

"Do you feel better, now?" Shawn asked her as he stroked the side of her face with his fingers.

"Yeah, I'm cool." Chanda replied in a whisper. They began making out before undressing each other for some night time fun. Afterwards, they lay in the bed talking and giggling. Shawn hushed Chanda when he heard someone coming up the stairs humming. Shawn immediately knew that it was his mother.

"Oh shit! Get up!" Shawn piped quietly.

"What?" Chanda asked, panicking.

"Get your clothes and go over by my dresser. My mom is coming," he told her.

Chanda leapt from the bed and hurried over to his dresser like she was told. Shawn threw on some sweat pants and opened his door.

"*Why did he open that damned door?!*" Chanda thought to herself.

"Mom, what are you doing here?" Shawn asked in a fake, sleepy sounding voice.

"I got off early. We had some kind of black out and all of the computers went down. I told those idiots they needed separate circuits for the systems. No telling how much info may get lost. Why are you up?" Ms. Keyona asked her son.

"I was about to get some juice when I heard you coming up the stairs," Shawn lied. But then he suddenly became thirsty.

"You used to do that a lot when you were younger; get up in the middle of the night and go downstairs to get something to drink." She smiled, reflecting back on those days. "Is Jamal asleep?"

"Yeah," Shawn replied.

"Well, I guess I better go do the same. Good night, baby."

Shawn kissed his mother on the cheek. "Good night, mom." He waited for his mother to go in her room and close her door before he went downstairs. He grabbed two cups and filled them with juice. He crept back to his room and turned the light on after he closed the door behind him. He gave one of the cups of juice to Chanda.

"Thank you," Chanda said. She drank some and asked in a whisper. "Where's your mom?"

"She's in her room getting ready to go to bed." Chanda's shirt was partially opened and her cleavage was exposed. Shawn couldn't help looking at her. "Ain't that a bitch?" he replied, getting back to the matter at hand.

"How the hell will I get outta here tomorrow?" she asked, as if she read his mind.

"I'll find a way. Right now, I'm ready to go to sleep." He grabbed Chanda by her shirt and pulled her in the bed on top of him. She buried her face in his chest to suppress her giggle before lying down and falling asleep.

The next morning, Tamera sat on her bed looking at the box of condoms that Deisha gave her the day before. She thought back to her encounter with Jamal and blushed over her first sexual experience with him. Ms. Niecie came into her bedroom and stopped dead in her tracks when she saw Tamera holding the condoms.

"Tell me that is not what I think it is." Ms. Niecie said. Tamera looked at Ms. Niecie and then looked back at the box of condoms and sighed. "I'll take that as a yes. You weren't just hanging with Jamal yesterday, were you?" she asked Tamera.

"No." Tamera replied quietly.

"I didn't think so." She sat down on the bed next to Tamera. "One thing Deisha must not have told you is that you don't have to hide anything. I won't scream or yell at you. And I certainly won't ridicule you for having sex at sixteen because I was much younger than you when I started. Yesterday was your first time?"

"Yes," Tamera nodded.

"We'll talk later on. Right now, get ready for school. And it's good that you're practicing safe sex. Make sure you get on birth control as a backup."

"I will," Tamera said as she stood up to gather her things for school.

Things were crazy at Shawn's house. Chanda was able to grab a quick shower and get dressed, but just as she was getting ready to make a break for the stairs, Shawn's mother opened her door. Shawn pushed Chanda back in his room and closed his door.

"Good morning, Mom," Shawn said, trying not to look suspicious.

"Good morning," Ms. Keyona said back. She made a face and then looked at her son. "Why do I smell Victoria's Secret?" she asked.

Shawn hesitated. "Oh, I knocked some over when I was taking a shower this morning." From inside of Shawn's room, Chanda let out a sigh of relief after hearing his response.

Yani

"Oh," she replied and then quickly dismissed it. She started going downstairs.

"Where are you going?" Shawn asked, almost panicking.

"I'm going downstairs to fix y'all something to eat," his mother told him.

"No!" Shawn piped, making his mother jump. "I mean, you don't have to. Usually, me and Jamal just grab something when we get to school."

"You have a little time for some bacon and eggs. Boy, I swear that junk food got you tripping. I can see I need to be home more often to fix you something to eat. Keep you from eating all that crap that y'all been eating."

Shawn peeped in his room when his mother disappeared down the steps. "Don't go anywhere," he told Chanda.

"Right, like I'm actually going to leave," Chanda said sarcastically as she rolled her eyes.

Shawn ran to Jamal's room. Jamal was laughing at him. "Nigga, you're caught."

"Yo man, help me out." Shawn pleaded.

Jamal laughed. "Man, if you get out of this one, you are one sharp boy."

"Stall mommy for me."

"How am I supposed to do that?" Jamal asked.

"I don't know. Get her upstairs and keep her in your room until I get Chanda out of the house."

"Alright, but if you get caught, I ain't got shit to do with this. I don't know nothing about nothing." Jamal told his younger brother.

Jamal went to the top of the stairs and called for his mother. "I need you to check something for me." His mother went upstairs and followed Jamal into his room. He wanted her to see if his DJ'ing CDs were any good.

Shawn knew his time was limited because his mother never left her pots unattended. She would want to keep a close eye on her food. Shawn got Chanda out of his room and they crept down the stairs. He opened the front door for her and was just about to let her out when he heard his mother approaching the top of the stairs.

"Oh shit!" Shawn said pushing Chanda out of the door. "Ring the doorbell in a couple of seconds." He closed the door quietly and then ducked down like he was tying his shoelaces.

Ms. Keyona looked at her son with an odd expression. "Shawn, I worry about you sometimes."

Shawn looked at his mother and smiled. Chanda rang the doorbell and Shawn opened the door. They looked at each other and started laughing.

Jamal walked over to them and said quietly, "Y'all owe me."

Shawn gave Chanda a kiss and led her by the hand to the kitchen so she could say hi to his mother.

"Mom, this is my girlfriend, Chanda. Chanda, this is the all famous Keys," Shawn chuckled.

Chanda smiled and spoke to Ms. Keyona.

"Aren't you Carmen's daughter?" Ms. Keyona asked Chanda.

Chanda's smile faded and she looked at Shawn. "Yes," she said in a whisper.

"I went to school with her." Ms. Keyona smiled. "She's pretty," she told Shawn as she elbowed him playfully. "Would you like something to eat?"

"No thank you," Chanda replied. "I gotta run back home because I forgot something."

Shawn and Jamal made them a sandwich. "Mom, are you coming to my game on Saturday?" Shawn asked.

"Yeah, I think I can make it."

Jamal kissed his mother on the cheek. "Bye, Mom."

"Bye, baby," she said. Shawn kissed his mother on the cheek also and he and his brother along with Chanda left so they could head to Chanda's house before going to school.

"When my mom said that she knew your mom, you lost all the color in your face," Shawn told Chanda.

"That's because I was thinking of what would've happened if we would've gotten caught."

"That shit was slick how y'all pulled that off," Jamal commented even though he knew they never could've done it without his help.

"That's because I'm that nigga," Shawn chuckled as he popped his collar.

"Shut your ass up, you're all hype and shit," Jamal joked.

They reached Chanda's house and she went inside. She joined her brother who was in the kitchen eating a bowl of cereal.

"Did mommy ask for me?" she asked her brother.

"Yeah, but I told her that you were sleep."

"Good looking out. Did she wake up yet?"

"Naw canon," Kareem replied trying to sound cool.

"Alright, I gotta go to school. I'll see you when I get home. Come straight home from school, I don't want you running with those little dudes from Blumberg."

"Okay," Kareem hesitated. "Mommy's pregnant."

"What? How do you know?" Chanda asked, completely unaware.

"She told me last night," Kareem replied as he shoved a spoonful of Frosted Flakes into his mouth.

"She ain't say shit to me about it. It's probably by that nut-ass dude she been hanging around with lately. Who cares? I'm out, Kareem. Don't forget what I said."

"Okay. Bye, Chanda."

Yani

While Chanda was talking to her little brother, Jamal was telling Shawn about what he did with Tamera.

"It's about time you hit that," Shawn said, slapping his brother a handshake.

"Shit, fucking real," Jamal chuckled.

Chanda came outside and locked the door behind her. "Y'all ready to leave?"

"Yup," Shawn answered as he threw an arm over her shoulder. They walked over to Ridge Avenue to catch the 61 bus.

When they got to school, Chanda told Deisha and Tamera about her wild night and morning with Shawn. Tamera filled Chanda in on her encounter with Jamal. They laughed at how Chanda barely escaped Shawn's house without getting caught.

While Chanda and Tamera were sharing their stories about the events that occurred the night before, Jamal was telling Maurice what he did with Tamera and of course Shawn was telling about his night and morning with Chanda.

CHAPTER 3
TROUBLE IN THE HOOD

Shawn played at the Recreation Center the Saturday after he snuck Chanda out of his house. His mother never showed up to his game but it didn't bother him. He knew she wasn't going to show. His team beat, 114-96. Shawn was awarded a trophy for being the high man of the game; he scored 39 points, had 15 rebounds and 8 assists. His brother and his friends were all there to support him. After the game, the guys from the neighborhood gave him his props also.

Spring kicked into gear in mid-April, bringing sun-shine and warm weather. Chanda was avoiding her mother at all costs. She went to school, and then afterwards, she hung out at Deisha's house or with Shawn if he wasn't playing basketball. She found a part time job working at Eternity Shoes during the week in the Gallery, which made it all the more easier for her to stay out of contact with her mother.

Jamal and Tamera became closer than ever. Jamal had a job working at Foot Locker, also in the Gallery. He took Tamera places whenever they had the time and brought her sneakers and clothes. He loved Tamera hard, and there was nothing that he wouldn't do for her.

One morning, Chanda ran into Deisha on her way to school.

"Chanda, if I tell you this, you can't tell anybody; not Shawn, Tamera, nobody." Deisha said after they spoke to each other.

"Alright, what's up?" Chanda asked.

"I'm pregnant. Or at least I think that I am."

Chanda looked at Deisha with wide eyes in total shock. "Are you serious?" she squealed.

"I'm so late, the shit ain't even funny. My period was supposed to come on two weeks ago." Deisha took a deep breath and tried to collect her thoughts. "I don't get it. Maurice always uses a condom and I'm on birth control."

"Have you talked to Maurice?" Chanda asked.

"No, I'm scared of what he might say."

"Girl please, you know that Mar loves you more than anything in this world and you can tell him anything. Why don't you just go get a pregnancy test?" Chanda suggested.

"That's what I'm going to do today. Either way, I'm going to have to go to my doctor. I scheduled an appointment for Monday."

"You talked to your aunt?" Chanda asked.

"I'll probably only tell her if it turns out that I am." She drew in another deep breath and sighed. "I told you that you'd be the first to know if something like this happened."

Chanda didn't respond at first. She then remembered that her mother was also pregnant. "Did I tell you that my mom is pregnant?"

"Yeah," Deisha replied as she took out her transpass after noticing the bus was coming.

"She's like three or four months. She's trying to be all buddy-buddy with me now. I still don't say much to her. I go to school, go to work, come home and do my homework. I check on Kareem to make sure that his homework is right, and that's it."

"Damn girl, don't you be tired?" Deisha asked.

"Not really." Chanda shrugged.

"What's up with you and Shizz?"

"We're just chilling with each other. We go out when we have time. He works at City Blue now so you know I'm just getting the hook-up from everywhere. Now all we need is for you to get that job at Victoria's Secret or Express." They sat in the back of the bus in silence. "If you are pregnant Deisha, and you need any support, I definitely got your back," Chanda told Deisha.

Deisha looked at Chanda and smiled. "Thanks, girl."

When Deisha arrived at school, she immediately called Maurice over to her.

"What's up?" he asked. He gave her a hug and a kiss.

"Nothing," she replied as she glanced away. "Actually, there is something. I need to talk to you." They went into the stairway so they could get away from eavesdroppers.

"What's wrong?" Maurice asked her.

Deisha was quiet trying to form the words. She finally just blurted it out. "I think I'm pregnant."

"Why do you think that?" Maurice asked her calmly but inside, his heart was racing.

"Because my period is two weeks late. I don't know if I am or not. I'm going to take a home pregnancy test and I have a doctor's appointment on Monday at 8:35AM."

"Did you talk to your aunt?" he asked.

Deisha shook her head and looked at the floor. "I'm too scared to."

Maurice hugged her and rubbed her back. "I'm still going to be here. I told you that if this were to happen, it wouldn't change anything. You didn't get pregnant by yourself," he let her go. "But if it turns out that you are pregnant, please don't go behind my back and have an abortion. It's my baby, too."

"That's why I love him!" Deisha thought to herself.

"Go to class," Maurice told her. He walked her to her class and then he went to his own. He sat down next to Jamal and propped his elbows up on the desk. He folded his hands together under his nose and sat there with a blank stare, thinking.

"What's up, nigga? It looks like you're in serious thought." Jamal said to his friend.

Maurice took a deep breath before answering. "Deisha might be pregnant," he told him.

"Aw shit," Jamal said in a low voice. "What are y'all going to do?" he asked.

"I don't know, yo." Maurice replied. "She's not sure but, you never know."

Class started but Maurice could barely pay attention. He prayed that Deisha wasn't pregnant, but was prepared to man up if she turned out to be.

During gym, Deisha, Chanda and Tamera were sitting on the bleachers waiting for the coach to finish in his office and get gym started. Track season was almost over for Deisha but she still ran during the summer with local teams from her neighborhood. While the girls were waiting, they decided to play rope. Just as Deisha was about to jump in the rope, the coach blew his whistle for the class to go to their gym spots. They sat down, laughing at a rap that Chanda wrote.

"Wow girl, you are so out of order for that one." Tamera giggled when Chanda finished.

Chanda put the piece of paper back in her sweat pants pocket. "Deisha, what's up with you and the coach?" she asked in a whisper.

"I don't know. But when I told him that I wasn't taking those pills, he got pissed off. Now he hardly lets me run anymore."

"If I was you, I'd step to him and tell him, yo dawg, get your shit together or I'm telling the principal how your punk-ass was supplying me with narcotics so they can fire your stupid ass." Chanda said imitating a Spanish accent.

Deisha and Tamera burst out laughing. "Girl, you're gone," Deisha said in between giggles.

The coach looked at Deisha and her friends and said, "If you girls are finished, we can start."

Deisha rolled her eyes. The gym class got up and began their exercises. From jumping jacks to stretches, the coach ridiculed Deisha about the way she did her exercises.

"If he says something else to me, I'm going the fuck off in here," Deisha mumbled to herself. They got down on the floor and began their sit-ups.

"Deisha, do you have a problem where you can't do your sit-ups right?" the coach sneered at her.

Deisha sat up on the floor. "I am doing them the right way," she retorted. "You ain't saying anything to anybody else."

"*You* weren't doing them the right way. Don't talk back to me, Deisha."

"Joshua wasn't doing his sit-ups at all and you ain't say shit to him," Deisha replied in the same tone, drawing attention to them. Tamera and Chanda looked at each other and smiled.

"Get up and go get dressed. You are not going to disrespect my class or me. You can go to the dean's office."

"I ain't going anywhere. The only reason you're tripping like this is because you're mad that I didn't want to take those fucked up diet pills you tried to give me," Deisha spat. The gym room became silent. The coach was pissed and you could clearly tell by how red his face became. He grabbed Deisha by her arm and tried to pull her into his office but she yanked away. She looked like she was about to hit him, so Chanda and Tamera grabbed her and started pulling her away. The gym class was instigating of course. They pulled her into the locker room so Deisha could get dressed.

"Girl, you better stop before they send security in here and lock your ass up," Chanda told her with a chuckle.

Deisha started putting on her shirt. "Man, he ain't going to do shit because he knows I'm 'bout it 'bout it and will sucker slide his monkey ass."

Tamera laughed. "I ain't heard that in a long time. Sucker Slide." Deisha began laughing also as she put on her jeans.

"Where are you about to go?" Chanda asked Deisha.

"To the dean and tell him how the coach gave me those diet pills and how they made me sick," she replied as she put the straps to her book bag over her shoulders.

"Alright, see you at lunch, Deisha." Tamera said as they headed out of the locker room. Deisha went through the doors while Chanda and Tamera went back to the class.

After gym class, Tamera was by her locker near the girl's bathroom fixing the shoe strings to the Air Force One's that Jamal bought for her. She had on a white shirt and a pair of Sergio jeans. Chanda was in the bathroom fixing her hair. A guy from another charter that did not know Tamera or Jamal, walked over to her.

"What's up, Slim? Can I talk to you for a minute?" he asked her.

Tamera closed her locker. "Naw, that's alright."

"Why, you have a boyfriend or something?" the guy asked.

"Yeah," Tamera was trying to keep the conversation nice and brief not wanting what happened outside of the Gallery a few months prior to transpire again.

"So, dude ain't here. I'm trying to see you. I can't have your number?" he pressed on.

"No," Tamera said, becoming aggravated.

"Bitch, who are you getting loud with?" the guy asked, not realizing who he was talking to.

"Bitch?" Tamera repeated. "Don't be calling me a bitch. You better go ahead with that nut shit before I have Jamal up here to whip your little punk ass!" Tamera yelled.

"I don't give a fuck about no Jamal. I'll knock him and you the fuck out. Don't no muthafucking body up here in Magnet put fear in my muthafucking heart. Go get Jamal. I'm a straight Canon! Go get him! Think it's a game?"

"Okay and when he comes up here, let's see just how much of a Canon you really are. Stay up here on the balcony and I bet you you'll get beat the fuck up," Tamera snapped.

The guy flagged her and walked away. Chanda came from out of the bathroom after hearing all of the commotion.

"What just happened?" she asked.

"He just called me a bitch because I didn't want to talk to him. Then he's going to say that he'll knock me and Jamal the fuck out because he's a Canon and all of this other shit. I'd like to see this," Tamera snapped.

"Are you going to tell Jamal?" Chanda asked.

"Hell yeah! He's not going to disrespect me and him all in one part. He must've lost his damn mind." They went down to the lunchroom and ran straight into Jamal.

"Why did this guy just call me a bitch because I didn't want to talk to him, and he said he was going to knock me and you the fuck out?" Tamera told Jamal.

"What? How did I get into this?" he asked her.

"He called me a bitch because I didn't want to talk to him and I told him I was going to get you to beat his ass," Tamera told Jamal.

"Man, where he at?!" Jamal asked. He looked around as if he knew what the guy looked like.

"I told him to be on the balcony after lunch."

"I'm tired of these niggas thinking everybody the fuck sweet because they're from the fucking bottom. I don't give a fuck about the bottom. I'll show him a Canon," Jamal hissed.

Shawn over heard what was being said and decided to be nosey. "What? Who's trying to start something?"

"Some dude was talking all this shit. I'm about to beat him the fuck up," Jamal told him.

Maurice came over to their table. "Did y'all see Deisha?" he asked his friends.

Yani

"Oh yeah, her and the coach got into an argument because he kept saying little smart shit to her about how she was doing her exercises. Deisha got tired of it so she snapped on him about how he was only acting that way because she wouldn't take his diet pills. He gripped her up and Deisha was about to knock the snot out of him, so we took her in the locker room so she could calm down and get dressed. She said she was going to the dean's office to tell him what happened." Chanda blurted it out in one breath. "Oxygen." Shawn laughed and kissed her on her cheek.

"She shouldn't have taken those damn pills in the first place," Maurice said.

Tamera saw Deisha coming through the lunchroom doors. "Here she comes now," she told her friends.

"She looks mad as shit," Jamal said as he watched her stroll over to them. She sat at the table, folded her arms and laid her head down. Her friends stared at her in silence.

"What happened?" Shawn decided to ask.

"Not a damn thing." She sat up. "I went to the dean's office, right? I'm explaining everything to him about how the coach gave me the pills and how when they started making me feel sick I gave them back to him and that's when he started acting funny towards me. So they called the coach downstairs. That muthafucka, I swear I'm ready to go up there and kick his fucking ass. He comes down to the office with this bullshit story about how I am an attractive girl, and I don't look like I need to lose any weight, and how he would never give diet pills to any of his track stars let alone any of his students because he knows that they could have some type of side effect on them," Deisha looked as if she was close to tears.

"Oh no he didn't," Tamera replied distastefully. Deisha sniffed and nodded her head.

"The dean didn't believe you, did he?" Maurice asked.

"He said that he did after he took me for a walk to calm me down because I started throwing things in his office. But I know he didn't," she wiped her face.

"Why didn't you tell him that me and Tamera found them in your bag?" Maurice asked.

"I did," Deisha replied. "But he said that wasn't enough because y'all didn't see him give the pills to me. So basically it would've been our word against his." A few tears spilled out of Deisha's eyes. She wiped her face.

"That's fucked up." Shawn sympathized.

"You dig me," Deisha agreed as she pulled her hair behind her ears and leaned on Maurice's shoulder.

"So what are you going to do now?" Jamal asked.

"I quit the track team. It's too late for me to get my class changed to a different elective because it's already fourth report period." She got up. "I'll be back. I'm hungry as shit." She went over to the ALA CARTE line to get something to eat.

"Now what about a fight that I heard is supposed to be happening?" Shawn asked, getting back to Tamera and Jamal's situation.

"Some dude was talking shit about how he was going to knock me and Tamera the fuck out like I'm Quame' or some shit. First of all, he's mad because he tried to talk to Tammy and she wouldn't give him any play, so he called her a bitch. But when she said she was going to get me to beat his ass, he started talking shit about how he's a canon. So after lunch, she going to point him out to me and I'm gonna steal the shit out of him and we're just gonna knuckle on the balcony. Then I'm going to class," Jamal told them.

"Damn he said it like he was meditating," Maurice said. Jamal laughed.

Deisha walked back over to their table. She put a cookie in Maurice's mouth and said, "Chanda and Tamera, come sit over here. I need to talk to y'all."

Maurice bit the cookie. "Thanks, babe."

Jamal glanced at Maurice and then looked at Deisha and smiled.

Deisha smiled back. "What are you grinning for?" she asked him.

"Nothing," Jamal replied with wide, innocent eyes.

Deisha looked at him suspiciously and then cut her eyes at Maurice. She followed Tamera and Chanda over to another table and they sat down together.

"What's going on?" Tamera asked.

"The only reason that I'm telling you this is because you live with me now and I don't want to leave you out. I would say don't tell Jamal but something tells me that Maurice already beat you to that punch." Tamera looked at Deisha oddly. Deisha sighed. "I think I'm pregnant." Tamera gasped and covered her mouth. Deisha looked at her hands. "I'm not sure yet. That's why when I get home I'm going to take a pregnancy test. I have a doctor's appointment on Monday."

"Oh wow, Deisha. What if you are?" Tamera gushed.

"Then we'll deal with it. Maurice already told me that he's not going to let me deal with this by myself."

"Aww!" Tamera gushed some more.

"It's time to leave. Let's finish talking in Mrs. Al's class," Chanda suggested. They grabbed their things and began leaving the lunchroom.

Tamera and Jamal were walking on the balcony when she spotted the guy who called her a bitch.

"That's him," Tamera told Jamal.

"Where?" Jamal asked her.

Tamera pointed through the crowd with her pinky finger. "Over there with the red Polo shirt on standing by the lockers."

Jamal went over to the guy that was pointed out to him. "Ay yo, you said you were going to knock me the fuck out?" Jamal asked.

"Who the fuck is you?" the guy asked as he looked at Jamal like he was some type of fool.

Jamal punched the guy in his mouth, making him fall into the lockers. "I'm that nigga bitch, now get the fuck up!"

A bunch of people started crowding around. The guy got up and Jamal hit him again. He was about to hit him once more but the guy ducked and hit Jamal.

"Oh shit!" Shawn exclaimed.

Jamal snatched his shirt off and they both threw up their hands. The guy swung at Jamal but he blocked it.

"What the fuck? I thought you said you were a Canon. You swing like a bitch," Jamal taunted.

Jamal swung again. The guy barely blocked it, so he held him there.

"Let him go 'Mall!" Maurice shouted.

"I'm not holding this nigga, he's holding me," Jamal said back. As soon as the guy let him go, Jamal hit him with a two piece. He was about to hit him again but an NTA grabbed him. They broke up the fight and Jamal grabbed his shirt. He kissed Tamera and then walked away willingly. The security guard took him straight to the dean's office.

"Mr. Williams, I haven't seen you in here in a while," the dean said when Jamal came into his office. Apparently, they had made acquaintances numerous times before. "For a moment I thought you had been transferred or got kicked out," he pulled out a folder and began flipping through Jamal's records. "Your grades and behavior have changed dramatically." He looked at Jamal over the rim of his eye glasses. "Are you sure that you're Jamal Williams?"

Jamal leaned back in his chair. "If I'm getting suspended, can we get on with it so I can go home and you can get back to whatever it is that you do?"

The Dean laughed a hearty laugh and shook his head. "Oh I'm not going to suspend you, Mr. Williams. I'll give you a few Saturday work details. It's either that or you could join the Big Brothers Association. We'll assign you to a little boy between the ages of 10 and 14. You'll work with them for two months and that'll be that. You'll also earn a credit for Community Service. So what's it going to be, Mr. Williams?"

Jamal never liked the dean and he especially hated the way he always called him by his last name. To Jamal, the dean was like one of those Blacks who swore he was accepted in the white man's world and his own people were inferior to him. Yet he did see to it that the students had a fair trial when it came to being punished. Jamal hoped that if he had to choose between being Black or White, he would certainly choose being Black.

"I'll do the Big Brother jawn, but under one condition. I get to pick the little boy," Jamal replied sitting up in his chair.

"What little boy do you have in mind?" the dean asked him.

"There's a girl who goes here. Her name is Chanda Johnson and she has a little brother named Kareem Johnson. He's been doing some things that may get him into trouble and hanging with some little dudes from Blumberg projects. He's 13 and I just want to show him better."

The dean nodded his head. "I know who Chanda Johnson is. She writes poetry." He reached into his desk drawer and pulled out a business card. "This is my associate. Her name is Ms. Roberts. Give her a call when you get out of school and let her know that I sent you to her. Give her Kareem's name and the school he goes to along with a telephone number and she'll set it up for you. I think you'll be a great influence on him seeing as though you know the downside of being in these streets. I don't know who the young lady is, but she's turned you around tremendously."

Jamal smiled and stood up. He shook the dean's hand and then left the office to head back to his classroom. He felt good inside knowing that he was about to do something positive as well as get a kid off the street.

Chanda didn't have to work after school but Shawn did. Since Deisha was having her own issues with her pregnancy scare, she decided to just go straight home. A moment after Chanda came home and went up to her room, her mother came in behind her. She was four months pregnant and was showing a little.

"Chanda, why is it that for the past couple of weeks, you've been coming home late on a school night?" she asked her daughter. "Where have you been?"

"Work," Chanda replied wanting to keep their conversation short and brief.

"You mean to tell me that you found a job and wouldn't tell me?"

Chanda looked through her closet for something to wear to school the next day since it was going to be warm and sunny outside, not responding to what her mother said.

"Why are you acting this way towards me, Chanda?"

Chanda stopped what she was doing and took a deep breath before turning to her mother. She looked at her for a space of heartbeats and then turned back to her closet.

"Chanda, I really need you right now," her mother said softly as she rubbed her stomach.

"Where were you when we needed you?" Chanda asked flatly making it sound more like a rhetorical question. She ran her fingers through her hair. "You know what mom? I really don't feel like arguing with you right now."

Yani

"I don't want to argue anymore either," her mother sighed. "I just want to talk."

"Well, I don't," Chanda said as she left her room.

Her mother followed her down the stairs. "Chanda, where are you going?"

"Nowhere," she said as she opened the front door.

"Chanda, you better not walk out of that door now and I'm talking to you!" Carmen yelled.

Chanda turned around and faced her mother. "Okay. You want to talk?" She closed the door. "About what? How every time we wanted to talk to you, you were too busy? Or how the only time you sat down and had a real conversation was when you found out that I was having sex. And then that wasn't really anything because the only thing you said was "don't slip up". And you think that now because you're pregnant, things are just going to automatically change like that? I don't think so."

Chanda's mother was stunned at what her daughter said and didn't know how to respond. Chanda could see that she had nothing to say so she left out and closed the door behind her.

Tamera walked Deisha to the store to pick up the pregnancy test. Deisha was scared out of her mind.

"Just pick one so we can leave," Tamera told her.

"I don't know which one to pick," Deisha said as she bit her nails.

"Just... pick one so we can get out of here," Tamera hissed. She looked around nervously, hoping no one that they knew would see that they were buying a pregnancy test.

"I don't know," Deisha said, continuing to look at her options.

"Get the Error Proof Test." Tamera whispered. Deisha looked at the box and then picked it up. "Come on, girl."

They went over to the counter and Deisha paid for the test. They left the store and went home. When they got in the house, the phone rang.

Deisha answered after the second ring.

"Hello?"

"Did you take it?" Maurice asked without saying hello.

"Hi Maurice, and no, I didn't take it yet. I just got back from getting it. I'm about to take it in a few minutes. You want me to call you when I get the results?"

"Yeah," Maurice replied.

"Alright babe," she hung the phone up and went in her room, leaving the pregnancy test behind. Ms. Niecie came in the house moments later.

"Hi Ms. Niecie," Tamera spoke as she sat on the couch and began flipping through a tabloid magazine.

"How are you doing, Tammy?" Ms. Niecie spoke back. "Where's Deisha?"

"She's upstairs."

Ms. Niecie sat her pocket book on the table knocking over the bag that had the pregnancy test in it. She picked the bag up and the test fell out onto the floor. Tamera stared with wide eyes when Ms. Niecie picked the test up also. She looked at Tamera. "Is this yours?"

"Ms. Niecie, I..." Tamera stammered.

Ms. Niecie interrupted her. "Is this yours?" she asked louder.

Tamera looked at the floor and hunched her shoulders. "No Ma'am."

"Whose is it then?" Tamera continued to stare at the floor not wanting to look up. "Come here, Deisha!" Ms. Niecie yelled up the stairs.

Deisha came down the steps but stopped when she saw the just bought pregnancy test in her aunt's hands. She knew she was in trouble.

"Aunt 'Chelle, I can explain."

"I don't want your explanation!" she yelled making Deisha jump. "Are you pregnant?"

"I don't know," Deisha replied in a low tone.

"You don't know?" her aunt repeated. She stared at Deisha. "What did I tell you when I first found out that you were sexually active? I told you that these sorry-ass niggas out here ain't trying to be a daddy and take care of no baby. I let you handle the responsibility because I thought you were mature enough. And you did exactly what I told you not to do. Maurice may seem like a nice guy, but he's probably just like all of the rest; checking out the back door instead of being a man and stepping up to the plate."

Deisha stood at the top of the steps with tears in her eyes. She blinked them away, refusing to let them fall. Her aunt noticed that so she took a deep breath so she would calm down.

"Take this." Deisha took the test from her aunt and retreated to the bathroom. She read the directions carefully and then followed them. She then sat on the side of the tub, tapping her foot as she impatiently awaited the results.

"Five minutes," she said to herself, looking at her watch. "Pink, I'm pregnant, blue- I have some type of malfunction with my organs." She sighed and rested her chin in the palm of her hands. "Please don't let me be pregnant. Lord, please. I'm too young for this shit." She looked at her watch again and saw that her time was up. She stood up and looked at the results from her pregnancy test. She closed her eyes and bit her bottom lip.

She then opened the bathroom door and came out.

"So what's the verdict?" her aunt asked.

Deisha handed the test to her aunt and then slid to the floor crying.

Her aunt looked at the test and then looked at Deisha. "I don't believe this shit, Deisha. You're seventeen years old. What the hell do you know about being a parent? I should've kept your head in those damned books and out of those damned boys' faces. You want to end up like your mother, because this is exactly how she got started? And now she's in those streets doing who knows what to get a hit off that pipe. She was beautiful and smart just like you are now, but she slipped up and now look at where she is. Is that how you want to end up? Is it!?"

Deisha shook her head and wiped her face. Her aunt was close to tears as well.

"I took you in to get you away from that life style. I tried to do right by you because I can't have kids of my own. The least you could do is do right by me."

Deisha moved her hair from out of her face and wiped it with the back of her hand.

"Get up and go clean yourself up. You sit in your room and think about how you're going to deal with this situation because you sure as hell ain't having an abortion."

Deisha got up and went to her bedroom. She couldn't make herself sit down. She just stared at the wall. Tamera knocked on the door, causing her to jump.

"Yes." Deisha answered as she wiped her face again.

"Can I come in?" she asked.

"Yeah," Deisha told her

Tamera came in and closed the door behind her. "You alright?" she asked.

"No. Why did she have to bring up that stuff about my mom? I don't want to be like her and I never will be anything like her," her voice trembled as she talked. "My mom is weak anyway. I'm stronger than she'll ever be. And if Maurice cops out on me then I'll do this by myself. Because I don't need no muthafucking man to take care of me. I can hold my own." She sniffed and ran her hands across her face.

"So what are you going to do now?"

"I'm still going to the doctors on Monday to make sure because sometimes those pregnancy tests can be wrong. Then I'll get a job and start saving up just in case Maurice splits."

"Are you still going to college?"

"Hell yeah, I want a future for me and my baby."

"That's what's up. I didn't know Ms. Niecie couldn't have children." Tamera sat on Deisha's bed and Deisha leaned into the wall.

"Yeah, she rarely brings it up so she must be really pissed right now," Deisha replied.

"Times like this make me wish I had held onto my virginity."

Deisha looked at Tamera and sighed. "You and me both."

That Saturday, Deisha was in the living room doing her homework and listening to music. For the first time in a long time, she was wearing her glasses instead of her contacts. Her hair was getting her neck hot so she pulled it back into a ponytail. "I'm ready to just cut this shit off," she said out loud to herself. She got up to take a break from her long hours of studying. She went into the kitchen to fix herself a bowl of cereal. Maurice knocked on the door just as she was pouring the milk. When she opened the door, he gave her a hug and a kiss.

"What's up Deisha?" he spoke to her after letting her go.

"Hey babe," she opened the door wider so he could come in.

He sat on her couch. "I didn't know you wore glasses."

She took them off and sat them on the table beside her. "That's because I always wore my contact lenses. If you tell anybody, I'll kill you." She smiled and they both laughed as she closed her books and sat next to him.

"What time is your appointment?" Maurice asked her.

"8:35AM Monday morning," she replied. They became silent for a space of heartbeats.

"So, what happened Thursday night?" Maurice asked, feeling uncomfortable about the silence. Deisha didn't come to school Friday and she wasn't home that night so he could get the information from her.

Deisha sighed. "My aunt found the pregnancy test and went nuts. She threw shit up in my face about my mom and had me in here crying, especially when the test came back positive."

"Positive?" Maurice repeated.

Deisha didn't reply. She started picking her nails before moving on to her next comment. "I still gotta go to the doctors to make sure that the results from the home pregnancy test were right because sometimes they can be wrong."

"Whatever happens, I'll still be here," Maurice said, trying to sound as convincing as possible.

Deisha shook her head. "The more you say that, the more I don't believe you."

"Why do you say that?"

Deisha stood up. "Because I can tell you don't want this baby. I don't want this baby." She thought about what she said and decided to re-word herself. "No, I'm not ready to be a mother yet. I'm just a kid."

"And so am I. But whatever happens, happens."

"You keep saying that. I don't want it to be that way."

"Well, what do you want me to say?" Maurice argued. "I don't even know how you got pregnant."

"How I got pregnant?" Deisha repeated with an attitude. "What the hell do you mean, how I got pregnant? I didn't get pregnant by my damn self." Deisha was losing her temper.

"Boo, you know what I meant. I'm talking about as far as protection and the birth control you're on. I'm not going to leave you to take care of my child… our child by yourself. Like I told you before, this is my baby too," Maurice said as he stood and held one of her hands.

"You say that now, but as soon as the baby gets here, you'll be looking for the back door."

Maurice looked at Deisha as if she had lost her mind.

Deisha pulled her hand away. "You know what? I have a lot of homework and studying to do so I need you to go home and we can talk later," Deisha said to him as she began gathering her things to go up to her room.

"What the hell did you just say?" Maurice asked, referring to her last comment.

"Could you just leave please?" Deisha asked.

Maurice stared at her for a space of heartbeats and nodded his head. "Okay, you've got it. I'll call you whenever." He left her house and closed the door behind him.

Deisha suddenly felt ridiculous for how childish she had just acted with Maurice. What her aunt said to her the other night was truly getting to her and causing her to have doubts in Maurice. She wasn't sure if she was pregnant but she was definitely sure that she needed to mature a little and start having more faith in her boyfriend.

Her cereal had become mushy after sitting in milk for so long so she poured it down the drain and then went up to her room to sleep off her anger.

Chanda was at work ringing up a customer when Tamera came in.

"Hey Chanda," Tamera spoke as she leaned into the counter.

"What's up, Tammy?" Chanda smiled. She gave the customer their change and then looked at Tamera sighing.

"You look tired as hell. What time do you get off?" Tamera asked.

"In a half hour," Chanda replied after looking at her watch. "I've been in here since 10 'o clock this morning." It was almost 7 o clock.

"Damn girl." Tamera said as she checked out a shirt on the rack.

"Only so I ain't gotta stay home and listen to my mom's bull-shit." Chanda stopped talking when a guy came over to the register with a handful of items. She began ringing him up trying to ignore the way that he was staring at her. When she handed him his change, he smiled at her.

"What's up?" the guy spoke.

"Hello," Chanda replied blandly.

"Is your name Chanda?" he asked.

"Yeah, how did you know?"

"Well, because I always see you at the Rec with Shizz. That's your dude, right?"

"He sure is," Chanda said as she smiled.

The guy smiled back. "Dag, I was going to try to talk to you, too."

"*Not if you want to keep your teeth,*" Chanda thought to herself while trying extremely hard not to laugh in his face.

"Can't knock a nigga for trying," he continued as the thought was running through Chanda's head. He looked at Tamera. "You got a boyfriend?" he asked her.

"How are you going to try to talk to me and then try to talk to my girlfriend?" Chanda laughed.

"Well shit, y'all both look good. I figured I'd walk away with one of y'all numbers," the guy explained, trying to display a charming smile.

"Niggas crack me up with that shit," Chanda said shaking her head.

Instead of responding to Chanda, the guy turned his attention to Tamera. "So who's your boyfriend because I'm ready to give dude a handshake?"

Tamera smiled bashfully. "Jamal," she replied.

"From Master Street? Shawn's older brother?" the guy asked. His facial expression completely changed.

Tamera became confused. "Yes."

"Damn, I know I can't fuck with you, then."

Tamera and Chanda looked at each other and started laughing. "That's a damn shame," Chanda giggled.

"Naw, don't nobody fuck with nothing Jamal got. That's like the law of the land around there."

"That don't make no sense," Tamera said as she shook her head.

"Naw, it's cool. See y'all later." The guy grabbed his bags and made a quick exit from the store.

Chanda and Tamera fell out laughing again. "That's crazy how Jamal got those niggas so uptight around there." Tamera giggled some more.

"He wasn't cute at all though. And he was just staring me in my damn face, like fall back, damn," Chanda said with a frown.

"What are you doing when you leave work?" Tamera asked.

"I was going to go to Shawn's house but he waited until the last minute to do that report in Ms. Jordan's class and its due on Monday. I'm definitely not trying to go back home yet so I might just hang down here for a little while."

"Well then hang out with me. Deisha's house is like a war zone ever since her aunt found out that she might be pregnant. And Jamal is hanging with his cousin, Samir."

"I don't think Deisha is pregnant," Chanda replied in a low tone so no one nearby could hear her.

"The pregnancy test said that she was, though." Tamera told her. "You can't go by what those things say because sometimes they can be wrong." She hushed when some more customers came to her register. She took care of them one by one quickly so she could get back to her conversation with Tamera. "Home pregnancy tests don't always be right all the time. Those things are just as wrong as the day's long," Chanda went on.

"She ain't have any business taking those diet pills." "I hope she's not pregnant," Tamera said.

"We all do."

"But why is her period so late?"

"Those diet pills. Doctors come up with a drug to cure one problem, only to start another one." She looked at her watch and realized it was time for her to clock out. "Jamillah," she called to one of her co-workers. "Where's Danielle?" she asked her.

"I think she's in the back. She just walked in from break," Jamillah told Chanda.

"Tell her I'm about to log off and count my drawer so she better come on. Shit I've been here since we opened and I'm ready to go."

"Alright," Jamillah chuckled.

"Hold up, Tammy. Let me go count my drawer. I'll be right back." Chanda said as she took her drawer out of the register when Danielle came out with hers. She went in the back to count it and to clock out. She came back out with her jacket moments later. "So where do you want to go?" "I don't know. But I definitely don't want to stay in this Gallery." Tamera said as she fixed the strap to her shoulder bag.

"Let's grab something to eat down South Street and then walk around."

"I'm with that," Tamera replied. They left the store talking and laughing and made their way over to South Street.

That Monday morning, Deisha woke up ready to face the possibility that she may be a young mother. After showering and getting dressed, she sat on the side of her bed watching television to waste time.

"What time is your appointment?" her aunt asked as she stood in her door way.

"8:35." Deisha replied.

"Well, I don't have to be to work until nine so I'll drop you off, okay?" her aunt told her as she straightened her rings out on her fingers.

Deisha nodded. As her aunt was leaving out, Tamera was coming in.

"Are you riding with us?" she asked.

"Aunt 'Chelle is giving you a ride to school?" Deisha asked.

"Yeah," she sat on Deisha's bed and asked, "Are you scared?"

"Oh yeah," Deisha replied, taking a deep breath. "And I wanted Maurice to be there, but after the way I acted on Saturday, I doubt if he'll even speak to me. I don't even know why I snapped on him like that."

"You were just scared, that's all. Are you coming back to school after your appointment?"

"Yeah, Mr. Gaines already knows that I'll be at the doctors and I'm coming to school late."

"Good luck," Tamera said as she gave Deisha a hug. She went downstairs to make a quick sandwich before it was time for them to leave.

Deisha came down moments afterwards and got her book bag.

"Are y'all ready?" Ms. Niecie asked as she came down the stairs.

"Yes," Tamera replied as she licked Miracle Whip from her finger before biting into her sandwich.

"Alright, let me get my bag." Ms. Niecie grabbed what she needed and then they went out to the car. They drove up to University City High School in silence. Tamera said good-bye to them both when she got out of the car. She then went over to Jamal and Shawn when she saw them.

She gave Jamal a kiss. "Hey babe."

"How come Deisha didn't get out of the car?" Shawn asked Tamera.

"Oh, she has to go somewhere," Tamera answered quickly, keeping her promise that she wouldn't tell about Deisha being pregnant.

Shawn frowned at her and then smiled. "Don't be trying to keep me out of the loop, Tammy. Maurice already told me anyway." He playfully licked his tongue at her. Jamal and Tamera laughed.

Ms. Niecie stopped at the Women's Medical Center to Pennsylvania Hospital off of 7th and Race Streets. "Do you want me to come with you?" she asked her niece.

"No that's okay," Deisha responded as she shook her head.

"No matter what happens in there, I'm behind you one hundred percent, you understand me?"

Deisha nodded. Her aunt gave her a hug and squeezed her. When she let go, Deisha got out of the car. She leaned in through the car window. "Thank you Aunt 'Chelle." She turned to go inside and her aunt drove away.

Deisha went through the normal procedure of giving a urine sample and getting her pap smear. She had a lengthy conversation with her doctor about her relationship with Maurice and what her plans were in the event that it turned out she was in fact pregnant. When the results came in, Deisha crossed her fingers and toes and said a prayer. Today appeared to be her lucky day because her prayer was answered. It turned out that she wasn't pregnant. But the question still remained; why hadn't her period come on? She asked her doctor that question.

"Were you taking any kind of pills that weren't prescribed to you?"

"Diet pills, but it was only for like two days," Deisha said. She didn't want her doctor to think that she was a pill popping fiend with a weight issue.

"That could possibly be it. The best thing for you to do right now would be to get on a vitamin C regimen, drink plenty of orange juice, eat plenty of fruits and vegetables as well as some fiber. It may take a couple of cycles, but you'll become regular again. If you notice any abnormal bleeding, cramping out of the ordinary, unusual bloating, come back here. And remember, the best way to stay in shape and control your weight is healthy eating as well as good exercise." Deisha's doctor explained.

"Okay," Deisha happily replied. Whenever her period did decide to show up, she would happily greet it.

After getting dressed, she left the medical center and walked over to 8th Street to catch the L train to school. When she got to school, her class was still in advisory. She went over to Tamera and Chanda and tapped them on the shoulder.

"What happened?" Tamera asked.

"I'm not pregnant," Deisha beamed.

"You're not?" Tamera squealed happily.

"Nope."

Tamera hugged her. "That's what's up."

"You should've seen how happy I was when the doctor told me that I wasn't pregnant. I was about to start bouncing off the walls."

"Are you going to tell Maurice?" Tamera asked.

"He should know since that would've been a part of his responsibility if you were pregnant," Chanda added.

Deisha sighed and looked at Maurice playing cards with his friends. She went over to him and tapped him on his shoulder.

"Yo!" he spoke, not looking to see who it was.

"I need to talk to you for a second," Deisha told him.

"Hold up, let me finish taking their money," Maurice did as he said he would and then went out to the stairway so he could hear what Deisha had to say.

"Are you apologizing for Saturday or you have something else you want to tell me?" he asked as he leaned into the wall.

"Both," Deisha said. She took a deep breath. "I'm sorry for Saturday. I was stressed over how my aunt reacted and the things she said and I took it out on you when all you were trying to do is be there for me and that wasn't fair. Do you forgive me?" she asked with a hopeful look on her face.

Maurice smiled and nodded his head.

"I just came back from the doctors," she smiled again for the billionth time that day. "I'm not pregnant."

Maurice looked Deisha over. "Are you sure?"

"Yup!" Maurice hugged her and squeezed her tightly. "I guess that's a relief, right?" Deisha asked him when he let her go.

Maurice thought about his answer before saying it. He didn't want to set her off again. "In a way, yeah. I mean, what's the point in pretending that bringing a child in this world is something we both wanted when the reality of it is, that neither one of us wanted you to be pregnant."

Deisha nodded her head in agreement just as the bell rang for their next period class.

A few weeks later, the gang of friends were sitting at their usual table eating and laughing. Chanda pinched Jamal on his arm.

"Ouch, damn what did I do?" Jamal asked as he rubbed his arm.

"Nothing I just felt like pinching you," Chanda laughed. "No but really, I wanted to thank you for taking my little brother under your wing the way you did. He really looks up to you and Shawn. If we could see my dad more, I don't think he would be acting out."

"It's all good. I know how it goes. You know I can relate. I didn't want to tell you, but he had some beef with some little Blumberg niggas. They tried to roll on him one day when he was coming from Vaux because he doesn't hang down there like he used to. He whipped one of the dude's asses and the rest kinda fell back. I told him not to even cut around there for anything because those little niggas are bad news." Jamal told Chanda.

"When the hell did this happen?" Chanda asked.

"This was like a week ago. I think they were trying to get him to hustle down there and he told them naw. Then when he stopped rolling through, they felt some type of way. But I talked to him. It should be squashed right now."

Chanda shook her head. "I've been telling him for months to stop fucking going down there and he didn't listen. I don't want to have to fuck nobody up over my little brother."

"Don't worry about it. I got Lil' Man," Jamal told her. Chanda finished her lunch and tried to calm down. But she had a gut feeling that something bad was about to happen very soon.

A few nights later Shawn was walking home from Chanda's house. As he was cutting over Thompson Street, three guys walked over to him.

"Ay yo, are you Jamal's brother?" one of the guys asked.

"Yeah, why?" Shawn asked. He had a feeling the confrontation wasn't friendly.

"Because we wanna know muthafucka, you got a problem?" another one asked.

Shawn stopped and looked the guys over. "No, but you're about to have a fucking problem. Don't step to me on some nut-shit. If you got a problem with Jamal then you deal with it when you see him."

"Yo, grab that nigga," the first one ordered. Shawn hit one and then dropped the other one. The third guy managed to catch Shawn with a right hook. When he swung the second time, Shawn ducked and rushed him. He started beating the guy up on top of a car when the other two jumped in it, knocking Shawn to the ground. They were about to jump him but an elderly lady came out of her house with a broom and chased them away.

"Got-damn devils," she hissed as she went over to Shawn to see if he was alright. "Somebody needs to whip on their asses." She helped Shawn up not realizing it was him. "Shawn!"

"Hi Ms. Ethel," Shawn spoke back coolly as if nothing happened.

"Shawn, why on earth were those guys trying to hurt you like that?"

Shawn wiped his mouth. "I don't know. I was coming from my girlfriend's house. Then one guy asked me if I was Jamal's brother. I said yeah and the next thing I know, one of them swings on me. Then the one that I knocked down was trying to stomp me because I was beating his friend up."

"Well, you go home and get cleaned up. It's late and you got school tomorrow. Tell your mother I said hi."

"Alright, I will." He started walking away.

"You be careful."

"I will." Shawn went home. When he walked through the door, Jamal was sitting on the couch falling asleep. He looked up at his brother and then became wide awake.

"Why is your lip bleeding?" he asked.

"These guys just tried to jump me," Shawn replied as if it was no big deal.

Jamal jumped up. "Who was it?"

"I'm alright."

"I ain't asked you that shit. Who was it?"

"I don't know. It looked like those niggas that be down Richard Allen."

"You're talking about Kirk and them."

Shawn didn't respond. Jamal was about to leave out but Shawn grabbed his arm.

"Get off me, Shawn." Shawn let him go. "These muthafuckas out here only starting shit because I don't roll with them anymore and they mad because I stopped selling. They're not going to have me or you running scared like two little bitches."

"I'm not scared of shit. They don't put any fear in my muthafucking heart. I fought in these streets plenty of times and I never had to pick up a gun and I'm not about to start now. You killed one nigga and now you act like that's what you gotta do every time you feel as though somebody steps outta line. That's the problem with too many of these niggas out here now; scared to take an ass whipping. Stop trying to take up for me all the time, Jamal. That's part of the reason why Raheem is dead."

"You're trying to say I got Raheem killed?" Jamal asked.

"What I'm trying to say is, stop thinking you gotta look for people when something happens because something always goes wrong."

"So you want me to leave this one alone?"

"Do that shit," Shawn replied with a nod.

"Fine, fuck it," Jamal said as he sat back on the couch.

"Is Mommy here?" Shawn asked.

"Naw, not yet."

"Good. I don't need to hear her bitching about why I look like this." Shawn went up to his room to get himself cleaned up.

The next day on Kareem's birthday, he decided to play basketball at The Recreation Center until it was time for him to celebrate with his family. He was bouncing his ball, practicing a cross-over that Shawn had taught him as he was walking down the street when one of his friends named Jerome came over to him and gave him a hand shake.

"Happy birthday my nigga," his friend said to him.

"Thank you, Rome."

"What are you doing today?"

"I ain't doing much, just hanging with my family, why what's good?"

"Walk me over to the Crazy Market. I'm about to grab a hoagie real quick. I'll treat you to one, too."

Kareem thought about it. He was told by Jamal and his sister not to go into Blumberg. The Crazy Market was across the street from the projects and he didn't want to get into any trouble. He figured he was only going to the store so it wouldn't be a big deal.

"Alright, I'll walk you." Kareem replied. They talked and made jokes as they headed over to the Crazy Market. Jerome lingered behind Kareem letting him go into the store first.

Jerome made a noise, "OOOOOOOH OOOOOH!" A few guys across the street from the Crazy Market looked over. Jerome pointed inside of the store letting them know that Kareem was in there. Kareem opened up a freezer and looked over the beverages to see if he saw something he wanted when three guys came into the store.

"What's all that shit you was talking now, nigga!?" one of them said.

Kareem turned around and the three guys rushed him. He did his best to fight them off but they caught him off guard.

Mr. and Mrs. Yang came from behind the counter and tried to break it up. Kareem scrambled to his feet and ran from the store. He cut straight down Jefferson Street hoping he made it to Jamal's house and Jamal was home. The three guys came out of the store looking for him.

"I'ma kill that nigga yo," one of the guys said as he pulled a pistol from his pants.

Jerome grabbed his arm. "Wait hold up, y'all just said y'all wanted to knuckle him."

The guy pushed Jerome away. "Which way did that little pussy run?"

One of the other guys looked up Jefferson Street and saw Kareem running. "There his bitch-ass go right there."

"Split up!" The main guy said as they all ran off.

Jerome was in a panic at the thought that he had just set his friend up and now he could possibly be killed. He started running towards Kareem's house to get his older sister Chanda.

Chanda was already on her way to The Recreation Center to get Kareem so they could go out for his birthday. When Jerome saw her, he started waving his arm for her and shouting.

"Hey Jerome, what's wrong?"

Jerome bent over and sucked in air to catch his breath. "They just jumped your brother."

"WHAT?!" Chanda yelled.

Jerome was too afraid to say he was the reason behind Kareem getting jumped. "These guys from Blumberg. I was in the Crazy Market getting a hoagie and Kareem came in. I said what's up, he went over to get a soda or something and the next thing you know, these three dudes rushed him," Jerome explained, lying through his teeth.

"What the fuck was he doing in the Crazy Market? I fucking told him not to go down there!" Chanda was hysterical and was stomping her feet as she talked. "Where is my brother now?"

"He ran down Jefferson Street towards 20th and they chased after him."

"He's going to Jamal." Chanda ran off and pulled her phone from her pocket book. She was haul-assing down the street as she called Jamal's house.

"YO!" Jamal answered on the third ring.

"Jamal! They just jumped my brother in the Crazy Market across the street from Blumberg!" Chanda screamed into the phone. She made it to 22nd street before she stopped to catch her breath.

"What the fuck do you mean? Who jumped your brother? Where's he at now?"

"I think he's running to your house," Chanda said close to tears.

"Alright, calm down. I got your little brother as soon as he comes through here." Jamal assured Chanda.

Chanda hung her phone up and started making her way to Jamal's house.

Jamal stood in his door way looking up the street to see if he saw Kareem coming. The phone rang and Jamal hesitated to answer it not wanting to miss Kareem. He thought that maybe it was Chanda again so he ran back in the house to grab it. Just as he was closing the door behind him, Kareem ran around the corner. He was half the way down the block and almost to Jamal's house when one of the guys cut him off. Kareem was scared and out of breath. He was about to cut through a parking lot but another guy was coming through. Kareem looked around him frightened.

Chanda was about a half of a block away in the other direction and saw her brother when he ran around the corner. She opened her mouth to scream his name but quickly closed it when she saw a guy come from another direction causing her brother to stop dead in his tracks. She watched in horror at what was happening. Just as she was about to start running, shots rang out. She dropped to the ground, screaming. People nearby looked at her as if she were crazy but then they ducked for cover also. When it got quiet, Chanda scrambled to her feet. She was out of breath, tired and her chest burned while her stomach was in knots as she feared the worst. She got up the street just as Jamal was coming out of the house. Her brother had run a couple of steps and collapsed in front of Jamal's house. Chanda stopped running and took a couple of steps towards her brother with her mouth wide open. She dropped to her knees and looked her brother over. She placed her hands on his bloody shirt and started screaming. Jamal ran his hands over his face cursing himself for answering the phone. He dialed 911 from the cordless phone in his hands and explained quickly what happened.

Shawn was coming from the bus stop when he saw the crowd. He pushed through, thinking that his brother had done something crazy, but then dropped the bags in his hands when he saw Kareem on the ground with Chanda holding him crying. He looked at Chanda and then looked at Jamal. Jamal shook his head.

The ambulance showed up and began loading Kareem in the back. They wouldn't let Chanda get in with him, which almost caused a fight. Shawn grabbed her and put his arms around her to calm her down.

"What happened?" he asked her as she pulled away from him.

"I don't know. I went to get him from the Rec and Jerome ran over to me telling me that these guys jumped Kareem inside of the Crazy Market. When Yang broke the shit up, Kareem ran and the guys came out and chased after him. I called Jamal..." she trailed off and burst into tears. "Then I was coming down the street and I thought he was going to be okay but these guys came out of nowhere. This is not happening. It's his birthday." She sniffed and wiped her face. She grabbed her purse off of the steps and pulled out her phone.

"Who are you calling?" Shawn asked.

"I have to call my mom." She waited a few moments. "Mom."

"Yeah Chanda, where is Kareem?"

Chanda burst out in uncontrollable tears. "They shot him, Mom!"

"What?" Ms. Johnson yelled bolting upward from her seat.

"They shot him, Mom! They shot Kareem!"

"Where is he?!" Ms. Johnson screamed.

"Temple Hospital," Chanda said, still sobbing.

"Where are you?" her mother asked.

"It happened off of Master Street. He was trying to run to Jamal for help and collapsed in front of his house. I'm over there now."

"I'm on my way."

Chanda hung up the phone from talking to her mother. She looked down at the blood on her shirt and on her pants. She plopped down on the steps and put her hands to her face crying uncontrollably. Shawn sat beside her and put his arm around her pulling her close to him. A few moments later, her mother pulled up.

"Shawn, Jamal, can y'all come with me?" she asked.

"Yeah." Jamal locked the front door and they climbed into the car. One by one Jamal made calls to Tamera, Maurice and Deisha so they could all meet at the hospital.

It seemed like forever for a doctor to update them on Kareem's condition. Chanda paced back and forth squeezing and ringing her hands. Every time she saw a doctor come by, she stopped to look, hoping they were coming to give her and her family good news about her brother.

Shawn walked over to her. "Do you want something to drink?" he whispered into her ear. Chanda nodded and they walked off. A couple of minutes later, they returned and then a doctor came in behind them.

"Good new or bad news?" Chanda asked. The doctor looked at her sympathetically. "Is he going to be alright?"

"I need to speak with the parent or legal guardian of Kareem," the doctor said, not answering Chanda's questions.

"Is my brother going to be okay?" Chanda asked louder.

The doctor looked at her and then looked at everyone in the room. He took a deep breath and said, "I am so sorry…"

Before the doctor could get the rest of the words out of his mouth, Chanda swung on him and grabbed him by his collar. "Y'all are supposed to be doctors and all you can say is I'm sorry?!" Shawn grabbed her to make her let the doctor go before security could be called. "THAT IS MY BROTHER IN THERE!!!" Chanda screamed as the doctor freed himself from her grasp. Shawn hugged her to muffle her crying.

"Where's my baby?" Ms. Johnson asked, almost hysterical.

"Ma'am, I want to offer my sincere condolences," the doctor started.

"Oh no…" Deisha said putting her hands over her mouth.

"We did everything we could. But it was too much damage and he lost too much blood…" the doctor trailed off. "We lost him. I'm truly, truly sorry."

Chanda collapsed in Shawn's arms crying hysterically. Jamal came over to her and helped Shawn stand her up. They both held her until she calmed down.

"I want to see him," Chanda said as she wiped the tears from her eyes.

"Yes, certainly, right this way," the doctor replied as he escorted them to where Kareem was. Chanda walked in the room with Shawn and Jamal at her back. She sobbed as she lay her head on his chest praying that she could hear his heart beat or feel his chest rise and fall from him breathing. But he was still, very still, not moving, not breathing. Chanda cried on her brother's chest. She kissed his hands and then kissed his face. She turned to Shawn and fell into his arms crying. Her brother meant more than anything to her in this world and now he was gone.

Chanda's neighborhood took the death of Kareem hard. His friends stopped by every day to pay their respects. Her mother walked around the house like a zombie. She worked feverishly with trying to get things together for Kareem's memorial service as well as his funeral. She was hardly getting any sleep and was barely eating. Chanda noticed how fatigue her mother was looking one afternoon when they were still cleaning out his room.

"Mom, maybe you should go lay down. You don't look so good. I can take care of anything else that needs to be handled," Chanda told her mother.

Her mother hesitated for a moment but then decided to do as her daughter suggested. As she was making her way down the hall, she caught a terrible cramp in her side. She leaned into the wall for support, taking deep breaths to gather up the strength to call Chanda for help. Just as she was getting ready to call for her, she caught another pain and screamed. Chanda ran over to her just as she was sliding to the floor.

"Ma, are you alright?" Chanda asked, wiping the sweat from her forehead.

"Call the ambulance, Chanda. Something is wrong with the baby," her mother panted.

Chanda ran down the hall to her room and called the ambulance. She let them know what the situation was so they could get to the house as quickly as possible.

All the way to the hospital, Ms. Johnson was hollering in pain from the contractions. She was hoping and praying they could save her baby.

Chanda stood outside in the waiting room waiting to get word from the doctors. She knew something was wrong but she was hoping that it wasn't bad. After almost an hour, the doctors were walking towards Chanda.

"Is the baby going to be okay? Is my mom okay?" she asked.

"Your mother is fine. At this time it appears to be a miscarriage. We are taking her over to get an ultrasound. If indeed it is a miscarriage, we will need to make sure everything was passed through and if not, we'll give her a DNC…"

Chanda stared at the doctor with a blank expression on her face. The room had gone quiet and nothing he was saying to her was audible. In less than a week, she lost her brother and sister. She left the hospital and walked all the way to Shawn's house, despite the rain.

Shawn opened the door and looked at her with a frown. "What happened?"

"My mother lost the baby," Chanda said blandly. Shawn hugged her slowly. "Why is all of this happening?" she asked in a shaky voice.

Shawn didn't reply. He let her go after feeling how soak and wet she was from the rain. He ran upstairs and then returned moments later with a t-shirt, a pair of his ball shorts and a pair of socks along with a towel and his mother's hair dryer. He took Chanda up to his room and undressed her, dried her off and helped her change her clothes. They sat on the floor with Chanda sitting between his legs while he blow dried her hair. When he was done, they lay on the bed with Chanda lying on his chest.

"I miss him so much," Chanda said as tears slid out of her eyes. "I don't know what I'm going to do without him... I don't have anything to fight for anymore. My brother was everything to me and those bastards took him from me." She sniffed and wiped her face. "I can't believe he's gone."

Shawn held her tight and let her cry. He didn't tell her it would be okay, or that it would get better, or that her brother was in a better place.

He just continued to hold her and let her cry.

When Chanda's mother was released from the hospital, things began to take a turn for the worse. Ms. Johnson would hardly say anything to Chanda. She just wandered around the house like a walking corpse, visiting Kareem's room late at night. It was as if she was checking up on him like she used to when he was alive.

Chanda's friends supported her by showing up to the funeral. But when it was time to say their final good-byes before the interment, Chanda snapped out.

"Don't close my brother in there!" Chanda screamed as she lay on top of Kareem, blocking them from closing the casket. Shawn and her father tried to move her but she fought back, scratching and slapping at their hands. Shawn grabbed a hold of her and held her tight, whispering in her ear to calm down. They were finally able to get into the cars and head over to the cemetery where Kareem was being buried. Chanda took one of the last roses, kissed the pedals and then laid it across his casket before rubbing her hand along the top. She said her final good-bye before turning to leave with her family and friends.

CHAPTER 4
HARD TIMES

The middle of July arrived quickly. Chanda was still shook up over her brother's death. She worked whatever hours she could at Eternity Shoes to keep herself from having a nervous breakdown. Shawn hardly ever got the chance to see her. She still wasn't on speaking terms with her mother. After the funeral, her mother began yelling at her for minor things and picking fights with her every chance she got.

One rainy Wednesday, Chanda was at work reading to pass by the time since it was a slow day with hardly any customers shopping. Shawn was passing through after picking himself up a new pair of basketball sneakers, and decided to stop in to pay her a visit.

"Hey beautiful," he said as he came over to her counter.

Chanda looked up at him and smiled. "What are you doing here?"

"I haven't really seen you all summer. Jamal and his cronies from 23rd and Turner Street went somewhere so I figured I'd come by and treat you to lunch or something." Chanda sighed and closed her book. "Bad timing?"

"No," Chanda told him. "I'm just tired. Not sleepy tired, my body is just tired."

"Because all you've been doing is working. You need to take some time for yourself and relax. When is your lunch break?" Shawn asked.

"Actually, I'm about to take it now," Chanda replied.

Shawn grabbed her by her hands and pulled her up. "Come on, I'm treating," he told her.

"Let me clock out." Chanda went into the back and then returned a few moments later. "How come you're not at work today?" she asked when she came back.

"I have off the next couple of days so I'm chilling. What do you want to eat?"

Chanda looked around. "Yo quierdo Taco Bell," she grinned. Shawn smiled also and they walked over to the Taco Bell booth. They ordered their food and then went to sit at their usual table to talk and eat. Shawn was glad to hear Chanda laugh. But suddenly she stopped. She placed her elbows up on the table and leaned on her hands. Shawn stared at her, noticing her sudden change.

"What's wrong?" he asked her.

Chanda shook her head. She waited a moment not wanting to share her tears for her brother in front of anyone. She took a deep breath and wiped her face. "Thank you for lunch." She managed a smile.

Shawn took a hold of her hand and intertwined their fingers. "Anytime you need me, you know I'm here for you no matter what. If you need to talk or cry or whatever, I'm only a phone call away."

"I know," Chanda whispered as her eyes became teary. She blinked to keep them from falling but to no avail.

"Are you finished eating?" Shawn asked as he stood up to clean off the table they were sitting at.

"Yes, I'm done." Shawn threw their garbage in the trash and then walked Chanda back to her job. She gave him a hug.

Shawn could feel how hurt she still was over everything that transpired with her brother's murder and her mother's miscarriage. He gave her a kiss and told her he would call her later when she got off of work.

After a lot of serious thought, Tamera decided she wanted to do something with her singing. She knew she had a great voice and did not want to waste her talent. She began taking singing classes at Freedom Theatre during July. She met another talented vocalist named Chineta, and they immediately became friends. The only problem that Tamera had with Chineta was that she was a complete weed head.

Every day while Chineta and Tamera were at the Historical building in Philadelphia, a young man who worked there named Aaron, and his friend Jamil, repeatedly tried to talk to them. Aaron was like a leader for trouble. He fought when "niggas got out of line". Jamil on the other hand, was nothing like him. He only led when it was in his best interest and only said something when someone else said something first. Basically, he was a follower.

One day, their instructor was running late so Tamera and Chineta sat talking about Aaron and Jamil.

"You should talk to Aaron, he's cute," Chineta suggested.

Tamera took a sip of her soda. "I already have a boyfriend."

"So? Girl please. Niggas do that shit all the time. They have their main jawn with a backup bitch riding the bench," Chineta replied. She was a medium brown-skinned girl with slight acne on her face that she tried hiding with make-up. She wore her hair short in a "Halle Berry" style, with large hooped earrings and kept her wrist adorned with bracelets and charms. Chineta saw herself as a young diva but most guys viewed her as the typical hood-rat with semi-quality fashion sense.

"Not all guys are like that, Chineta." Tamera laughed and shook her head. "Besides, even if I didn't have a man, Aaron would be the last kind of nigga that I deal with. He's funny, but his whole attitude is just too reckless."

"Says the chick whose boyfriend is Jamal Williams," Chineta remarked as she gave Tamera the screw face.

Tamera laughed, "Yeah well, why you won't talk to Jamil?"

"Because that nigga doesn't have a back-bone. He's a nut. He needs to be more like Aaron."

"That's his problem. He's so busy trying to be something that he's not, he doesn't know who he is anymore. And if it's all like that, how come you won't talk to Aaron?"

"Because Aaron doesn't like me, he likes you." Just as the words fell from Chineta's lips, they saw Aaron and Jamil walking through the door. "And speak of the damn devils."

Tamera spotted them also. "Aw hell."

They walked over to Chineta and Tamera. Jamil was about to sit next to Tamera but Aaron grabbed him by the back of his shirt. "Naw nigga, get your ass up," Aaron told him. Jamil laughed and sat next to Chineta.

"If y'all don't have class, how come y'all always in here?" Tamera asked.

"Because we work here. Plus, I come to see you," Aaron said as he displayed a charming smile. "So when are we going to hook up?"

"I told you, I mess with Jamal," Tamera said for the millionth time.

"Why do you keep saying that nigga's name like I know him or something?" Aaron replied. The truth was, he had heard of Jamal but he didn't give a damn. He wanted what he wanted and he wasn't going to let another hood nigga's hyped legend make him back down. He was shorter than Tamera and dark skinned with a cleft in his chin. His eyes were dark brown and he wore his hair in braids that came close to his shoulders. Aaron was a handsome guy with a sharp tongue and quick wit. Tamera flagged him and ignored his last comment.

"Where's y'all instructor?" Jamil asked.

"She said she was going to be late," Chineta told them.

"Ay yo Chineta, you got that?" Jamil asked referring to her usual stash of weed. He was a tall skinny individual who struggled to fit in with the "in" crowd. He was a light brown-skinned young man with slight freckles on his nose and rusty brown hair. His chipped front tooth gave him a rugged look and though he tried to act tough, he actually was a kind hearted teen who followed the wrong crowd.

"Nigga when don't I ever have any?" she replied with a grin.

"Why don't y'all come chill with us over Jamil's crib?" Aaron asked.

"Because we have class and I am not trying to be seen with the likes of you," Tamera smirked before laughing.

"Yeah whatever. That sarcasm shit doesn't work with me. Because once I bite that, it's a wrap," Aaron said with confidence.

"You ain't biting shit," Tamera frowned at him. Aaron laughed.

Yani

"Come on Tamera, we might as well. Ms. Freeman won't be here for a while and I'm getting tired of sitting here," Chineta insisted.

"You go with them. I'll stay here," Tamera frowned.

"Stop being a punk, dag. Come on," Aaron said as he pulled her up from her chair.

"Get off me boy, what tip are you on?" Tamera snatched away from him.

"Please Tammy, please?" Chineta begged.

Tamera sighed and gave in. "Alright, damn. Let me get my bag."

They grabbed their things and left the Freedom Theatre. Tamera didn't normally leave with a group of people that she wasn't familiar with but she figured since her and Chineta had become close and she didn't plan on smoking weed or doing anything with Aaron, things would be okay.

When they arrived at Jamil's house, Tamera sat on the couch with her things close by. She watched as Chineta and Jamil sat on the love seat and immediately started rolling blunts. She ran her fingers through her hair trying to get over how uncomfortable she felt. She was beginning to wish that she had stayed for class.

Jamil, Chineta and Aaron were passing blunts back and forth as they laughed and talked about nothing of importance.

"Tamera, you look like a spare man, here," Aaron said as he tried passing a blunt to her.

"Chill, I don't do that shit," she replied as she waved her hand in front of his.

"One hit and I'll leave you alone. I swear," he insisted.

Tamera sighed becoming annoyed and then took the blunt from his hand. She looked at it for a moment and then turned her nose up at the smell. Aaron and the others laughed. She took a deep breath and then took a hit. She then took another hit and passed it back to Aaron. The sensation she felt wrongly gave her the impression of feeling "nice", so when they passed the blunt back to her, she didn't decline. Before she knew it, she had a partial buzz. She leaned back on the couch and ran her fingers through her hair. When she glanced over at Jamil and Chineta, she was shocked to see them making out and feeling each other up. She was even more surprised when she felt Aaron's lips touch her neck as his hand moved over her breasts. Since Jamal was the only person that she had ever allowed to touch her that way, she became a little tense but didn't say anything. Before she knew what was happening, Aaron was leading her upstairs to a dark room and was trying to lay her on the bed.

"No Aaron, stop," she told him.

Aaron forced her onto the bed and started licking and sucking on her neck. She tried to push him off of her but he threw his weight onto her.

"Stop Aaron!" she screamed louder, still trying to push him off of her.

Aaron put his hand around her throat to make her stop fighting him and continued to feel her up before trying to unbutton her pants.

Tamera decided not to panic. She knew that panic would make her situation worse so she pretended to give in. She rubbed her hands across his back and over his chest, kissing and tonguing him. She conjured up moans to make him believe that he was pleasing her entirely. When he loosened up the grip he had on her, she slid her hands down his pants, rubbing and jerking him back and forth until she got the erection from him that she wanted.

"Let me ride you, baby," she said in a sexy voice.

"You wanna ride this dick?" he asked in the same tone.

"Oh yeah," Tamera grinned. She rolled him over on his back and then climbed on top. Aaron lifted her shirt up and massaged her breast while she continued to jerk him off. When she felt like she had him in the palm of her hands, she squeezed him unmercifully. He let out a high-pitched howl and grabbed at his privates. He reached for her throat again so Tamera squeezed harder, digging in her nails.

"You fucking bitch," he squealed.

"Let me go or I'll rip this shit right the fuck out!!" she yelled as she squeezed him harder. He let her go and Tamera leaned so close to his face, he could smell her breath.

"You think this hurts? If you come near me again or so much as speak to me, if I catch you even looking at me, what I did to you today will seem like Vanessa Del Rio just gave you a fucking blow job." She let him go and jumped off of the bed. She ran out of the room and bolted down the stairs. When she got to the living room, Chineta had her head in Jamil's lap and he was leaning back with his eyes closed and his mouth opened. Tamera snatched her bag from the chair and left out of the house in disgust.

Deisha was in Wildwood with Maurice and his family for the weekend. It was their last day there and Deisha decided to spend some time with his sister, Keisha.

They were walking along the beach when Deisha started firing questions.

"So what neighborhood hoodlum has your eye, Keisha?"

"What made you ask me that?" Keisha giggled.

"Just figured we could have some girl talk," Deisha replied as they walked. When Keisha didn't answer, she elbowed her playfully. "Come on, I know you like somebody around there."

Keisha giggled bashfully. "Alright, just don't tell my brother or he'll flip out."

"Your secret's safe with me." Deisha smiled.

"I like this guy named Manny that graduated from Vaux a year before I did. I said I would tell him one day but every time I see him, I just freeze up," Keisha explained.

"Manny? Are you talking about Kiree's little brother?" Deisha asked.

"Yeah, how do you know him?"

"Because I beat up his sister for talking shit one day. Maurice let Kiree know that if her and her ugly-ass friends jumped me, then him and his little squad of cronies would get fucked up."

"Dag," Keisha replied.

"You want me to get y'all hooked up?"

"No!" Keisha exclaimed.

"Why not?" Deisha asked, confused.

"Because, I don't know how he's going to react. What if he laughs at me or he doesn't like me?" Keisha said in fear of rejection. She was almost the splitting image of her older brother Maurice, with the same exotic features making her appear as though she was Dominican. They both had the same medium brown skin complexion, chinky, brown eyes and dimples. Keisha was a little shorter than him, and she was curvy with wide hips, large breasts and long legs. She didn't look 14 at all, and had Maurice not been her older brother, the older neighborhood guys would have tested her to see if they could get into her pants.

"Then, oh well. There's another guy out there. Don't let getting turned down by one guy make you second guess yourself." Keisha didn't respond so Deisha asked her again. "Do you want me to get y'all hooked up or what?"

"I guess so," Keisha replied.

They walked on some more in silence. Deisha cleared her throat and asked, "Are you still a virgin?"

Keisha waited a few seconds before answering, "You really want me to answer that?"

"I'll take that as a no. So, who got lucky?"

"Dominique," Keisha said blandly.

"Please tell me it's not the Dominique that I'm thinking about," Deisha said as she put her hands to her face.

"Dominique from 18th Street," Keisha confirmed.

"Damn, how'd that happen?"

"We were talking for like a month and he started buying me stuff. He would pick me up from school and take me places. Me being naïve, I thought I was in love and all of my girlfriends envied me because I had this popular boyfriend who was older, cute, drove a car, and had money. Then one day in March, I went to his house, he got what he wanted and I haven't heard from him since then. I only called him once after that but he claimed he was busy but I could take a hint," Keisha explained.

"Do you regret that day?" Deisha asked.

A THUG'S REDEMPTION

"Every minute of it. No wonder Maurice didn't want me hanging around him."

"Don't worry about it. Most girls who lose their virginity at a young age wish they had waited. But whoever you decide to be with, don't let them cap your head up with no fake-ass love line to try to get you in bed. Only have sex when you're ready to take it to that level. And if they can't wait then, oh well. They aren't worth your time."

"Aren't you and my brother having sex?" Keisha asked.

Keisha's bluntness made Deisha hesitate. "Yes, we are."

Keisha looked at her and noticed the *Raheem* chain around her neck. "Who's Raheem?"

Deisha looked at the chain and touched it. "My first love. I was 14 when I lost my virginity to him. He got killed a little while after that and told Jamal to give this chain to me. Shawn, Jamal Raheem and Maurice were really close."

"It doesn't bother Maurice that you still hold onto it like that?"

"He knows he's number one. It's just some things I still cherish about Raheem. All Maurice needs to know is that I love him and nobody is taking his place." They walked on some more enjoying their stay away from home, the breeze and the scenery.

When Deisha returned home, her aunt approached her. "What's wrong with Tammy?"

"What's really wrong with her?" Deisha asked back.

"Her instructor at Freedom Theatre called and said that she skipped class today. She's been up there sleeping all day. Her room is all dark and she wouldn't even take calls from Jamal. I hope she isn't pregnant."

"You want me to talk to her?" Deisha asked.

"Yeah because I tried and she told me that she just wanted to be left alone." Deisha got a soda from out of the refrigerator. "How's Chanda doing?"

"I'm not sure. All she does is work or sit up in her room. Her mom's been a real queen "B" since her brother got killed. You'd think she would be a little more sympathetic since Chanda watched him get gunned down," Deisha replied as she cracked open her beverage.

"That's a damn shame. I saw her in the Gap earlier and she looked so sad. That's why I asked," Ms. Niecie said.

"Well right now she's probably thinking that nothing else could possibly go wrong."

"For now, let's worry about Tamera," Ms. Niecie said.

Deisha went upstairs and knocked on Tamera's bedroom door.

"Yes," Tamera answered.

"Can I come in?" Deisha asked.

"Yeah," Tamera replied.

Deisha came into the room and stumbled into the dresser. "Got-damn girl, you have all kinds of booby traps in here. Can I turn on a light or something?"

"Sure, go ahead," Tamera mumbled.

Deisha turned her light on and then sat on the side of Tamera's bed. "What's wrong?"

"Nothing," Tamera sulked.

"You're eyes are blood shot red like some Ridge Avenue wino and you're telling me nothing is wrong? Don't bull-shit me. Aunt 'Chelle said that you skipped singing classes and you wouldn't talk to her. You wouldn't even accept calls from Jamal. Did he do something? Am I going to have to fuck him up?" Deisha joked as she nudged Tamera playfully.

"No," Tamera moped.

Deisha crawled over beside Tamera and lay next to her. "Then what's wrong?" she asked as she rubbed Tamera's hair.

Tamera sniffed and then wiped her face. "If I tell you this, you have to promise that you won't tell anyone."

"It depends on what it is," Deisha replied.

"Please, Deisha. I don't want anybody to know." Deisha nodded in agreement after seeing that her friend was under a lot of stress.

Tamera sat up and hugged her pillow to her chest. She told Deisha everything about Aaron, from the time she met him up until their encounter today.

"I don't know if it was my fault for leaving with them in the first place knowing that that's what he wanted. Then I made matters worse by smoking weed," Tamera finished.

"Are you going to tell Jamal?" Deisha asked.

"No, I can't tell him that. He'd probably kill Aaron."

"Do you want to file a report or something?" Deisha asked.

"No! I just want to forget that it happened," Tamera said sternly.

"Well what are you going to do about the singing classes?"

"I'll quit. I don't want to go back after what happened today. I don't want to see *him* either."

"Considering what you did to him today, I doubt that he wants to see you."

"I just want to lie down. If Jamal calls again, just tell him that I'm not avoiding him. I just don't feel good and I'll call him tomorrow."

Deisha got off of Tamera's bed. "Alright, Tammy. Goodnight."

"Goodnight. And could you tell Ms. Niecie that I'm okay. I was just a little exhausted."

"Sure, I'll tell her," Deisha said before closing the door behind her as she left.

The next day, Jamal and Maurice were walking through the Gallery. They were in there getting sneakers and clothes while bussing on people as they moved throughout different stores.

"What did you and Deisha do while y'all were in Wildwood?" Jamal asked.

"Not a damn thing," Maurice told him. Jamal started laughing. "Naw because man, my mom was off with her dude and they were doing their thing. Deisha was out with Keisha mostly, so I hung with my cousin and we just walked around fucking with people.

"You're telling me that you were in a room with Deisha by yourself at night for three nights and you ain't hit once?" Jamal asked in disbelief.

"Oh, hell yeah; just not like I wanted to because my mom's nosey ass kept stopping by."

"I called Tamera yesterday to see if she wanted to go to that Nelly concert since she's so in love with that nigga, but she wouldn't take any of my calls."

"Oh, you got the tickets?" Maurice asked.

"Yeah but she wouldn't bring her ass to the phone. She claimed she was tired. Had she known I had those damn tickets, her ass would've been wide awake."

"Damn homie, what did you do now?" Maurice laughed.

"Why it always gotta be me? I ain't do shit," Jamal replied.

Maurice checked out a girl as they were walking past Sneaker Villa. "Damn, that girl got a fat ass," he commented.

Just as Jamal spotted the girl and was about to comment himself, the girl turned around and he changed his mind. "Damn her face just fucked up the moment. She looks like Blanca from Street Fighter 2."

He and Maurice laughed as they headed over to the food court to get something to eat.

Chanda called out of work the day Jamal and Maurice were walking through the Gallery. She woke up that morning with a serious stomach virus and couldn't stop vomiting. She was huddled over the toilet bowl crying and vomiting at the same time. Ms. Johnson wouldn't even come into the bathroom to see if she were okay. Chanda got up and fixed herself a cup of water. She took a deep breath and drank the water slowly. She looked at her reflection in the mirror and saw how tired she looked. She had been grieving hard for her brother and it felt like it wasn't getting any easier. Her heart hurt and her soul ached. She wished like hell things had been different and she could hang with him like she used to.

Chanda went downstairs and made herself a pot of tea and some chicken noodle soup. While her food was cooking, she threw on a pair of sweat pants and a t-shirt and swept her hair into a pony tail. She sat at the table with her head down thinking of her brother while she waited for her food to finish. When everything was prepared, she went back to her bedroom and turned on her TV. Her mother knocked on her door moments later.

"How come you're not at work?" she asked without saying good morning.

"I called out because I have a stomach virus," Chanda told her.

"Oh," Ms. Johnson replied. Chanda looked up at her ceiling and then shook her head at her mother's lack of concern. "Your Aunt Rachel is coming over so I want you to mop the downstairs floors and clean the bathroom."

"Mom, did you just hear a word I said? I have a stomach virus. I've been vomiting all morning," Chanda replied.

"If Shawn were to come over here right now you know your stomach would not be bothering you. It was probably just something that you ate. Do what I told you to do before your aunt gets here."

Chanda looked at her mother and then got off of her bed. She snatched her inhaler off of her dresser and stormed out of her room. She went into the bathroom and closed the door behind her.

"I swear to God, I can't wait until I get the fuck out of here because this shit is ridiculous." She moved everything into the hallway so she could sweep and mop the floor. Just when she was about to fix a fresh bucket of water so she could do the downstairs floors, she vomited all over the freshly mopped bathroom floor.

"Oh, I don't believe this shit, man!" Chanda was now furious and almost in tears as she re-did the bathroom. When she went downstairs to do the living room, dining room and kitchen floors, her mother was sitting in the kitchen smoking a cigarette; a habit that she picked up after Kareem was killed.

"You and Shawn going anywhere?" she asked after taking a drag on her cigarette.

"No mom, I'm sick," Chanda mumbled.

Ms. Johnson looked her over. "I sincerely hope you're not pregnant because if you are, you're getting an abortion. I am too young to be a grandmother and I'll be damned if you're running around here shaking babies at 18."

"Just because I'm sick that doesn't mean that I'm pregnant. And no I wouldn't have an abortion if I were. Just because you lost your baby doesn't mean you have to take mines away *if* I were pregnant," Chanda sneered at her mother.

"Who the hell do you think you're talking to, Chanda? I've told you before about that shit."

"Mom!" Chanda yelled as she slammed the mop down. "You're doing things to me that's not even making any sense. I told you that I had a stomach virus and all you said was 'oh' like you didn't even care. Then you're making me mop these floors and it's not even me that's having company!

"Ever since Kareem died all you do is take everything out on me like everything is my fault. You scream at me for little stuff. You scream at me for stuff that I didn't even do. Half the time you're screaming at me and I don't even know why. You never stop to see how I feel. It's always about you and your FUCKED UP LIFE!" Chanda screamed as she slid everything off of the table and onto the floor out of anger. She started wheezing.

Her mother looked at her and then looked at the mess on the floor. Chanda took out her inhaler and used it. Before she knew it, her mother advanced to her and punched her in her face. Chanda held her face with tears in her eyes as she looked at her mother, appalled. Her mother was about to hit her again but Chanda blocked it and punched her mother back. They started fighting wildly, cursing and screaming at each other. Chanda's aunt heard the commotion outside and used her key to get in. She ran over to her sister and her niece and tried to break them up. Chanda had her mother by her hair but her mother had her in a headlock.

"Carmen, let that girl go!" Rachel screamed, still trying to separate them.

"Bitch, get the fuck off of me!" Chanda screeched.

"Carmen, let that girl go, now!" Rachel begged.

Ms. Johnson pushed her sister out of the way. "Stay out of this, Rachel. She wants to be grown so damn bad!" Carmen pushed her daughter onto the floor and got on top of her, beginning to choke her. Chanda kicked her legs as she tried to get in air and free herself but was unsuccessful.

"You're going to kill her and she's all you have left!" Rachel pleaded. She pulled Carmen off of Chanda and Chanda scrambled to her knees. She put her hands to her throat as she gagged. She was trying desperately to get in air but couldn't. She then pulled her inhaler from off of the counter and used it until she could breathe easily

"Get your shit and get the fuck out of my house!" her mother yelled.

"Where am I supposed to go?" Chanda cried.

"I don't give a shit where you go but you're getting the fuck out of here."

"I hate you!" Chanda screamed.

Her mother picked up a glass and threw it at her barely missing because Rachel grabbed her arm. "Get the fuck out!" she yelled.

Chanda ran upstairs and put her sneakers on. She combed her hair and put it into another ponytail. She listened as her mother bad-mouthed her to her aunt. Shaking her head, she grabbed her book bag and a duffle bag and put her clothes and all of the rest of her belongings that would fit. She zipped it up, sniffed and wiped her face. She then called her father, seeing that she had no other place to go. When he answered, Chanda broke down in tears as she told him everything that happened.

"So she's kicking you out because you're tired of her shit," her father concluded.

"Basically, yeah. She knows that I've been messed up since Kareem got killed and she's been taking it out on me like it's my fault."

"I know sweetheart, I know," her father consoled her.

"Daddy, you told me that if I ever needed a place to stay or if it got that bad here that I could stay with you. It been got that bad but I was only hanging in there for Kareem. He's gone now and I have no other reason to stay." She sighed as she paced her bedroom floor.

"Chanda if you want to stay with me I'll come get you right now," her father told her.

"Thank you daddy," Chanda said as she let out a sigh of relief. She hung up the phone and then waited patiently for her get out of jail free card.

Later that day, Tamera was at Jamal's house after he came back from the Gallery with Maurice. They were reminiscing about old songs and childhood memories when it dawned on Jamal that Tamera was supposed to be at Freedom Theatre for her singing lessons.

"How come you're not in class today?" Jamal asked.

"I quit," Tamera said.

"How come?"

"I really don't want to talk about it. It was just some stupid stuff that was going on and I didn't feel like dealing with it so I just quit."

"Oh," Jamal dismissed it. He knew something was bothering her about the classes by the way her expression changed when he asked her about it, but he decided not to pry. He moved her hair to the side and kissed her ear and her neck. When he moved his hand up her tank top, Tamera thought back to what happened with Aaron and she moved away.

"Stop," Tamera said as she wiped her hand across her neck where Jamal had just kissed her.

"What's wrong?" he asked.

"It's a girl thing," Tamera replied. She forced a smile.

"A girl thing?" Jamal asked suspiciously.

"Yeah you know, bloating, cramps, all the stuff that prevents females from having sex certain times out of every month," she said nervously.

"Oh," Jamal replied again. He gave her a kiss. He could tell that she was lying to him. "You don't have to lie about it. If you didn't want to do it, all you had to do was say, no."

"Who said I was lying?" Tamera asked defensively.

"Your facial expression. You look like you have a lot on your mind. You have something that you want to talk about?"

"Not really."

"I don't keep shit from you. Why do you have to keep shit from me?"

Tamera sighed. She tried to decide if she should tell Jamal the real reason she quit her singing classes but she didn't want to piss him off. She knew it could set off his temper but she decided to be honest with him. She took a deep breath and told him why she really quit her singing classes.

"You've gotta be fucking kidding me," Jamal said as he got up from the couch when she finished. "Why you ain't stop him before he got started?"

"What?" Tamera asked confused.

"Why the fuck didn't you stop him before he got you upstairs?" Jamal was pissed that Tamera would be foolish enough to let something like that happen.

"I was scared," Tamera replied.

"You weren't scared to smoke weed. You weren't scared to leave with a group of people that you barely fucking know and then go to a house that you've never been to before. How do I know if more happened than what you said?"

"So you're saying I'm lying now?" Tamera asked.

"I don't know. You tell me."

"No I'm not lying! You're making it sound like it's my fault!" Tamera was beginning to wish that she never told him.

"You knew what he was after," Jamal argued.

"He tried to rape me, Jamal! He choked me. He fucking choked me!" She was close to tears and extremely angry at how Jamal was reacting. Jamal tried to calm down seeing how upset Tamera was over the situation. He tried to give her a hug but she pushed him away. Tamera snatched her purse from his couch and stormed out of his house.

Since the summer, Maurice's mother had been home more than usual. She worked for the school district which meant whenever the students had off, she had off as well. This was a distraction for Maurice because he and Deisha couldn't do all of the things that they normally did. It was also annoying to Deisha. She knew that Maurice's mother did not like her. No matter how respectful Deisha tried to be, Ms. Brown continued to show her dislike for her every chance that she got.

They were sitting on his couch play fighting with plastic baseball bats from Wildwood. Every time Maurice tried to steal a kiss, Deisha wacked him with the bat and they started play fighting again. He held her arm down and stole a long kiss from her. He stopped when he heard his mother coming and Deisha wacked him with the bat again.

"Hi Ms. Brown," Deisha spoke as she was hitting Maurice.

"Hey Deisha. Maurice, y'all better not break anything in here," Ms. Brown warned.

"We're not," Maurice replied.

"So how are you?" Ms. Brown asked in a tone that showed she didn't care actually. She was never too fond of Deisha being her son's girlfriend.

"I'm fine," Deisha smiled.

"That's good. Let me know if Maurice gives you any trouble," she said meaning the total opposite. She went into the kitchen.

"Why it gotta be me?" Maurice asked as he kissed Deisha on the cheek.

"He's alright," Deisha replied, giggling.

"Are you staying for dinner?" Ms. Brown asked. She prayed that she wasn't.

"No, my aunt wants me in at a certain time because she needs my help with something," Deisha lied. There was no way in hell she was breaking bread with Maurice's mother.

"You don't live with your mother?" Ms. Brown inquired.

Deisha hesitated. "No."

"Why?"

"There were some problems when I was little. My aunt wanted to give me a better life so she took me in," Deisha explained. She wasn't comfortable with Ms. Brown prying into her personal life. Maurice kissed her on her cheek again when he saw how uncomfortable she was becoming.

"Oh. Exactly what kind of problems could you have with your mother when you are a child?" Ms. Brown asked in a distasteful manner.

"Mom," Maurice interjected.

"No Maurice, it's okay." Deisha licked her lips and took a deep breath. "My mom was on drugs and most of the time I was in the house by myself. From the age of five to eight, I thought it was normal. Until I realized what my mother was doing on her knees wasn't. My aunt got tired of only taking care of me part-time and despite everyone telling her to mind her business she put my mother through DHS and took custody of me. Now my mom is running the streets doing who-knows-what to get a hit off that pipe and I'm studying my ass off so I don't have to be like her." Deisha got up, ready to go home earlier than she had anticipated.

"I'm sorry to hear that," Ms. Brown lied feeling as though that would explain Deisha's promiscuous behavior. "I never would've guessed you were the product of a drug addict."

Deisha looked at Ms. Brown as if she had lost her mind. Instead of engaging in an argument that she obviously was trying to start, Deisha left the house.

"I knew it had to be something wrong with that girl. Maurice, of all the girls you could have picked for a girlfriend, you go and choose a sexually promiscuous crack-baby."

"Mom, number one Deisha is not promiscuous. Number two she is far from a crack baby. You don't know what that girl went through in her mom's house but got the nerve to judge her. Deisha is one of the smartest girls at that school and was chosen to take college courses at Drexel University during our senior year," Maurice was furious with his mother.

"That might account for something if you were going to an academic high school but look at what school you attend. It's not Central or Engineering and Science. It's University City, in one of the worst neighborhoods in Philadelphia!" His mother shook her head at him.

"You can say what you want, mom. It doesn't matter if you don't like her. I love her." Maurice left out the house to go after Deisha to make sure that she was okay.

Chanda grabbed her book bag and her duffle bag when she heard a knock at the door. She rushed downstairs just as her mother opened it.

"What the hell are you doing here?" Ms. Johnson sneered at her ex-husband.

"I came to get Chanda. Is she ready?" he replied.

"You ain't getting shit," Ms. Johnson contested. Chanda came downstairs and walked over to the front door.

"Are you ready?" her father asked.

"Yeah," Chanda replied, as she fixed the strap to her duffle bag over her shoulder.

"You ain't do shit for her in the last 15 years and because she doesn't want to listen to a damn thing in here and I knocked her on her ass, you think you're going to just come in and sweep her up out of here!" Ms. Johnson was trying to cause a scene, which was one of the many things that drove her husband away.

"This shit ain't about me sweeping her anywhere, Carmen. This girl watched her brother get gunned down in the got-damn streets and all you're doing is giving her hell. She doesn't need to hear your constant bull-shit. Chanda, let's go."

"You're not going no damn where," Carmen said as she tried to snatch Chanda by her arm. Chanda yanked away and walked out of the door. "The only reason you're taking her now is because she only has one year left. You were a sorry muthafucka when I met you and you ain't changed a bit yet!" Carmen yelled.

"The only thing that hasn't changed is your attitude. You always wanted to control things and have shit your way. But when the time came, you fucked things up and then blamed everybody but yourself. You're doing exactly that now. You let your child deal with this whole situation by herself. This is not Carmen's world and you need to understand that."

"I'm the one who lost two of my babies and she's dealing with this on her own? Don't hand me that bullshit!" Carmen was furious.

Chanda and her father went over to his jeep. She sat her stuff in the back seat and climbed in the passenger side. "I'm sorry about your miscarriage, Carmen. But maybe if you hadn't been such a heartless bitch, you and Chanda could have helped each other through this." He got into his jeep and drove away.

Carmen went into her house and joined her sister in the kitchen. They began to talk. "I rightly don't give a shit. He ain't done a damn thing for her in the last 15 years and all of a sudden, she wants to go running to him. Let him take her. Shit, I've done my part. I'm finished." She lit her cigarette and took a long drag.

"It's your own fault," Rachel told her.

Carmen blew out smoke and looked through it with piercing eyes. "How the hell is it my fault?"

"Would you shut up and listen for a change? That's your problem; you're so quick to spit your piece but you don't ever want to hear what the other person has to say. You ran that girl out of here. All you do is yell and scream at that girl. She can write some beautiful poetry and stories. Do you know how talented your daughter is? Of course you don't know because you don't show any interest, do you? You don't even at least try to see what she has been up to. You're doing the same thing to her that Mommy did to us except she's not running the streets to get away from it like we did. She's writing and trying to go to college. She's the only thing you have left and now she's gone. And I don't blame her if she doesn't come back. It's not fair, Carmen. It really isn't." The telephone rang and Rachel picked it up. "Hello?"

"Hello, is Chanda there?" Shawn asked.

Rachel shook her head and looked at her sister. "Chanda isn't here right now. As a matter of fact, Chanda won't be here anymore."

"What?" Shawn asked. He didn't recall her saying anything about moving earlier that day when he talked to her.

"Is this Shawn?" Rachel asked.

"Yes."

"She doesn't live here anymore. She just moved out."

"Where did she go?" Shawn asked, confused.

"I don't know. She's staying with her father right now. But if she calls, which I doubt that she will, I'll have her call you."

"Okay, thanks." Shawn hung up the phone and looked at it with a puzzled expression on his face.

"What's wrong?" Jamal asked.

"I just talked to Chanda this morning and she ain't say anything about moving," Shawn said.

"She moved? Where did she go?"

"I don't know. That's what her aunt just said. It's probably because of something that jumped off with her mom. She's been real bitchy since Kareem got killed."

"Don't Chanda have a cell phone now?" Jamal asked.

"Yeah, I keep forgetting about that." Shawn picked up the phone again and dialed Chanda's number. It went straight to voicemail so he left her a message. "Yo, call me when you get this and let me know what's up?" He hung up and sat back on the couch.

When Deisha got in, her aunt and another lady were sitting in the kitchen talking.

"Hi, Aunt 'Chelle," Deisha called from the living room. She was trying to see who the other lady in the kitchen was. The other woman that was sitting with Deisha's aunt turned around and smiled. She got up slowly and advanced towards Deisha. Deisha backed up. She couldn't believe she was staring at her mother.

"What is she doing here? Aunt 'Chelle?!" Deisha was furious beyond anyone's imagination.

"Janelle was in rehab and has been clean for almost three years, Deisha. She just wants to see you."

"I wish I could say the feeling is mutual," Deisha snapped. She was feeling the irony of running into her mother after the talk she had with Maurice's mother.

"Watch your mouth," her aunt sneered.

"It's okay, Deisha. I just came by to say hi and to see how much of a fine young lady you grew up to be," Janelle replied.

Deisha took a step back, holding her tongue from another sarcastic remark.

"Deisha please," Michelle pleaded.

"She can't do this to me. She can't just come back here and pretend like nothing happened and then think she can just pop back into my life. No!" Deisha refused. She was completely against the little reunion they were trying to pull.

"It's not like that, sweetheart. I just wanna talk," Janelle said.

"You left me, Janelle. I don't wanna talk to you," Deisha said acidly.

"She's not asking you to come back home. She only wants to talk to you," Michelle pleaded.

Deisha was aggravated and it was evident in her face. "Alright man," she said giving in with a sigh.

Janelle smiled. "Can I have a hug?" Deisha wanted to punch her in the face more than she wanted to hug her. But she swallowed her anger and gave her mother a hug. Her aunt smiled, happy to see the two of them together again. They sat down on the couch. "So, what's been happening? Fill me in."

"Well, I have a job working at a daycare. I'm on the track team and the Honor Society. I won a few trophies in the last two years at the Penn Relays. Colleges are sending me recruitment letters and I got a scholarship offer from Truth University in Atlanta. Other than that, nothing has really been happening."

"That's wonderful," her mother perked. "Do you have a boyfriend?"

Deisha blushed. "Yes, his name is Maurice."

"And he treats her like the queen she is. That boy really adores her," Michelle chimed in.

"Are you two... you know?" Janelle asked.

"I'm 17 and we've been together since I was 15. Yes," Deisha replied looking at her mother as if she had asked a stupid question.

"Oh, you don't have any kids do you?"

"No. We're careful," Deisha said having an idea where the conversation was headed.

"Good." Janelle let out a sigh of relief. "That's what messed me up," she slipped. Deisha looked at her angrily. Michelle winced knowing how her niece was going to react. "I'm sorry. That's not what I meant."

"No, that is exactly what you meant. Look, why did you even bother to come here, Janelle? I'm almost a grown-ass woman. What the hell would I need to see you now for when you never did a damn thing for me?"

"Deisha, watch your mouth," her aunt warned.

"For what? She just admitted that I was a mistake. As far as I'm concerned, she's just another nigga off the street."

"Deisha, I didn't mean to offend you in any way. And I didn't come here to pick up where we left off. I just wanted to let you know that I understand now what it must've been like for you."

"Please! You wouldn't understand if I relived it for you and the roles were reversed." Deisha stormed up to her room and slammed her door.

"I'm sorry," Michelle apologized. She had hoped that the reunion would have turned out to be a good thing.

"No, you don't have to apologize Niecie, she's right. If I had let that stuff keep going on, imagine how she would be now."

Michelle gave her sister a hug. "Give her some time. She'll come around."

"Thanks for taking care of her," Janelle said.

"No problem." Michelle rubbed her hands together. "Are you staying for dinner?"

"Yeah, I can't remember the last time I had a home cooked meal."

Janelle sat in the kitchen while Michelle cooked. She filled her sister in on Deisha's teenaged years and they talked and laughed like they did when they were younger.

Chanda received Shawn's message just as she was entering her father's home.

"Your room is right next to the bathroom," her father told her.

"Okay," Chanda replied as she looked around. She went upstairs to the room, which was much bigger than the one she had at her mother's house. She had a queen sized bed with huge closet space. She also had a full-bodied mirror on her bedroom door. She sat her bags down on the floor and went back downstairs.

"You like your room?" her father asked.

"Yes," Chanda replied.

"Good. Renee got it ready for you about a year ago just in case this day ever came.

"Who's Renee?" Chanda asked.

"I haven't told you about her?" her father asked with a raised eyebrow.

"No." Chanda shook her head.

"She's my fiancée. We're getting married next April. Yeah, she's wonderful. I think you're going to like her."

"Daddy, can I use the phone?"

"You don't have to ask me. It's one in your room on your dresser."

Chanda smiled and went up to her room. She picked up the phone and dialed Shawn's number beginning to think that maybe moving in with her father wasn't such a good idea after all.

"Hello?" Shawn answered.

"Shawn?" Chanda replied.

"Yeah, what's going on?"

"My mom kicked me out because of an argument we got into," Chanda explained.

"Where are you now?" he asked her.

"I'm at my dad's house but I'm wishing that I weren't."

"Why do you say that?" Shawn asked.

"I have a bad feeling about this. He's about to marry some chick that I never even met let alone heard about. It just doesn't feel right."

"Maybe you just have to adjust a little bit since you're not used to living in a house with your father," Shawn suggested. "You'll be alright."

Chanda sighed. "I guess. So what are you doing on this merry day?"

"I'm not doing anything. I'm just chilling in the house under the air playing NBA 2K1. So what happened between you and your mom?"

"Well I told you that I had the stomach virus earlier when we talked. She started her dumb shit and we got into an argument. I got tired of her snapping on me ever since Kareem got killed and I went off. Then we started fighting."

"Fist fighting?" Shawn asked.

"Yeah, and she started choking me too," Chanda added.

"Wow, that's crazy..." Shawn cleared his throat. "So um, who won?"

"What?" Chanda asked.

"Who beat the fight between you and your mom?"

"How are you going to ask me some shit like that?" Chanda chuckled.

"Naw because I know you have rumble game but you had to get it from somewhere," Shawn laughed with her.

"Who do you think won? Shit, I did. But she was fucking me up though," Chanda admitted as she laughed.

"Chanda, could you come downstairs for a minute?!" her father yelled up the steps.

"Shawn, I have to get off the phone. I'll call you later on."

"Alright, babe," Shawn hung up the phone and Chanda went downstairs to see what her father wanted.

"Chanda, there's someone that I want you to meet. Renee, this is my daughter, Chanda. Chanda, this is Renee."

"How are you?" Chanda said extending her hand to Renee.

Renee shook Chanda's hand and said, "I'm fine. So you are the young lady that your father is so proud of?"

"I guess so," Chanda smiled.

"How old are you again?"

"I'll be eighteen August 6th."

"You're going to the 12th grade, right?"

"Yes," Chanda turned to her father. "Dad, can I run back up North Philly for a minute to get something from my girlfriend, Deisha?"

"Sure, just one thing before you go; I don't mind you going out and I'm not going to set some outrageous rules and curfews for you. If you're going to go out, just come back at a reasonable time or let me know what time you'll be back. If you're going to be later than the time you gave me, call me and let me know. I know your mom had you doing all kinds of crazy cleaning like you're Cinderella or something. All I ask is that you help out around here."

"No problem, Daddy." Chanda replied.

Her father handed her a key. "Get yourself a key made while you're up there." Chanda took the key and left.

Tamera burst through the front door and ran upstairs to her bedroom.

"What is wrong with that girl, now?" Michelle asked as she looked towards the stairs.

"Who's that?" Janelle asked.

"Deisha's friend; I took her in also because her father had a problem with his hands. He wasn't molesting her or anything. I just saw him slap her in the face and I knew I couldn't let her stay with him anymore."

"Oh," Janelle replied as she sipped her coffee.

Tamera lay on her bed and looked up at the ceiling. Deisha knocked on the door a few moments later.

"What?" Tamera asked with an attitude.

"Damn girl, I just wanted to see if you were alright," Deisha snapped back.

"I'm sorry. You can come in."

Deisha opened the door and closed it behind her. "So what's wrong now?"

"I was talking to Jamal today and he found out that I quit my singing classes. I ended up telling him about Aaron and the whole day when I was down there. He actually thought that I was lying. Then he tried to make it seem like it was my fault for leaving with them."

"In a way it is. But don't worry about it. Jamal is probably just mad that you lied to him the night it happened. This is one of those situations where you might want Jamal to kick someone's ass," Deisha told her.

"Yeah, but you saw what he did to the guy at school on the balcony. And all he did was call me a bitch. Imagine what Jamal would have done to Aaron," Tamera said, frightened at the thought. She ran her hands over her face and took a deep breath. "Who's that lady downstairs?"

Deisha sighed. "My infamous mother, unfortunately."

"That's your mom!" Tamera said with her eyes wide and her mouth gaped open in shock.

"Yeah and she got a lot of nerve bringing her crack-head ass back here like everything was going to be cool. She must've bumped her muthafucking head on one of those twelve steps of that program that she was in," Deisha snapped.

Tamera laughed, "That was not nice."

"Deisha, Tamera, come downstairs to eat!" Michelle called to them.

Tamera and Deisha went downstairs giggling. Deisha stopped when she saw that her mother was sitting at the dinner table. She quietly fixed her plate of stuffed pork chops smothered in gravy, with rice, string beans and biscuits, and poured herself a glass of lemonade.

They were sitting at the table eating silently when Janelle cleared her throat and asked, "So Deisha, have you decided what college holds your attention the most?"

Deisha nodded her head, refusing to talk to her mother.

Not seeing her head movement, Michelle said, "Deisha, do you hear her talking to you?"

"She said yes, Michelle," Janelle told her sister. "So which one is it?"

Deisha sighed, becoming annoyed with her mother's small talk. "Penn State."

"Why not go to one of the schools that offered you a scholarship?" her mother asked.

"Because they don't have my major. Why are you concerned now all of a sudden? You ain't been around for four years and now you just want to pop out the blue like some revived jack in the box trying to be what you were never good at."

"Deisha, you better watch your damn mouth!" Michelle warned her.

Yani

"For what? If she really gave a damn about me, she never would've let things get as bad as they were. And how is she going to come here and try to hold a conversation with me like everything is okay? Sorry Janelle, everything is not okay. Can I be excused?" Deisha said as she got up from the table.

"No you may not. Sit your ass down. I don't know where you think you are but you better watch your damn mouth and show me as well as your mother some respect. Regardless of what happened when you were younger, she is still your mother," Michelle scolded Deisha.

"No Michelle, it's okay," Janelle interjected.

"No it's not. I taught Deisha better than that."

"Maybe this wasn't such a good idea after all." Janelle got up from the table and grabbed her purse. "Deisha, I'm sorry about the way things fell apart when you were younger. I really am. I didn't know how to be a mother to you and I was battling a lot of demons. I'm truly, truly sorry and I hope that one day you can forgive me." She left out of the house.

Michelle got up to follow her out the door. "Deisha, I'll deal with you later."

Feeling the heat from the conversation at the dinner table, Tamera grabbed her plate and made a quick exit to her bedroom when Michelle left.

Deisha tossed her fork onto her plate and folded her hands over her mouth. The doorbell rang a moment later. "Who the hell is this now?" Deisha asked out loud. She went over to the door and opened it.

"Hey," Maurice spoke. "I just ran into your aunt and she told me you were here. She said she was mad at you. What did you do now?"

"I ain't do shit. She's mad because my mom came over and I didn't treat her like it was a reunion that I was looking forward to. My aunt should know by now I don't pretend for anybody. Shit ain't sweet and I don't sugar coat it for nobody." Deisha was beyond pissed off.

"Your mom was here?" Maurice asked, as Deisha let him in.

"Yeah, but fuck that bitch," Deisha said acidly.

"I'm sorry about earlier with my mom. She was out of pocket for that," Maurice said as he sat at the dining room table.

"Yeah, and I don't appreciate that shit either. And I know she doesn't like me."

"How do you figure?" Maurice quizzed. He took her biscuit from her plate and bit into it. Deisha shook her head at him.

"Come on Maurice," Deisha said, looking at him crossly. "Don't act like you never noticed how she talks to me and how she looks at me when I come over. I remember when we first started going together and I called one time, I heard her say in the background, 'that girl you talk to now is on the phone. What do you see in her, anyway?' What ever happened to if you don't have anything nice to say, don't say shit at all?"

"Deisha, you rarely have anything nice to say about people," Maurice replied. "But don't worry. I checked her for you. And I let her know that regardless of how she feels about you the only thing that matters is how I feel about you." He got up from the table and stood behind Deisha. "I gotta go. I know my mom is pissed so I might as well deal with the fall out." He rubbed her neck and kissed the side of her mouth.

Deisha walked him over to the door. "It's real ironic how after I had that discussion with your mom about why I don't live with mines, mother dear shows up unannounced and uninvited."

"I know, but don't worry about it. The stress is not needed." He gave her a kiss. "I'll call you later on, okay?"

"Okay," Deisha watched him leave and then closed the door behind him. She and her aunt needed to have a very serious conversation about her mother.

A few nights later, Jamal and Shawn were sitting on the porch talking about sports, their upcoming senior year of high school and new video games that were coming out, when their cousin Samir pulled up in his Black Expedition. Shawn hadn't seen or heard from him since Jamal had been shot almost a year before.

"What's up Shawn?" Samir spoke.

"What's up nigga? Where you been?" Shawn asked knowing that if his cousin was coming around, it was for a specific reason.

"I been around, handling business as normal. You still running ball?"

"When am I not?" Shawn chuckled.

"I don't see a rock in your hand right now, you slacking?" Samir asked.

"Naw, never that!"

"Jamal, let me put a bug in your ear real quick."

Jamal came off the porch and got into Samir's truck. Shawn watched from the porch.

"I need you to do me a favor."

Jamal stopped him before he could finish. "If it's what I think it is, you know I can't. I just got cleared with my P.O and I'm trying to keep shit straight for college."

"Yeah that's all well and good but you still owe me. You never finished selling that package because you got locked up the other year. I let you chill so the cops would get off your back, but I could've lost a lot of money over that. Then when I needed you again, you turned around and got shot. Not to mention I'm still fixing that shit your brother pulled when he took that gun."

"Yeah, trying to hold shit down for you. And if it wasn't for Shawn, I'd probably be dead right now," Jamal argued.

"No, if it wasn't for Shawn, your ass would've had the burner on your way to my house instead of looking for him," Samir argued back. Jamal fell silent knowing that he was right. "Don't go making it seem like you're doing shit to help me out nigga, I'm the one that helped you out. You never held up your end of the deal," Samir said sternly. Jamal shook his head. "It's only for a couple of weeks. One of my young bols got snatched and I need to keep his corner flowing until his lawyer gets him out. That should be in two weeks. He didn't have anything on him but they are claiming that he missed a court date and had a bench warrant out on him," Samir explained.

Jamal took a deep breath. He was beginning to wish that he had left well enough alone when Raheem got killed. It seemed as though he would be in debt forever to Samir with no way out soon. "Alright man, but only two weeks. I'm not going back to jail again. And I for damn sure ain't taking another bullet. Not for you, not for nobody."

"My man," Samir said as he gave his cousin a handshake. "I'll see you in a couple of days with the details."

Jamal said his good-byes and got out of his cousin's truck. He went back over to the porch and sat next to his brother. Shawn looked at him for a moment knowing what he was about to do. Before he could get the words out of his mouth to convince his brother otherwise, Jamal stopped him.

"Don't even bother, Shawn. Just mind your business."

"Whatever man, I knew that was the only reason he came by." Shawn shook his head and left the porch to go to the store.

Jamal had been selling drugs again for his cousin for two weeks. He had a couple more days to go before he was supposed to be done with the favor and he could hopefully move on with his life.

He was standing on the corner of 25th and Montgomery Avenue when he got a funny feeling. He went over to one of his friends. "Yo Mark, I need you to do me a favor."

"What's up 'Mal?" Mark spoke.

"I got a bad feeling yo, and I'm dirty right now. Hold my stuff for me and I'll be back to get it in an hour or so," Jamal told his friend.

Mark took the drugs from him and Jamal went back down the street to walk towards his house. When he got close to his block, it dawned on him that he forgot to give his money to Mark as well. Just as he was patting his pockets, the police rolled up on him and stopped him.

"Aw shit man, what I do now; jay-walk?" Jamal asked sarcastically. He recognized one of the cops as one who had locked him up previously.

"Where are you going, Jamal?" the cop asked him.

"I'm going the fuck home. It's hot as shit out here. Why what's up?"

"You better watch your mouth, boy," the white cop said to him as he got out of the car.

"Boy? Nigga I'm a grown ass man," Jamal spat as he gave the cop the screw face.

"That's it," the White cop said as he grabbed Jamal and pushed him onto the hood of the car. He pulled his hands behind his back and slapped handcuffs onto him.

"What the fuck, man? I ain't even doing shit!" Jamal said angrily.

The cop patted him down and reached into his pocket, pulling out the wad of money that Jamal had. "Oh, then what the fuck is this shit? You've been dealing again?"

"I ain't been doing shit but working."

"Working where, the corners again, huh, smart ass?" the White cop taunted.

"Yo man, this is harassment," Jamal said as they put him in the back of the squad car.

"Yeah, well we're going to take a trip down to the police station to do some questioning." The two cops got into the front of the cop car and drove to the police station.

After questioning Jamal repeatedly about some shootings that had occurred in the neighborhood, as well as questioning him about rumors of dirty cops on the force and not getting any information out of him, they left him in the interrogation room to verify his employment. After seeing that he had been working at Foot Locker, they gave him his money back and allowed him to make his phone call. Jamal decided to call his mother.

"Mom?" Jamal asked when he heard her voice on the phone.

"Who's this?" his mother asked sounding as if sleep had distorted her voice.

"It's Jamal, mom. Can you come get me, please?"

"Come get you from where?" Jamal hesitated for a moment before answering her knowing that his mother was going to be pissed. "Jamal, where are you?"

"Jail," Jamal sighed.

"JAIL!" Ms. Keyona screamed. "Jamal, what the hell are you doing in jail? Or should I even bother to ask."

"Mom, it wasn't even my fault this time, I swear. Punk-ass cops rolled up on me talking shit because I had $1100 on me."

"You better watch your damn mouth! And what the hell were you doing with $1100 on you?" Jamal's silence infuriated her. "Are you at the same place as before?" she asked.

"Yes."

"I'm on my way."

Keyona took Shawn with her to go get Jamal from the police station. They rode up there in silence but Shawn could tell that his mother was very angry. Ms. Keyona signed the necessary papers and they released Jamal to her. She looked at her son furiously.

"Nice seeing you again, Jamal," the cop who had arrested Jamal before smirked. Jamal eyed the cop as if he wanted to punch him in his mouth.

"Come on Jamal!" Ms. Keyona snapped. They walked out of the police station and got into the car for the drive home. "How long has this been going on, Jamal?"

"Not long," Jamal replied.

"Not long? So you were selling again. You're lying to me, too? Exactly how long is not long?" Jamal didn't answer soon enough so she yelled, "How long?!"

"For a couple of weeks," Jamal replied.

Ms. Keyona angrily drew in a deep breath and sighed as she tapped the steering wheel while she drove. They stopped at a red light. "And you knew about this Shawn, and you didn't say one word to me."

"Because I didn't think it was any of my business," Shawn replied.

"What if something happened to your brother besides him getting locked up? Supposed he'd been shot again or killed this time? I bet you would've wished you had said something then, huh?"

Shawn didn't respond. He didn't care one way or another. Jamal never listened to him or anybody else. But the thought of him losing his only brother hurt him. He pushed the thought out of his mind and thought about Chanda and what she might be doing instead.

The car became silent as they continued their drive home. Ms. Keyona then spoke in a sobbing tone. "Why Jamal? Why do you keep doing this to yourself? You even have a job now so it's not like you need the money. You're doing so well in school now, getting good grades, you have a nice girlfriend. What are you running from? What is wrong?"

Jamal sighed and looked out of the window, not answering his mother. They drove the rest of the way home in silence. Shawn got out of the car first and went into the kitchen to get something to drink. His mother and Jamal followed behind.

"Pass me a soda Shawn," Jamal said to his brother.

"Jamal, you have to go," his mother told him.

"What?" Jamal asked, startled.

"I'm not putting up with this shit anymore, Jamal. The drug dealing, the streets, I'm tired of it!"

"It was a favor for Samir," Jamal tried to explain.

"I don't care. I'm sick of Samir and the way you run up behind him. I raised you. But if you want to continue to do favors for him, then you stay the hell there!"

"I'm not going to do it no more, mom. This is my last year of school and I don't have anywhere to go."

Shawn stood in the kitchen doorway watching to see if his mother was really going to throw Jamal out the door.

Ms. Keyona sighed and gave in. "Fine Jamal, but this is it. The next thing you do, you're gone. And I mean it. You are skating on thin ice."

Jamal gave his mother a hug. "Thanks Mom."

"Stay out of trouble, honey. Y'all all I got left." She looked at her two sons and realized at that moment how much they looked like their father. Her eyes became teary as she thought back to how quickly he was taken from her and her sons when they were too young to remember him. Since then, everything about Samir disgusted her and she did her best to detach herself from that side of the family. She refused to lose her son the way she lost his father because of Samir. History was not going to repeat itself…

CHAPTER 5
STARTING OVER

August rolled around bringing humidity and anxiety among Deisha and her friends as they prepared for their senior year of high school. Their vacation was slowly coming to an end. A few days before Chanda's 18th birthday, Deisha and Tamera were sitting in Deisha's bedroom planning what they were going to do for her. They wanted her to feel special on her birthday since she was still torn up over her brother's murder.

Deisha lay on the floor. "So what are we going to do? We should drag her ass out of the house to a strip club. Nah, I think a surprise party would be better. I'm not old enough to see any butt-naked men and neither are you."

Tamera grinned. "We can do that for my 18th birthday."

Deisha grinned with her. "I've gotta give it to Jamal. He turned my sweet and innocent girlfriend into an innocent freak. He done turned your ass out."

Tamera laughed, "We're not talking about me right now." "I think we should throw her a birthday party so she can be around everybody that cares about her," Deisha suggested.

"What if she doesn't want to be around a bunch of people on her birthday?"

"Believe me, it's not good to constantly be by yourself when you lose somebody that you love," Deisha told Tamera.

"Well, first we need to find out if it's alright with her dad. Then we need to get Shawn to get her away from the house so we can set everything up."

"I have an idea. We should pretend like we didn't even remember her birthday," Deisha suggested.

"Um, I don't think that is going to make her feel better." Tamera said as she looked at Deisha as if she were crazy.

"Listen, that'll throw her off. We can get her dad and his fiancée to pretend they forgot about her birthday. That'll really piss her off. Then Shawn can take her out and listen to her whine and complain about it all day. He'll bring her back to the house and then we'll bust out with the surprise."

"I guess that'll work," Tamera replied.

"I'm still tripping on Jamal renting a hotel room for you and him for your birthday," Deisha smiled. Tamera began to laugh. "My aunt still thinks you spent the day with your Godmother. You know you owe me, right?"

Tamera laughed even harder. "How I owe you when you used me as a decoy so you could spend the night with Maurice that time?"

"Yeah, true that." They laughed together. Deisha looked at her watch and then hopped up from the floor. "Well I have to run to work. I have exactly forty minutes to get there or I'll be late. See, if Aunt 'Chelle had let me get that car, this wouldn't be an issue."

"Next time CYA," Tamera said.

"CYA? What the hell is that?" Deisha asked as she put on her shoes.

"Cover your ass, nigga," Tamera giggled.

Deisha laughed as she left her bedroom to go to work.

The next day, Deisha was on her way out of the house to grab items for Chanda's birthday party when her phone rang.

"Hello?" Deisha answered.

"Can I speak to Deisha?" Maurice asked.

"Who's this?" Deisha asked, being smart.

Maurice smiled. "It's David."

"Hey David," Deisha giggled playing along. "I haven't heard from you in a minute. What's up, boo?"

"Get the fuck out of here," Maurice laughed. Deisha laughed with him. "You're playing right?"

"Yeah, I don't even know anybody named David. I knew it was you."

"Then why'd you ask me that?"

"Because I love fucking with you," Deisha replied before laughing louder.

"Whatever," Maurice replied. Deisha giggled. "What are you doing?"

"I was about to go grab some stuff for Chanda's birthday party."

"You should come keep me company. I have to watch my little cousin so come chill over here with me."

"At your house?" Deisha asked in a disgusted tone.

"Yeah, where else?" Maurice asked, confused.

"Hell no, I'm not coming back to your house. I told you, your mom doesn't like me and I don't like her."

"That's fucked up," Maurice said as he sucked his teeth.

"Yeah well, tell your momma that," Deisha laughed.

"Alright Deisha, be like that. Just call me later on."

"Alright," Deisha hung up the phone, grabbed her keys from off of the table and left the house.

She was half the way down the block when she saw Manny and some of his friends coming up the street. She then remembered that she promised Keisha that she would get them hooked up and decided to hold off on going to the store.

"Manny, come here for a second!" Deisha shouted over to him.

"Damn yo, who's that?" one of Manny's friends asked as he licked his lips and looked Deisha over.

"That's Deisha from 26th and Turner Street," Manny replied.

"Is that you, because if not...?"

Manny cut his friend off. "Chill yo, that's Mar's girl." Manny went over to Deisha to see what she wanted. "What's up?"

"Hey Manny what's up?" Deisha smiled at him immediately seeing why Keisha liked him. She thought they would look so cute together.

"Nothing much, just chilling," Manny replied.

"Do you know a girl named Keisha?" Deisha asked, cutting straight to the point.

"I know a lot of girls named Keisha. Which one are you talking about?"

"I'm talking about Maurice's little sister," Deisha replied.

"Oh yeah, I remember her. She was in my cousin's class over at Vaux. She used to mess with Dom. Why, what's up?"

"Do you like her?" Deisha asked.

"She's cool peoples," Manny said. He actually did like her but thought she was a little young. He also saw how Maurice whipped Dominique's ass and wanted no parts of that.

"Look, Keisha likes you. I mean, really likes you. She said she was scared to say anything because of the whole rejection thing. So why don't you give me your number and I'll give it to her so she can call you," Deisha said as she pulled out her cell phone to put his number inside.

"Yo, you're dead serious!" Manny laughed.

"Um, yeah I am," Deisha smiled at him.

"I'm not going to be able to talk to her. That's Maurice's little sister. And I saw what he did to Dom. I'm cool," Manny said as he shook his head.

"What Maurice doesn't know won't hurt him. Don't worry about him. I'll handle Mar," Deisha told him. Manny became quiet for a moment. "So do you like her or what?"

"Yeah, she's cool."

"Then why don't you talk to her?"

Manny thought for a moment. "I'll call her tonight."

"Don't bull-shit me, boy. You don't even have her number," Deisha retorted.

"My cousin has it in his year book from when she signed it," Manny explained as he backed away.

"Alright Manny," Deisha said as she turned to head to Maurice's house so she could share the good news with Keisha.

Chanda was in her bedroom lying across her bed when her father knocked on her door. "Yes," Chanda replied.

"Dinner is ready if you want to eat," her father told her as he peeped into her room.

"Is it okay if I eat a little later on? I'm not really hungry right now."

"Okay. Well, there is also someone here to see you." Chanda got off of her bed and followed her father downstairs. "I meant to tell you that your mother called here for you earlier."

"She shouldn't have wasted the phone call," Chanda replied blandly.

"I figured you'd say something like that. That's why I didn't bother to call you to the phone." Chanda's eyes locked on Shawn and a huge grin spread across her face. "Oh my God, she's actually smiling!" her father teased. Chanda laughed. "Go out on the porch."

Chanda walked out to the porch and Shawn followed behind her. He gave her a big hug and squeezed her tightly.

"Are you alright?" Shawn asked.

"Yeah, I'm straight," Chanda replied.

"What were you doing?"

"Chilling, thinking about what I'm going to do for my birthday. What made you come down here?" Chanda asked as she sat in one of the chairs.

Shawn sat beside her. "I wanted to see you. What do you want for your birthday anyway?"

"I don't know, truthfully. I just want to do something that will take my mind off of all the dumb shit that's happened these last few months." She laid her head on Shawn's shoulder. "I just wish somebody would come and take me out of here."

"Where do you wanna go?" Shawn asked her.

"Anywhere but here." They sat on the porch talking about the upcoming school year. Shawn managed to make Chanda laugh which was good to hear considering she had been so down since her brother's murder.

"Babe," Shawn said as he kissed her forehead.

"What's up?" Chanda replied.

"I love you, you know that."

Chanda didn't know how to respond. That was the first time that he told her that and it made her heart sing.

"I know, and I love you too, Shizz," Chanda replied.

Shawn stood up and stretched. "I gotta run home. I'll call you later on okay," he told her.

"Okay," Chanda smiled. Shawn kissed her and cupped her face in his hands. He leaned his forehead onto hers. He didn't need to say anything else. Their feelings were understood between the two of them.

Deisha knocked on Maurice's door. Maurice looked at her surprisingly.

"What are you doing here? I thought you weren't coming," he asked.

"Something came up. Is Keisha here?" Deisha asked as Maurice let her inside of the house.

"Yeah, she's upstairs. What do you want my sister for?"

"Because I need to tell her something. Stop being so nosey. Can I go upstairs?"

"Yeah, but wait, hold up. What do you have to tell her?"

"Girl talk," Deisha smiled as she ran up the stairs.

"How are you going to come in my house, you didn't give me a hug or a kiss, but you go straight up to my sister's room for some girl talk? That's some bull-shit," Maurice laughed. "You better not be getting her hooked up with none of these knuckle-headed niggas around here!" he yelled upstairs.

"You need to stop!" Deisha yelled back at him. She knocked on Keisha's door.

"Yes," Keisha replied.

"It's Deisha, can I come in?" Deisha asked.

"Sure, what's up Deisha?" Keisha replied as Deisha came into her room.

"Hey Keisha, I just saw Manny." Keisha's face lit up. "Be expecting a phone call soon."

"What did you do?" Keisha asked as she blushed.

"I was coming down the street when I saw him and basically told him that you liked him but was scared to talk to him, blah, blah, blah, and asked him if he liked you." Keisha covered her face and fell back onto her bed. "He said he did but never said anything to you because you're Maurice's little sister. So I told him to call you so y'all can hook up."

"Aw man, I can't believe you told him!" Keisha shrieked as she covered her face.

"Girl, you better learn to be aggressive and start going after the guys that you like. Chicks are not waiting for guys to ask them out anymore, we're beating them to the punch," Deisha told her.

"Thank you Deisha," Keisha replied. She was extremely excited.

"You're welcome. Now let me go see your brother since he's feeling some type of way that I came to see you instead of him," they giggled as Deisha left the room and went back downstairs. When she got down there she looked around.

"I thought you said you were watching your little cousin?" Deisha asked when she didn't see any kids.

"You don't see him?" Maurice asked as he played NBA 2K1 on his PlayStation 2. "He's lying on the couch sleeping."

Deisha sat next to him and watched him play the game. "So what did you want me to come over here for?"

"I wanted to talk to you about something," Maurice told her. He paused the game and stood up. "I forgot what it was now."

"It must wasn't important then," Deisha teased.

"Yeah well, we'll never know now will we?" Maurice pulled Deisha up by her hand. "What were you and my sister talking about?"

"You're so nosey. I told you that it was girl stuff."

"I swear man, you better not be getting her hooked up with none of these pickled-headed muthafuckas out here." Deisha laughed. "You laughing and I'm serious as shit. None of these niggas around here are about shit."

"Then what about you?" Deisha asked with a smirk on her face.

"I'm an exception to that rule," Maurice replied, sitting back on the couch.

"I only told her something she needed to hear. It might even make her happy." Maurice pulled Deisha onto his lap. "We're throwing a surprise party for Chanda. Are you coming?"

"Yeah, that girl needs a picker upper. Besides you, I never saw anybody grieve so long for somebody," Maurice replied.

"She watched her brother get gunned down in the streets, Maurice. That's not something you'd get over in a short period of time. Then her mom was treating her like shit afterwards like it was her fault. I'm surprised she didn't have a nervous breakdown."

"Yeah well, if she did, she could come straight to you, Oprah," Maurice teased.

Deisha smacked him on his arm. "That wasn't funny." She got up to leave.

"Where are you going?" Maurice asked as he grabbed her arm.

"I told you, we're planning her party. I have a lot to do being the fact that I only have today off from work."

"That's all the more reason why you should stay here with me. I barely see you that much as it is." He pulled Deisha back onto his lap.

"I can't stay, Maurice," Deisha whined as he kissed her neck. Maurice put his arms around her so she couldn't get up. "Maurice?"

"Yeah?" he mumbled as he nibbled on her neck.

"Your little cousin is watching us," she whispered.

"Lil Man, I thought you were sleep," Maurice said as he slid Deisha from his lap onto the couch.

His cousin scrambled off of the couch. "I'm not no more," he looked over at Deisha. "Hi," he said sweetly.

"Hi," Deisha spoke back with a smile.

"Do you want some cookies, young bol?" Maurice asked as he got off the couch.

Yani

"Yeah, and some juice too. Please," he added on leaving the 'L' out so it sounded more like he said 'pease' instead.

Maurice took his cousin into the kitchen with him and then came back moments later with a napkin full of chocolate chip cookies and two cups of juice. He handed one to Deisha.

"He's so cute. What's your name?" Deisha asked.

"Christopher," the little boy replied as he stuffed his mouth full of cookies.

"How old are you?" she asked him.

Christopher held up three little fingers and then drank his juice.

"He is so cute, Mar. How long do you have to watch him?"

"Just until tomorrow night," Maurice replied.

"I'll chill with you for a little while, but as soon as your mom comes home, I'm going to have to roll," Deisha said sternly. Maurice nodded his head in agreement.

They played with Christopher out front for the rest of the afternoon. And as soon as Maurice's mother pulled up, Deisha gave him a kiss and hugged Christopher before she left, as promised.

The day of Chanda's birthday arrived quickly. Her dad and his fiancée were already hip to the surprise birthday party plan. They came into her bedroom with a small slice of cake that held an "18" candle inside of it, waking her up. Chanda tried to hide under the covers but her father snatched them away.

"We can't really do anything special for you this year because our money is tied up in the wedding and everything." Her father handed her an envelope. "Happy birthday, sweetheart. That's $180. Don't spend it all in one place."

"Thanks Dad. Thank Renee." Chanda got out of her bed and stretched just as the doorbell rang.

"That's probably your friends," Chanda's father said.

"I doubt it," Chanda moped. "They haven't mentioned my birthday coming up or said anything about it. Some friends they are." She brushed her hair into a ponytail and then followed Renee and her father downstairs.

She went into the kitchen while her father answered the door.

"Well, isn't this a surprise?" he said blandly.

"Who is it?" Chanda asked from the kitchen. Her father ignored her as he glared at his ex-wife.

"Good morning Ty. I just stopped by to say happy birthday to Chanda and give this to her," Carmen said politely.

"You've got a lot of damn nerve coming here after the shit you pulled, Carmen." Tyrone said acidly.

"Come on, can we just put that all behind us. I'm sorry about that, I really am. I just want to see her." Tyrone continued to stare down at her. "She's my daughter, too."

"It's up to Chanda whether or not she wants to see you," he told her as he opened the door wider so she could come in.

"I know," Carmen replied as she stepped inside.

Tyrone went into the kitchen. "Chanda, there's someone here to see you."

"Is it Deisha and Tamera?" Chanda asked as she poured herself a cup of juice.

"No, it isn't."

"Shawn?" she asked as she took a sip of her juice.

"I'm afraid not," her father mumbled.

Chanda sat her cup on the table and looked at her father. "Who?"

Her father sighed. "Go see for yourself."

Chanda stood in front of him for a moment and then walked into the living room. She stopped dead in her tracks when she saw her mother. She glared at Carmen and Carmen stared back.

"I'll leave you two alone," Renee said before going into the kitchen.

"What are you doing here?" Chanda sneered.

"I wanted to see you on your birthday," Carmen replied.

"For what, to choke me again?"

"I'm sorry about us not having that mother-daughter relationship. I was just trying to deal with the situation with your father," Carmen said after a moment.

"Why can't you admit to your mistakes instead of always trying to push the blame off on someone else? You put me through hell for as far back as I can remember. Why would I want to see you on my birthday?" Chanda asked angrily.

"Chanda, with everything that was going on with your brother getting killed and me losing the baby, and then almost losing you, I understand now that life is too short to be holding grudges against the people that you love. I'm sorry for everything that I put you through." She reached into her bag and pulled out a black box. She tried to give it to Chanda but she refused it.

"I don't want it," Chanda told her as she shook her head.

"Please take it," her mother pleaded.

Chanda stood for a brief moment and then sighed before taking the box from her mother. She opened it and inside was a decorative frame with multiple photos. The picture in the top right corner was of her mother holding her as a baby. Next to it was a photo of Kareem when he was a baby. Under his picture was a photo of Chanda and Kareem when they were young and next to that was the three of them together. That was the last picture they all took together three weeks before Kareem was killed.

"I love you, Chanda. You may not believe me, but I do. Eighteen years ago when I held you in my arms for the first time, I knew you were the best thing I could've ever hoped for. I can't take away the pain that I caused you, but I can try to make it right."

Chanda tried to fight back the tears but they fell anyway. Her mother walked over to her and hugged her tightly. Chanda hugged her back.

"Happy birthday, sweetheart," Carmen said.

"Thanks mom," Chanda replied back.

"So what are you doing for your birthday?" Carmen asked as she let her daughter go.

"Shawn said he's going to take me shopping and out to dinner. We might catch a movie, too."

"That sounds nice. We can hang out next weekend. I have some coupons to a new spa that just opened in Center City. We can go and do our girly thing."

"Sounds like a plan," Chanda smiled. She walked her mother to the door.

"Have a good time tonight," her mother told her.

"I will," Chanda replied. Her mother left and she closed the door behind her.

Tamera was in Deisha's bedroom. They were talking and trying to make sure they had everything straightened out for Chanda's birthday party.

"Her dad and his fiancée said they are just giving her some money and a card and leaving it at that for the time being. Then they're going to basically talk about spending the day together instead of doing anything with her for her birthday," Deisha explained.

"Don't you think Chanda will be mad about that?" Tamera asked.

"A little. I mean, that is her dad. She'll probably be thinking how fucked up that is that he can chill with his fiancée before he'll spend time with her on her birthday especially after everything that's happened."

"True," Tamera agreed. "Shawn said he'll take her out for a while so we can set up."

"But he has to have her back by 6:30." Deisha told Tamera.

"I know, he knows, we have it covered. All of our friends from school are coming. We have the decorations and your aunt cooked, right?"

"Yeah, she made shrimp salad, fried and steamed jumbo shrimp, buffalo party wings, and some other things. You know how my aunt gets down," Deisha replied.

"That's what's up. I'm hungry just thinking about it." Tamera and Deisha laughed.

"So, I purposely left my purse over there so I could stop by and talk about all the "fun" I'm going to have with Maurice today." Deisha smiled mischievously as she picked up her phone to give Chanda a call.

"Hello?" Chanda answered as she slipped an earring in her ear.

"What's up Chanda?" Deisha perked.

Chanda hesitated. "Nothing much. Hey Deisha." She looked at herself in the mirror and then splashed some Mary Kay *Elige* perfume on.

"Listen, I left my bag over there and it has some stuff in it that I need. Is it alright if I come by to get it today?"

"It's cool. Are you coming to get it, now?" Chanda asked her.

"Yeah, because I have some other stuff to do and Maurice is supposed to be taking me out. I can't wait," Deisha gushed. Tamera covered her mouth and giggled.

"Alright, I'll just see you when you get here," Chanda sighed when she hung up the phone. She was hurt that her best friend since the 5th grade had forgotten her birthday. She looked at herself in the mirror again. She was looking dapper in a pair of faded, partially torn hipster jeans, a strapless tank top and opened toe three inch wedges. She grabbed her small hobo purse and was about to put her cell phone in it when it began to ring.

"Hello?" she answered as she left out of her bedroom.

"Happy birthday, beautiful," Shawn said in her ear.

"Hey babe, thanks," Chanda smiled. The sound of Shawn's voice always had a good effect on her.

"You're an old head now," Shawn joked.

"I'm not old," Chanda giggled.

"Shit, you're older than me. You can go to jail for messing with a minor," he said.

"Shut up," she laughed out loud.

"Are you ready?"

"Yeah, but Deisha is on her way to get her bag that she left here the other day. Can you believe that cow forgot my birthday? She pretended like she had something more important to do. Tamera didn't say anything either," Chanda ranted.

"Apparently, everybody forgot. Don't worry about it. I remembered."

"I know and thank you. But even my dad is tripping. He and Renee gave me a card with some money in it but they're spending the day together like my birthday is trivial."

"Yeah well, that's family for you," Shawn replied. Chanda had no idea that Deisha was on three-way listening in. Everything was going according to plan. "I'll be there around 12:30 alright?"

"Okay," Chanda replied. Shawn kissed in her ear before he hung his phone up.

"Deisha, are you there?"

"Yeah boy, you deserve a damn Academy Award," Deisha laughed. "Leave in like 20 minutes so we'll get there one after the other," she instructed.

"Alright," Shawn agreed.

"See you when I get there."

Shawn hung up with Deisha. "Jamal!" he called out to his brother.

"Yo!" Jamal answered from his room.

"Go to Deisha's house around three with Maurice so y'all can get to Chanda's house to set up."

"Shit man, I can't go to Deisha's house. Tamera is going to be there and she's still mad at me. She ain't trying to see me until I come up with a reason why she should forgive me." Jamal and Tamera still hadn't patch things up from the fight they got into over why she quit her singing classes.

"Shit, she was able to get along with you long enough to go out on her birthday. Work that shit out," Shawn told him as he grabbed his keys and his wallet so he could leave out.

Chanda was sitting on the porch waiting for Deisha to come get her bag so she could leave with Shawn. As soon as the thought passed, she saw Deisha get off of the bus and head over to her house.

"What's up girl? I like that shirt," Deisha said as she sat next to her.

"Thank you," Chanda replied. She picked up Deisha's bag and handed it to her.

"Thanks. So what are you doing today?"

"Nothing really," Chanda replied as Shawn came up to the porch.

"Hey," he said as he gave her a kiss. "What's up Deisha?"

"What's up, Shizz? Are y'all going out?" Deisha spoke back.

"Yup," Shawn replied.

"Well, let me go. I have so much to do today."

"Alright Deisha," Chanda said as Deisha left the porch and walked to the bus stop. "Did you see that shit?" Chanda hissed.

"Don't worry about it," Shawn told her.

"That's fucked up," Chanda said. She was extremely hurt at the thought of her best friend not even mentioning her birthday.

Shawn kissed her again. "I told you not to worry about it." He grabbed her hand and pulled her up. "Come on. Are you ready?"

"Yeah, I gotta let my dad and Renee know that I'm leaving first." She went upstairs to her father's room. He and Renee were lying across his bed watching television. "Daddy, I'm about to leave." Her father pretended as if he didn't hear her. "Dad..?"

"Yeah, sure honey," her father said, waving his hand at her. She stood there for a moment and then went back outside with Shawn. Renee and Tyrone looked at each other and giggled.

"What's wrong?" Shawn asked when he noticed how sad Chanda looked.

"Nothing," Chanda moped.

"Are you sure?" Shawn double checked. Chanda nodded her head. Shawn took her by the hand and they left the porch. "So what do you want to do first? Shop, go to the movies, walk around South Street, eat?"

"Shopping," Chanda said as a huge grin spread across her face.

"I knew you would say that," Shawn laughed.

While Shawn and Chanda were on Chestnut Street shopping for sneakers, Jamal was waiting for Tamera to come to the door so they could talk.

"What?!" Tamera shouted as she banged open the screen door.

"What?" Jamal repeated. "Yo, why are you talking to me like that?"

"Well, what do you want?" Tamera asked.

"I wanted to talk," Jamal replied.

"Talk?" Tamera asked with a frown on her face. "Oh so now you want to talk about this after it's been more than two weeks?" Jamal looked at her without responding. "I'm listening."

"All I wanted to say is I'm sorry for saying that I don't care because I do. I didn't mean that I didn't care what happened to you or to us. What I meant was, I didn't care anymore about the situation because it was done and over with. It's no point in dwelling on it anymore. If I see that nigga, I'm still going to fuck his shit up, but I just want us to be cool again. So I'm sorry," he grabbed her by her hand. "Do you forgive me?" he asked.

"Let me think," Tamera said as she touched her chin with her finger, pretending she was in deep thought. "No." Jamal looked at her surprised, thinking that she was serious. "Sike naw, I forgive you. Just don't let that shit happen again."

"So we're cool now?" Jamal asked just to be sure.

"Yeah, we're cool."

Jamal kissed her. "I missed that."

"I just bet you did. It's probably a lot of other things that you missed, too."

Jamal looked down at her breasts and smiled, "Hell yeah!"

Tamera smacked him on his arm. "You are so nasty." Jamal kissed her again as Deisha came over to the door.

"Oh for the love of beans, will y'all take that shit somewhere else? Gross," Deisha joked.

Tamera giggled and licked her tongue at her.

"Didn't your aunt cook, Deisha?" Jamal asked with a grin.

"Yeah and I need y'all to come taste some stuff for me," Deisha said as she went back in the house towards the kitchen.

Jamal followed behind her. "Oh, hell yeah!" He rubbed his hands together in greed. "Ms. Niecie can throw down in the kitchen."

Chanda and Shawn were trying to have fun, but Chanda kept spoiling it by bringing up the fact that everyone had forgotten her birthday.

"Damn, why are you still complaining? That's not going to change the fact that they forgot. Just get over it and enjoy now," Shawn told her.

Chanda tried to perk up and smile as they sat by the water fountain in the Gallery. Shawn leaned over and kissed her again. "Happy birthday."

"Thank you," Chanda said as she kissed him back. Shawn stopped and looked at his watch. "What's the deal with the watch?" Chanda asked him.

"Huh?" Shawn asked.

"The watch, you keep looking at it like you're pressed for time. Are you going somewhere?"

Shawn hesitated. "Naw, I just wanted to see what time it was," he lied.

"Oh, what time is it anyway?" Chanda asked him.

"It's a quarter after four. What do you want to do now?" he asked her.

"Let's go down Penn's Landing. I haven't been down there since I was a kid."

Meanwhile, back at Chanda's house, all of her friends were there setting up for the party. Deisha was with Renee and Tyrone in the kitchen placing the food on the table.

"Your mother did all of this cooking?" Renee asked.

"Actually, my aunt did the cooking. She's like a mother to me though," Deisha replied.

Renee licked her finger and looked at Deisha. "What do you mean?"

"It's a long story. My mom was on drugs when I was little and my aunt was tired of taking care of me part time so she fought to get custody of me and has been my guardian since I was twelve." Deisha explained.

"Oh," Renee replied. She could tell that it was a very sensitive topic for Deisha. "She did a wonderful job because you turned out terrific just like the food."

Deisha giggled, "Thank you." She picked up the birthday cake and carried it into the dining room. She sat it on the table as Maurice walked over to her.

"Hey babe," he greeted her as he kissed the side of her mouth.

"Hey," Deisha replied.

"What's wrong?" Maurice asked her.

"Nothing," Deisha said as she put the last of the candles into the cake.

"Are you sure?" Maurice asked. He noticed she seemed a little uneasy.

Deisha took a deep breath and then smiled at him. "Yeah. Excuse me." She made her way over to Jamal. He was standing next to another friend from school named Rasheem and they were comparing ideas on the music being used for the party. "What's up y'all?" Deisha spoke to them.

"What's up Deisha?" Rasheem spoke as he held his headphones to his ear.

"I thought you weren't DJ'ing?" Deisha asked Jamal.

"I'm not. I told you, I don't do local shit. No offense Rasheem." Rasheem stuck his middle finger up at him and Jamal chuckled.

"That was not nice, both of y'all," Deisha laughed with them. "I know you're going to DJ at my birthday party though, right?"

"How much are you paying?" Jamal asked with a grin.

"Damn Jamal, that's a shame. I'll remember that when you need help in Physics this school year."

"I'll think about it," Jamal said, still grinning.

"So what time is Shawn bringing Chanda back to the house?" Maurice asked.

"In a little while," Deisha told him. "By now, if Chanda is doing what I think she's doing, she's probably getting on his damned nerves," Deisha laughed.

Tamera looked out of the window and saw Shawn and Chanda coming up the street. It looked as though they were arguing. "Yo, they are super early!" Tamera called out to her friends.

"Who?" Deisha asked as she ran to the window. She spotted Chanda and Shawn also. "Didn't I tell his punk ass not to bring her back until 6:30!? Everybody get y'all stuff and hide. Somebody hit the lights!" Everyone scrambled to duck somewhere and Tamera shut the lights off.

Shawn and Chanda were crossing the street. Apparently they had gotten into an argument because of all of the complaining that Chanda was doing.

"I know you're mad because you think that everyone forgot your birthday. But you're taking it out on the one person that didn't forget: me. That's not cool, babe."

"I never said you forgot. But those are my best friends and my dad and his fiancée acted like they didn't even care. How could they do something like that to me after everything that's happened these last few months?" Chanda explained. They walked onto the porch. Chanda noticed that the lights were out and she sucked her teeth. "Damn, they rolled out on me, too!" She said angrily. Shawn looked at her and shook his head. Chanda stuck her key in the door and pushed it open. She moved her hand along the wall to find the light switch and screamed when she felt a hand. Tamera turned the lights on and everyone jumped up screaming "Surprise!" Chanda was startled. She covered her face and leaned into Shawn.

"Mmm hmm, you thought we forgot, didn't you?" Deisha asked as she gave Chanda a hug. "I'll never forget, so happy birthday, bitch!" she whispered in her ear before kissing her on the cheek.

Jamal put a birthday hat on her head and also gave her a kiss on the cheek. "Happy birthday, old-head. I can't even lie. I did forget your birthday was today until somebody reminded me to come here earlier."

Chanda looked at him with her mouth gaped open, feeling disappointed.

"I'm just joking," Jamal smiled as he gave Chanda a hug.

After everyone said their individual happy birthdays to her, she made her escape into the kitchen. Shawn followed behind her.

"What's wrong?" he asked her. Chanda shook her head. "Babe, I'll never know what to do for you if you don't let me in."

"I'm alright," Chanda insisted. She leaned over the counter with her head down. "You knew about this, didn't you?" she asked as she looked at him.

"Yeah, when we were on the phone earlier, Deisha was on three-way listening in."

"Damn, and I talked all that shit about everybody today," Chanda replied as she hung her head. She truly felt horrible and embarrassed.

Shawn kissed the side of her mouth and rubbed her neck. "Babe, trust me, it's no beef and everybody understands. We expected you to be pissed. It made the surprise even better. Come on so everybody ain't partying without us," Shawn said as he took her by the hand and led her back to the party.

After the party was over and people began to clear out, Chanda's friends stayed behind to help clean up the house.

"Thanks y'all, I needed that," Chanda said as she swept the living room.

"You're welcome. You know you're my homie and I had to go all out for you," Deisha said. Chanda gave her and Tamera a hug.

"See y'all," she said as they were leaving.

Shawn gave her a big hug and squeezed her tightly. "Happy birthday, babe," he told her once more.

"Thank you," Chanda replied before letting him go and giving him a big kiss. "I'm so sorry about earlier. I acted like a spoiled, ungrateful brat and I'm really sorry."

"Naw boo, it's okay. Trust me, I understand. I'm about to go home because I have to work tomorrow. I'll call you as soon as I get in, okay?"

"Okay," Chanda agreed. She watched Shawn and Jamal head over to the bus stop and then closed the door.

The next day, Keisha was walking down the street. It had rained earlier leaving a cold chill in the air for early August, so she threw on a pair of dark blue Express jeans, a short sleeved button up blouse and a pair of white Adidas shell top sneakers. She was planning on hanging out with some friends at the Gallery later on, hating to stay in the house because it rained. As she walked past Nicholas Street on her way to Ridge Avenue, Manny recognized her and walked up beside her.

"What's up, Keisha?" he asked, playing with a tooth pick in his mouth.

Keisha looked at him and began to blush, getting butterflies in her stomach. "Hey Manny."

"Where are you getting ready to go?" he asked.

"I'm on my way to the store."

"Let me talk to you real quick," he said sweetly.

"About what?" Keisha asked, pretending not to know what was coming next.

"Deisha said that you were into me," Manny teased. Keisha smiled bashfully. "Don't get quiet on me now." He nudged her with his arm. "So what's up?"

"What do you mean?" Keisha asked.

"When are you going to let me take you out some time?"

"Whenever you're not busy. I know you be out here with your homies. So you let me know what's up," Keisha told him, trying to sound confidant and cool.

Manny smiled at her as he twirled the toothpick in his mouth. "Well look, my cousin lost his year book so I don't have your number. Do you have a pen and some paper?"

Do I look like I have pen and paper? Keisha thought to herself. Instead of saying that, she shook her head.

Manny spotted one of his friends. "Yo Akeem! You got a pen and some paper, homie?"

Akeem patted his pockets and then shook his head, "Naw yo!"

"Hold up, don't go anywhere," Manny told her before going into a nearby corner store. Moments later he returned with a scrap of paper and a pen. He scribbled his number down on it. "You're going to call me, right?" he asked as he gave her the paper.

"Yeah, I'll call you." Keisha looked at the paper before folding it up and putting it in her back pocket. "See you," she said as she walked away. She felt like she was on cloud nine and ended up heading back home instead of going to the store for what she really wanted. When she got back in the house, she hopped on the phone to call Deisha.

"Hello," Deisha answered. She sounded groggy as if sleep was distorting her voice.

"Thank you Deisha!" Keisha said excitedly.

"What? Wait a minute, who's this?"

"It's Keisha," she giggled.

"Oh what's up Keisha? What are you thanking me for?"

"For the hook up with Manny!"

"Y'all are talking now?" Deisha asked as she sat up in her bed.

"I just saw him near Ridge Avenue. I got his number and I told him I would give him a call." Keisha was blushing and beaming all over the place.

"See, I told you." Deisha was happy for her.

"My heart was beating all fast. I had butterflies in my stomach."

"You got it, you got it bad," Deisha sang from Usher's song, *You got it bad*. They chuckled together. "Where's Maurice?" Deisha asked.

"He was sleep when I left to go to the store. I didn't even get what I was supposed to after seeing Manny."

Maurice actually woke up when he heard her run in the house and decided to listen in on her conversation to find out who she was getting hooked up with.

"Oh, well I'll call him later on."

"Alright, Deisha thanks again for talking to Manny for me."

"You're welcome," Deisha said. They said their good-byes and hung up.

Keisha walked over to the stairs to go down so she could grab a soda from the refrigerator but was stopped when she saw Maurice standing on the steps.

"Boy, you scared me. I was just talking to Deisha. She said she was going to call you later on."

"What the hell is Deisha doing playing Love Connection with you and Manny?"

"Why were you listening to my conversation?" Keisha snapped.

"You better watch who you're talking to and don't answer my question with a question." Keisha stared down at her older brother. "Don't stand there like you don't know how to talk."

"It ain't any of your business."

"Who the hell do you think you're talking to like that?" Maurice asked as he came up the stairs and got into Keisha's face. "Don't let me catch you around him."

"Why not?" Keisha asked.

"Because I'm not trying to have my little sister out here fucking with no drug dealers."

"Manny is not a drug dealer," Keisha said in defense of her hopeful boyfriend.

"Yo, you heard what I said. You know you ain't got any business out here trying to run the streets with these dumb-ass niggas around here in the first place."

"Ain't nobody…"

A THUG'S REDEMPTION

Maurice interrupted her. "Keisha, don't go there because I know what you did with Dom." Keisha stared at her brother with her mouth partially gaped open. She was appalled as well as embarrassed. "And he was going around bragging about that shit not realizing that it was going to get back to me. After I took my foot out of his ass, he thought twice before he spoke to you again. Don't listen and watch what happens to you." He walked past his sister and left the house to go pay Deisha a visit.

Deisha ran down the stairs when she heard her doorbell. "Coming!" She walked over to the door and opened it. "Hey Maurice, I ain't know you were coming over."

"Anybody here with you?" he asked.

"No, my aunt had to work late and Tamera is out with Jamal somewhere. I figured I'd get some sleep since the house is quiet for a change."

Maurice gently pushed Deisha into the house. "Let me talk to you for a minute."

"What?" Deisha asked as she stumbled backwards.

Maurice closed the door behind them. Deisha knew this look. He definitely was not pleased about something. "Why are you getting my sister hooked up with Manny and you know that nigga sells drugs?"

"Manny doesn't sell drugs," Deisha told Maurice.

"How do you figure?"

"Because he's too busy busting his ass in school so he doesn't have to end up like Kiree and his cousins."

"And how do you know? My sister ain't ready for these streets. You should've known that from what happened with her and Dom."

"Who said she's running the streets? And that was one mistake. You're not even giving her the chance to show that she learned from that mistake. You can't stop your sister from liking who she likes just like your mom can't stop you from liking me."

"That's different," Maurice argued.

"No it's not. And stop kicking every dude ass that shows interest in your little sister. She's gonna end up hating you."

"Look Oprah, Dom was running around talking about how he ran up in my sister. What, I wasn't supposed to say nothing? You're fucking right I kicked his ass and I'll do it again if anybody talks about my sister like she's some neighborhood hoe."

"Don't call me Oprah," Deisha smiled.

"Then stop acting like her," Maurice retorted.

"Manny is nothing like Dominique."

"Yeah, we'll see."

Deisha laughed at Maurice and shook her head at him. "If you come barging up in my house like that again, I'ma kick you in your teeth."

Yani

"Yeah whatever," Maurice chuckled. "I'm going back home. I'm still sleepy like shit and all of this is giving me a damn headache." He gave Deisha a brief kiss before he left. Deisha closed the door behind him and laughed some more.

A few days later, Tamera was in her room with her earphones on singing Alicia Keys' *Fallin*. Ms. Niecie was coming home from work and heard her so she decided to listen. Tamera looked up and was startled. She took her earphones off and turned down her music.

"I didn't mean to scare you," Ms. Niecie told her.

Tamera smiled and shrugged her shoulders. "It's okay."

"You have a nice voice. How come you didn't stay in the singing class that you were taking?"

Tamera fidgeted for a moment before answering. "There were some things going on that I wasn't comfortable with so I just decided not to go back."

"Oh, well it's not like you needed lessons anyway. Is Deisha anywhere around here?"

"No. She went to pick up her paycheck." Tamera replied.

"I need to talk to her so when she comes in, tell her to knock on my door." Ms. Niecie said.

"Okay."

"And keep singing because you really do have talent. Have you ever thought about singing in a choir?"

"No, not really. I used to sing in one with my mom when I was younger."

"Well, let me go lay down. I'ma needs my rest. I have a date later on tonight," Ms. Niecie gushed.

"How Ms. Niecie got her groove back," Tamera joked.

"Hey, Stella was forty. I'm barely pushing thirty-three." Ms. Niecie said as she placed a hand on her hip.

"Okay Ms. Niecie," Tamera smiled. Ms. Niecie chuckled as she went to her room.

Tamera lay on her bed and stared up at the ceiling. School was getting ready to start but for some strange reason, she wasn't thrilled about going back like she had been in the previous years. She was becoming bored so she went into Deisha's room and got her phone so she could call Jamal. Jamal answered on the third ring. "What's up?"

"Hey," Tamera said in a sad voice.

"Who's calling Jamal?" he replied playfully. He knew that it was Tamera.

"Me," Tamera replied.

"Me who?" Jamal said in a kiddy voice.

"Tammy, who else?" she giggled.

"I know. I was just fucking with you. What's up baby girl?"

"Nothing," Tamera sighed.

"Can you call me back later on? I'm about to run up Erie Ave with Shawn and Maurice."

"Alright," Tamera said. The sadness in her voice was obvious. She was about to hang up the phone when Jamal called her name. "Yes," she said as she put the receiver back to her ear.

"What's wrong?" he asked.

"Nothing, I was just thinking about school and my mom," Tamera told him.

"Aw babe. Well look, we're going to talk as soon as I get back in. If you want I'll come chill with you, we can order some Chinese food and talk, okay?"

"That sounds perfect. Thank you," Tamera managed to smile.

"No problem, babe. I'll talk to you in a bit. Love you."

Tamera hesitated before responding. "Ditto," she said in return.

Jamal smiled before he hung the phone up. Tamera stayed in Deisha's room looking around when Deisha came in behind her.

"Ms. Niecie said she wanted to talk to you when you got in," Tamera told Deisha.

"Aw what the hell did I do now?" Deisha asked as she tossed her pocketbook onto her bed.

"I don't think she's mad or anything. She said something about having a date tonight."

"Here we go with the Stella shit. I bet he's younger than her too," Deisha teased.

"I didn't know your aunt was thirty-three."

"Thirty-three? Nigga, she's been thirty-three for the last two years. Thirty-three must have been her prime years."

"That's not right Deisha. I'm going in my room, you are so mean," Tamera chuckled as she went back to her room and Deisha went to knock on Ms. Niecie's door.

Shawn, Jamal and Maurice headed over to Erie Avenue to check out a basketball game in a nearby playground. Shawn was scoping out the competition to see who he would be up against in his senior year. As he, his brother, and Maurice were by some of the benches talking, Jamal noticed that one of the guys was watching him and pointed him out to a couple of the other guys. Maurice noticed it, too.

"Yo Mal, did you just see that shit?" Maurice asked as he turned to the side.

"Yeah," Jamal replied as he looked at the guy who pointed him out dead in the eye. "I saw that shit."

"What's going on?" Shawn asked. He was so into the game that he had no idea what was about to transpire.

"Don't look, but it's four niggas across the court, one of them got a white Du-Rag on. He just pointed me out to his homies like they scoping for me," Jamal said as he continued to watch the guys.

"Damn 'Mal, what the fuck did you do now?" Shawn asked.

"I ain't do shit," Jamal said in a low tone.

"Do you even know those niggas?" Maurice asked.

"Hell no. But one of them looks a little familiar. I just don't know from where."

They stood there for a minute as Jamal thought about his options. He knew if it came down to a rumble, Maurice and his brother would be down. But now-a-days, niggas didn't fight anymore and he wasn't carrying. He definitely didn't want to get another cap busted in his ass and he for damn sure didn't want what happened with Raheem to happen to Maurice or Shawn.

"Let's roll yo," Jamal said as he tapped Maurice on his chest.

"You sure?" Maurice asked as Jamal started heading towards the school yard's exit.

"Yeah, let's go just in case anything pops off. It's kids in here."

They started walking out of the school yard. Jamal had a hunch to look behind him and wasn't surprised to see the guys leaving out behind them.

"Fuck," Jamal mumbled. He wasn't in the mood for any drama. He had a hunch to stop and turn around. When he did the guys were rushing him. It happened so fast, Maurice and Shawn didn't have a chance to react. The guys were so focused on jumping Jamal that they weren't expecting Maurice and Shawn to do anything. Maurice and Shawn jumped in it and they were all fighting on the corner of 17th and Venango. It looked like a mini riot as people gathered to see the action. Despite Jamal having two on him, he was holding his own and kicking some serious ass. The guy that pointed him out to his friends became frustrated and pulled a gun from his waist. Shawn caught a glimpse of the gun and ran over to his brother. He pushed him out of the way just as the gun went off five times. Shawn was hit twice; once in the back and once in the thigh. People screamed as they ducked to the ground and dove behind cars for cover. The shooter and his friends ran.

Maurice got up slowly and looked around. He walked over to his two friends fearing the worst. He was getting ready to call out their names when a woman began screaming.

"Shawn?" Jamal asked as he rolled his brother over.

Shawn grimaced and reached towards the wound in his back with a shaking hand. "Fuck..." he murmured with a painful groan.

"Got damn it, Shawn! Why'd you do it, man? Why'd you do it?!" Jamal yelled as he looked his brother over.

He was about to pull him into his arms when Maurice yelled, "Don't move him, 'Mal! The bullet might travel. Don't move him."

Jamal was kneeling over his younger brother feeling helpless, not believing that the roles had been reversed from the time he was shot.

"I took it 'Mal, I… I had you, man. I took it," Shawn said weakly.

"Shhh, don't talk," Jamal told him as he held his brother's hand. He looked up at Maurice with tears in his eyes. "Call the ambulance, yo!"

Maurice reached into his pocket and pulled out his cell phone but saw an ambulance with no sirens coming in their direction. He ran in the middle of the street waving his arms. The EMT driver slammed on the breaks.

"Sonuva bitch!!" the EMT driver exclaimed. He stopped the ambulance and jumped out. "Are you nuts? I could've hit you, son!"

"My friend's been shot and he's over there with his brother," Maurice explained. They rushed over to Shawn.

"What happened here?" one of them asked as they began helping Shawn.

"These guys tried to jump me after the basketball game. They started shooting and my brother got hit in the back and in his leg," Jamal explained quickly.

"He was only shot twice?" they asked.

"That I know of, yeah," Jamal said. His head was spinning and he was dizzy with worry.

One of the EMTs got on his radio, "Black teenager around 16 years of age, GSW to the back and leg. No exit wound apparent, victim still conscious, we are en route to Temple University Hospital."

The cops pulled up just as Shawn was being placed in the ambulance and Jamal climbed in the back with him. An oxygen mask was placed over his face. Jamal held his hand and talked to him all the way to the hospital in between answering the questions being asked by the EMTs. Once in the hospital he pulled his phone from his back pocket and tried desperately to remember his mother's work number.

"Can I speak to Ms. Keyona Williams?" he asked with a sniff once someone finally picked up the phone. He was placed on hold and then moments later, his mother picked up.

"This is Keyona Williams, how may I help you?"

"Mom, you gotta leave work early. You gotta leave now," Jamal said, trying to sound as calm as possible.

"Jamal? You know what type of shift I work. Asking to leave early is like asking for a kidney; it's just not going to happen. Why, what's the matter? Is everything alright at home?"

Yani

"No... Shawn is in the hospital," Jamal told her. He was trying extremely hard not to cry. He knew she was going to immediately blame him when she found out how he was put into the hospital.

"Shawn is in the hospital for what?" Ms. Keyona panicked.

"He got shot, Mom. We were..."

His mother interrupted him. "Got shot for what?!! Y'all were what, Jamal? What were y'all doing?"

"We were at a basketball game near Erie avenue and on our way to the bus stop, I got jumped. Somebody pulled out a gun and started shooting and Shawn pushed me out of the way." Jamal explained briefly.

"Bull-shit, Jamal! You're selling again, aren't you? I could put my foot up your ass through this damn phone!" Ms. Keyona fumed.

"No, I'm not," Jamal replied.

"Oh my God, my baby... what hospital is he in?"

"He's in Temple," Jamal replied.

"I'm on my way. And you better hope that nothing happens to him, Jamal." She slammed the phone down. Jamal waited a moment before hanging up. He was furious at Shawn for doing what he always told him not to do, and furious at his mother for continuing to feel as though everything that went wrong was his fault but what was right never had anything to do with him.

Jamal went over to Maurice when he saw him come through the waiting room doors. "I swear to God man, let something happen to my brother and I'ma get every last one of those pussies, watch." Jamal was seething.

"Did you call your mom?" Maurice asked.

"Yeah and she blamed me as usual but, fuck her. I know what really happened. This time it wasn't even my fault. I didn't say shit to dude, and I don't know why they were fucking scoping me out like that."

"This shit is crazy yo," Maurice said as he shook his head. "Do you want me to call Chanda?"

"No, she's been through enough. She doesn't need to hear about this."

"She's gonna find out eventually and will be pissed that you didn't tell her," Maurice reminded him.

"Shit! This don't make any fucking sense, man!" Jamal snapped as he put his hands to his face.

Maurice left the waiting room and stepped outside so he could call Chanda.

"Hello?" Chanda answered after the second ring.

"Chanda, are you busy?" Maurice asked.

"Who's this?" Chanda asked not recognizing Maurice's voice.

"It's Maurice. What are you doing?"

"I was just watching TV. Why, what's up?"

"Shawn got hurt a little while ago," Maurice began to tell her.

"Shawn got hurt how?" Chanda asked as she sat straight up in her bed.

"Calm down Chanda," Maurice said, trying his best not to alarm her.

"No, I want to know what happened."

"It's a long story and I'd rather tell you in person. You need to get to Temple hospital's emergency room as soon as possible.

"Maurice, what happened to him?" Chanda asked with her voice trembling. Her heart was racing and she felt fear all over.

Maurice waited a moment before answering. "He got shot."

"No Mar… Maurice, are you sure? Are you sure it's him? Was it because of Jamal?" Chanda asked as she began to feel sick with worry.

"Only because he pushed Jamal out of the way," he explained.

"Where's Jamal? Is he okay?"

"He's here waiting to hear how Shawn is doing. He's in surgery right now. Their mom is on the way."

"Got damn it," Chanda mumbled. "I'm on my way."

Maurice hung up the phone and went back to Jamal in the waiting room. "You alright?" he asked his best friend.

"Yeah, I'm straight."

"Why'd he say that earlier?"

"Say what?" Jamal asked as he put his hands to his face and leaned on his knees.

"He said he took it this time and that he had you."

"Because back when I got shot it was because I pushed him out the way. I guess he was returning the favor." Jamal looked down the hall and saw his mother coming towards him. He stood up to greet her but when he opened his mouth, his mother slapped him in it.

"I told you this shit was gonna happen. Exactly this!" she said, as she was wailing on him."

"It wasn't my fault!" Jamal said as he tried to restrain his mother.

"Then whose fault is it, huh? Why is my son lying up in the hospital after being shot? Why Jamal?" She hit him some more.

"Because he pushed me out of the way! Because he was looking out for me like I always had to look out for us because you were never the fuck there!"

Ms. Keyona was getting ready to swing on him again but Maurice grabbed her. People had begun to watch. "You better watch your mouth after what you did to my baby! Don't think for one second I won't see your ass in jail for this. I don't give a damn if you are my son!"

"I don't give a fuck no more. Lock me up shit, ain't like I never been to jail before. You're talking about what I did to your son. You never did shit to protect us! All this time, who the fuck do you think looked out for Shawn? Me!! You never seem to give a damn about us until some shit like this goes down." He walked away from his mother and stood outside to get some air. Maurice knew that he was hot so he let him go. He stayed in the hospital and waited for Chanda to arrive. Fifteen minutes after the dispute between Jamal and his mother, Chanda was tapping him on the shoulder.

"That was fast," Maurice said. He got up and gave her a hug.

"Where is he? Is he okay?" Chanda asked hastily.

"He's still in surgery. I don't know anything else."

"His mom isn't here?"

"Yeah, her and Jamal just had a big fight. She went to get some coffee and Jamal went outside to get some air."

Chanda sat next to Maurice. "What happened?"

Maurice was getting ready to tell her when Jamal's mother came over to them. He stood up with Chanda. "I'll tell you later," he whispered.

"Did the doctors say anything?" Ms. Keyona asked.

"No," Maurice told her.

"Did you see Jamal?"

Maurice shook his head. "He ain't come back in yet."

"Hi Ms. Keyona," Chanda spoke.

"Hi sweetheart," Ms. Keyona spoke back.

Chanda followed Maurice outside so she could talk to him. "What happened?"

"We went up Erie Ave so we could see this basketball game when for some reason, this dude pointed Jamal out to these other three dudes. When we left, they just jumped Jamal out of nowhere. Me and Shawn jumped in it and then the next thing I know, Shawn rushed Jamal and a gun went off."

"Where did he get shot?" Chanda asked with tears in her eyes.

"He got shot in his back and in his thigh, I think. He told Jamal that he took it this time and that he had him. Jamal told me that he said that because back when he got shot, it was because he pushed Shawn out of the way so he wouldn't get hit."

"He returned the favor…" Chanda shook her head and Maurice hugged her as she cried harder.

Jamal walked over to them. "What's the word?"

"Nothing yet," Maurice told him as he let Chanda go.

"The doctors ain't say anything yet?" Jamal asked. Maurice shook his head.

Jamal looked down at Chanda. "I'm sorry," he apologized.

"I don't blame you, Jamal. It's not your fault."

"Tell my mom that," Jamal said as they walked back into the hospital. "Mom, did they say anything?"

"He's fine. He's going to be okay," she told her son. "We can see him in a little while."

They sat in the waiting room and waited patiently for the doctors to give them the word as to when they could visit Shawn. A little while later, a doctor came over to them. "Is there a Chanda Johnson in here?"

"I'm Chanda," she said as she stood up.

"Could you come with me, please?" the doctor asked.

Chanda followed the doctor to Shawn's room. She went inside and pulled up a chair beside him.

"What's up?" Shawn asked weakly.

"Nothing, are you okay?" Chanda asked him.

"I've been better." He looked her over. "Why were you crying?"

"Because I thought you were going to leave me," Chanda explained.

"Naw, I ain't going no-where. Who's all out there?"

"Your mom, Jamal and Maurice. We didn't call anybody else yet."

"My mom cursed Jamal out didn't she?" Shawn asked.

"From what Maurice told me, yeah."

"She needs to chill out. Could you do a favor for me? When you go back out there, tell her that it wasn't Jamal's fault. I was just looking out for him like he's been looking out for me all these years. And tell them that I'm alright."

Chanda smiled and shook her head. "You better not had left me. I would've kicked your little dead ass in here." They laughed together. Chanda leaned over and kissed Shawn on the forehead. She then left his room and delivered the message as he requested.

"I'm sorry baby," Ms. Keyona said to Jamal as she tried to hug him.

Jamal rejected her and then backed away slowly as he shook his head. "No mom, you always blame me when shit goes wrong but you ain't never there when I'm doing something right unless you want to brag to your friends and make it seem like you've done so much when you haven't done anything. You stay grilling me for selling drugs. But not once did you ever turn down the money that I was giving to you to help with the bills, now did you?"

"Jamal, I'm sorry if I wasn't there the way you needed me to be. It's just that times were tough and I needed to make a choice. Try and find a better life for you and Shawn or stay on welfare."

"Don't lay any guilt trips on me. The fact of the matter is, you are never there," Jamal hissed.

"I was always there," Ms. Keyona argued.

"When mom?! When?!" Jamal yelled.

"Jamal, all the times I used money that I was saving for us to bail you out of jail! And don't you dare try to talk down to me about money you gave me. I didn't know where it came from."

"But you took it all the same. You never bothered to ask where it came from. And as for you bailing me out of jail, all you did was throw me into the next one because with you, I'm always guilty until proven innocent." Jamal walked out of the hospital and over to the bus stop. He didn't have any change on him when the bus pulled up so he was going to put a five dollar bill in, but the bus driver stopped him.

"You can't get on the bus without a shirt on, son," the driver told him.

"My brother just got shot and I didn't want to walk around with blood on my shirt. I just need to get home so I can get showered and changed and go back to the hospital."

The driver looked him over and decided to let him on. "Come on." Jamal climbed onto the bus and paid his fare. He sat down in an empty seat near the driver as the rest of the passengers looked at him, hoping he would talk about the shooting.

"So where do you have to go?"

"Ridge Avenue and Master Street. I live on 18th and Master though."

"My niece doesn't live too far from there. Do you know a girl named Tamera?"

"Tamera Harrison?" Jamal asked.

"Yeah, that's her. She's kind of tall, light brown skin, can sing and has long hair," the bus driver described.

Jamal chuckled, "Small world. That's my girlfriend."

"No kidding, huh? How long have y'all been together?"

"Since last October."

"Do you love her?" the bus driver asked.

Jamal suddenly felt embarrassed. The embarrassment subsided and he decided to tell the bus driver the truth. "Yeah, I love her."

"Why?" the bus driver pressed.

"Because she's the only person I can talk to and not hold my tongue and I actually feel like I'm being listened to for a change. Plus, she's the only person that really understands where I'm coming from."

"Coming from? What do you mean by that?" the driver continued with his questions as more people got on the bus. The original riders were already eaves dropping.

"I used to sell drugs my freshman and sophomore years of high school. But I stopped the summer before my junior year because I was getting into too much trouble, a lot of my friends were getting killed or going to jail. That's not how I wanted to spend my life. I'm hoping to go to college."

"That's good," the driver commented.

"Then when I got shot..."

"You were shot?" the driver interrupted Jamal.

"Somebody was trying to start something. To make a long story short, I pushed my brother out of the way and got hit right here," Jamal said as he pointed to the bullet wound that almost cost him his life.

"You were lucky," the driver told him. Other passengers agreed with him.

"Some people say that I'm too lucky. But luck always runs out." Jamal fell silent for a moment before speaking again. "Anyway, I was in the hospital for a while and despite what her friends and father was telling her about me, she stayed with me anyway. If it wasn't for her, I wouldn't even be considering college."

"Oh, so you're the young guy that Darnell was talking about."

"More than likely, yeah."

"Well after listening to what you have to say about the two of y'all relationship and what he was saying, I don't see what the big deal is with y'all being together. You treat her right and it's good that you recognized your mistakes and corrected them instead of being oblivious to them and making them over and over again. It's a rare trait in young, Black males these days." Jamal nodded his head in agreement. He stood up as his stop was approaching. "I take it that you two have been through a lot," the driver assumed.

"You have no idea," Jamal replied.

The driver stopped the bus at Ridge and Master. "Well, all good relationships has their ups and downs. What makes them last is how you deal with them. Take it easy. I hope your brother pulls through this. And tell Tamera that it wouldn't hurt for her to give her Uncle Roger a call some time and pay me a visit."

"Alright," Jamal said as he got off of the bus. He started walking down the street towards his house when he noticed a few boys trying to jump another little boy. They had him surrounded when Jamal went over to them.

"Ay Naeem! Why don't y'all chill with that shit?!" Jamal scoffed.

"We were only playing," Naeem said as he and his friends backed off.

"So what, stop fucking with people all the time before the shit gets serious and somebody fucks you up for that." Naeem and his friends backed off and strolled down the street. Jamal turned to the little boy who was about to get beat up. "Yo Anthony, don't let nobody back you up in no corner like that. They come at you like that again, swing on the person with the biggest mouth cause nine times out of ten, he's only ramming because his friends are around. Don't let them try to play you like no bitch. You hear me?" Jamal schooled the little boy.

"Yeah," Anthony replied as he wiped his shirt off. The little boy walked up the street opposite the direction that the other boys went in.

Jamal looked around and shook his head. "I've gotta hurry up and get the fuck from around here. This shit is crazy." He went to his house to get cleaned up so he could head back to the hospital to see his brother.

CHAPTER 6
TROUBLE IN PARADISE

After getting shot, Shawn had to spend extra time in the weight room during gym to strengthen his back and legs in order for him to be ready for the basketball season. It was a painful and grueling experience, but Shawn refused to give up and was determined to have his strength back at 100%. He knew college scouts would be keeping an eye on him and he wanted to be a Georgetown Hoya more than anything in the world.

In the beginning of October, Chanda seemed to be happier than ever. Since her and Shawn had gym together, she went to the weight room with him every day to help him with his work-out. She started applying to colleges early to get as many acceptance letters as possible. Her main focus was on University of the Arts. She often told Shawn that if she couldn't go there, she didn't want to go anywhere else.

Maurice and Jamal were at the Arcade playing video games trying to decide what to buy on a Saturday afternoon. Two girls were watching them from another game console nearby.

"Dana, why won't you go talk to him?" one girl asked the other.

"Because Iesha, I can't." Dana replied to her girlfriend. She was shy and timid and never would have imagined approaching a guy and asking him for his number.

"Don't be a nut. You better hurry up before they leave." Iesha told her. Dana shrugged her shoulders and continued with her game but she couldn't keep her eyes off of Maurice. Iesha grabbed her friend's hand and pulled her over to them.

"Nigga, I done whipped your ass like five times. Give that shit up," Maurice chuckled not noticing the two girls standing near them.

"Naw nigga, put two muthafucking quarters in the machine and stop talking shit so I can bust your ass." They both started laughing.

Just as Maurice was getting ready to put his change into the slot, Iesha interjected. "Excuse me, can I get the next game?" she asked sweetly.

Maurice and Jamal exchanged looks. Jamal backed off of his game with a sly grin on his face immediately seeing what the two girls were up to.

"Yeah, you can have mine," he told Iesha.

"Actually, my friend wanted to talk to your friend," Iesha said with the same look on her face as Jamal's. She recognized him from the neighborhood and immediately was attracted to him. Maurice smiled and rubbed his chin. "What's your name?"

"I'm Maurice," Jamal lied. "And this is my homie, Jamal."

"Well, this is my friend Dana and my name is Iesha. She's kinda shy but she still wants to talk to you." She looked at Jamal and grinned again. Dana started blushing.

"Shorty, how old are you?" Jamal asked Dana.

"Fourteen," Dana replied bashfully.

"You're fourteen, too?" Maurice asked Iesha.

"No, I'm fifteen. How old are y'all?" Iesha asked.

"I'm eighteen," Jamal replied.

"I'm seventeen," Maurice said.

Iesha looked at Dana and smiled. "How come you're not talking, Dana?"

"She's cool. She's just shy," Maurice said. "It's cool because I already got a girl."

"Do you have a girlfriend, too?" Iesha asked Jamal.

"Yeah," Jamal replied as he licked his lips.

"I won't tell if you won't tell," Iesha said in a sexy, defiant tone.

Maurice laughed sarcastically. "It's on you, dawg." He laughed some more as he moved onto another game. Jamal looked at him and then turned his attention back to Iesha.

"Why did he say that?" Iesha asked, confused.

"Ignore him," Jamal told her.

"So what's up?" Iesha flirted.

Jamal felt like telling the girl to slow her hot-ass down because she was way out of her league. "Why don't you write your number down and I'll call you if I'm not busy," he said instead.

Iesha took a pen out of her bag. "What, you hustle or something?" Iesha asked, looking for adventure and money.

"Naw actually I've got a real job," Jamal replied, seeing what the girl wanted.

"Oh," Iesha wrote her number down and gave it to him. "Aren't you going to give me your number?"

Jamal shrugged his shoulders. It didn't matter if she did call him. He had used one of their tricks against her by giving her Maurice's name. He wrote his number down and gave it to her.

"Are you going to call me?" Iesha pressed.

"Yeah," Jamal replied absent mindedly.

"When?" she asked as she looked him dead in his eyes.

Suddenly Jamal became annoyed with the girl. He sighed and said, "Tonight, tomorrow, whenever."

"You're not going to call me," Iesha said, becoming doubtful.

Jamal chuckled as he backed away to Maurice. "You'll hear from me again." He turned to his friend and shook his head. "That girl's scattered."

"I won't tell if you won't," Maurice mocked. He started laughing and leaned onto the game. "I don't believe her young ass came off like that. That girl probably still got shit stains in her draws, she's so young. You better watch it, nigga. You're going to need a do not enter sign on your ass if you get caught messing with that."

"I ain't fucking with her. Can you say, *Tammy*?" Jamal replied as he looked at Maurice crossly.

"Yeah those quiet girls can rumble. They're crazy, too."

"I think I'm gonna pass on that one," Jamal said as he shook his head and tossed her number in the trash.

"You never should have considered it. You should've told her young ass to stay in her lane and go finish playing with her Barbies." They started laughing as they went to play another video game.

The next day, Keisha was walking home from seeing Manny. She saw Dominique on the corner in front of a store but pretended she didn't notice him.

"Come here Keisha," he demanded, sweetly.

Keisha ignored him and continued on her way home. Dominique rushed to catch up to her and walked besides her.

"What's up girl? Why are you acting like you don't know a nigga now?"

"Why are you talking to me?" Keisha asked, acidly.

"I can't talk to you no more?" Dom asked in his same sweet tone.

"You gave that right up when you went around bragging about how you had sex with me. No, let me rephrase that: fucked my young ass up." Dominique didn't reply to her. "You ain't answered my question. Why the fuck are you talking to me?"

"What are you going to do, go get your brother on me again? He's lucky I ain't shoot his ass."

"No, you're lucky he ain't shoot yours. And I ain't get him. He heard about it on the streets because you talk too fucking much. I guess you didn't think it would get back to him. That shows just how little pussy you get if you're running around bragging about hitting off a fourteen year old."

"Actually your age ain't had anything to do with it. Just the pleasure of having Maurice's little sister was enough."

Keisha stopped and looked at him angrily. "I'm going to pretend that I didn't hear that shit."

"Look Keisha, I didn't stop you to argue about that. I just wanted to see how you were doing and actually apologize. I know I didn't do right by you and I wanted you to know that I miss you."

Keisha was at her doorstep. "Bite me. And you better get off my damn porch. You must really think I'm going to be dumb enough to let you play me again." She opened her front door and slammed it in his face.

"What the fuck are you slamming the door for?" Maurice snapped as he was doing his homework on the couch.

"Dominique… never mind," Keisha mumbled.

"Dominique what? Is he still fucking with you?"

"No, he just wanted to apologize."

"Whatever. I guess I ain't whipped his ass good enough. He should've apologized sooner. Where are you coming from anyway?"

"No-where," Keisha smiled.

"Alright, don't get young bol fucked up."

"Whatever," Keisha sucked her teeth as she hung up her jacket.

"Some chicken-head called for you," Maurice told her.

"Why she gotta be a chicken-head?" Keisha asked as she giggled. Maurice smiled and got up from the couch. He closed his books and stretched. "Who was it?" Keisha asked.

"I don't know. Some girl," Maurice replied. "She ain't leave a name."

"What did she say when she called? Did she ask if I was here or did she ask if she could speak to me?"

"She asked if you were here."

"Oh, that was Marcella. She ain't want anything important. She just wanted to be nosey."

"Yeah, yeah, yeah. Mommy said to take the chicken out and have it cleaned by the time she comes home."

"Dag man, why didn't she say that before I left?" Keisha smirked with an attitude.

"Yeah well, just make sure you get it done before she comes home. I ain't trying to hear her shit."

Keisha went upstairs and changed into some sweatpants. She then washed her hands and came back downstairs to clean the chicken like her mother told her to.

"See if you were smart, you would clean that chicken and leave before Mommy gets back in," Maurice told his younger sister.

"I'm not like you. I can't just leave when I want."

"All you gotta do is leave a note with a good excuse," Maurice told her.

Keisha continued to clean the chicken. "But it's Sunday. I'm not allowed to stay out late on Sundays."

"You just want to stay here with her," Maurice said as he tied his sneakers.

"No I don't," Keisha replied.

"Tell her you're with me." When Keisha didn't say anything, Maurice shook his head. "Stay here if you want to. I'm out, peace." He grabbed his jacket and left the house.

Chanda, Deisha and Tamera were at Chanda's house listening to music, talking and laughing when Shawn called. Chanda turned the radio down and answered the phone on the third ring. "Hello," she said still laughing from the last comment that Deisha made.

"Chanda?" Shawn asked.

"That would be me. Hey boo, what's up?"

"Nothing, I just got home from work and wanted to call you. Are you busy?"

"No why?" Chanda asked.

"Hey Shawn!" Tamera and Deisha yelled through the phone.

"Tell them I said what's up," Shawn replied.

"He said what's up y'all. So what's up with you, Shawn? Why do you sound like that?"

"I would ask you to leave the room but you're gonna tell Tamera and Deisha what I'm about to tell you now anyway so…" Shawn trailed off.

"Okay, so tell me."

"Remember back when Jamal got shot and the cops traced that gun back to me and took me in for questioning and everything?" When Chanda didn't respond, Shawn cleared his throat. "Remember Khalil?"

"Yeah ain't he the dude everybody was saying killed Raheem?" Chanda asked. Deisha became all ears when she heard Raheem's name mentioned.

"Yeah, well you know Jamal killed him, right?"

"I heard rumors about it. Why are you telling me all of this?" Chanda asked. She had a feeling something eerie was going on.

Shawn sighed. "The gun that I had was the gun Jamal used. He never got caught because Samir is connected. I mean he has connections in all kinds of places. The problem is, the cops that came on the scene when Jamal was shot weren't apart of Samir's team. And the gun Jamal used is a rare caliber that only cops are supposed to have. The only way for the gun to have gotten on the street is…"

Chanda interrupted him, "Is if a cop leaked the weapons. Jesus."

"Exactly," Shawn agreed. "They knew of three murders that occurred with that kind of gun. Khalil's was one of them which was why they were grilling me so hard about where I got it from. The only reason I was let off the hook is because I made a call to Samir and he made a couple calls and they let me go. Samir must've had a Sergeant in his pocket or something, I don't know but, the brass came down on him. He's ready to flip shit unless Samir moves a shipment for him. And from the sounds of it, this shit is big. I mean Columbian kinda big. The Sergeant is telling Samir if the shipment isn't moved, the evidence is going to fall on me for Khalil's murder. So now…" Shawn trailed off.

"What? Now what?" Chanda asked as her heart raced.

"I owe him." Shawn replied in a low tone.

"Owe him how?"

"Because if he doesn't move the shipment for this dude, I'm going to jail. He's doing this to keep me out of trouble so he wants me and Jamal to work for him."

Chanda interrupted him. "Wait a minute though. Jamal killed him, so it should just be Jamal's ass not yours."

"What? Who did Jamal kill?" Deisha asked, eaves dropping.

"Shhh!!!" Chanda said as she put a finger up to silence Deisha.

"Yeah, but if I never took the gun to begin with, the cops never would've been able to trace the gun back to me."

"But how do they know it's the murder weapon?" Chanda asked.

"I told you, it's because the gun is a rare caliber that only cops are supposed to have. This shit is coming down because there are crooked cops on the force and Internal Affairs is asking questions."

"No Shawn, this is bull-shit! This is Jamal's mess, let him clean it up." Chanda was fuming.

"If I didn't take the gun that day, Jamal would probably be dead," Shawn replied.

"Shawn, what about the basketball season? What about school and college and everything else? You better tell Jamal to handle his B.I or tell Samir to fuck off."

"I can't, babe. I'm looking at a murder charge right now," he told her as he shook his head.

Chanda slammed the phone down and pushed it to the side. "I don't fucking believe this shit!"

"What? What's wrong?" Tamera asked.

Chanda waited a moment before speaking so she could calm down. "The gun that Shawn had when Jamal got shot was traced back to Khalil's murder. Cops are supposed to be the only ones to have the type of gun that was used. So now they know that cops are supplying weapons to the niggas on the street. So because the heat is coming down on them, they are coming down on Samir so he is coming down on Shawn and Jamal. Now Samir is trying to muscle Shawn and Jamal into being his little street soldiers. If they don't, Samir is just going to sit back and let Shawn go to jail for a murder that Jamal did."

"So Jamal did kill Khalil. I always knew he did but I was so angry at the fact that Khalil killed Raheem, I never cared," Deisha said.

"I told Shawn he better tell Jamal to get to confessing because if he would've left that shit alone none of this would be going down. I wanted Khalil dead for what he did to Raheem, too. I'm sure we all did. But now look at what's happening. It's not worth it. I'm not going through that shit, man. Tammy, I don't see how you can do it because ain't that much love in the world. I don't see how you can stay with Jamal knowing the shit that he's doing," Chanda snapped.

"What's that supposed to mean?" Tamera asked in a hostile tone.

Yani

"It means exactly what I said. That either you got to be desperate or pretty fucking stupid."

"I'm no-where near the fuck stupid or desperate so you better watch who the fuck you're talking to!" Tamera snapped back.

Deisha winced, never hearing Tamera talk to anyone like that.

"Tammy, he's a murderer and he's about to let Shawn go down for some shit he did three years ago. Open your eyes, Tammy because I can got-damn guarantee you that if you stay with him, you will not live to see your eighteenth birthday," Chanda told her.

"Don't say that, Chanda. It's a reason why they're together," Deisha said.

"Man fuck that! As much as I miss my brother, I am not trying to join him anytime soon. I'm out! Because when the walls are tumbling down, and they will tumble, I am not gonna be there to watch them fall."

"Can we talk about something else? Damn!" Tamera snapped.

Shawn was sitting in his room still pondering his situation. He knew if he did the favor, he would risk losing Chanda and could possibly go to jail. He also knew that if he didn't do it, he could go to jail for murder or Samir was destined to do something stupid. He tossed his ball in the air trying to find a reasonable solution.

Jamal stood in his doorway and looked down at him. "What's wrong?" he asked Shawn.

"Nothing," Shawn said flatly.

"I know that look. I see through your little ass like glass, nigga. You're worried about that gun situation, aren't you?"

"Yeah man, this is some bullshit," Shawn replied as he tossed his ball in the air repeatedly.

"Look, it's only for a couple weeks. Once it's over, we go off to college and move on with our lives," Jamal told his younger brother.

"You really think Samir is just going to let this shit be over and done with? Now the cops are trying to muscle Samir and get more out of the deal by bringing in shit for the Columbians. This shit ain't gonna stop after one shipment and you know it. They're not going to let us slide. They're going to keep hanging this over our heads so they can get us to do what they want us to do for them. This shit ain't about helping us. This shit is about helping them and getting more paper." Shawn shook his head and threw his ball at the wall angrily.

Jamal thought about what Shawn said. He knew his younger brother was right because it was a thought that crossed his mind quite a few times since this all hit the fan. He was beginning to understand what Samir's motives were and how he damned himself the minute he asked for help with carrying out the hit on Khalil. Samir wanted him to be his soldier, not a part-time help. He wanted Jamal sucked into the game simply because

Jamal was so ruthless when it came to certain matters. Jamal was trying to humble himself and move past all of that. Unfortunately, Samir wasn't trying to let him go.

The damage that he had done by killing Khalil was becoming clear. Family or not, Samir was never going to let him go and that murder was his leverage to control him. The only problem was, now his brother was paying for his need for revenge though he had nothing to do with the situation.

Anger took over him quickly.

"You know what? Fuck this shit. I lived that street life, not you. And I'm not about to let Samir keep thinking that he can control me behind some shit that happened three years ago, trying to make it seem like I owe him because I don't owe him shit. When I talk to him, I'ma let him know to leave you out of this. I don't want you or nobody else to pay for what I did.

I pulled the trigger, not you. And if it comes down to it, I'll take the fall. Don't worry about it. I got this."

"Alright," Shawn replied, not really knowing what else to say.

Jamal left and went straight to Samir's house. He knocked on his door and waited patiently for an answer knowing that he was home because it was collection day.

Samir opened his door and peeked out. "What's up, Jamal? I ain't know you were coming by." He opened the door wider so Jamal could come in.

"I'm not going to stay long because I have a lot of stuff to do at home. I just wanted to say that y'all need to leave Shawn out of this, for real. He didn't have nothing to do with Khalil getting killed, that was all me. Just leave him out of this and let me do this like I always do. He's trying to go to college, just let him chill."

"What the fuck does that have to do with me? Now I know that your little brother is trying to do his thing with his basketball and everything, but that shit he pulled taking that gun just brought on more problems than I was trying to have to fucking deal with. I got fucking heat on me now, 'Mal! The muthafucking pigs is looking for a reason to pinch me and because of that shit, I got to do business with these spick ass Columbians, bring their shit in on my turf and on top of that shit, divvy out more of a cut to keep muthafuckas quiet. Shawn doesn't know what fucking trouble he's causing right now behind that shit he pulled last year. So I don't give a fuck what he's trying to do. He can either man up on this shit or…" Samir trailed off.

"Or what?" Jamal asked, having an idea what Samir was thinking.

"Let me just say if y'all had been any other niggas on the street, I would've saved myself the aggravation and killed both of y'all," Samir said with a straight face.

Jamal looked at Samir as if he were crazy. "You're really going to come out of your mouth and say some shit like that? We're supposed to be family."

"Fuck that family shit, Jamal. This is business. Everybody is expendable."

Jamal became furious. "It's the fuck like that? How about we do the shit like this? I'ma turn myself in and tell the cops I killed Khalil, fuck it. And when they ask how, I'm telling everything. Fuck that family shit you say? Since it's fuck me nigga, now it's fuck you, too."

Samir snatched Jamal up by his neck and pushed him into the wall. They struggled with each other in a grip pushing back and forth until Samir managed to pin Jamal down on his dining room table. "You're a snitch now, nigga? Huh?! Is that what the fuck you just said, pussy? IS IT!?" He pulled a gun out and turned Jamal over so he could face him and pushed the gun into his face. "I'll blow your muthafucking scalp off right here, nigga! After everything I did for you, you're whipping your dick out and telling me to suck it by trying to snitch?"

Jamal looked Samir dead in the eye and said calmly, "I ain't scared of you, Sa. You're just another motherfucker off the street."

Samir cocked his gun. "You ain't scared nigga? Yeah, just like your fucking pop. That nigga was fearless, too. Ready to ride at the drop of a hat and had niggas shook around here. But unlike you, the nigga was reckless and sloppy until I shut his shit down."

Jamal looked at Samir wide-eyed making sure he understood what he had just said to him. Samir had just admitted to killing his father. A man he vaguely remembered. A man that he thought had just upped and left his mother struggling to take care of him and his brother. The room swam as Jamal tried to process what Samir just said.

"That's right. I got him the fuck out of here so what makes you think I won't get you and Shawn the fuck out of here, too? Y'all niggas ain't shit to me," Samir said in a low and threatening tone. Jamal trembled with anger. "Now dig this shit and dig it good, muthafucka. I cleaned up after your punk ass too many times for you to come in my face talking about some snitching shit. Talking about that shit alone is enough to body your bitch ass right now. I'ma leave Shawn out of this. But you nigga, I own your muthafucking ass like I'm your daddy, nigga. I'ma even be nice and let you wait until the end of the school year. Because the more I clean up after you, the more your bitch-ass is going to owe me." He took the gun away from Jamal's head and smacked Jamal on the cheek slightly as he smiled. "So we're cool now? We have an understanding?"

Jamal looked at Samir angrily. "Yeah."

"Good," Samir said as he put his gun away. Jamal started walking to the door. "You know, Tamera is too gorgeous to be caught up in something like this. It would be a shame for something to happen to her. After all, danger isn't for pretty little girls." He looked at Jamal with a sly grin on his face when he turned to face him. "I'm just saying."

"You better leave her the fuck out of this. You got a problem with me. Leave the shit with me." Jamal said through clenched teeth. He swore if he was carrying he would have blown Samir away right then and there.

Samir smiled but then his expression became very serious. "You heard what the fuck I said. If you even try some slick snitching shit, I'ma kill you, Shawn and your fucking wifey."

They stared daggers at each other for a moment and then Jamal left. He was beginning to think that he had just made matters a lot worse.

Maurice stopped off at Shawn and Jamal's house to hang out so he didn't have to be at home when his mother returned.

"Hi Maurice," Ms. Keyona said when she opened the door for him. "Are you here for Jamal?"

"Yeah, how are you, Ms. Keyona?" Maurice spoke.

"I'm hanging in there. Jamal's not here. Do you want to see Shawn instead?"

"Yeah, that's cool," Maurice replied.

"He's upstairs. He hasn't come down almost all day. I don't know what's wrong with that boy. I don't know where Jamal is either. He shot outta here like a bat outta hell earlier without saying one word to me. I swear these boys think they can just come and go as they please and don't say a word to me. They swear they can handle their problems on their own. That's why their asses stay in so much trouble. Come on in."

Maurice came into the house and stood in the living room. Ms. Keyona went to the stairs and called up to Shawn. "Maurice is down here to see you!" She went into the kitchen to finish cooking her dinner. "So how's school coming along, Maurice?"

"It's alright." Maurice replied.

"Have you started applying to colleges yet?"

"Not yet. I'm still looking for one that has my name on it," he told her.

Shawn came downstairs and gave Maurice a handshake. "What's up, Mar?" He then whispered. "Is my mom in there?"

"Yeah," Maurice replied. Shawn motioned for him to come up to his room.

"Shawn, do you know where Jamal went?" Ms. Keyona asked as she came out of the kitchen.

Shawn hesitated. "No, he just said he would be right back. He probably ran to the store or went to see Tamera real quick." He looked at Maurice and they made a grand exit up to his bedroom. Shawn closed the door behind them once they were inside.

"What's up with you?" Maurice asked as he sat in the chair at his desk.

Shawn leaned into the wall and told Maurice the entire story about the gun, Samir and the cops that he had on the take and the kind of trouble they were in. "Now Jamal is at Samir's house trying to see if he can get us out of this shit."

"Y'all stay in more shit than a little bit. I thought you just told your mom you ain't know where Jamal was?" Maurice replied.

"If I would've told her he was with Samir, she would've started bitching and I don't feel like hearing her shit."

"I feel you. That's why I left my house." They heard the door close downstairs and listened. Jamal exchanged a few brief words with his mother and then came upstairs. He knocked on Shawn's door and then came in.

"What's up, Maurice?" Jamal spoke. Maurice nodded his head at him and Jamal closed the door.

"What did he say?" Shawn asked.

Jamal was quiet before he said anything. He was still trying to get over the shock of finding out that his cousin, whom he had trusted all of these years, had murdered his father. "I've got good news and I've got bad news. And I got some shit that you won't fucking believe. What I say in this room doesn't leave this fucking room." He looked at Maurice and Shawn both so they could see how serious he was. "Shawn, you don't have anything to worry about. I got this. But that nigga put a gun to my head and told me he doesn't give a fuck if we're family or not. He straight said he would kill me, you, -and get this- Tamera, all because I told him I would take the fall for Khalil's murder rather than see you go to jail for some shit you didn't do, or have him keep thinking he can jerk me the fuck around like he's been doing these last three years."

Shawn's mouth was partially open in disbelief.

Maurice shook his head. "That's some fucked up shit yo," Maurice commented.

"Yeah, he's on our ass now. So it's two things we gotta do: stay outta the way and get you and Tamera the fuck outta here after graduation or our asses are gonna be dead before we see college."

Shawn buried his face in his hands. "This shit ain't cool, man."

Jamal looked at his brother for a moment, debating on whether or not he should tell Shawn that their father was murdered by Samir. He cleared his throat. "Shawn, it's something else."

Shawn looked up at his brother. "Does it get any worse than this?"

Jamal looked at his brother as his eyes watered. He shook his head and then blinked his tears away. "Samir killed our father…"

The silence in the room was loud and painful as Shawn and Maurice looked at Jamal in disbelief. Neither could believe the words that came out of his mouth.

"How do you know? What the fuck do you mean Samir killed our father? That nigga told you that shit!?" Shawn said loud and angrily.

"Shawn, calm down. I don't know the details. But when he put that gun to my head, he basically told me it wouldn't faze him if he killed us just like it didn't faze him when he killed our dad." Jamal shook his head.

"You can't be fucking serious, Jamal. Y'all cousin killed your fucking dad? Do your mom know?" Maurice asked.

"That's a good question," Jamal replied as he thought about how much their mother hated Samir. It was beginning to become clear.

"We need to go fucking ask her then," Shawn said as he moved towards the door.

Jamal stopped him. "No. Let me talk to her first. Something is going on with this family. It's a bunch of secrets and shit going on that's about to hit the fan and blow around. If Mommy knew all this time that Dad got killed and Samir did it but she didn't say anything…" Jamal trailed off unable to finish his thought. Too much was going on in his mind. "I'ma talk to her Shawn, alright? But you need to calm down and chill."

Shawn was fuming but he took heed to his brother's warning.

Later that night after Maurice went home and Shawn had gone to bed, Jamal knocked on his mother's door.

"Yes?" she answered, sounding tired.

"Mom, I need to talk to you," Jamal replied through the door.

"Come on in, Jamal," Ms. Keyona told him.

Jamal opened the door and came into her room. He closed the door behind him and then leaned onto her dresser. He stared at her for a long time.

"What's wrong, honey?" Ms. Keyona asked him. She could tell that something was deeply troubling her son.

"Tell me about my father?" Jamal asked in a low flat tone.

Ms. Keyona looked him in his face and then looked away. "What do you want to know?"

"Just tell me about him. I want to know who he is. I want to know his name. Who knows, maybe one day I'll find him." Jamal studied her facial expressions to see how she would react.

"There's nothing to tell. His name was Andre Williams. When Shawn was about two years old, he left and never came back."

Jamal stared at her quietly before he said anything. "You know what? It's a damn shame that I'm 18 years old, Shawn is 17 and you still won't tell us the truth. You still won't tell us the whole story about our father."

"Watch your mouth!" Ms. Keyona replied.

"Where's my father?" Jamal asked again.

"I don't know," Ms. Keyona replied.

"You don't know?" Jamal took a couple steps towards her. "Tell me why you never liked Samir, Mom?"

Yani

"I never said I don't like Samir. I just know what he's into and I don't want him in my house," Ms. Keyona answered. She was becoming nervous.

"Mom, all these years you let me and Shawn believe our father left you. You let us believe that our dad was this no good bum who walked out and didn't give a fuck about us. But you knew all along that he was dead." Jamal's voice cracked as he continued to talk. "You knew Samir killed my father and you never said anything."

Ms. Keyona looked at her son wide-eyed. "Who told you that, Jamal?"

"How come you never said anything, Mom?" Jamal asked. The pain could be heard in his voice.

Ms. Keyona put her hands to her face and started sobbing. "Jamal, I couldn't say anything." She continued to sob, unable to say another word.

"Mom, what happened to my father?" Jamal asked again.

Ms. Keyona wiped her face. She waited a moment before she began speaking. "Your father was out there in the streets hustling. He worked for a man named Smitty, but he was like his right hand man. I never really nagged him about his business because he told me from the door that as long as I took care of home, he would take care of us. So I stayed in my place and played my part as you kids would say today. He was respected because he didn't take any shit. Just like you, Jamal. I swear, the two of you are so much alike, it frightens me." Ms. Keyona cleared her throat and continued.

"Samir was trying to come up in the streets under Smitty's rival, Kristoff. Out of no-where, Smitty got locked up one night, so your father started taking care of business for him. There was a rumor that someone snitched and that was how Smitty got knocked. A lot of people said Samir snitched to the cops to take the heat off of him and Kristoff. Out of nowhere, Smitty was killed in his cell; knifed in his sleep if I remember correctly. I think they figured if he was dead, that would give them the opportunity to take his territory. But your father maintained things. Samir wanted your father to work for him and Kristoff. Your father turned him down and things got heated. There was supposed to be a truce. One night, Samir came by the house. I remember I had just put Shawn to bed and you were sleep. You were about four and Shawn had just turned three. I remember they were getting loud and normally I would stay upstairs when he was conducting business, but I never trusted Samir and had a feeling he was going to do something dirty. I never would've thought that he would kill your father, I mean at the time he was only sixteen at best.

"I heard your father say something that alarmed me and I came downstairs. I saw Samir pull the gun. I screamed out something and before I knew it, he shot your father in the chest. He killed your father right in front of me. Kristoff was there, too. They told me if I wanted to see both you and Shawn grow up, I'd better keep my mouth closed about what I saw." Ms. Keyona became silent for a moment. "And so I did."

"Your father was everything to me. And Jamal, I swear you are the splitting image of that man. Seeing you in the streets like this scares the hell out of me because I don't want the same thing that happened to your father to happen to you. I hate Samir for what he did. God knows I do. And I wish something could have been done but he has too many cops in this city at his back."

Jamal looked at his mother with mixed emotions. A part of him was angry that she had kept that kind of secret from him and his brother. Another part of him was furious that all of this time Samir had been playing him, using him. The man he trusted and admired for so long was really a back stabbing fraud that murdered his father right in front of his mother and had her living in fear and living a lie for so long.

Jamal walked over to his mother and gave her a hug without saying anything. He kissed her on her forehead and said, "Everything will be fine, Mom. Don't worry." He went back to his bedroom and sat down. He didn't want to do anything rash that would cause his brother and girlfriend to be killed. But one thing was for certain and two things were for sure, Samir was going to pay for what he put his family through.

Tamera saw Jamal in the hall the next morning at school and stopped him at his locker. "I need to talk to you, Jamal," she said with seriousness in her voice.

"About what?" Jamal asked as he closed his locker door.

"When I ask you this, promise me that you'll give me a straight answer. No beating around the bush or trying to sugar coat any of this." Jamal looked down at her and shrugged his shoulders. She swallowed and then took a deep breath feeling the butterflies in her stomach as she thought about what she was getting ready to ask him. "Did you kill Khalil?" she asked innocently.

Jamal looked past her. "Why did you ask me that?"

"Because I wanna know. I need to know."

Jamal continued to stare past her. "Don't worry about it." He leaned over and planted a kiss on her forehead.

"Answer me Jamal," Tamera insisted.

Jamal sighed, "If I did, I had a good reason."

"There's never a good reason to take someone's life besides self - defense."

"So he had a good one for killing Raheem?" Jamal shot back.

Tamera hugged her books to her chest. "I thought you said that you didn't have anything to hide from me?"

"I don't," Jamal said in a low tone finally looking her in the eye.

"So why won't you give me a straight answer?" Jamal hugged her. "What are you trying to protect me from?"

"Nothing. It's just some things aren't meant to be known to some people and this is one of them and you are that person." He kissed Tamera for a brief moment and then walked her to class.

Later that day during lunch, Jamal and his friends were sitting in their usual seats. Chanda still wanted answers to the latest fiasco that was going down. A small argument started between her and Jamal over it.

"Chanda, you need to leave this alone," Shawn said in a low voice as he put his hands to his head and leaned onto the table.

"No Shawn, because it sounds like Jamal got y'all in some deep shit and if it's something crazy that's about to go down, let a nigga know now so I can get the fuck out of dodge. No offense, but you niggas got a strange attraction to bullets. First Raheem, then Jamal, Shawn, you just got a cap busted in your ass and I'm even hearing Khalil's name mixed up in there somewhere," Chanda replied angrily.

"Jamal, did you kill Khalil?" Deisha asked Jamal. He looked her in her eyes for a moment and then looked away without responding.

"Don't nobody know how it felt that day to watch Raheem die in my arms," Jamal finally said in a low calm voice. "To see him fall from that gate when that punk-bitch shot him right in front of me, to hear him gasping for air in my arms; y'all don't know what the fuck that shit did to me. Every fucking time I closed my eyes, I saw that shit happen again and again. Raheem was a friend to all of us and yeah we were all hurt and mad when he got killed. A lot of y'all blamed me and to this day I still believe it was my fault. So yes I wanted that nigga dead. I wanted to kill that muthafucka even if it cost me my life. I didn't give a fuck." Jamal took a deep shaky breath as tears filled his eyes before he continued. His friends were shocked at the emotion he was showing.

"So, I got my cousin to help me. We rode up on them niggas the night before Raheem's funeral and it didn't matter who was with him, nigga or bitch was getting it that night. I promised Samir I would sell drugs for him. I didn't think it was that big a deal, I mean he just helped me kill a nigga and covered it up for me. At the time I thought, cool, I can make some money and help my mom because we were struggling. When Shawn took that gun and I got shot last year, everything came out. The gun I used to kill Khalil is not supposed to be on the streets. Only cops are supposed to have those guns. But one was linked to three homicides and now it's linked to Shawn because of his finger prints. So now it's some shit where crooked cops are supplying street niggas with weapons and it's all coming to a head. All this time, I thought Samir had our backs and wouldn't let anything happen to us…" He trailed off and put his hands to his face in anger.

Maurice shook his head knowing what Jamal was thinking. Shawn put his hand on his brother's back. "It's alright 'Mal. It's cool."

"This shit ain't fucking cool yo," Jamal sobbed. "All this time this nigga been in my face, claiming to be on our side and he looked me in my muthafucking face and told me he killed my fucking father."

"Wow, are you serious?" Deisha asked with her mouth hanging open.

"This nigga threatened me, he threatened Shawn and…" Jamal trailed off when he looked at Tamera.

"What Jamal? What?" Chanda asked. Her heart was racing after hearing everything. "Who else did he threaten?"

Tamera looked at Jamal as he stared back at her. "Me…" she said in a low voice. "He threatened me."

"He probably wasn't even serious, Tammy. He probably just said it because he was mad," Jamal said quickly.

"Bull shit, Jamal!" Tamera hissed. "This man killed your father and threatened to kill you and Shawn and y'all are his family. What makes you think he'll have a problem killing me? I ain't nobody to him!" she exclaimed. She snatched her book bag from off of the floor and stormed out of the lunchroom.

When their last period class began, Deisha sat with Tamera to calm her down.

"Are you going to break up with him?" she asked her quietly while they did their work.

"Hell yes," Tamera said angrily. "I'm not getting caught up in that mess. He got Raheem killed, got himself shot, got his brother shot and now I'm getting threatened by a nigga that I don't even know."

"He might need you to help him get through this. I mean, I know I gave Jamal a hard time after Raheem got killed, but after hearing everything he said during lunch, I don't think anybody was more hurt than Jamal when Raheem got killed."

"That's too bad. He should've thought about this shit long before now. So tell Ms. Niecie if Jamal calls, don't call me to the phone. Just let her know that we broke up."

"Alright," Deisha replied. "But, you know he's not going to let you go so easily."

"He doesn't have a choice," Tamera mumbled.

Later on that day after school, Tamera was in her bedroom doing her homework. She constantly kept thinking about Jamal, which was a major distraction for her and it kept her from being focused. She used the latest drama of his to get herself back on track so she could get her assignments done. Just as she was getting down to business, Deisha knocked on her door.

"Yes," Tamera replied.

Deisha opened her door. "Can I hold your pink finger nail polish?"

"It's over there on my dresser with the rest of my colors. Did Jamal call?"

"Nope, maybe he finally took a hint." Just as Deisha spoke, she heard a tapping noise at the window. "What the hell is that?" Deisha asked.

"Probably just a bird," Tamera said, dismissing it.

Deisha shrugged it off and started picking through Tamera's polish again. "Damn, you have all the colors. Maybe I'll take a couple more."

"Just make sure you bring them back, Sticky Fingers," Tamera giggled.

"Whatever," Deisha said, laughing as well. The tapping noise came again. Annoyed with it, Deisha went over to the window and opened the blinds. She screamed and almost dropped the polish she was holding in her hands. Deisha snatched the blinds up and opened Tamera's window. "Boy! You scared the shit outta me! And why the hell are you in our backyard?"

"Who is it?" Tamera asked as she got off of the bed.

"Who do you think?" Deisha said as she smiled. She knew Jamal wasn't going to walk away from their relationship of a year so easily.

Tamera walked over to the window cautiously and looked out. Jamal motioned Tamera to him with his hand but she shook her head, refusing him. He put his hands together as if he were praying and poked his lip out. Tamera sighed and closed her blinds. She grabbed her jacket and went downstairs. When she opened the back door and looked around, Jamal was gone. She stood in the middle of the backyard and saw him walking down the alleyway so she called out his name. He turned around and came back to her.

"What do you want?" she asked him.

"I want to talk to you," he told her.

Tamera looked at him for a moment trying to decide if she wanted to give him that opportunity. She sighed and gave in. "Well...?"

"I don't blame you for being mad at me because of everything that's going on. But I need you to understand, when I did what I did back then, I didn't think it was going to turn out like this. And I swear I wasn't trying to put you in any of this. I know you've given me enough chances but, I can't get through this without you. One more chance please, that's all I'm asking for." He grabbed her by her hands and pulled her closer to him.

Tamera shook her head, hating the effect he had on her. "I hate you, you know that?"

"No you don't," Jamal said as he hugged her. "I'm not going to let nothing happen to you as long as I have breath in my body, please believe me when I tell you this."

"I believe you," Tamera replied as she wrapped her arms around him and buried her face in his chest. Jamal kissed the top of her head. "What's going to happen to us, Jamal?"

"I'm working on something right now. I thought about just turning myself in but, I got a feeling Samir will still come after Shawn if I do and honestly y'all are safer if I'm on the streets and not locked up. What were you doing before I came around here?"

"I was doing my homework."

"Okay. I need to go home and do the same." Tamera looked at the ground when he looked at her. Jamal smiled. "I never noticed that before."

"Noticed what?" Tamera asked.

"You hardly give me eye contact unless you're mad at me. You're shy."

"No I'm not," Tamera blushed.

"Yes you are. I'm surprised I didn't break you out of that. Oh well, I broke you out of something else though…" Jamal smirked. Tamera looked up at him and punched him in his chest playfully. "I knew that would get your attention," Jamal laughed. He backed up as Tamera tried to hit him again.

"Whatever. You are so nasty." Tamera giggled.

"But you love me anyway," Jamal said as he gave her another hug.

"I don't hardly love you, boy," Tamera said with a huge grin on her face.

"I love you, though." Jamal kissed her. "I'll call you when I get in the house."

"Okay," Tamera watched him walk out of her backyard and down the alley until she couldn't see him anymore. She caught a chill that wasn't attributed to the autumn air and then saw a brief flash of Shawn yanking her to the ground. She shook her head and frowned, not exactly sure what she saw or why. She went back into the house to finish her homework.

Jamal was walking down the street towards his house when he heard a girl repeatedly shouting Maurice's name. He looked around to see if he saw Maurice but when he didn't, he continued on his way.

"Maurice!" Iesha shouted again.

Jamal turned around and spotted the girl from the arcade. "Shit man," Jamal mumbled to himself as the girl hurried over to him.

"What's up?" Iesha spoke cheerfully when she finally caught up to him.

"Nothing. What's up with you?" Jamal asked back trying to mask his annoyance with her.

"Nothing really. I'm calling you like, Maurice! And you just kept right on walking."

"I was looking around to see who was calling me but I didn't see you," Jamal lied.

"How come you ain't call me?" Iesha asked.

"I told you if you didn't hear from me it was because I was busy."

"Oh, I called you a couple times but some dude kept saying you weren't there. I was like damn this nigga wasn't lying when he said he's busy."

"That was my brother," Jamal lied. Sometimes it was him telling her that he wasn't home. He had already warned Shawn that if a girl called looking for Maurice to just tell her he wasn't there."

"You have a brother?" she asked.

"Yeah we're in the same grade but I got him by a year."

"Oh." Iesha began to play with her nails. "Can you walk me home?" she asked innocently.

"Where you live at?" Jamal asked, not recognizing her as a girl from around the way.

"25th and Turner Street."

Jamal frowned at how close she was to Tamera. Not thinking that he would get caught, he shrugged his shoulders and gave in while thinking of a good excuse if Tamera did see them together.

Iesha asked him little questions about his relationship with Tamera while they walked to the house, which was beginning to annoy the hell out of him. "Do you want to come in?" she asked when they got to her house.

"Naw, I need to make a run real quick," Jamal said, shaking his head.

"Please. I just want some company for a little while. Please," Iesha begged. She gave him a sexy smile.

Jamal sighed, thinking *"This young-girl about to get her ass in some serious trouble if she don't slow her role."* He walked in behind her and sat on her couch. They talked for a moment and then suddenly Iesha got up and started walking towards him, slowly. She unbuttoned her shirt and then unclipped her bra. Jamal couldn't believe how the young-girl was coming on to him, nor did he stop her. She leaned over top of him so that her large breasts were in his face. He put his hands on them and squeezed them before putting one in his mouth and sucking on her nipple. Before he knew it, Iesha was on her knees giving him a blow job and moments later he was ejaculating all over her chin and chest.

Jamal finally got a grasp at what just happened as he caught his breath. He fixed his pants and then walked over to her door.

"You're leaving?" Iesha asked seductively, stupidly believing that she had Jamal in the palm of her hands.

"Yeah," Jamal fumbled. "I told you I had some runs to make."

"Oh," she replied as she walked him to the door. "Are you going to call me later on?" She finished fixing her shirt, purposely doing it in the doorway so whoever was walking by could assume something happened.

"Huh?" she asked when Jamal didn't answer fast enough.

"Yeah, I'll holla," Jamal said as he backed away.

"See you Maurice," Iesha closed the door and Jamal turned around running into Chanda, who happened to have seen and heard enough to know what was going on.

"I sure as hell hope for your sake that you got some unknown sister we don't know about... Maurice."

Jamal knew he was caught then. "I can explain. It ain't even…"

Chanda interrupted him, "What it looks like? Don't even hand me that shit, Jamal. Who the fuck was that? Why are you coming outta that bitch's house and why do she wanna know if you're going to call her later on? And why the hell is she calling you Maurice? Jamal, I know you ain't have sex with that girl!"

"Not exactly," Jamal said, trying to make the situation not seem as bad as it was.

"What the hell do you mean *not exactly*?" Chanda asked, confused.

When Jamal didn't answer fast enough, she thought for a moment and then Bill Clinton and Monica Lewinsky came to mind. "You let her suck your dick?!" Chanda shrieked, disgusted. Jamal shushed her. "Don't shush me, Jamal. I don't believe you. You always got your ass in some shit. What's the matter? Tamera wouldn't do it for you?"

"I ain't go over there intending for that to happen. I was just walking her home."

"What the fuck for? I don't believe you, Jamal," Chanda said as she shook her head at him.

"Don't tell Tammy," Jamal pleaded.

"Why, are you going to tell her?"

"No, I…"

Chanda cut him off again. "I'm not about to let you lie or keep some shit like this from her so you can go around and get your dick sucked whenever a little hood rat bitch wants to do it for you." She shook her head again and looked at Jamal distastefully. "I ain't got time for this." She walked down the block as if she was going to catch the 3 bus home but then doubled back to Tamera and Deisha's house.

Deisha happened to be opening the door to look outside when she saw Chanda coming up the block. "Hey girl, I ain't know you were coming over."

Chanda came onto the porch. "Is Tamera here?" she asked, hastily.

"Yeah," Deisha said as she let her inside. "She's upstairs, why?"

"I need to talk to her. Tammy!" Chanda shouted up the steps.

"What's going on?" Deisha asked.

"Come here, Tammy!" Chanda called out again.

Tamera came downstairs. "What? What's wrong?"

"I hope you didn't get back together with Jamal," Chanda said as she crossed her arms over her chest and tapped her foot angrily.

"Why?" Tamera asked, sounding worried.

"Did you?" Chanda asked impatiently.

Tamera looked at Deisha and then looked at Chanda. "Yeah, why?"

Chanda threw her hands in the air in frustration. "What, Chanda?"

Yani

"Jamal just cheated on you." Chanda wasted no time in breaking the bad news.

"What? How… how, he just came from my house not too long ago?" Tamera asked as she caught a sinking feeling in her stomach.

"Yeah, well he just came from some girl's house over on 25th and Turner Street." Tamera stared with a hurt expression on her face. "And when I stopped him and asked him why the hell the girl was asking him to call her back, he ain't say anything. Oh and get this shit, the bitch was calling him Maurice." Tamera looked at Chanda confused.

"Maurice?" Deisha asked as she looked at Chanda.

"Yup, and when I asked him if he had sex with her, this nigga says not really," Chanda continued. Tamera's confused look became even more confused.

"In other words Tammy, she sucked his dick," Deisha said to her. Tamera covered her face and sat on the arm of the sofa. "Are you alright?"

"Where did you say you saw him again?" Tamera asked.

"25th and Turner Street," Chanda told her. Tamera got up and yanked the front door opened. "Where are you going?"

"I'ma beat her ass," Tamera said as she stormed out of the house.

Deisha and Chanda looked at each other surprised by Tamera's intentions. They had never seen her that angry before. They followed Tamera down the street.

"Which house?" Tamera asked angrily.

"I'll show you," Chanda told her. They walked on silent for a moment.

"Trifling bitch. She wants to suck on something, she's about to suck on my muthafucking fist, watch," Tamera spat.

"You're going to fight her?" Deisha asked.

"Over Jamal?" Chanda added.

"For the simple fact that everybody around here knew I was fucking with him and she's going to try to play me like my shit's the fuck sweet! I'ma kick her sweet ass! Don't think I'm sweet because I'm fucking quiet!" People that were nearby began to creep behind them sensing a fight.

"Right here," Chanda said, pointing to the house she saw Jamal come out of.

Tamera stopped a girl that was walking by. "Ay girl, what's the girl's name that lives here?"

"Iesha," the girl said. She looked at Tamera oddly as she took off her earrings.

Tamera pulled her hair back into a ponytail and then rolled it into a bun. "Hold my stuff," she told Deisha. "How old is she?" she asked the girl.

"Fifteen, I think." She sensed a fight also and decided to stick around. She never liked Iesha anyway and would be delighted to see her get her ass whipped.

Tamera frowned at how young she was and looked at her friends. "You know what? I don't even care. Tell her to bring her ass out here."

Chanda grabbed Tamera's arm. "Tammy…"

Tamera yanked away. "No, fuck that. I'ma kick a bone outta her young ass." She cracked her knuckles as she waited for the girl to come out. People started watching from across the street. Not sure what was about to happen, Iesha came to the door. The other girl told Iesha that another girl was out there because her brother wanted to talk to her. Like a fool, Iesha fell for it and came off of her steps.

"What's up?" Iesha asked Tamera.

"Is your name Iesha?" Tamera asked sweetly.

"Yeah," Iesha replied.

Tamera hauled off and punched Iesha in her mouth making her stumble back. "Trifling bitch!" She kicked the girl in her stomach. Iesha acted fast and grabbed Tamera's shirt and started swinging on her.

"Get her, Tammy!" Chanda screamed as her and others crowded around. Tamera slung the girl around and started giving her body shots as well as punches to her face, making her lose her balance.

"Fuck her up, Tammy! That's right!" Deisha screamed. Tamera got the girl on the ground and started stomping her.

"Somebody stop that fight before that girl breaks something," a witness chuckled. It looked like Tamera was trying to break her ribs.

"No don't stop the fight. I never liked that bitch no way!" another person yelled.

Two guys grabbed Tamera and started pulling her away. Tamera struggled against them telling them to let her go. Chanda and Deisha took a hold of her and started walking her down the street to calm her down while others helped Iesha up off the ground.

"Where my rings at?" Tamera asked as she tried to catch her breath. Deisha handed them to her. "Here."

Tamera looked through them and then took the one she wanted and gave the others back to Deisha. "Hold these for me."

"Where are you about to go?" Chanda asked.

"To Jamal's house. Wait for me at home." She walked around the corner.

Chanda looked at Deisha and they both started laughing. "They always said those quiet girls are the crazy ones."

"I never knew she had it in her," Chanda chuckled.

"Hey, like she said, don't fuck with her thinking she's sweet just because she's quiet," Deisha giggled.

"I think I want to come back around your way for when Tamera gets back," Chanda said. They chuckled more as they walked to Deisha's house.

Tamera walked to Jamal's house and knocked on the door. She fixed her hair, smoothing it to the back as best as she could as she waited patiently for him to come to the door. Shawn opened the door and looked at her.

"Hey, what are you doing here?" Shawn asked. He had just finished hearing the story from Jamal and knew she couldn't be there for a good reason.

"Is Jamal here?" Tamera asked, ignoring his question.

"Yeah, what's wrong?" Shawn stalled.

"Nothing, I just need to talk to Jamal for a moment. Can you tell him to come to the door?"

Shawn let Tamera in the house and closed the door behind her. He then went up to Jamal's room. "Tamera is downstairs and she does not look pleased. She looks like she just fucked somebody up. Or is about to," Shawn warned his brother.

"What did she say?" Jamal asked nervously.

"She just asked for you to come downstairs so she can talk to you."

Jamal got off of his bed. "Stay up here," he told his brother as he headed downstairs. When he saw Tamera for himself, he knew he was caught. "Hey," he said pleasantly.

"Fuck you, Jamal!" Tamera yelled as she threw the ring he gave her for her birthday at him.

Jamal looked down at the floor and then looked at her. "Can't we just talk about this?"

"You cheated with some bitch that's fifteen fucking years old that lives right up the fucking street from me and you want to talk! What the fuck do we have to talk about? Huh?!"

"I'm sorry," was all that Jamal could think to say.

"Sorry that you got caught? You come to my house talking that bullshit about you needing me to get through this shit you've got going and no less than the time it took for my stupid ass to forgive you, you go behind my back and cheat! How long has this shit been going on? How long have you been playing me like some nut?"

"It's not like that and you know it. It just happened today, I swear."

"Then what is it? What, I wasn't good enough for you so you had to let some fifteen year old bitch suck your dick?!"

"Damn," Shawn mumbled as he listened from upstairs. He had never heard Tammy that angry or use that much profanity in one conversation.

Not knowing what to say, Jamal tried to hug her to calm her down so he could talk to her but she hit him. She started wailing on him as she cried.

He grabbed her so she would calm down.

"GET OFF OF ME!!" Tamera screamed. Shawn came to the middle of the stairs to make sure they weren't fighting. Jamal let her go. "Don't come near me, don't call me, nothing! Fuck you and that bitch. And since you wanted to be so bold as to fuck her knowing how close she lived to me, maybe you wanna go pick her ass up off the ground." She yanked open his door and slammed it behind her. She walked back to Deisha's house trying not to cry. People recognized her from the fight and laughed about how she stomped Iesha. When she got into the house, she went up to her room, closed the door and laid in the bed crying into her pillow.

The next day, Tamera took the day off from school. Deisha tried to convince her to go but she refused, claiming she needed a break.

While at school, Jamal looked for her in advisory so he could try to talk to her. When he saw Deisha come to first period alone, he knew Tamera wasn't coming to school.

Jamal got into a small argument with Chanda in their second period Spanish class. He argued that she needed to mind her own business.

"You need to stop robbing cradles, letting jail bait suck your nasty dick." The class instigated but Jamal ignored them. He wasn't in the mood to be whipping anybody's ass.

Deisha had other things on her mind. She wanted to know why the girl was calling Jamal by Maurice's name. She knew that he had some type of involvement in whatever was going on. They sat by themselves during their lunch period.

"What did I do now?" Maurice asked as they sat down with their food.

"Who said you did anything?" Deisha replied.

"Because you've been looking at me all day like I did something."

"You wouldn't be thinking that way unless you did," Deisha told him.

"So you think because Jamal cheated that I cheated, too?" he asked her as he took a bite of his sandwich.

"No, but I know you know something about it. Why else would Jamal give that girl your name instead of his own? Did you know that little smut?"

"Man listen, me and Jamal were at the game store when these two girls walked over to us like they wanted to play the game we were playing. The chick Iesha tried to get me to talk to her friend but I told her that I had a girl already."

"Probably because she was ugly," Deisha smirked.

Maurice laughed. "Anyway, before they asked us if we had girlfriends, Jamal told the one chick his name was Maurice and I told the other chick that my name was Jamal. He told the chick that he had a girl but she came off all aggressive talking about I won't tell if you won't. I walked away after that. When Jamal came to where I was, I told him not to fuck with the girl and he said he wasn't because he didn't want to hurt Tammy. I ain't even know what happened until Chanda had that outburst in Spanish earlier. I heard Tammy was fighting last night but the dude told me he didn't know why. He just knew that she stomped the shit out of the girl," Maurice explained.

"Yup, and I was daring a bitch to jump in it because they would've gotten some of the same."

"So what all did Jamal do because he wouldn't say when I asked him?" Maurice asked.

"Jamal didn't do anything. Let's just say the girl did it all for him."

Maurice laughed. "Oh shit," They went back to their friends to finish having lunch with them.

When Deisha came home from school, she saw Tamera sitting on the couch watching T.V. She looked through the mail to see if she had anything and then tossed it on the counter.

"You look like hell," Deisha said as she looked Tamera over. "What did you do all day?"

"Nothing really. I just did my hair and went to the nail salon to get my hands and my feet done." Tamera was trying hard to show that she wasn't upset or hurt but Deisha could tell that she was.

"Your hair is cute," Deisha complimented.

"Thank you." She sat up on the couch. "So what happened in school today?"

Deisha dropped her book bag on the floor. "Nothing really. Chanda and Jamal were arguing."

"About what?" Tamera asked.

"Oh just how Chanda needs to mind her business and how Jamal should have enough class to at least cheat with a girl of age that didn't live up the street from you."

The phone rang as Deisha finished her last statement. "Hello," Tamera answered. The person on the other line wouldn't speak. "Hello…" Tamera said again. When she got the same results, she hung the phone up. "I hate when people do that."

"What, somebody was playing on the phone?" Deisha asked.

"Yeah," Tamera replied. The phone rang again and Tamera picked up the receiver with an attitude. "What?!"

"Tamera?" Jamal stammered, not expecting such hostility.

Tamera didn't respond right away. "Did you just call here?"

"Yeah," Jamal replied.

"Why you ain't say anything? No skip that, what do you want?"

"Can we talk?" Jamal asked.

"No, go talk to Iesha," Tamera snapped before hanging the phone up on him.

"That was Jamal?" Deisha asked.

"Yeah," Tamera mumbled as she ran her hand back and forth across the table and then looked up at Deisha.

"Why you ain't talk to him?"

"Deisha, if Maurice got his dick sucked by some little young bitch, would you be so forgiving?"

"Good point," Deisha replied. Tamera went up to her bedroom to start the homework that Deisha brought home for her.

Shawn and Chanda were in his bedroom. She was helping him with one of his English papers as she filled out college applications. They were barely talking and Shawn wasn't appreciating the silence.

"Why are you so quiet?" Shawn asked her.

"Huh?" Chanda asked, looking through some of her college applications.

"Why are you so quiet?" Shawn asked again.

"This whole situation with Jamal and Tamera is making me mad."

"It ain't got nothing to do with you, so you might as well not worry about it. That's between Jamal and Tamera. I been stopped trying to give him advice on his relationship let alone whatever else he does. He never listens to me anyway." Chanda looked at Shawn for a moment, tapping her pen. "What?"

"Nothing," she said as she looked back at her applications. "Well, I guess it's a good thing that Jamal pulled a bone headed move like that. Maybe since they broke up, Samir will leave Tammy out of this." Chanda shook her head. "I bet money that they get back together, though."

"No, I don't think they will. If you would've seen Tamera here that day, I think she's had enough."

"Shawn, I saw the ass whipping she gave that bitch, trust me, I know Tammy was pissed. But I also know she loves him hard. And I believe Jamal loves her a lot, too. I think when she gets over the anger, she'll forgive him and they'll be right back together." Chanda said.

The next couple of days at school were very uncomfortable for Tamera. It was hard to concentrate with Jamal constantly staring at her. She continued to ignore him despite her urges to hear what he had to say and forgive him.

She was standing on the balcony a week after her fight waiting for Chanda and Deisha to come out of the bathroom so they could go to lunch when Jamal stood next to her.

"What's up?" he asked her. Tamera looked at him as if he were crazy.

"Can we talk, now?"

"I thought I told you not to say anything to me," Tamera snapped at him.

"Babe, I know you're mad at me, but I'm trying to make it up to you. I love you, Tammy. And I know you love me, too. If you didn't, you wouldn't still be standing here."

Tamera fixed the straps to her book bag over her shoulders. "You are so right." She turned to walk away from him but he grabbed her by the arm.

Yani

She yanked away from him looking as if she was going to swing on him. Jamal backed away feeling hurt and began thinking that he had truly lost Tamera for good. Deisha and Chanda came out of the bathroom.

"What did he want?" Chanda asked, distastefully.

"He wanted to talk but I told him to leave me alone," Tamera explained.

Deisha could see the sadness in her face. "Come on y'all. I'm starving," she told her friends.

They went to the lunchroom to get their food. Not wanting to eat anything from the lunchroom, Tamera sat away from her friends. She put her earphones on and laid her head down on the table. Shawn saw her when he was coming back from the ALA CARTE line with his chicken, fries, juice and cake. He sat next to her and tapped her on her shoulder.

"Are you alright?" he asked her when she looked up.

Tamera smiled. "Yeah, I'm just a little tired, that's all." She laid her head back down.

"What are you listening to?" he asked. He leaned his head against hers and started bobbing his head to *Rock the Mic*, from the *State Property* Soundtrack. She laughed at how silly he was acting before resting her head back on the table. Shawn went to the table that Maurice and Jamal were sitting at.

"What's wrong with her?" Jamal asked.

"Why don't you go ask her?" Shawn suggested.

"She won't talk to me," Jamal replied as he took a bite out of his cheese pretzel.

Chanda and Deisha were coming from the ALA CARTE line also and saw Tamera sitting at the table by herself, so they sat with her. She looked up to see who it was and then laid her head back down.

"What's wrong, Tammy?" Deisha asked.

"I can't believe he did this to me," Tamera mumbled through tears.

Deisha started rubbing her back. "It ain't have anything to do with you personally. Jamal is just one of those guys who is greedy and won't pass up the opportunity to have some pussy."

"The only thing better than some pussy is some new pussy," Chanda said mocking Terrance Howard from the movie *The Best Man*. She was trying to make Tamera laugh.

Instead, Tamera stood up and blurted out, "I fucking hate his ass."

"What?" Chanda asked as Tamera started walking away.

"Tammy?" Deisha called after her. She grabbed her arm.

Tamera yanked away. "Get off of me," she snapped.

Deisha looked at Chanda, confused and then they followed her to the bathroom.

Maurice looked at Jamal and then continued eating his food without saying a word.

"What is wrong with you?" Deisha asked.

Tamera got a wet paper towel and wiped her face. "This is real crazy, man. He talked all of that trash when he thought I did something with Aaron and here he is going behind my back letting another bitch suck his dick."

"Look, this is bullshit. Don't be crying over his punk-ass. You knew he wasn't shit from the door when you first started talking to him. And we warned you but you didn't listen," Chanda said angrily.

Deisha stopped her. "I don't think she needs to hear this right now."

"And I don't want to hear it either. Don't comment on my shit," Tamera tossed her paper towel in the trash and snatched open the bathroom door as two girls were about to come in, scaring them. "Sorry, y'all." Tamera left the bathroom and went back to her seat. She put her earphones on to drown out the activity of the lunchroom.

As the weeks rolled on, things began to change a lot among Jamal and his friends. Both he and Shawn got their driver's license around the same time that their mother received a settlement from an accident she was in. She was going to buy Jamal a car but he declined stating he would rather have the money. Shawn took a car instead. Ms. Keyona bought him silver 1998 Ford Taurus. Shawn felt like he was on top of the world and used every opportunity he could to get behind his new wheel. He soon started teaching Chanda how to drive once she got her learner's permit.

Before Maurice's 18th birthday, he and Deisha had begun to argue more and more and it always seemed to be about Jamal. His birthday fell on a Saturday so Jamal made plans for them to hang out that weekend. Because of that, Maurice and Deisha celebrated his birthday the Friday before.

After Jamal and Tamera broke up, he started hanging on the streets again, shooting craps on 23rd and Turner Street with his friends, smoking weed and going back to his old ways. The night that Jamal and Maurice hung out for his birthday, they were in Jamal's bedroom smoking weed.

"I'ma get you blunted tonight," Jamal told Maurice. They spent a couple of hours in his room smoking weed, talking and laughing. Maurice found out that Jamal was still sleeping with the girl Iesha on a regular basis.

Within the next hour, Maurice was so high, he could barely see straight. What made it worse was he had to work the next day. Shawn had come home from work and as soon as he hit the top step, the smell of weed was so strong he could have gotten a partial high. He was about to open Jamal's door but Maurice staggered out. He almost bumped into Shawn. He smiled and nodded his head at him. His eyes were so small that they barely looked open. Jamal wasn't looking any better.

"What the hell, man?" Shawn coughed, waving his hand in front of his face. "Yo, Jamal you better do something about this shit before Mommy gets home. I don't feel like hearing her mouth tonight." Jamal and Maurice staggered down the steps laughing at nothing. Shawn followed behind them.

Maurice fell out on the couch and Jamal went into the kitchen looking for something to snack on. He grabbed the large size bag of Sour Cream and Onion potato chips and went back into the living room, munching on them. "Naw nigga, get your ass up. You ain't staying here."

"Hold up man," Maurice waited a moment before speaking again. "Yo, drop me off at my crib, Shawn."

"Naw canon, I'm tired. You better call Deisha and tell her to come walk you home. Plus my brakes acting funny," Shawn told him.

"Call her for me?" Maurice asked as he closed his eyes and put his arm over his face.

"No, get your ass up and call her yourself," Shawn retorted.

"Yo, you're drawing like shit right now. Damn, call her for me." Maurice laughed a little. "Ay yo 'Mal, I'm fucked up."

"You dig me," Jamal chuckled with him.

Shawn went into the kitchen and dialed Deisha's number. Tamera answered instead.

"Tammy, let me speak to Deisha real quick."

Tamera handed the phone to Deisha who had fallen asleep while she was studying. "Huh?" she answered in a sleepy voice.

"Come get Maurice from my house," Shawn said to her.

"What's wrong with him?" Deisha asked.

"Come see for yourself."

"Let me guess, Jamal?" When Shawn didn't respond, she sighed angrily. "I'm so sick of this shit." She hung the phone up and grabbed her coat. Shawn stayed in the kitchen until Deisha arrived. When she did, Jamal and Maurice had fallen asleep on the couch.

"They are high outta their muthafucking minds," Shawn told Deisha as he opened the door for her to come in.

Deisha looked at Maurice angrily trying not to be overwhelmed with how handsome he looked sleeping. She tapped him on his shoulder and he looked up. "Come on so I can walk you home." She tried to sound as calm as possible. *"Damn he looks good!"* she thought to herself. "Get up, boy."

"Alright," Maurice snapped. He leaned up slowly and then stood up. When he stretched, Deisha handed him a stick of gum. Maurice looked at it and then snatched it from her. "You ain't funny, Oprah."

"I'm not trying to be funny. It's just that weed don't smell that hot on you. And I told you about that Oprah shit." They left Shawn and Jamal's house and started walking towards Maurice's. He put his arm around her and started saying perverse things in her ear.

Deisha moved his arm. "Stop," she told him.

"What's your problem?" Maurice asked her.

"You're high," Deisha said with a frown.

"No I'm not," Maurice argued.

"Yes you are and it's pissing me off."

"Wow, one time and you're acting like this is an everyday thing. I was just trying to have fun on my birthday. My bad."

"You don't need to get high to have fun for your birthday, Maurice," Deisha replied.

"Here we go again, Oprah. I'm not even going to get into this shit, tonight." Maurice huffed as they walked down the street.

Deisha rolled her eyes at him. "Then don't," she snapped.

"You always gotta have the last fucking word."

"Who the hell are you cursing at?" Deisha retorted.

"Who the fuck do you think I'm cursing at? I'm getting tired of your mouth. You think I won't base the shit outta you. You need to be a fucking shrink because you have some serious issues. Go on Oprah and help some muthafucking body since you swear up and down that you are her." Maurice was heated.

"I'm going to ignore that shit. That weed got you talking tough," Deisha said angrily as she stuffed her hands in her coat pockets and walked ahead of him.

"No you're ignoring it because it's the fucking truth. They say the truth always comes out when a nigga drunk or high. You of all people should know that with your mom and all."

Deisha stopped walking again and stared at him. "I can't believe you just said that shit," she said in a hoarse voice as her eyes became teary. She began walking towards her house instead of Maurice's.

Maurice ran to catch up to her. "I'm sorry, I ain't mean it," he said as he tried to stop her.

"Get off of me," Deisha mumbled as she snatched away from him. "You meant that shit. You know you meant it."

"I'm sorry." Maurice apologized.

"I don't even know why I bother sometimes. Every time you get around Jamal…"

Maurice interrupted her, "Why is it always about Jamal?"

"Because it is! We never argue until he starts going through his shit. And then his shit rubs off on us because when you're around him you act like you can't think for yourself. I'm not high or drunk but that's the honest to God truth. And I'm not dealing with it anymore. Walk home by yourself." She walked away from him thinking he was going to come after her so they could talk it out. When she got to the next corner and he hadn't stopped her by then, she knew that he wasn't. She marched home alone as the tears fell from the hurt she felt over his comment about her mother.

Yani

Things weren't the same between Deisha and Maurice after his birthday and his remark on her mother. Deisha barely went to visit him at his house and their conversations on the phone were very brief. She was becoming miserable and the hope that their almost three year relationship could be saved, was dwindling.

While Tamera was out with her God Mother on Christmas Eve, Chanda hung out with Deisha as she wrapped her gifts.

"I don't know what to do," Deisha was saying. They had been talking about Maurice for the last hour. "I'm still not ready to talk to him yet because of what he said about my mom and he knows that shit was wrong," Deisha explained to Chanda. "It's like we don't click anymore after that."

"I don't know what to tell you. Maybe it's time for y'all to move on or maybe it isn't. Y'all have to decide. When you first told me what he said about your mom that blew my mind. I know you don't want to let him go because he's been the best thing that happened to you since Raheem died, but all good things don't last forever."

"I know," Deisha mumbled. "I was just hoping that something was still there." She curled a bow on one of the gifts that she wrapped.

"Then again, who knows? Maybe y'all need some time apart to see how much y'all mean to each other," Chanda told her.

Deisha sighed as the phone rang. She picked up the receiver. "Hello?"

"Deisha?" Maurice asked.

"Hey Maurice," Deisha smiled.

"What are you doing?" he asked her.

"I'm just wrapping up everybody's gifts. Why?"

Maurice was silent for a moment. He sighed and said, "We need to talk."

Deisha became quiet also and Chanda noticed her facial expression change. She knew that whatever Maurice said couldn't have been good.

"About what?" Deisha asked as she sat on the couch.

"This fighting and shit boo, it's not cool. Normally we make up and then everything is fine from there but this shit ain't fine. And I know what I said about your mom was fucked up, but our fighting goes further back than that. I try to talk to you but it don't seem like I'm getting anywhere. I don't know what to do anymore."

"And you think I do?" Deisha asked.

"I'm not saying that."

"Then what are you saying? Or what are you trying to say but are beating around the bush with it?"

"See, here we go again with the smart shit. All I wanted to say was maybe we need to separate for a while until we both are ready to see eye to eye. I mean, don't get me wrong, I still love you and everything. I just…" Maurice trailed off not knowing what else to say. Deisha couldn't believe that he was breaking up with her. "Are you still there?"

"Yes," Deisha said hoarsely.

Maurice sighed, knowing that he was hurting her. "I gotta go. I'ma holla at you later, alright?"

Not wanting to hear his voice anymore, Deisha hung the phone up without saying goodbye and stared at it.

"What happened?" Chanda asked.

"We just broke up," Deisha said in a low voice with tears in her eyes. She blinked them away, refusing to let them fall and got up so she could put the gifts under the tree.

"Are you alright?" Chanda asked her.

"I'll be okay," Deisha told her.

When Christmas arrived the next day, Deisha was not in the holiday spirit. Family members such as other aunts, her grandmother, and her cousins came over for dinner. She got dressed in a red and white sweater with a pair of straight leg jeans and stiletto shoes. Tamera was wearing a black and grey sweater with light blue denim jeans and her black hiking Timberland boots. She was trying to cheer Deisha up, but nothing seemed to work.

"Look on the bright side," Tamera said to Deisha. "Tomorrow we can go man hunting at Franklin Mills and shop." Deisha smiled but was still upset over her breakup with Maurice. She stayed upstairs in her room while her family was downstairs after dinner. Her aunt knocked on her door.

"Yes," Deisha answered as she wiped her face.

Michelle opened her door. "Why aren't you downstairs with your cousins?" She walked over to her and sat on her bed. "What's the matter?"

"Me and Maurice broke up yesterday," she leaned on her aunt's shoulder as the tears spilled out of her eyes.

"Aw baby," Michelle said as she rubbed her niece's shoulder. "Why?"

"Because we were constantly fighting and he was tired of it. He acted like I wasn't tired of it, too. I wanted to try to work it out but he didn't." Deisha hadn't told her aunt what Maurice said about her mother. That would have taken him out of her good graces.

"Honey, it will be okay. One thing I am sure of is that boy loves you more than anything in this world. And I knew that by how he kept you company when Raheem was killed. He'll come back around. You two just need to sit and talk things out. You can't have a successful relationship without communication. Maurice just better hope when he comes back that it isn't too late. And trust me he will be back, crawling on his ashy hands and knees."

Deisha laughed a little and sniffed. "Thank you, Aunt 'Chelle."

"You're welcome, sweetheart."

Tamera knocked on her door.

"Yes," Deisha answered again.

Yani

Tamera peeped into the room. "It's hard to entertain your family, y'all. They're getting restless. Oh, and Deisha you have a guest."

"Who is it?" Deisha asked.

"Maurice," Tamera smiled.

"I told you," Michelle said as she winked at her niece. Deisha got up and wiped her eyes, smiling.

"Told her what? I wanna know. I want to do some female bonding," Tamera pouted.

"Girl, we bonded with you when you and Jamal broke up," Michelle said, following Deisha out of her room. Deisha went downstairs and into the living room where Maurice was waiting for her.

"Hey," Deisha spoke.

"What's up?" Maurice spoke back.

"Nothing. What are you doing here?" Deisha asked.

"I came to drop off your gifts."

"Why did you buy me anything if you wanted to call it quits?"

"Because I already bought it for you before we talked last night and I never said that I wanted to call it quits. I just said that we needed some space from each other."

Deisha looked at the floor. "Same thing."

"No it's not."

She waited a moment before speaking. She couldn't help the smile that spread across her face when she asked, "What did you get me?"

Maurice smiled back at her and reached into his duffle bag. He pulled out two wrapped boxes and a wrapped gift on top of them.

"Damn," Deisha chuckled. "I know you didn't wrap these."

Maurice laughed as Deisha tore open the first gift which was a new pair of Timberland boots. The second box had a hat and scarf set that Deisha liked when they were passing through Old Navy a few weeks before. The last gift was a silver locket with Deisha and Maurice's name on a heart. She looked at it without an expression on her face.

"What's wrong?" Maurice asked as he stared at her. Deisha shook her head. Maurice took it from her and walked behind her. She pulled her hair up as he fastened the chain around her neck. There was a light clanking noise as it touched the *Raheem* chain that she wore. "Don't take this off," he instructed.

"I won't," Deisha said as she shook her head side to side.

"Damn man, can a nigga get some love on Christmas? You have all your peoples here. I should be getting my black ass home so my peoples don't think I'm pulling a disappearing act." Deisha laughed and gave him a hug. "I love you," he told her as he squeezed her tightly. "I've gotta go. But before I do," he reached into his pocket and pulled out a misled toe and dangled it above their heads. Deisha looked up and started laughing. He leaned over and kissed her for a brief moment before letting her go. As he walked to the door, Deisha remembered that she had a few gifts for him also.

"Hold up," Deisha told him as she went over to the tree. She grabbed three wrapped packages after rummaging through the ones that hadn't been opened and gave them to him. "There's one in there for Keisha, too."

"Alright," he replied as he put them in his duffle bag. "I'll call you later on so we can talk about everything," he told her as went to the front door.

"Okay," Deisha agreed.

"Tell everybody that I said Merry Christmas and all that other good shit. I know your aunt cooked too, so you better save me a plate."

Deisha laughed again, "I will." She closed the door behind him, still smiling. She gathered up the things he bought her for Christmas and went to her room to put them away when Tamera knocked on her door again.

"Yes?"

Tamera peeped in the room. "What did Maurice get you?" she asked.

"I'll show you later after everybody leaves. We might get back together, though." Deisha smiled.

"That's what's up. Well, you have another visitor, Ms. Popular."

"Damn, who is it now?"

"It's a surprise," Tamera smiled.

Deisha started following Tamera downstairs. "Y'all better not be getting ready to start any dumb shit. Y'all know I do not like surprises," she said just before reaching the bottom step and coming face to face with her mother.

"Merry Christmas sweetie," her mother said excitedly as if Deisha would be happy to see her. She moved over to hug her but Deisha took a step back with a look on her face that suggested she might start swinging.

"Deisha," her aunt called out to her with a look of warning on her face.

Deisha looked at her aunt as if she would hit her too for allowing this set up. Eavesdropping from the kitchen, her aunts and grandmother noticed the silence and suddenly felt uncomfortable. She shook her head. "I know it's Christmas and everything, but I'm not about to give up any false pretenses and act like her being here is giving me a merrier Christmas than I was already having." She turned and went back up to her room. Michelle was going to stop her but Janelle intervened.

"It's okay Michelle. No need to try to make her do something she doesn't want to do."

Michelle sighed seeing that the situation was hopeless. "Well, come on in the kitchen and fix yourself a plate. Momma is here with Natalie and Shantell."

They went into the kitchen. Their mother Erica, originally had five children; the twins Natalie and Shantell who were the oldest, a boy named Lamar who was killed when Michelle was 15, Michelle and the youngest,

Janelle. Her eyes lit up when Janelle came into the kitchen. The last time she laid eyes on her was before she went into rehabilitation four years prior. She hugged her daughter tightly.

"Hi Ma," Janelle spoke as she squeezed her mother back.

"Hey baby," Erica said as she took a step back to get a good look at her. Janelle hugged her other sisters. They felt the same as Deisha did about her visit but decided to be more pleasant. Neither was pleased with her drug addiction and the effect that it had on Deisha but didn't intervene like Michelle had. "You look good," her mother commented.

Janelle posed with her hands on her hips. "I just took it one day at a time."

"Well, sit down and eat so we can talk," her mother told her. Erica had a few words for her daughter. "So how long have you been back?" she asked. She really wanted to ask how long she had been clean but didn't want to be so blunt about it.

"Well, it was a two year program that set us up with new jobs after we finished the 12 step program. That was one thing I started that I was able to finish. So anyway, they set me up with this secretarial job at a law office and they gave me an apartment. It felt so good to be able to do something positive with myself that I just told myself there was no way I was going back to that stuff. So I've been clean for more than three years."

"That's wonderful," her mother told her, with her other three daughters chiming in with agreement. "So, how does Deisha feel about all of this? Is she still bitter about it or is she coming around?"

Janelle was quiet for a moment and then cleared her throat as she swirled her fork around her collard greens. "She's still angry. I'm hoping that she'll come around and understand how much of a hard time I was having during that period."

"Well there are some things you need to understand too, sweetheart. Not that I'm coming down hard on you or anything, but I always taught you how to be responsible and strong and to never start anything that you can't finish. Now you say that was a hard time for you, and I'm sure you have many excuses for why you turned to that white powdered devil, but the fact of the matter is, you gave up. You let that girl down and put her through some serious hell. So don't think that you're the only victim here because lord only knows how that poor girl would've turned out if Michelle hadn't stepped in," Erica scolded her daughter.

Erica's daughters were silent for a moment, waiting to see if Janelle would respond. Janelle wanted to defend herself but found no defense for her actions. They continued to sit quietly when Deisha purposely came into the kitchen to slice herself off a piece of cake, hoping to start a conflict.

"That's a sharp set that you have on," Shantell complimented her.

"Thank you," Deisha smiled as she grabbed the vanilla ice-cream out of the refrigerator to add to her cake.

"How old are you now?" Natalie asked.

"I just turned 18 back in September."

"That's right you and Tiffany are around the same age. You know, she just had a baby not that long ago. She had a little boy."

"Oh, that's nice," Deisha replied not at all surprised by the news. She always thought of her cousin as being a hot ass.

"Yeah, Deisha runs track and has all kinds of colleges looking at her. This girl is going to be special." Janelle bragged as if she had something to do with how good Deisha turned out.

Deisha frowned her face and was about to make a smart remark but caught her Aunt Michelle looking at her, letting her know to keep her mouth shut.

"I can't wait until the day comes when she makes me a grandmother," Janelle added.

That right there was enough for Deisha. She couldn't hold her tongue any longer. "Why? So I can turn out like you. And correct me if I'm wrong but wouldn't that make Aunt 'Chelle the grandmother. She was more of a mother to me than you were."

"Got damn it," Michelle mumbled and shook her head.

"Deisha, please don't do this," Janelle begged.

"Do what? I didn't do shit. Excuse my mouth, Nana."

"Deisha!" Michelle yelled. "You better watch your mouth and show your mother as well as the rest of us some respect in my house."

"Respect? How do you expect me to respect a crack-head? How do you expect me to respect a woman who clearly had no respect for herself? She left me in that house by myself starving while she went out to get high and party. Yeah, she deserves a lot of respect for that."

Tamera and Deisha's cousins listened from the living room while they played her Playstation 2.

"Baby, if you would just listen and try to understand how hard those times were for me especially after I had you." Deisha looked as if she was about to slap the color out of her mother's face so Michelle grabbed her.

"I know you're not trying to throw blame!" she screamed hysterically. "You want somebody to blame, blame yourself for your weaknesses! Don't try to put that shit off on me! I didn't ask for that shit!" Deisha began to cry as she yanked away from her aunt so she could snatch her mother bald. Her other aunts got up to help keep Deisha from getting to her mother.

"Tamera, come get her and take her upstairs, please." Michelle called into the living room.

Tamera's heart was racing as she watched the family conflict. She put her arm around Deisha and took her up to her bedroom so she could calm down.

Shantell, Natalie and Erica looked at Janelle as if they could finish what Deisha didn't get the chance to start.

"Why y'all looking at me like that? She ain't get her mouth from me," Janelle said defensively, missing the big picture.

"That's not the point," Shantell argued. "It's a good thing she didn't pick up any of your other habits."

"What are you trying to say?" Janelle retorted.

"You know damned well what I'm trying to say. What you fail to realize is that it was you who abandoned that girl like that. You made those decisions. Instead of owning up to what you did, you wanna point the finger at everyone else not realizing you got three coming back at you," Shantell replied.

"I don't even want to think of how that girl would have turned out if Niecie ain't stepped in," Natalie added.

"Oh, will y'all cut the shit? I am so sick of everybody acting like I'm the devil and Niecie is Jesus fucking Christ," Janelle hissed.

"You better watch your damned mouth around me, gal. Don't use the Lord's name in vain because believe it or not, He's been damned good to you despite your sins," Erica snapped.

"And I never said I was Jesus, Janelle. I did what I thought was best for Deisha."

"What you should've done was minded your own business. Nobody asked you to intervene. Y'all talking about what a good job Niecie did with Deisha when her mouth is grotesque. But do I see y'all thanking her for that?"

"No, her mouth is like that because I taught her not to be afraid to speak her mind and to not let anyone think they can just walk all over her and treat her anyway they want to. I also taught her self-respect, something that you should've done your damn self," Michelle retorted.

"You should've minded your own business just like I said," Janelle said again.

"How can you say that? DHS was bound to step in sooner or later. What would you rather have: some stranger taking Deisha and not knowing if she was safe or having family take her and know she's in good hands?"

"Oh bull-shit, Michelle. The only reason you took her is because you can't have kids of your own. Can you say, *abortion*?" Janelle said with an evil expression on her face.

A vein in Michelle's neck had begun to show from her anger. Her mother and her sisters looked at her having no idea what Janelle was talking about. "You fucking crack-head bitch!" she shrieked. She picked up an empty pot and threw it at Janelle barely missing, but catching her on the shoulder. "Get out of my house before I rip your fucking head off!"

"You ain't got to tell me but once. I don't mind leaving this raggedy muthafucka," Janelle said as she grabbed her plate.

"For it to be so raggedy, you're marching kinda fast with that damned plate. You better savor the flavor because that's the last time you'll ever eat in this house," Michelle yelled as her sister left out of the house and slammed the door behind her. She was breathing heavy, feeling embarrassed, hurt and ashamed.

"I didn't know you had an abortion, Niecie," her mother said as she looked at her. Michelle glanced at her mother and sighed. "And I certainly didn't know that was the reason why you couldn't have children. When did this happen?"

"When I was fifteen. It was a little while after Lamar was killed."

"Why didn't you tell me?" her mother questioned.

"I was scared, momma. We were still grieving over Lamar and I didn't want to add to the pain we were feeling," Michelle said with tears in her eyes.

"See that's the problem with you all. You're too damn distant. You're always thinking you got to handle things by yourselves and that you can't come to one another when you need help. I didn't raise you that way. I raised you to stick together no matter what. Now you may think that having that abortion would give you a chance to put the wrong things right, but you killed the chance of you ever being able to have life beyond your own. I'm not downing you. I know you thought what you did was for the best and maybe it was. But you have got to start finishing the things that you start," Erica told her children.

"That's one of the reasons why I took Deisha in," Michelle said as she became choked up. Shantell and Natalie comforted her.

"I know, and you did a wonderful job, despite what your sister said. So don't you even worry about it. Now wipe your face and slice me off another piece of cake. And I know that you stole my recipe." They laughed as Michelle sliced off cake for everyone and they sat down to enjoy the rest of their Christmas, reminiscing on their youth.

At Chanda's house, mostly all of her father's family was there. A few of Renee's family members came over also to spend the holiday with them. Chanda was sitting in the living room watching old episodes of Martin as she patiently waited for Shawn to arrive. Despite her disdain for the school uniform colors, she found herself wearing a white sweater and a pair of black leather pants and her black Timberland boots. She twisted the front and the back of her hair up and left the ends spikey. One of Renee's nephews was immediately attracted to her. He came into the living room also and sat in a chair across from her.

"How are you doing?" he spoke.

"What's up?" Chanda asked as she continued to watch Martin act a fool on television. She began to laugh. "This nigga is stupid."

"I know right? But he's still funny as shit though." Chanda nodded her head in agreement. "What's your name?"

Yani

"Chanda."

"Oh, my name is Chris," Chanda didn't reply and that made him feel a little uncomfortable but he still tried his luck. "How old are you?" he asked.

"Eighteen," Chanda replied, sure to keep the conversation short and sweet.

"Damn, you're that old?"

Chanda looked at him crossly. "How old did you think I was?"

"Fifteen or sixteen. Damn, I guess it's no point in me asking you if you have a dude."

"Actually, he should be here any minute," Chanda smiled.

"Damn, let me take my little young ass back downstairs with my brothers before I play myself. Nice talking to you anyway." Chris made his escape into the basement. Chanda shook her head at the boy that tried to talk to her. Moments later, the doorbell rang. She looked at herself in the mirror to make sure that she looked okay before she opened the door.

"Merry, merry," she said with a huge grin on her face.

Shawn threw his arms around her and squeezed her tightly. "Merry, merry," he said back to her. "I got all the stuff you asked for; those CDs, the jeans you were looking for and those movies."

"Aww thanks babe. I got your stuff too. I had to go to like three different game stores to find NBA 2k2." Chanda told him after they kissed.

"Thanks babe," Shawn looked in the kitchen. "You got a lot of people in here. Can a nigga still eat?" he asked.

"Yeah I already put a plate to the side for you," Chanda told him as she grabbed his hand and started leading him to the kitchen.

Shawn heard a lot of noise coming from the den. "What's going on in there?"

"Oh, Sixers and the Lakers are playing."

"Aw shit, I forgot. Can I watch, too?"

"You're supposed to be keeping me company, not watching the game with them," Chanda moped.

"And I am, boo. But I've been waiting for this game for a minute." He tapped on the door and went inside. He shook Chanda's father's hand and said hello to everyone before sitting down to watch the game. Moments later Chanda came in and brought Shawn his plate. She sat next to him and they watched the game, hype, loud, cheering and cracking jokes. Even though her brother wasn't there with her, it was one of the best Christmases that Chanda had in a long time.

CHAPTER 7
SLIP UPS

Jamal was finally ready to swallow his pride and do whatever it was that he had to do to get Tamera back. He realized how miserable he was without her and knew that the only reason he was acting the way he was again was because he wasn't with her anymore. He was willing to do any and everything he had to do to get her back. He wrote her a letter, which she tossed in a dresser drawer pretending that she never received it. He gave her shout outs on the radio and dedicated songs to her but she continued to treat him like just another brother that she was passing by. He was ready to give up but continued taking suggestions from Maurice and Shawn. Shawn suggested he ignore her and give her the impression that he was no longer interested.

Tamera was beginning to get worn out by the different tactics that Jamal was using to get her attention. Just as she was ready to get back together with him, she noticed the silent treatment he had begun to give her. She was starting to get confused. She wanted to get back together with him but refused to be the one doing the crawling. She was trying to come up with a plan to make him come to her. Valentine's Day was approaching and she refused to spend that day alone like she did Christmas, so she knew she had to act fast.

While sitting in advisory one morning, Tamera heard an announcement on the loudspeaker about a talent show/musical that the school was having in honor of the small learning community Excel, for all of their performances throughout the city and decided to audition. Before she had a chance to, Chanda came over to her and suggested she sign up.

Tamera declined, wanting to keep her performance a secret. She went into the auditorium and auditioned singing *Fallin'* by Alicia Keys and blew the director of the talent show away. Little did Tamera know, a guy from Philly International Record label was in the auditorium to meet with the director and she caught his attention. He scribbled her name down planning on coming back to see her perform during the show.

A few days later, Shawn and the rest of the University City Jaguars ripped the Franklin Electrons apart. Without their starting guard, they didn't have a chance. Shawn was going to celebrate with Chanda but she told him to celebrate with his team since they were still undefeated for the season.

The day of the talent show came quickly. Tamera came to school in her usual uniform of a white button down blouse with a black and white striped tie, a pair of black Dickie pants with her black Timberland boots. She pinned her hair up in a fabulous style and pretended it was a normal day. Chanda and Deisha were waiting for her after their third period class so they could go to lunch, but she told them to go without her because she was staying behind to get help with her Physics II lab. When her friends were gone, she went straight to the auditorium to get changed for the program.

Tamera changed into a pair of faded, light blue skinny jeans with gray knee boots and a matching gray form fitting sweater. Another young lady that was performing sat next to her to see if she was ready. They talked while the auditorium was filling up.

"Have you seen Tamera?" Deisha asked her friends.

"Naw, she said she was going to meet us down here because she was getting help with a Physics Lab or something," Shawn said.

"I told her she should've been in this talent show but she told me she didn't want to," Chanda said.

"You didn't see her, Jamal?" Maurice asked.

"Nope," Jamal replied, still acting as if he could care less about her.

The curtains were drawn so the performers couldn't be seen. Tamera peeped from behind them to see if she saw her friends. When she saw Jamal easing his way into a row to sit down, butterflies filled her stomach. She began to pace back stage.

Her friend Angie came over to her when she noticed how nervous she had become. "What's wrong, girl?"

"I don't think I can do this. I'm nervous," Tamera said with a helpless look on her face.

"Oh no girl, I'll be damned if you back out now as good as you sound on that stage," Angie told her. She began imitating Ike Turner. "Now what I need is for you to get out on that stage Anna Mae, and sing the song like I told you to sing it." Tamera roared with laughter. "You've got to g-e-e-eet up from WAY in here. You better put some stink on this muthafucka."

They both fell out laughing. "Seriously though, you gotta go out there. You have an awesome voice and people need to hear it. Your voice is beautiful. You sound too good to back out," Angie told Tamera before giving her a hug.

The lights were dimmed and the Principal quieted the students down. Tamera was the first act for the show. A piano was rolled out to the center of the stage behind the curtains. Though the person could not be seen because the curtains were drawn, it was obvious that someone was lying on top of the piano.

Tamera started *Fallin'* off Acapella. When she got to the chorus, the curtains were drawn and Tamera sat on the side of the piano as her friends cheered for her loudly and clapped.

"I'll be damned, that little bitch said she wasn't going to be in it!" Chanda exclaimed. She glanced over at Jamal and wasn't surprised to see the blank expression on his face. That was the first time he heard Tamera sing. He knew she had a voice, but he had no idea she was that good. When she was done, she received a standing ovation.

At the end of the assembly, Tamera's friends were waiting outside for her. When she came over to them, Chanda pinched her.

"Ouch, what was that for?" Tamera asked as she rubbed her arm.

"Because you told me that you weren't going to be in the show and you lied," Chanda said as she wagged her finger at her.

"I wanted to surprise y'all," Tamera smiled as she glanced at Jamal.

"Shocked the shit outta me," Maurice said. "I was like damn, look at Tammy trying to be all sexy on the piano and shit. With her fuck 'em girl boots on." They laughed together.

"I really sounded okay?" Tamera asked her friends.

"Hell yeah," Shawn told her as he pulled his car keys out. "Somebody needs to sign you or something."

"Well I'd love to shoot the shit with y'all but this little nigga gotta get to work," Maurice told his friends. He slapped Jamal and Shawn a handshake.

"You and me both. Shawn can you take us to the Gallery, please?" Deisha asked sweetly.

"What the fuck do I look like, a got damn taxi driver? Are you giving me money for gas?" Shawn asked playfully.

"Hell no, I'm not giving you money for gas as much as you eat at my aunt's house, nigga," Deisha retorted.

"Shit, you ain't giving me no gas or ass so what the fuck… joke, joke!" Shawn said as he jumped back when he saw the look on Maurice's face. They laughed as they walked to his car, leaving Tamera and Jamal standing alone. She cleared her throat and started to walk past him but he stopped her.

"Are you ready to talk now?" he asked her.

"I didn't say that," Tamera replied meaning quite the opposite.

"Judging by the song you were singing, I think you are. Plus you act like you were waiting for me to say something to you."

"Call me tonight and we can talk then. Right now I need to get home and watch this tape so I can see my performance."

"Alright," Jamal agreed as he watched Tamera walk away feeling good that they were at least on speaking terms.

Later that evening, Tamera and Jamal talked on the phone for over two hours, deciding to give their relationship another try. They also had a chance to discuss the situation with Samir.

"So far, me and Shawn came up with a plan to take you to my uncle's house in Germantown. I told him about what was going on and I asked him if he could let y'all stay there until all of this is straightened out just in case Samir's threats were real. He doesn't have a problem with it. He just told me to make sure I covered my ass."

"This is scary. I feel like I'm in a movie or something," Tamera replied.

"Naw boo, this shit is real. And like I said before, I'm sorry about dragging you into this. I ain't think he would take it this far."

"Well, what's done is done," she told him. "So what are you getting me for Valentine's Day?" Tamera asked with a huge grin on her face.

"Who said I was getting you something?" Jamal joked as he smiled also.

"You're trying to get back in my good graces you must have something special planned for Valentine's Day."

"I'm already in your good graces. If I wasn't, you wouldn't have been on the phone with me this long."

"Not hardly," Tamera smirked.

"Well if it's not that, it's because you still love me," Jamal said arrogantly.

"Boy, I don't hardly love you," Tamera lied.

"We'll see on Valentine's Day."

"Where are we going? What are we doing?" she asked.

"It's a surprise. But look, I have to get this homework done. I just want to tell you that I missed you like crazy. I messed up big time when I did what I did with that girl, but I want you to know I never meant to hurt you. You're the best thing that's happened to me and if you hadn't seen past the streets, and the hustling and trouble that I was getting into and gave me a chance, I don't know where I would be right now. I love you babe, and I don't want to lose you again. You're it for me, okay?"

"Okay," Tamera blushed. Her heart fluttered as she listened to Jamal pour his heart out to her.

"Damn you're not going to tell me you love me back?" Jamal asked her. Tamera laughed. "Alright, be like that. You're going to tell me one of these days. I'ma make you say it one way or another. I have my ways. And you know of them well. And in case you forgot, I can refresh your memory."

Tamera laughed even harder at how perverse Jamal was being on the phone. "Get off the phone you little freak," she told him.

"Alright, see you in school tomorrow." He hung up the phone and Tamera sighed. She felt good now that they were back together. She took the phone back to Deisha's room.

"So what happened?" Deisha asked.

"We're going to get back together. I think we'll get through this," Tamera replied

"Yeah, Jamal loves you and he was so miserable without his boo," Deisha told her with a smile.

Tamera blushed. "I need to finish my homework, but I'll be back so we can talk some more."

"Okay. And by the way, girl you were so awesome on stage today. I mean you're voice is really great," Deisha said.

"Thanks girl," Tamera smiled before closing her door and going back to her room.

Valentine's Day came quickly. Jamal had special plans for Tamera. He had her favorite flowers, white roses, delivered to her house that morning. He picked her up and took her to see *Diary of a Mad Black Woman* by Tyler Perry at the Merriam Theatre. Afterwards, they went to dinner and Jamal took her to another hotel room where they spent the rest of the night intimately.

Chanda and Shawn weren't too big on Valentine's Day. They showed how much they loved each other every day out of the year, so to them it was just another day. They stayed at Chanda's house playing video games and enjoying each other's company.

Deisha and Maurice went to the movies and grabbed an early dinner at Maggianos. They went to his house to be together since Keisha was out with Manny for Valentine's Day and his mother wasn't home either. They began kissing, caressing and undressing each other, getting into it. While Deisha was on top, Maurice's mother came in without knocking. She gasped at what she saw. Deisha screamed and jumped off of Maurice, covering herself with the sheets. Ms. Brown left his room and slammed the door behind her.

"Oh-my-God!" Deisha squealed. "I can't believe she just caught us." She jumped out of his bed and started throwing her clothes on faster than a runway model in between sets.

"I don't believe this shit, man. I ain't never going to hear the end of it. I swear man, I ain't." Maurice said as he put his clothes on as well.

"Oh my God, oh my God," Deisha repeated. She brushed her hair to the back and snatched a rubber band off of Maurice's wrist and put her hair into a ponytail. She looked at him and sighed. "I'm not going down there."

"You have to, boo. We gotta face the music."

"Can't I just crawl out of your window or something?"

Maurice laughed and grabbed her hand. "Come on." They walked downstairs and Maurice looked around. He was about to make a clean break for it but was stopped in his tracks by the sound of his mother's very angry voice.

"Maurice, I know damn well you are not about to walk out of my house and not say anything like nothing happened," she said furiously. Maurice turned to face his mother and sighed. "One of y'all better say something."

"Mom, I'm sorry," Maurice replied, not knowing what else to say.

"I don't want to hear it, Maurice. How dare you disrespect my house like this? What the hell do you think this is; a got damn motel?"

"Mom," Maurice said.

Ms. Brown interrupted him. "Not one damn word. You better not bring her here anymore. And I mean that shit," she stormed back into the kitchen and began slamming things around. Maurice left the house and walked Deisha home in silence. He didn't say anything until they got to her doorway.

"You know my mom doesn't like you," he said.

"Wow, tell me something that I don't know. I just never knew why."

Maurice touched her *Raheem* chain. "Because of this. She feels as though you shouldn't be wearing it if you're with me."

"Well, this isn't any of her business or her concern. Ain't like I'm cheating because he's dead."

"Well, that's why. But all that matters is I love you. And even though she just caught my naked ass boning the girl that she's not too particular about, happy Valentine's Day anyway." He leaned over and gave her a kiss. "Damn man, if I would've known she was gonna tell me not to bring you back, I would've just finished what I was doing."

Deisha smacked his arm. "Go home Maurice, before you get me in even more trouble." Maurice laughed as he walked off of her porch and started going home.

Jamal kept his promise of reminding Tamera that he had ways of making her tell him she loved him. He worked her over better than he ever had. It was the best sex that Tamera had ever experienced.

The next morning, Deisha knocked on Tamera's door. It was past twelve o'clock and she was still asleep. She drew the blinds so the sun would shine in. "Wake up, girl!" Deisha yelled playfully.

Tamera opened her eyes and squinted. She rubbed them and then threw the blankets over her head. Deisha pulled the covers back and sat next to her.

"Damn girl, what time did you get in last night?" Deisha asked.

"Like 2 o'clock," Tamera said in a husky, sleepy voice.

"Jamal must've put something on your ass, girl. What did y'all do and where did y'all go?"

Tamera chuckled. "We went out to eat. He took me to see *Diary of a Mad Black Woman*. He bought me flowers and he rented a hotel room. He gave me a massage with coconut oil and we... you know," she covered her face and laughed. "Then we fell asleep. We woke up like twelve something and took a shower together and ended up doing it again in the shower. He washed my hair, we got dressed and then he brought me home."

"Damn girl, I told you Jamal had it bad for you. Well, you had more fun than me," Deisha said as Tamera grabbed some under clothes and a towel to take her shower.

"Why? What happened between you and Maurice?"

"We went out to the movies and we got something to eat, too. We went back to his house and started getting into it. Why did his mom come busting up in his room and catch us?" Tamera gasped and covered her mouth before breaking out into a hysterical laughter. "It's not funny. She told Maurice not to bring me back to the house. We left and he walked me home laughing like it was a joke."

Tamera laughed some more. "I'm sorry. I don't think that lady likes you."

"She doesn't. And her reason is really stupid."

"What's her reason?" Tamera asked.

Deisha tapped the *Raheem* chain that was hanging around her neck. "She thinks it's inappropriate for me to be wearing this if I'm with her son."

"That ain't none of her business," Tamera replied as she put on her shower cap.

"Yeah, my words exactly. But fuck her, shit. I don't like the bitch either. Then Maurice little silly ass says if he knew his mother was going to get like that, he would've just finished what he was doing." Tamera burst into laughter again. "That shit is not funny. Hurry up and get dressed. I need you to go to this lady house with me so I can see how my prom dress is coming along.

"Alright," Tamera replied.

A few weeks later, Shawn and the U-City Jaguars played against Gratz in the championship. Chanda wasn't able to attend because she came down with the flu. Shawn sat in the locker room rubbing his hands together, feeling nervous

His coach sat next to him. "Are you alright, Shawn?" he asked.

"Yeah, I'm cool. I'm just a little nervous," Shawn replied.

"Well, just remember that you have college scouts there. Bring you're A game and don't hog the ball. Pass the ball, play defense and don't be scared to take the open shot. Okay?"

"Okay Coach," Shawn agreed. The team left the locker room and started warm-ups. Shawn immediately got excited and began showing off before the game. It started off with him and Rasheem Burton hitting three 3 pointers back to back. They were neck and neck at the beginning of the first quarter but by the end of the first half, they were losing by 15 points.

When they got to the locker room, their coach began snapping on them.

"What the hell is wrong with you guys? You act like you haven't had a lick of practice." Shawn was leaning up against some lockers with a towel over his head. The coach looked at him and Rasheem. "And what's the matter with you two? You're supposed to be the heart and soul of this team and you're playing like you don't give a damn. What's with the damn turnovers? You're throwing up so many got-damn bricks you'd think you were rebuilding homes for Temple. Now I don't know about you, but I didn't come this far to lose and go home with absolutely nothing. Shawn, you're the captain of this team, you better talk to these guys." He left the locker room, pissed.

Shawn remained quiet. He felt as though he wasn't the only one on the team and he shouldn't have to always take responsibility when things went from bad to worse. He waited until it was time to come back onto the floor before he said, "Y'all know what we have to do." They went back on the court and started shooting around until the whistle was blown.

The Jaguars were making an incredible come up in the third quarter. They were making plenty of stops, forcing turnovers and dominating in the paint. By the middle of the third quarter, they had gone on a 26-8 run and by the end of that quarter the Jaguars had a 3 point lead making the Gratz Bull-Dogs sweat.

As soon as the final quarter started, a junior named Kevin got the steal and threw it to Shawn for a fast break. Just as Shawn was about to drive through the lane for an easy lay-up, one of the players gave him a hard foul, which the U-City fans felt should've been a flagrant. Shawn was on the floor holding his wrist. Rasheem and another player, who was also a junior named Antoine, received technical fouls for arguing with the referee about not calling the flagrant.

Shawn was helped over to the bench. "Yo, that shit was outta order, man!" he piped.

"I know, Shawn. This is not good. This isn't good at all," the coach was saying. He called the reserved guard Michael over to him. "I want you in for Shawn."

"Wait Coach, you can't take me out of the game," Shawn contested.

"And why can't I? You look like you have a sprained wrist. You still have colleges here to look at you and they've seen enough, which wasn't bad. I'm not going to risk your future, win or no win," the Coach explained to Shawn.

The whistle was blown for the players to come back onto the floor. Gratz made their two foul shots, cutting the lead down to one. Shawn put an ice pack that was given to him on his wrist and threw a towel over his head as he watched the game unfold. The Jaguars were struggling to keep their lead. Shawn kept insisting that the coach put him back in the game but was refused. With only a minute and a half left in the game, Gratz took a two point lead after going on an 8-0 run. The Jaguars called a time-out.

Once again, Shawn tried his luck. "Coach Snyder, you gotta put me back in the game."

"Shawn, I already told you no, now don't ask me again. I am not going to risk your future."

"You're not going to be risking my future. I'll be alright. Look, you just said at half time that you didn't come all this way just to go home with the 'L'. Put me in the game if you really feel like that."

The coach looked at Shawn and sighed. Finally giving in he said, "Alright, Shawn. You're coming back in at the point. But if you get hurt any more than you already are and we still lose, I'ma rain on your ass like white on rice, you understand me?"

"Yes sir," Shawn snickered.

Coach Snyder drew up the next play for them to run, which was a pick for Shawn on the left side with Rasheem setting the screen. He didn't want to take any chances with Shawn getting hurt trying to drive through the lane. The plan worked like magic with Shawn hitting the 3, putting the Jaguars up by 1. The fans were already going crazy when Shawn came back onto the floor. Chants of "SHIZZ, SHIZZ, SHIZZ!" could be heard throughout the crowd.

A lay-up by Gratz put the Jaguars down by 1 with less than a minute to go in the game. They double teamed one of the players from Gratz that was killing them from the inside, leaving another shooter open who made the jump shot. Coach Snyder called another time-out.

"Alright guys, there's a few things that I need from you. Do not foul, do not double-team and stay on that small forward Rockler because he is kicking our ass. And that's the same little twit that gave Shawn that hard foul in the beginning of the fourth quarter and he's been playing Shawn kinda close. And lastly, draw the foul. Those guys are sloppy on the defensive end. We're not that far from winning, guys. I want that damn trophy. Defense on three, 1-2-3 DEFENSE!"

The Jaguars ran back onto the floor with the ball in their possession. They ran a play with Shawn driving through the lane to draw the foul thinking that Rockler was covered. But he spun around his coverage and fouled Shawn anyway, knocking him to the floor. He had a smirk on his face as he walked away. Rasheem bumped into him purposely and when he turned around, the expression on Rasheem's face let him know he was two seconds away from catching a North Philly ass whipping.

Shawn went to the foul line holding his wrist. The referee threw him the ball and he bounced it for a moment. He shot the first free-throw but missed. Groaning from U-City fans and cheers from Gratz fans were heard throughout the Liacouras Center. Shawn walked away from the free-throw line to shake off his jitters. His wrist was bothering him but he tried to ignore it. He bounced the ball and shot it, making the second free throw and cutting the Bull-Dogs lead to one. Rasheem and the other teammates gave him handshakes and rubbed his head. With only 20 seconds left in the game, Gratz began to run the clock trying to make the Jaguars foul, but their coach yelled for them not to. Seeing the time running down, Rasheem told Shawn to run to their end of the court. He crept up behind the guy with the ball and made the steal, quickly throwing the ball to Shawn as he ran up the court. Shawn caught the ball and then slammed it in the hoop at the buzzer, snapping his wrist but winning the game. Teammates that weren't in the game as well as students that came to the game from University City ran onto the court to celebrate their first Championship. Shawn was on his knees grimacing in pain as his friends were jumping all over him as well as each other. He was voted MVP and his friends lifted him into the air as he held up the teams' trophy.

After being checked out and learning that his wrist was fractured in two places, a cast was placed on it and the Coach dropped him off at home. Jamal heard him come in and came down the stairs to congratulate him on his win. Their mother didn't show up to his game again, but Shawn didn't let it bother him.

"Sorry I wasn't at your game. They wouldn't let me off work for shit. But we had that jawn turned on and I taped it here," Jamal apologized.

"It's cool. At least I know you were trying to make it, unlike mommy. Did anybody call for me?" Shawn asked as he sat down on the couch. He was exhausted.

"Yeah, Chanda called. She sounded hella-bad, man. I hope whatever the fuck she got I don't get that shit. But the phone's been blowing up with everybody from school."

Shawn laughed, "Where's Mommy?"

"Who the fuck cares as long as she ain't here?" He looked at Shawn's wrist. "Are you alright?"

"Yeah, I just fractured it."

"Dude lucky I wasn't there. I would've fucked him up for that shit. But, I'm about to go see Tamera. She's sick, too."

"What's wrong with Tammy? Is she still upset about the University of Arts thing?"

"Naw, actually they're reviewing her application. They never got her demo and now that they do have it, she might get in. But she was saying something about a stomach virus. She might have eaten something bad because she's been throwing up all crazy. I told her to leave that damn Chinese food alone." He grabbed his coat and opened the front door. "If Mommy gets here before I get back, just tell her I left, you don't know where I went and you don't know when I'm coming back."

"Alright," Shawn replied. He took his trophy up to his room and sat it on the dresser next to the other ones that he won. He laid across his bed thinking back to when he was younger before Raheem was killed. His thoughts were interrupted by a knock at his door. "Yo!" he answered.

His mother came in. "Hey Shawn."

"Hi mom," Shawn spoke back.

"I thought you would be out with Chanda."

"No she's sick," Shawn explained.

"Oh," she saw the cast on Shawn's wrist and gasped. "What happened to you?"

Shawn looked at his mother and then shook his head when he realized that once again she forgot about a game that he constantly reminded her not to forget to show up to. "I fell," he told her as she sat next to him on his bed.

"Are you lying to me?" Ms. Keyona asked.

Shawn thought her question over. Technically he wasn't lying because he did fall. "No."

Ms. Keyona rubbed his cast. "Are you alright?" When Shawn didn't reply she got up from his bed and cleared her throat. "Where's Jamal?"

"I don't know."

"He didn't say where he was going?"

"No."

"Well, I'ma go start dinner. I have a taste for some peppered steak with rice and corn." She left Shawn's room and closed the door behind her. Shawn looked up at the ceiling and shook his head.

That Monday, when Shawn and his friends were on their way to school, they stopped at the usual food stand to buy something to eat for breakfast. Just as Shawn was about to order, he caught a glimpse of the Daily News. There was a huge picture of him being held in the air with a caption that read: Shawn Williams; Breakable but Unstoppable.

Shawn paid for the newspaper and then yelled to his friends. "Yo y'all, I'm in the paper!" He took it over to his friends and showed it to them.

They crowded around as other students who were passing by decided to be nosey and have a look as well. They laughed and gave Shawn handshakes and pounds. Inside the article, there were two more photos of Shawn as well. One showed him sitting on the bench with a towel over his head and the other showed him hanging from the rim after he dunked the ball in at the buzzer. Other teammates had their picture in the paper as well, but they were mainly focused on Shawn and Rasheem.

When they arrived at the building, other students were standing around looking through the paper. Shawn received many handshakes as he moved through the building throughout the day.

Because of the pills stopping him from driving, Shawn caught public transportation home. People that had newspapers stared at him. One guy stopped him while he was on the 61 bus. "Are you Shawn?" he asked. Shawn nodded his head. "That was a helluva game y'all played yesterday. I wasn't expecting y'all to win, especially after they took you out of the game. But they were salty as shit when you came back and the young guy got that steal and you made that dunk. That shit was hot!" the guy said excitedly.

"Thanks yo," Shawn said as he got up to get off at his stop. He got off the bus and walked home shaking hands of neighborhood guys that either saw him play in the game or saw him in the newspaper. When he got in the house, he saw his mother sitting on the couch with the newspaper in her hand.

Ms. Keyona looked up at her son. "Why didn't you tell me you had a game yesterday?"

"I did tell you. I told you all last week that I was in the championship. It's not my fault you don't pay attention."

"Shawn!" Ms. Keyona piped.

"It ain't like you would've came anyway," Shawn said as he dropped his book bag on the living room floor.

"I was at work. People had newspapers asking me questions. Do you know how it made me feel not being able to answer them?"

"Nobody told you not to participate or show interest in the things that we do," Shawn replied blandly.

Ms. Keyona didn't respond knowing that what her son said was right. "And why did you lie about your wrist?" she asked instead.

"I did fall," Shawn said.

"Not like how you said," Ms. Keyona argued.

"I never said how I fell," Shawn looked at her confused wondering why she was trying to pick an argument.

"Well you still should've told me," Ms. Keyona said.

"Why's that?" Shawn asked.

"Because I'm your mother, I had a right to know."

A THUG'S REDEMPTION

"Yeah like you should've told us that Samir killed our father!" Shawn yelled angrily, making his mother recoil. He trembled as he glared at her. "I get so tired of telling you things and afterwards it's like I never even opened my mouth. It's like the only time you do listen is when one of us gets hurt or Jamal gets locked up. And not even then because you're too busy assuming." With that last comment, Shawn left the house and took a chance driving his car so he could go see Chanda.

The end of March came quickly and excitement was all around. Most of the seniors were excited because graduation and prom would be drawing near while others were excited because they were receiving college acceptance letters. But Tamera had become edgy and jumpy. For the past couple of weeks, she had been checking the calendar and counting the days since her last period. She was a couple of weeks late. She sat on her bed thinking over and over what could be wrong. The last time her and Jamal had sex was on March 17th. But her period was due March 3rd. It was now March 23rd.

"But didn't we use a condom...?" she thought to herself. She thought some more and then Valentine's Day popped in her head. She remembered it was something different about that time but was never able to put her finger on it. It dawned on her that Jamal didn't use a condom. She thought back to the box of condoms that she had. There were twelve in the box and if she included Valentine's Day it should have been 3 left. She flipped through the box and saw that she had four. "No, no, no. That can't be right. Her eyes started to get teary so she went over to her calendar. Her last period was February 5th and it went off on the 9th. It usually came every 27-28 days. She was two weeks late and if her calendar was telling her what she thought it was telling her, she was five weeks pregnant. She suddenly felt light-headed so she lay across her bed. She started crying, beginning to panic. She tried not to cry too loudly because Deisha would hear her.

A knock came at her door. She knew she wouldn't be able to hide the fact that she was crying so she decided to play possum and not say anything, hoping it would make whoever it was go away. She hugged the teddy bear that Jamal bought her for Valentine's Day close to her face.

Deisha knocked again. "Tammy, I know you're not sleep because I just heard you moving around." She knocked again. "Tammy?"

"What?" Tamera asked, sucking her teeth.

"Can I come in?"

"Why?" she was trying not to sound like she had an attitude.

"Because I want to talk," Deisha replied.

"Can't it wait until later?"

"It's important," Deisha insisted.

Tamera laid there for a couple of seconds. "Hold up." She got off of her bed and looked in the mirror. She wiped her eyes but it was no use.

Yani

"Fuck it," she mumbled as she flagged the mirror. She laid back on her bed. "Alright."

"What was that all about?" Deisha asked as she came in and looked around.

"I had to move a chair because I didn't want you to trip over it like last time," Tamera lied.

"It was dark then," Deisha replied, knowing that she was lying. She decided to wait before she asked why she was crying.

"What did you want to talk about?"

"Well, they are looking for people to sing in the graduation and I figured since you have such an awesome voice, you might want to sign up."

"That's it?" Tamera frowned.

"Well yeah, I figured you might want to hop on it now before some other wanna-be diva tries to step in with a voice like Brandy, fucking everything up," Deisha smiled.

"Okay, fine," Tamera said as she shook her head.

Deisha looked Tamera over. "Now why were you crying?"

Tamera looked at Deisha, startled. "What?"

"What my ass, you heard me."

Tamera thought up a quick lie. "I was thinking about my mom and I was starting to realize how much I miss her."

"Oh, it's going to be alright," Deisha said as she rubbed her back to comfort her.

"Did Jamal call?" Tamera asked.

"No, but if he does, I'll give you the phone."

"Okay." Deisha left the room and Tamera sat thinking. She decided to take a home pregnancy test until she could get to the doctors to see if she really was pregnant. She grabbed a jean jacket since it felt like spring outside and took twenty-five dollars out of her wallet. She went downstairs.

"Where are you getting ready to go?" Deisha asked as she was sitting on the living room floor studying.

"Just to the store. I have the munchies. Why, do you want something?"

"No, that's alright." Deisha went back to her homework and Tamera left the house. She walked over to 23rd and Ridge Avenue to the Ridge-Way Market. She grabbed some chips, a soda, a few candy bars and some Tasty Cakes. She picked up an Error proof test and sat everything on the counter. The cashier began ringing everything up but gave Tamera a funny look when she got to the pregnancy test. Tamera returned the same look.

"$19.67 is your total," the cashier told her. Tamera paid for her items and the cashier handed her the change. She put it in her pocket, grabbed her bag and left the store.

When she got to the house, she was relieved to see that Deisha had gone to her room. Tamera went up to her own room and closed the door. She drank her soda hoping what happened to Deisha didn't happen to her and she would get an accurate result. She held her urine until she couldn't hold it anymore and then ran to the bathroom with the test. She squirmed around as she read the directions to the test and then she tried as best as she could to follow them. She then stuck the test in its protective case, washed her hands and took the test box and the test to her bedroom.

Tamera sat on her bed and tapped her foot as she patiently awaited the results. When the five long minutes were up, she went over to her dresser and picked up the test which showed a blue plus sign. She trembled inside as she feared the worst.

"I'm pregnant," she mumbled as she began to shake all over. She stared at the test for what seemed like an eternity. Finally she put it in a bag with the box and stuffed it under the trash. She knew she needed to get to her doctor to confirm it but since it was Sunday, she wouldn't be able to make an appointment until Monday after school.

The phone rang and Deisha answered it on the third ring. A few moments later, she knocked on Tamera's door. "Yes?" Tamera answered.

"It's Jamal," Deisha told her.

Tamera opened the door just enough to take the phone and then closed it back. She cleared her throat and took a deep breath before answering, "Hello."

"Ay babe, what's up?" Jamal spoke.

"Nothing," Tamera said in a low voice.

"What are you doing?"

"Reading."

"What's wrong?" Jamal asked, noticing how short she was being with her answers.

"Nothing," Tamera told him.

"Then why do you sound like that?"

"Sound like what?"

"Like you just lost your best friend or something," Jamal replied.

Tamera giggled. "No I'm alright." She wanted to tell him that she thought she was pregnant but she decided to wait until she was sure.

"Let's go out somewhere," Jamal suggested.

"Now?" Tamera asked.

"Yeah, it's nice outside."

"I can't," Tamera refused.

"Why?"

"Because I don't feel good," Tamera lied.

"Babe, I asked you what was wrong and you said nothing. Tell me what's wrong?"

Tamera thought for a moment. "I'm just tired that's all."

"Are you sure?" Jamal asked.

"Yes, I'm sure."

"Alright. I'ma let you sleep. I'll call you later on tonight."

"Okay," she agreed.

"I love you," Jamal smiled, knowing she wasn't going to say it back.

"Ditto."

Jamal sighed. "I swear you're going to tell me one day instead of that ditto shit."

Tamera laughed, "You'll hear it eventually."

"I better," Jamal replied.

They hung up and Tamera lay across her bed. She closed her eyes and had a flash of herself dropping something on the ground and Shawn passing it to her. It left as quickly as it came. She shook her head frowning, wondering if it was the memory of a dream. She dismissed it as she closed her eyes to go to sleep.

The next day at school, Tamera was quiet for the entire day. She did her school work as usual but didn't say anything to anybody. At lunch, she sat at the table with her head down and her earphones on. Her friends sat with her talking and laughing but she remained silent.

"What's wrong, Tammy?" Chanda asked. Tamera shook her head refusing to look up.

"How come you're not talking to anybody?" Deisha asked. Tamera shook her head still refusing to speak or look up.

Jamal stared at her for a moment knowing that she was lying. She hadn't given him eye contact all day and wouldn't talk to him. He figured he would find out when they got home and he could talk to her alone. He knew from previous experiences that when she went silent it was because something had triggered the memory of her mother's death and she was in pain all over again.

Tamera couldn't wait until she got home so she could make her doctor's appointment. When she got to the house, she got her phone book and called Dr. Jefferson's office. She was shocked that she was able to get an appointment for the next day at 1 o'clock. She went back to her room to do her homework and then laid down for the rest of the night.

The next day at school, Tamera was acting the same as she did the day before; silent and withdrawn from everyone. During advisory, Jamal saw her sitting at her desk with her head down and went over to her. He tapped her on her shoulder.

Tamera looked up at him. "Huh?"

"How come you went to bed so early yesterday?" he asked.

"I was tired," Tamera said as she lay back down on her desk.

"What was wrong with you yesterday?"

"Nothing," she replied, refusing to look at him.

"Why are you lying to me?" Jamal asked in a low voice.

"I'm not lying to you, Jamal," she replied.

"Then why you're not talking to anybody? Why aren't you talking to me?" When Tamera didn't say anything, he pulled her up by her arm. "Get up." Tamera sat up and looked at him. "Come on." She followed him into the stairway. "Talk to me, Tammy." Tamera looked at the floor so he tilted her chin so she would give him eye contact. "What's wrong?" he asked again.

Tamera looked at him with tears in her eyes. "Jamal, I'm pregnant."

Jamal looked at her wide-eyed for a moment. He looked at her stomach and then looked at her. He put his arms around her and hugged her. "Are you sure?"

Tamera let Jamal go. "I'm two weeks late and I took a home pregnancy test yesterday. It came up positive. Valentine's Day, Jamal. We didn't use a condom." Tamera wiped her eyes and took a deep breath.

"It's going to be alright," he told her.

"What about college?"

"You can still go to college."

"How, because I don't want to have an abortion?"

"And I don't want you to," he looked at his watch. "Look, it's almost time for first period so we're going to talk about this at lunch, alright?"

"I can't, I have a doctor's appointment."

"Damn well, I don't have to work today so call me when you get the results." Tamera nodded and Jamal kissed her. "And stop crying like it's a bad thing because it's not. We're in this together." They went to their class. Tamera sat down at her desk and tried to do her work but couldn't focus. She slammed her papers down and pushed them to the side before resting her head on her desk in frustration. Jamal looked at her from across the room and went over to her. He rubbed her neck and kissed the side of her mouth. "Baby, it's okay. Do you want me to sit with you?"

Tamera leaned her head onto his and sighed. "Yes please."

Jamal got his books and sat next to her so they could do their work together.

When it was time to go to the doctor's appointment, Tamera prepared herself for the worst. She knew she wasn't going to luck up like Deisha did because she hadn't been taking any pills. The positive sign came up on the pregnancy test almost immediately. Tamera looked at the test results with tears in her eyes.

"Could I have a glass of water, please?" she asked in a trembling voice. The doctor handed her a paper cup full of water and called one of the Medical Assistants over to get a panel of blood work from Tamera once she let it be known that she was not going to have an abortion. Once the blood was drawn, Tamera went to the front to make another appointment. She took the prenatal pills that were given to her as well as a prescription to get more and the new mother's baggy and went home.

When Tamera got in the house, she plopped down on the couch and burst into tears. She looked at the papers over and over again trying to come to grips with the fact that a baby was growing inside of her. Deisha came in and tossed the mail on the coffee table.

"Hey," Deisha spoke to her before she realized Tamera was crying. When she did, she sat next to her. "What's wrong?"

Tamera wiped her face and then handed Deisha the envelope. Deisha opened it and immediately recognized the paperwork from when she had to take the pregnancy test. She scanned over the papers until she got to Tamera's results and gasped.

"You're pregnant?" Deisha asked.

"Yup."

"Oh my God! Does Jamal know? Is that why you've been so quiet and not talking to anyone?"

"Pretty much and yeah I told Jamal this morning." She began to cry silently. "I don't want to be pregnant while all of this is going on this summer."

"Are you going to have an abortion?"

"No, that's not something I could ever live with." She stood up and sighed. "Now I have to face your aunt."

Deisha hugged Tamera. "Don't worry, we're going to be here for you."

Tamera gave Jamal the okay to tell Shawn and his mom as well as Maurice about the pregnancy even though he had already told them. When he told his mother, she tried to convince the both of them that it would be in their best interest if they aborted. When they refused, she practically called them stupid.

Even though Deisha had been accepted to almost every school she had applied to, she still waited to hear from Penn State. When the letter finally arrived, it was only to let her know that she had been rejected. Despite the fact that she had been accepted to great Colleges and Universities such as Spelman and Immaculata, she took the news rather hard and turned into a complete study-freak.

The morning sickness phase kicked in for Tamera rapidly. She had to get up an entire half hour earlier just so she would have enough time to do her hair, shower, dress and get something to eat so the bus ride to school wouldn't make her sicker than she was when she first woke up. Chinese food no longer appealed to her. She often had to run out of class and pray that she made it to the bathroom in time before she made a complete fool of herself. She was lucky if she could keep a bowl of cereal down.

One afternoon during lunch, she was leaning on Jamal's chest as she ate strawberries, grapes and cherries.

"Do you think you'll be able to keep that down?" Shawn teased.

"I hope so. I don't get it. What's the point in being so hungry that I'm ready to eat beans straight from a can if I'm not going to be able to keep it down?"

"You know it's not good for you to keep throwing up like that," Chanda told her.

"How do you know?" Tamera asked as she sucked on a strawberry.

"Well Renee is pregnant too, and her doctor gave her a prescription to help with her morning sickness. She's also on a strict diet because she has gestational diabetes. You might want to be tested for that also," Chanda suggested.

"Is your pants hard to buckle yet?" Deisha asked.

"Sometimes, but it only hurts when I bend over so a lot of times I zip but I don't button." Tamera replied.

"Well, swimming is also good for pregnant women. And I have to use the swimming pool tomorrow to make up my Gym classes that I missed so I can get my credit. Y'all should come with me," Deisha suggested.

"I'm down," Jamal said. "Babe, you wanna come?"

"Yeah, sounds like fun. I haven't been swimming in a while."

"Okay, then it's a bet." Deisha looked at Maurice. "You should wear those sexy, black speedos that I like."

Jamal and Shawn looked at Maurice as if he were crazy.

"Nigga, if you roll up to the pool with some damn speedos on I'm fucking you up, real rap," Jamal said as he laughed.

"Yo, she's lying; I don't wear no damn speedos. You play too much, Deisha." Maurice shook his head as he laughed. They laughed together, cracking jokes until the lunch period was over.

The next day as agreed, they all met at the school's swimming pool. When Tamera put her two piece swim suit on, she was shocked to see that she had a small pouch even though she was barely three months pregnant. Chanda and Deisha groped her stomach and argued over who was going to be the God Mother. Shawn rubbed on it saying that was his niece in there. Jamal argued it was a boy. Tamera glowed, loving all of the attention.

Once in the pool, Tamera doggie paddled around for a while from one end of the pool to the other end while Jamal and the others played keep away. It was fun at first, but then she started feeling nauseous. Just as she was getting over in the five feet end of the pool, she began to get dizzy. Her face felt hot and her head felt like it was swelling. She fought hard to keep her eyes open but before she could call out for help, darkness took over and she passed out in the water.

Jamal and the others hadn't noticed that Tamera wasn't doggy paddling around anymore until Chanda was almost hit by the ball that Jamal was trying to throw to Shawn.

"Hey watch where you're throwing that damn ball, boy!" Chanda yelled. She looked around and noticed that Tammy wasn't in the pool.

"Where did Tammy go?"

"She probably went to go get dressed early," Deisha assumed.

"She could've let somebody know," Chanda mumbled.

"Well maybe she was starting to get sick and didn't get a chance to let anybody know. I'll go check on her." Deisha climbed out of the pool and went into the bathroom but didn't see Tamera there. As she was looking around, Chanda decided to play keep away with the others when she saw Tamera floating face first in the water.

She screamed, "Jamal! She's drowning!"

"What?" Jamal asked as he wiped water out of his eyes.

"Tammy!" Chanda yelled as she pointed to where she was.

Deisha heard the commotion and ran out of the locker room almost slipping and falling from the wetness on the floor. Jamal swam down to where Chanda was with Maurice and Shawn following behind. Chanda was trying to lift Tamera up, but she was too heavy.

"Let her go," Jamal told her. He went under water and then pulled Tamera up himself. Shawn and Maurice helped him lay her on the side of the pool. Jamal climbed out and scrambled beside her. "COACH!" he yelled.

"He stepped out," Shawn told him.

"What happened to her?" Deisha asked, panicking.

Jamal listened closed to her mouth. "Shit," he mumbled. He opened her mouth and started pushing down on her chest trying to get her to breathe. He breathed air into her mouth and listened again. "Come on man, breathe. This shit ain't funny," he said as he started pushing down on her chest again. He breathed air into her mouth and listened again. He frowned when he didn't hear anything. He started pushing down on her chest again, breathing heavy as tears filled his eyes. "Help me, Shawn." Shawn was in a stupor, not believing what he was seeing. "Help me Shawn!" Jamal screamed. "My baby is in there."

Shawn knelt down and started pushing down on Tamera's chest. Jamal breathed air into her mouth once more. Her head jerked to the left and then to the right. She let out a dry, ragged cough and spit water out as she choked. Jamal cradled her head so she could breathe.

Tamera looked up at him. "What took you so long?" she gasped.

Jamal wiped the water out of her face and smoothed her hair back.

Deisha and Chanda let out sighs of relief before helping her to the locker room so she could shower and get dressed.

"You better not scare me like that again," Chanda told her as they gathered up their things to head down to Shawn's car.

"I know girl, I almost bust my ass running out that locker room when they said you were drowning," Deisha added. They piled into Shawn's car.

"Are you alright?" Jamal asked Tamera as he stroked her head when she laid on his shoulder.

"Yeah," Tamera replied in a soft voice.

"Damn, it just dawned on me that we all came close to dying except for Maurice and Deisha," Shawn said as he pulled out of the parking lot.

"That's because Maurice punk-ass always running," Jamal teased. His friends laughed.

"You got-damn right. And I have yet to catch a bullet, unlike some. So you're damn right this nigga will run when the bullets start flying. Unfortunately, I've been there every time one of y'all almost bought it. When Raheem died, I was there, When Shawn and Jamal got shot, I was there, Now you Tamera," Maurice replied.

"Yeah well let's just hope it's not your grave that we'll all be standing over, speedy Gonzales," Deisha chuckled.

"Shawn, drop us off at Hahnemann Hospital," Jamal instructed.

"Why?" Tamera asked.

"Ain't that where your doctor is?" Jamal asked.

"Yeah."

"Drop us off, Shawn. I want to make sure both of my babies are okay."

Shawn drove them over to the hospital like Jamal said and he and Tamera went inside to find Dr. Jefferson. She tapped him on his shoulder.

"I'm Dr. Jefferson," she said as Jamal turned around. "What's the problem?"

"Tamera almost drowned and I wanted make sure they both were okay," Jamal explained.

"You must be Jamal. Where is she?"

"Right here," Jamal said as he pointed to Tamera sitting in a chair. Dr. Jefferson walked over to Tamera and tapped her on the shoulder. She looked up with tired eyes. "Tammy, sweetie I want you to come in the back with me okay?"

Jamal put his arm around her and helped her to the back room that the doctor went into.

"What happened?" Dr. Jefferson asked as she took out a hospital gown for Tamera to put on.

Jamal started helping Tamera undress. "We went with a friend to the school pool so she could do some make-ups. I was doggy paddling around while they played keep away. I started feeling nauseous and then my face got real hot and my head felt like it was swelling. I was trying to hurry up and get to the end of the pool but everything went black," Tamera explained as she slipped the hospital gown on.

"You said you felt dizzy, your face started getting hot and your head felt as if it were swelling? Has this happened to you before?" the doctor asked as she pulled an ultrasound machine near her.

"Yeah when I stand up for a long time or if I get up too fast, or if I don't eat anything for a while. A few times I almost passed out at home and in school, but I was always able to shake it off. If I drink an orange juice or something, I feel better," Tamera replied.

"Sounds like gestational diabetes," Dr. Jefferson replied as she rubbed warm jelly on Tamera's stomach.

"You're saying I have diabetes?" Tamera asked, frightened.

"Gestational diabetes. It happens to a lot of women when they are pregnant. You just need to be on a more controlled diet and take your prenatal vitamins regularly. You've got to take it easy because the first trimester is the most dangerous and a spontaneous miscarriage can happen very suddenly."

Jamal saw a tear slide out of Tamera's eye so he held her hand. They both looked at the screen.

"See, there is your little baby right there," Dr. Jefferson said as she pointed to the screen. She let them listen to the heartbeat. "Everything looks and sounds normal." She turned the monitor off and gave Tamera a towel to wipe the jelly off of her stomach. Jamal helped her get dressed. After blood was drawn to test her for gestational diabetes, she was given a few prenatal vitamins to take with a cup of water. When they left, Jamal hailed down a taxi for them and made sure that she got home safely. As Tamera was coming in the house, she caught another flash. A loud noise went off and she fell back onto the ground. Again like the last time, as quickly as the flash came, it left. Tamera stood in the doorway of the house staring, trying to focus. Again she wasn't sure what it was; if it were a dream that she had before. It gave her the chills and was beginning to scare her.

CHAPTER 8
PREPARING FOR THE WORST

It was now the middle of May. Jamal was becoming a little antsy as he knew it was close to the time for everything to jump off with Samir. He wondered why Samir had not been harassing him about the upcoming events. When he brought it to Shawn's attention, Shawn told him that it was probably because Samir was waiting for them to fuck up.

Tamera kept her job at Sam Goody even though Jamal told her that if there was anything she needed he would get it for her. She wanted money for herself. Her hours had been cut down due to her pregnancy and Jamal was finally able to convince her that it made no sense for her to work those few hours making a little bit of money when he was giving her that and more. After thinking it over, she decided to quit and rest at home. Jamal continued to spoil her, making sure she had whatever she wanted and needed. They both couldn't wait to start shopping for the baby.

Ever since Deisha found out that she was rejected from Penn State, she turned into a complete study freak trying to make sure she kept her grades up to get a scholarship to Immaculata College. She made sure she had practically all A's on her last two report cards.

Maurice could barely keep Deisha from the library. Most times when he called she was either studying or sleeping due to being exhausted from studying so much. One day, he happened to catch her sitting on her porch listening to the radio, enjoying the night air.

"What? You're not studying?" he teased.

"No, but I should be. Finals are in two weeks. Those bastards had the nerve to make them the same week as the Prom.

"Damn girl, you're studying enough for both of us." He pulled Deisha up by her hands. "Come chill with me up at The Rec?" he asked her sweetly.

"Why can't we chill here?" Deisha whined, not wanting to be anywhere near The Recreation Center because of the constant fighting they did up there.

"Because I don't want to chill here. And why have you been avoiding me?" he asked.

"I wasn't avoiding you, babe. I've just been studying."

"You've been acting like this since my mom caught us. Just because she doesn't want you at the house no more don't mean you gotta cut me off." Deisha sighed knowing that he was right. "So are you coming?"

"I gotta put the radio back in the house." She went inside and put her radio in her bedroom. She then came back outside and walked with Maurice to The Recreation center hand in hand.

"One more month boo, are you ready to say goodbye?" Maurice asked.

"No," Deisha sulked.

"No? Aren't you the one that said you would blow this bitch up if you could get away with it?" Deisha laughed. "How come you're not ready to go, now?"

"Memories; everything that happened to me happened here. Everybody that I love is leaving after we graduate. My best friend is about to start a new life when she gives birth in November," Deisha sighed.

"How do you think I feel? You're talking about going all the way down South to Truth University and shit."

"No I'm not. I'm going to Immaculata. I thought I told you."

"No, I guess you were too busy studying," Maurice teased. "That's what's up because that's where I'm going, too."

Deisha playfully punched him on his arm. "Babe, you didn't tell me! That means we can still see each other. Aww!" Deisha gushed as she wrapped her arm around his.

"So what made you choose Immaculata?"

"Because they're the next best thing to Penn State when it comes to compensating my major."

"And what's that?" he asked.

"Child Psychology," Deisha said, glancing at him.

Maurice fell silent not knowing what to say. He didn't want his next comment to bring up what he said regarding Deisha's mother.

Deisha understood his silence so she decided to change the subject as they approached the Recreation Center. "One thing I won't miss is this pissy-ass neighborhood." She spotted a man urinating in a corner. "See, look at that shit. The trifling bastard. And I bet you he's going to go to the Chinese store, order some chicken wings and won't even wash his hands before he eats. Nasty ass," Deisha said distastefully.

Maurice laughed and snatched her close to him. "See, that's the Deisha I remember."

That next Friday afternoon, Deisha was in her room looking in the mirror. She looked at the chain that Raheem left her when he died and the chain that Maurice gave her for Christmas. She began to think that the reason she wasn't able to take Raheem's chain off was because she never told him how she felt about him. She figured that since she was getting ready to go off to college that it wasn't any time like the present to get what she had to say off of her chest.

She went downstairs and was about to head out the door when her aunt stopped her.

"Deisha, where are you going?" Michelle asked.

"To finish something I should've ended a long time ago," Deisha replied.

"Do you want to talk about it?" her aunt asked.

"Maybe when I get back."

"Alright, don't stay out too late."

Deisha left the house and headed over to Raheem's burial spot. As she walked towards it, her palms started to sweat and her mouth dried. When she reached the actual site, her entire body began to tremble. Just as she was squatting down and clearing away the grass that had begun to grow around his tombstone, it dawned on her that she didn't bring any flowers.

"Don't think that because I don't come to visit on a regular basis that my feelings for you changed," she sighed. "God, how can a person possibly love two people at the same time? I don't know. It's weird for me to say that after all these years, I still love you. I miss you so much and the only reason I'm doing as well as I am is because of Maurice." She smiled. "It's ironic that I ended up with your best friend. Maybe it's because you knew he would be good for me. Sometimes it feels like you're watching over me."

Deisha touched the *Raheem* chain and became quiet as she listened to the silence surrounding her. "No matter how hard I try, I can never take this off. I never even got the chance to tell you that I loved you, too. But that's why I'm here now; I love you, Raheem. I don't think I will ever stop." She sat there for a little while longer thinking back to their times together because he was abruptly taken from her. Finally, she stood and ran her finger across the top of his tombstone. "We'll be together again in another time."

Deisha walked to the bus stop and got on when it pulled up. She took a seat in the back and then unclipped the *Raheem* chain from around her neck. She looked at it for a moment and then closed her hand around it, holding onto it tightly.

When she arrived at her house, she went up to her room and put the chain in her jewelry box, never to really look at it again. She went back downstairs feeling refreshed.

"You've got this weird glow like you just lost your virginity," her aunt joked. Deisha laughed. "Where did you go?"

"I went to pay my respects."

"To who?" Michelle asked as Deisha sat on the couch.

"To Raheem," she replied.

"Oh."

"I never really had a chance to say goodbye and I never really told him how I felt about him so I decided to do it now which is stupid. He's gone."

"Well, what did you tell him?" Michelle asked.

"I said how I could never take the chain off without feeling like I was hurting him."

"But, you're not wearing it now," Michelle noticed.

"I took it off on my way back home. I miss him a lot, Aunt 'Chelle. It's hard to believe I still love him but I love Maurice, too."

"You're in love with Maurice, there's a difference. You can love anybody. But falling in love is much stronger."

"I know." They fell silent. Deisha cleared her throat and asked, "Aunt 'Chelle, how come you never told me that you got an abortion when you were younger and that's the reason why you can't have kids now?"

Michelle was startled by her niece's question. "That's something that I felt as though you didn't need to know."

"It's more to it than just that," Deisha assumed.

"No it's not. It really was something that I didn't want people to know about me. I was ashamed and embarrassed and that was a secret that only your mother knew."

"Why did my mom bring it up on Christmas?"

"To get back at me for doing such a fine job raising you; a job that she should've done herself." She walked behind Deisha and kissed the top of her head. "I'm going to run to the store. I'll be back." She left the house and closed the door behind her.

A few days later, Deisha and her friends were heading out of the building when a girl that didn't like Deisha bumped into her on purpose. Deisha knew the girl didn't like her and was trying for the longest time not to beat her up, but this time was too much.

"Bitches always starting shit but never sticking around to finish it," Deisha said loudly so the girl could hear her.

"Who the fuck is she talking to?" the girl asked her friend.

"Bitch, I'm talking to you!" Deisha hissed as she dropped her book bag, ready to rumble.

"No the fuck you're not," the girl hissed back.

"Yes the fuck I am. Bring your nut-ass over here and I'ma show you who the fuck I'm talking to." Maurice tried to pull Deisha away when he saw the girl advancing towards her but she yanked away and socked the girl when she got close enough. An N.T.A that was normally referred to as "Toy Cop" pulled Deisha into the building and took her to the principal's office.

Maurice and his friends went over to Shawn's car to wait for her.

"What happened?" Chanda asked

"Some girl bumped into Deisha on purpose. They exchanged some words and when the girl came over to Deisha like she was tough Deisha knocked the shit out of her. I think she's the chick that's been starting stuff with Deisha for a while," Tamera told her friends.

"Damn girl, listen to your mouth," Jamal joked as he put his hand over her mouth.

"She just better hope she don't get kicked out of school or graduation," Maurice said as he sat on the trunk of Shawn's car.

"I just noticed something," Shawn said. "Deisha's not wearing that *Raheem* chain."

"Damn, I ain't even noticed that shit," Jamal replied.

"Me neither," Maurice said.

"That's something I thought you would've picked up on first," Chanda said. They sat outside and waited for Deisha.

The Principal was having a conversation with a teacher while Deisha waited in her office. When she finished, she joined Deisha and put her glasses on. She began to give Deisha her usual bull-shit speech about how graduation was on the way and how she didn't want to kick her out or suspend her because it could affect the scholarships that Deisha had coming her way.

"Why would you wait until you're so close to graduation to get into some mess like this, Deisha? I'm surprised at you." Deisha didn't reply so the principal sighed. "What do you think I should do? I mean, let me know."

"I don't know," Deisha said as she shrugged her shoulders.

"Well," the principal said sighing, "I'm not going to kick you out of graduation because from 9th grade until now, you have not been a problem. But it wouldn't be fair to the other seniors if you didn't receive some type of punishment. I hope you're tired Deisha; five days suspension."

Deisha looked at the principal wide-eyed. "She started with me!" she piped.

"You threw the first punch, Deisha. You know the rules in this school and you broke them." She wrote Deisha's name out on the pink slip and put it inside of the envelope. "What's your aunt's name?"

"Michelle Burton."

The principal put Deisha's aunt's name on the envelope and handed it to her. "Come back next Wednesday to get reinstated. Bring your aunt with you. And the next time you decide to handle a situation by throwing hands, you'll be on the first thing smoking out of here."

Deisha sighed with annoyance and left the office. She walked out of the building and over to Shawn's car.

"You're suspended?" Shawn asked.

"Yup, I got five days and the bitch started with me, oh hell no. Don't let me catch her ass. She thinks I went across her muthafucking eye last time. Wait until I see her." They got inside of the car and started towards home.

"I need to talk to you," Maurice said to her.

"Why?" Deisha asked. Maurice didn't answer her so she didn't say anything else. She already had an attitude and didn't feel like arguing with him.

Shawn stopped at his house and everyone went their separate ways.

Maurice and Deisha started walking towards The Recreation Center.

"What did you want to talk about?" Deisha asked him.

"Why you ain't tell me that you took off Raheem's chain?" Maurice asked.

"You just now noticed? You spent all of this time complaining about the damn chain and you're just now noticing after it's been almost a week?" Deisha snapped.

"But why did you take it off?"

"Does it matter?" Deisha asked back.

Maurice looked at her for a moment before he asked his next question. "When did you take it off?"

"Last Friday."

"What made you finally take it off?" Maurice continued to question.

"Damn, you're asking a lot of questions." They walked on some more before Deisha answered him. "I was looking in the mirror at the chain you gave me for Christmas and the chain he gave me when he died and it dawned on me that I never actually said goodbye and I never told him how I felt about him.

"So...?" Maurice asked.

"I went to his grave and told him what I should've said almost four years ago," Deisha explained.

"And what was that?"

Deisha looked at Maurice becoming annoyed with his nosiness. "It's personal, Maurice."

"Oh, it's like that?" Maurice asked as he nodded his head. Deisha laughed. "So that's what made you finally take it off?"

"Yeah because I ended it. It was like after he died, his chain was a part of him that he left behind to remind me how much he cared about me. I guess after I finally was able to tell him how I felt about him, I was able to take it off and set him free." When Maurice didn't comment, Deisha asked, "Why are you so quiet now? I thought you said you needed to talk to me."

"I did," Maurice replied.

"That's all you wanted to talk about?" Deisha asked as she looked at him.

"Pretty much," Maurice replied.

Deisha stopped and looked at him. "I'm about to hit the shit out of you." Maurice laughed and Deisha smacked him on his arm. "It's not funny. I thought you wanted something important. I'm going home."

Maurice grabbed her arm." I'm sorry." He pulled her close to him. "Stay with me, please."

"I can't."

"Why not?" he asked.

"Because I'm suspended and if I go home late and tell my aunt, she's going to chew me a new ass-hole for fighting and getting suspended and not bringing my ass straight home. So I've gotta go." They kissed for a moment. "Call me later on."

"Alright, chump." He smacked her on her butt as she walked away.

"Ya momma," Deisha smiled as she walked away. She went home and awaited her aunt so she could inform her of her suspension.

While Deisha and Maurice were going for their walk, Jamal was walking Tamera back to her house. They began to talk about their plans for June 20th.

"Did you start packing yet?" Jamal asked her.

"No, not yet," Tamera replied.

"Why not?"

"Because it's still a month left. And I don't want Deisha's aunt to come in my room and see all of my stuff packed up. I'll pack up two days before graduation."

"I'm going to have to come get you at night, though." Jamal told her.

"Why?" Tamera asked as she looked at him.

"Because Samir got hip to our plan."

"What do you mean, Samir got hip to the plan?" Tamera panicked.

"I mean he knows I'm planning on taking y'all somewhere while I handle this business with him," Jamal explained.

"How does he know that?"

"Because he thinks like I do. He knows I would die before I let anything happen to you or Shawn so he figured if he planned on doing something to y'all, I wouldn't be dumb enough to leave y'all down here."

"Does Samir know exactly where you're taking us?" Tamera asked.

"No. My Uncle is one of the few people on my dad's side I actually socialize with and keep in contact with. Samir is on my mom's crooked ass side of the family. His mom and my mom don't get along because she knew that Samir killed my father and didn't do anything. I just found that out."

"Jamal, does Samir know that I'm pregnant?"

"No, I hope not," Jamal said as he shook his head.

Tamera let out a deep sigh. "This is so out of order."

Jamal waited before making his next comment. "Maybe you should've stuck to your guns and stayed away from me."

"Maybe, but it's too late to be worrying about that now because you've got more to look out for besides me and Shawn," Tamera told him as she rubbed her stomach. They walked on some more in silence. "Baby, are you scared of Samir?"

Jamal waited a moment before he answered. "Not really."

"Just a little bit?"

"I'm scared of what he's capable of. I'm scared because he has more protection than I do. These niggas out here are more loyal to him than they are to me and if it comes down to choosing sides, of course they are going to choose him." They arrived at Tamera's house. Jamal hugged her tightly and held her close to him. As normal, Tamera put her face to his chest so she could smell his cologne. She exhaled and smiled. When she closed her eyes, another flash came of Shawn trying to pull her to the ground but losing his grip. She shuddered in Jamal's arms.

"What's wrong?" Jamal asked her.

Tamera looked up at him trying hard to remember what she saw but like a dream, it faded as quickly as it came. She shook her head. "Nothing."

Jamal kissed her and then knelt down and kissed her stomach. "I love you," he said as he looked up at her.

"I know," she smiled as she rubbed the back of his head. Jamal smiled at her and then left. Tamera closed her eyes trying hard to remember what she saw and wondered why she kept seeing it. She shuddered again feeling uneasy and went into the house to get some ice-cream.

Later at Tamera and Deisha's house, Michelle went berserk when she found out that Deisha had been suspended for fighting.

"What the hell were you fighting for?" she asked furiously.

"It wasn't my fault, Aunt 'Chelle. I was standing outside minding my own business…"

Michelle interrupted her. "Since when do you mind your own business?"

"I was. This girl that's been acting like she wanted to fight for the longest time bumped into me for no reason."

"And I bet you said something to her, didn't you?" her aunt asked as she placed a hand on her hip.

"But it wasn't even a fight. I just socked her and then security grabbed me," Deisha said as she tried not to laugh.

"Well, did the other girl get suspended?"

"No," Deisha replied.

"Well why the hell not?" her aunt asked furiously.

"Because she never swung back and because I threw the first punch. That's the reason why I was suspended."

"You know what? I am so sick of your damn principal. I'm glad this is your last year at that damn school. She's always pulling some shit like this."

Michelle looked at Deisha with anger in her eyes. "You're lucky you ain't get kicked out of graduation."

"I know," Deisha agreed.

"How long are you suspended for?"

"Until next Wednesday. You have to bring me back so I can be reinstated."

"You wait until you have a month left to get suspended. If you have homework, go do it."

Deisha went up to her bedroom even though she didn't have any homework. Just as she was putting her Ashanti CD on, Tamera burst into the bathroom and started vomiting. She was huddled over the toilet bowl coughing and breathing heavy. Deisha stood in the bathroom doorway looking down at her.

"Are you alright?" she asked.

Tamera shook her head, "No." She was getting ready to say something else but vomited instead. She sniffed and began to sob. "I hate throwing up." She pulled her hair behind her ears and wiped her face. Just as she was about to get up, the vomiting attack came and she was forced back over the toilet bowl again. She began to cry. "Deisha, can you rub my back, please?"

Deisha sat on the side of the tub and rubbed her hand across Tamera's back, trying to calm her down. She got a paper towel and wet it so she could wipe her face. When she felt a little better, she got up to fix herself a cold cup of water, and drank it slowly.

"Are you alright now?" Deisha asked again.

"Yeah," Tamera sighed. She followed Deisha to her room and sat on her bean bag chair. "So what's the deal with the chain?"

"What is that, the topic of the day or something?" Deisha frowned.

Tamera frowned back at her. "I was just asking, damn."

"I know. I just decided that it was time to let go, that's all."

"So where is it now?"

"In my jewelry box," Deisha said as she pointed to it. "Are you ready to go off with Jamal?"

"No not yet. It some issues he has to work out first." Tamera sighed.

"What issues?" Deisha asked.

"Samir figured out Jamal was planning on taking me and Shawn somewhere safe while he carried out this favor. Even though he doesn't know where exactly, Jamal is playing this like a chess game."

"Why don't he do what the hell needs to be done so this shit can be done and over with?" Deisha asked as she shook her head.

"It's not that simple. It's a lot to this that Jamal won't talk about. He's scared about something and I think the fact that he knows Samir killed his dad changes everything."

"Well he needs to figure something out so you don't get hurt because y'all have a baby on the way."

"We know and he's trying. It's just that it's not a lot of people he can turn to because these niggas out here are more loyal to Samir than they are to Jamal. And like he told me earlier, if they have to choose sides, they're going to choose Samir's side." Tamera got up to leave Deisha's room. "I'm going to go lay down for a bit. We'll talk later."

"Alright Tammy," Deisha said as she turned her TV on and lay across her bed.

Keisha and Manny were walking down the street in his neighborhood the next day. They had been talking for eight months and Keisha was glad to see he wasn't so quick to have sex with her. Another side to her wondered why he didn't try her or at least bring up the topic.

Every time they walked past a group of people, guys would shake Manny's hand and nod at Keisha or say hello to her. The females, however, would smile and speak to Manny but looked at Keisha as if they had a problem. Keisha tried not to pay it any mind but it was starting to get annoying.

Manny was the hot guy in his neighborhood that all of the girls wanted. He was handsome; standing a little over 6 feet tall with a medium brown complexion. His eyes were almond shaped and the color of burnt sienna. He was always dressed in the latest trend and always had the hottest sneakers. Most of his friends called him a "Sneaker Head" and you never caught him without a fresh haircut that made his hair so wavy, it could make a person sea sick. He had swag, was smooth and confident. Seeing him with Keisha, who was not from their neighborhood, pissed the girls off.

Manny noticed her facial expression and asked, "What's wrong with you?"

"Nothing," Keisha said.

"Why do you look like that, then?" Manny asked her. Keisha shook her head and they walked on some more. Another group of girls were walking towards them and they spoke to Manny. When he let Keisha's hand go to speak back, one of the girls gave Keisha a dirty look and cut between them, bumping into her on purpose. Keisha turned around and looked at the girl, ready to punch her in the back of her head. Instead, she kept walking. It was obvious that she was pissed by her heavy stroll. Manny looked at her and slowed down so he could watch her walk.

"You're evil as shit," he said, laughing.

"No, I'm not." Keisha replied.

"Then why are you walking like that?"

"Because man, these girls are going to keep trying me and I'ma end up smacking the shit out of one of them."

"What do you mean?" Manny asked.

"They keep giving me dirty looks like they want to fight me or something."

"That's because they are intimidated by you," Manny told her.

"For what? They don't even know me," Keisha said with an attitude.

"Exactly. You're this new girl that came up in the neighborhood and took one of the dudes they've been trying to take but couldn't get. And look at your height. Shit, if I was a girl, I would feel slighted every time I saw you, too." They walked on some more. "Stop walking like that, man." Manny laughed some more.

"I can't help it," Keisha chuckled. They arrived at his house and sat on his steps talking.

"You're mom know about me yet?" Manny asked.

"She been knew about you," Keisha replied.

"Is that a good thing or a bad thing?"

"It's not a good thing because sometimes she'll come out of no-where and ask some embarrassing questions.

"Like what?" Manny asked, playing stupid.

Keisha looked down the street and waited a moment before she answered his question. "She asked if we are having sex." She waited to see if he was going to comment and when he didn't, she went on. "Other than that, she doesn't show the slightest interest in what we're doing. She doesn't ask to meet you. I doubt she even remembers your name and I plan on keeping it that way."

"Damn, it's like that? When did she find out?"

"A little after Valentine's Day when she came in my room and saw the balloons that you bought for me taped to my wall." They fell silent again.

Manny made Keisha stand in front of him while he was sitting on his wall. He had his hands on her waist and was staring at her but she looked past him.

"Keisha?"

"Yo," she replied as she continued to look up the street.

"Are you a virgin?"

The question caught her off guard and she almost choked on her chewing gum. "Why?"

"Because I want to know. Don't I have the right to know since I'm your man?"

Keisha smiled. "Yes."

"So are you?" he asked again.

"Sorta..." Keisha replied nervously.

"Naw boo, it's either a yes or a no."

Keisha smiled feeling embarrassed that he had put her on the spot like that. "Then I guess it would be a no." Manny's silence made her feel uncomfortable. Someone drove past playing *Ether* by Nas and Manny rapped along with it.

Yani

"That was the shit," he said.

"You're not going to ask me anything else?" Keisha asked him.

"Anything else like what?"

"I don't know. I just thought you would ask me something else about it."

"I just wanted to know whether you were or not. Who took it isn't my business and most dudes not gonna wanna know who was hitting their girl off before them. You wouldn't want to know who I was knocking off before you, would you?" Manny asked her.

"No," Keisha replied in a low voice. Manny kissed her neck and then nibbled on her chin making her laugh. He hugged her close to him.

"I've gotta get ready to go make this money, okay?" he told her.

Keisha let him go and looked at him. "You're still hustling?"

"Not as much as I used to. Why? Do you want me to stop?" Keisha didn't respond. "If you want me to stop, I'll stop." He grabbed her by her hand and stood up. "Come on so I can walk you home." They started towards her house, walking hand in hand when a guy stopped Manny.

"Yo, what's up, Manny?" the guy spoke.

"What's the deal, yo?"

The guy noticed Keisha and nodded at her. "How are you?"

"Hello," Keisha spoke back.

"Yo Manny, let me rap to you real quick."

Manny told Keisha to wait a moment and he walked off to the side with his friend. "What's up?"

"Yo man, some shit is about to go down. D-Ball just told me and some other bols to get off the court because they are about to come through there and anything in their way is getting hit and I'll be damned if it's me. Take your girl home yo, and don't come back out even when the smoke clears," his friend warned him.

"Who are they after?" Manny asked.

"Dominique stole like three stacks from him. Plus he was going around bragging about how he fucked his little sister and what-not calling her all kinds of bitches and shit. You know how D-Ball gets. I'd find a place to chill because those niggas are not playing."

"Alright yo, good looking," Manny thanked him as they shook hands.

"No problem," his friend replied. He sprinted down the street and disappeared around a corner. Manny went back over to Keisha and put an arm around her waist, guiding her towards her house.

"What was that all about?" Keisha asked.

"Nothing," Manny lied. "Is it alright if I chill at your house?"

"I thought you were going to hustle?" Keisha asked in a smart tone.

"Change of plans," Manny said, being short with her.

Keisha stopped walking. "What is going on?"

"Nothing, why?"

"Then why are you in such a rush to get to my house?"
"Because…"
"Because what?" Keisha interrupted him knowing he was about to lie.
Manny sighed. He had heard of her past with Dominique and didn't want her to know that he was a target. "Something is about to go down and I don't want you to get hurt." He grabbed Keisha by her hand and they rushed to her house.

About an hour and a half later, Shawn and Chanda were sitting in his house playing video games. They were laughing and cracking jokes when they heard a commotion outside of Shawn's living room window. Shawn paused the game just as Jamal was coming downstairs to see what was going on. They walked over to the door with Chanda following behind them. Jamal looked out the door with Shawn and noticed Dominique arguing with two other guys like they were about to fight.

"I wanna see," Chanda said, squeezing in between them.

"What the hell?" Jamal asked as he looked one of the guys over. Shawn was scanning the guys and saw when he reached under his shirt to pull his gun. Jamal noticed it also.

"Get back," Shawn said as he pushed Chanda back into the house. Chanda stumbled in almost falling over her foot when Shawn slammed the door. Shots rang out as well as some cursing. Shawn, Jamal and Chanda ducked for cover. One of the bullets came through the window just as Chanda ducked under it. Shawn turned his head and saw her covered in glass. He waited for things to get quiet before seeing if she was okay. He went over to her and brushed the glass out of her hair and off her neck and shirt. She looked up at him startled, scared and breathing heavy. Shawn hugged her and rubbed the back of her neck.

Someone outside began to scream so Jamal opened the door. He wasn't surprised to see Dominique lying in the middle of the street in a puddle of blood. His hands were around his neck gasping for air as he kicked his leg out. Jamal looked down at him from his step. Slowly, Dominique stopped. His hands slid partially to his chest and his head turned towards Jamal. Jamal closed his eyes and sighed deeply. Shawn and Chanda looked at him.

"Fuck MAN!!" Jamal exclaimed as he swung himself around and stormed into the house. He knocked over a chair in anger. As usual, people came to the sidewalk to see who the victim was.

A moment or so later, Keisha ran around the corner. Manny had tried to stop her but she was too fast for him. She pushed through the crowd and her mouth gaped open when she saw Dominique lying on the ground. Shawn darted off the porch and grabbed onto her, remembering the story Maurice told him about Keisha losing her virginity to him. She tried to yank away from him but he held her tightly trying to muffle her screams. She had his shirt in a tight grip, crying hysterically. Manny came around the corner and looked at Keisha and then Dominique's body on the ground. He turned away and walked back to his house.

Shawn looked at Chanda. "Do you have Maurice's number?" he asked her.

"Yeah," she replied. Her heart was racing from everything that was happening.

"Call him and tell him to come get his sister, now!" Chanda went into the house to do as she was told. "What the fuck are y'all standing around for? Somebody call the fucking cops or something! He ain't on display! What the fuck is wrong with y'all?!" Shawn snapped as he continued to hold Keisha in his arms.

"Reese?" Chanda asked when she was finally able to get Maurice on the phone after three tries. "What are you doing?"

"You just woke me up, why? Who's this?" Maurice asked, sounding hoarse from his late afternoon nap.

"It's Chanda. You didn't just hear those gun shots?"

"Naw, where at?" Maurice asked as he rubbed his eyes. He looked at his watch to see what time it was.

"Right in front of Jamal and Shawn's house. They just killed Dominique and if I didn't duck when I did, a bullet that came through the window would've took me with him."

"Get the fuck outta here!" Maurice said now fully awake.

"Yeah and your sister is around here tripping. Screaming and crying and what-not," Chanda told him.

"What is she doing around there?"

"I don't know. She ran around here."

"Alright, I'm on my way." He hung up the phone and Chanda went back outside with Shawn. He was sitting on the steps holding Keisha, rocking her from side to side. A few minutes later the cops arrived. They watched them conduct their investigation in silence. Two of the cops came over to them.

"I'm Detective Davidson and this is my partner Detective Adams from the 22nd precinct. Did you happen to know the victim?"

"Only from around the way," Chanda replied as she looked down the street.

"Do you know what happened?" Detective Adams asked.

"No, we were sitting in my living room playing the game when we heard gun shots. One of them came through our window. By the time we got to the door, Dominique was on the ground and whoever did it was already gone." Shawn told them. He was leery about talking to any cops now that he knew a lot of them were being paid off by Samir.

Detective Davidson looked at Keisha. "Miss, do you know anything about the incident?"

"No, I got around here after it happened." Keisha replied in a shaky voice.

"We could use your help. It seems like you know the victim well. If you know something that could give us some leads…"

"I said no!" Keisha yelped. She buried her face in Shawn's shirt and began to cry again.

The detective sighed and handed them all a business card. "If you happen to remember anything, please don't hesitate to call us." The detectives walked away. They crumpled the business cards up and tossed them onto the ground. Maurice came around the corner and walked over to Shawn's porch.

"Maurice," Keisha said as she wrapped her arms around him.

"I'ma come back around after the heat dies down and I make sure that she's alright," Maurice told his friends.

"Alright," Shawn replied. Maurice and Keisha walked off to their house and Shawn looked over at Chanda. "Come here," he told her. She walked over to him and he hugged her tightly. "If you had ducked a split second later they might be putting you in a body bag right along with Dom."

"Don't remind me," Chanda replied as she hugged him back.

"Let me get a plastic bag and some tape. My mom is going to trip when she sees this shit."

Jamal walked back into the living room. "The cops still out there?"

"Yeah, they're circling bullets and stuff," Shawn told him.

"Where is the broom and dust pan so I can sweep this glass up?" Chanda asked.

"It's in the kitchen." Jamal told her.

Chanda went into the kitchen to get the broom. She also called her father to let him know she was going to be home a little late because of what happened.

"Look in the corner and pass me a bag, Chanda. It should be some tape on the counter, pass that to me too," Shawn called into the kitchen.

"I don't believe this shit, man." Jamal said as he stepped over the glass. "And we got school tomorrow, too. What time is it?"

"Almost 9:30pm. Which means Mommy is going to be home soon. So we gotta hurry up," Shawn replied.

"Hurry up for what? And try to hide a bullet hole in the window? Like Mommy isn't going to notice that," Jamal said sarcastically.

Chanda picked up the bullet shell and looked at it. "Damn, that nigga had a Desert Eagle." She sat it in the window sill and began sweeping up the glass as Shawn taped the plastic over the window where the bullet hole was. Right after they finished up and was about to go back outside, Shawn and Jamal's mother came in the house.

"I just heard Dominique got killed. Are y'all alright?" she asked.

"Yeah, but one of the bullets came through the window. We fixed it though," Shawn told her.

Ms. Keyona went over to the window and looked at it. "I'll have Ronnie come and put a new one in on Friday. As long as y'all are okay. Chanda, it's getting kinda late. You might wanna go home with all of this shooting going on around here and you have to go all the way to South Philly."

"I called my dad and let him know what happened and that I would be home a little late," Chanda told her.

"I'll give her a ride mom," Shawn replied.

Ms. Keyona went over to the steps. "All of this damn shooting and killing going on don't make any damn sense." She went up to her bedroom.

"At least she ain't start bitching," Jamal stated. They went outside and waited for Maurice to come back around as they watched the cops finish up. A moment after they sat out there, Maurice came back around the corner. He pulled up a chair next to them.

"How's Keisha?" Chanda asked.

"She's going to be alright. Her and my mom got into an argument and then it got worse because Keisha called Deisha to come get her and you know her and my mom don't click like that. So she waited for my mom to go to bed and she grabbed some clothes and went over to Deisha's."

"Yeah, she was going through it when she saw Dom on the ground." Shawn told him.

"What happened, yo?" Maurice asked.

"I don't know. I guess they were arguing or some shit," Jamal said.

"They who?" asked Maurice.

"D-Ball, Dom and some other dude," Shawn said.

"Yeah," Jamal continued. "So you know us, we're nosey as hell. We went to the door and were watching when I noticed one of them niggas was about to pull a gun so I jumped back in the house and Shawn slammed the door. Like two seconds later, somebody started shooting and a bullet came through our window right after Chanda ducked under it."

"I saw D-Ball the other day in the Chinese store and he asked me if I saw Dom. I told him naw. He told me he was talking shit about his little sister and if he caught him, it was curtains. I thought he was just going to whip his ass or something," Maurice told his friends.

Shawn noticed that Chanda had fallen asleep on his shoulder. He nudged her so she would wake up. "Come on so I can take you home."

Chanda stood up and stretched. "Tell Deisha to call me." Maurice nodded and Chanda and Shawn went to his car so he could drive her home.

Tamera was in Deisha's room with Keisha. Even though they had school the next day, Michelle didn't mind her staying the night since the term was almost over and she could see the girl was distraught over Dominique's murder.

"What happened?" Tamera asked.

"I don't know," Keisha replied. "I was at Manny's house talking and he started walking me home. Some guy pulled him to the side and was talking to him. The next thing I know, he's in a rush to get to my house. I asked him what was wrong but all he told me was something was about to go down and he didn't want me to get hurt. We were at my house watching TV when I heard the gunshots. I don't know what made me run around there, I just knew that something was wrong." Tears slid out of her eyes as she shook her head. "I can't believe he's gone."

Deisha handed her a tissue. "You shouldn't have ran out there like that. What if something had happened to you?"

"Keisha, did you see Jamal around there?" Tamera asked.

"Yeah, he was in the house, but I could tell he was just as mad as I was. Right after I got around there, his brother, I forget his name…"

"Shawn," Deisha told her.

"Yeah, him… he grabbed me and was hugging me. Man, I hate when shit like this happens. They're always killing the good ones but never do anything about the ones that be doing all of the dirty shit." She threw her tissue on the floor and put her hands to her face, crying uncontrollably.

Deisha got up and unfolded her chair bed. She took some sheets out of her closet and gave Keisha one of her pillows from off of her bed. "If you want, you can have my bed and I'll sleep on the chair bed," Deisha offered.

Keisha wiped her face. "No, it's okay. Can I call my brother?"

"No need, he's not home," Deisha told her.

"How do you know?" Keisha asked.

"Because he said he would call me when he got in the house." Her phone rang just as she finished her sentence. She picked up the receiver. "Hello?"

"Hey Deisha," Maurice said to her. He sounded exhausted.

"Hey babe," Deisha spoke back.

"Is my sister still up?"

"Yeah, is everything cool around Shawn and Jamal's way?"

"The same scenario whenever somebody popular gets popped. Not to say it like that but, it is what it is. I know she's still crying."

"Yeah," Deisha sighed.

Maurice shook his head. "After he tried to do her dirty, she got the nerve to be crying over that nigga. Put her on the phone," Maurice told her. Deisha handed Keisha the phone.

"Hello," Keisha spoke.

"Keesh, are you alright?"

"No," her voice trembled as she answered her brother.

"Don't try to stop yourself from crying because it's only going to make it worse." Keisha broke down in tears. Deisha rubbed her back to calm her down.

"Who did it?" she asked.

"I don't know," Maurice lied. "Look, just get some sleep and I'll see you in school tomorrow. Do you want me to bring you anything?"

"I don't have any lunch money," Keisha told him.

"Come to my advisory tomorrow and I'll have some money for you, alright?"

"Okay, thank you." She hung the phone up and wiped her face again. "Is it alright if I make a quick phone call?"

"Sure," Deisha replied as she put her night shirt on.

Keisha picked the receiver up and dialed Manny's number. He answered after the first ring. "Hello?"

"Manny?"

"Keisha? Are you alright?" Manny asked her as he sat up in his bed.

"I've felt better," she told him.

"Why were you crying like that earlier?"

"It kinda goes back to what you asked me earlier when we were sitting on your porch," Keisha said as she twirled the phone cord around her finger.

"Oh. But are you alright though? Because I called your house three times and nobody answered.

Keisha figured he would call so she turned the ringers off in the house. "Yeah, I'm okay for now. I came over to Deisha's because my mom was getting on my nerves."

"I'll pick you up tomorrow after you get out of school, okay?" Manny assured her.

Keisha smiled, "Okay." She waited for Manny to hang up and then she put the receiver down.

Deisha looked at Keisha and began to smile herself. "That's got to be one sharp dude to get you to smile after all of the crying you just did."

Keisha giggled bashfully before retreating to the bathroom so she could change into her night clothes. When she returned, she and Deisha talked for a little while until she fell asleep.

Michelle peeped into the room moments later. "Is she alright?" she asked.

"Yeah, for now. But when it starts to sink in that he's gone and she starts to think about it, it's going to hit her hard. But she'll be okay," Deisha told her aunt.

"Who was Dominique to her?"

"Her first love."

"Well, how old is she?" Michelle frowned.

"Fifteen." Deisha noticed the look on her aunt's face. "She was the same age I was when I lost my virginity to Raheem, Aunt 'Chelle."

"Well, I hope she's careful. I'm getting ready to go to bed so, goodnight." She kissed Deisha on her forehead and left her room.

The next day, Keisha went to school as normal. She tried to pretend as if everything was okay but all of the memories of her and Dominique flooded her mind. She thought about the last few times she saw him and how he tried to apologize and make up with her, but she shot him down maliciously. She began to feel guilty. She fought off her tears, not wanting to share them with anyone while she was in class. But when she went to lunch, instead of sitting with her friends, she went over to her brother.

"What's wrong?" Maurice asked her when he saw the expression on her face.

Keisha tried to speak but couldn't get the words out and began to cry. "I keep thinking about all the times that Dominique was trying to apologize to me and how I treated him like dirt and the way I talked to him. I was so nasty to him and all he was trying to do was say he was sorry. And now I won't get the chance to forgive him." Keisha sobbed as she sat next to her brother with her hands to her face.

Maurice was upset that his sister could have that kind of remorse for Dominique after the way he dogged her out in the streets and tried to make her out to be some type of smut. "I'm sorry to say this, but fuck that nigga. He ain't give a shit about you after what he was running around doing. And I guarantee you, the only reason he was trying to apologize was to get back in your good graces because he found out you were messing with Manny and he figured if you forgave him, he can hit again. That nigga wasn't sorry, he was fucking sneaky and that's why his ass got popped. Fuck that nigga, straight up."

Deisha shook her head at Maurice. "Don't say that, Mar. For real that's not what she needs to hear."

"It's the fucking truth," Maurice hissed at Deisha as he cut his eyes at her. She had never seen him that angry before.

"So what, no matter how you feel about Dom, he meant something to your sister. Dogging him out after he got killed isn't helping and it's not making her feel better. Let her grieve!" Deisha said back to him.

"No he's right, Deisha. Y'all are both right. I know Dom didn't care about me. But he was still my first. And no matter what he did, nobody deserves to die like that." Keisha wiped her face. "I'm going to get something to eat." She left their table and went to the ALA CARTE line.

"I'm so mad at you for saying that Maurice," Deisha said.

"Look Deisha, don't start. I'm not in the mood for this shit, for real." Deisha fell silent not wanting to argue with him. She knew he was angry and did not want his anger directed towards her.

During Keisha's last period class, the grief she felt over Dominique's murder was so overwhelming she knew she had to leave. She went over to her teacher's desk.

"Ms. Gregory, I'm not feeling so well," Keisha said to her teacher.

"What's the problem?" Ms. Gregory asked.

"A friend of mines was killed last night and…" Keisha trailed off and put her hands to her face to hide her tears. Her teacher walked her out to the hallway.

"Oh sweetheart, I'm sorry to hear that. Is there anything I can do for you?"

"Can I just go to my brother's class to get my mother's work number so I can go home?" Keisha asked as she sniffed and wiped her face.

"Who's your brother?" Ms. Gregory asked.

"Maurice," Keisha replied.

"Not Maurice Brown?" the teacher gasped. "I always wondered if you two were related to each other. Now it's coming together. The two of you do look alike now that I think about it. You'll need a hall pass and then you can go right over," Ms. Gregory told her.

Keisha took the hall pass and then went to Maurice class. Tamera saw her peeking into the classroom and looked around for Maurice.

"Reese, your sister is at the door," she told him.

Maurice got up and walked over to the doorway. His teacher called out to him.

"Maurice, where do you think you're going?" his teacher asked.

"My sister is outside," Maurice told her.

"Maurice, sit down right now," the teacher instructed.

"No man, get outta here." He waved the teacher off and went to the door to see what was going on. Keisha hugged him unable to keep her tears in. Maurice tried to talk to her in a hushed tone to calm her down. He was also trying to stay calm himself.

His teacher came to the doorway. "Maurice, you know you have no business running out of class…"

Maurice interrupted her already pissed off that Keisha was as upset as she was over Dominique after the way he treated her. "What the hell are you talking about? This is my business, this is family."

His teacher recoiled as if someone had cut the blood from her. "I think you better watch who you're talking to," his teacher warned.

Maurice sighed. "Okay, my bad, just chill, please. Her friend got killed last night."

"Do you want to talk about this? Maybe you should send her to the councilor," the teacher suggested.

"She doesn't need any damn councilor. She needs to go home," Maurice snapped.

"Well, you can't stand out in the hall like this. And if you continue to talk to me this way, both of you will be going home."

"I said alright! Damn! They're just going to have to suspend me then. Go back in the classroom and mind your business. We're not doing shit in there anyway."

"You need to calm down," his teacher replied.

"No you need to calm the fuck down. You see me out here with my sister, I just told you somebody she was close to was killed last night and you're out here trying to start an argument."

"Mr. Brown!" the teacher piped. Maurice shook his head as he held his sister. "Don't stay out here too long."

"Whatever," Maurice mumbled. His teacher closed the door. "Keisha, do you want Mommy to come get you?"

"She won't come get me for this," Keisha moped.

"Well, I'm about to hook it up." He peeped in the room and told Chanda to come over to them.

"What?" she asked when she got to the door way.

"In five minutes, ask Ms. Tate if you can go to the bathroom. Take your phone with you," Maurice instructed.

"For what?" Chanda asked.

"My sister is going to go to the office and call you. I need you to pretend like you're our mom so she can get an early dismissal."

"Alright." Chanda got a piece of paper and scribbled down her cell number. She gave it to Keisha and then went back to her desk.

"Alright Keisha, call this number in like five minutes and pretend like you're talking to Mommy," Maurice told his little sister.

"What if I get caught?" Keisha asked as she looked at the number.

"Trust me, it's been done before," Maurice assured her.

Keisha went to the coordinators office and explained the situation. She called Chanda and pretended to talk to her mother like she was told. She hung up before the coordinator could ask to speak with her.

"Well, I would've liked to talk with her to make sure that it was okay to release you, but I trust you. I'm sorry for your loss, Ms. Brown. Be careful going home," he told her as he wrote out her early dismissal slip.

"I will," Keisha replied thinking how easy it was to pull that off and planning on using that tactic to get out of school more often. She went back to her Math class and gathered her books together and put them in her book bag.

"You're leaving?" her teacher asked her.

"Yes," Keisha replied.

"Get your homework from one of your classmates."

"I will," Keisha said as she left out of the classroom. She stopped back at her brother's class. He got up and went over to the door.

"I told you it would work. You're going home?" Maurice asked her.

"Yeah but I'ma stop by Dominique's mom's house and see if she needs any help with anything."

"Alright, I'll see you when I get in from work later on." Maurice hugged his little sister and she left.

Dominique's mother was pleased to see Keisha more than any of the other people that came to the house to offer their condolences. She always liked Keisha more than the other girls that Dominique claimed to be his girlfriends because she was respectful and had a good head on her shoulders. She wished they had stayed together longer hoping that would have changed her son's behavior as well as his attitude. Keisha helped out the entire week of the funeral, cleaning the house and watching Dominique's daughter while his mother ran errands.

The funeral was the hardest part. It was an extremely long line of people there to pay their respects to Dominique. Maurice was shocked that D-Ball had the nerve to show up but he didn't say anything. The closer Maurice and Keisha got to the casket to view his body, the more Keisha trembled.

"Are you alright?" Maurice asked as he put his arm around her shoulder.

"Yeah," Keisha mumbled as she rubbed her hands together. There were three people ahead of them and Keisha could partially see him. She began to cry silently. But when they finally approached the casket and she saw him lying inside looking peaceful, she buckled forward and almost collapsed from grief. Maurice held her up and helped her to her seat. She spent the majority of the service with her head resting on her brother's shoulder letting the tears fall as she thought back to the brief time she and Dominique shared together.

Keisha went back to Dominique's mother's house after the burial to help with his wake. She knew his mother would need all the help and support possible since Dominique was her only son.

After the funeral, Tamera was at Jamal's house keeping him company. He was lying on her chest as they lay on the couch together. Tamera looked at him when he fell asleep and smiled as she admired how handsome he was. Her thoughts drifted off to Dominique, Kareem, Raheem and her mother wondering if there were a Heaven and they were there, what were they doing at that moment. She then began to think of herself, Jamal and their unborn child and what the future held for them. Before she knew it, she had fallen asleep.

It was partly cloudy as Tamera walked down the street with Shawn. She was holding something in her hand as they approached a car. She dropped the items in her hand onto the ground. Shawn bent over to pick them up. Tamera heard screams and a loud noise. She felt Shawn's hand reach for her, trying to pull her to the ground but his grip slipped. Tamera then fell backwards onto the ground...

Ms. Keyona tapped Jamal. "Boy, get up." Jamal looked at his mother but didn't move. "How long have y'all been in here?"

"Since after Dominique's funeral," Jamal told her. Ms. Keyona looked at him suspiciously. "We wasn't doing anything."

"I sincerely hope not. Y'all already got one on the way. I ain't trying to be shaking no damn babies. I did my crime and I did the damn time." Jamal looked at his mother and shook his head as she headed upstairs to her bedroom. He then looked at Tamera admiring her beauty and thought of how lucky he was to have her. He saw a tear slide out of her eye and down the side of her face. He was about to wipe it away when a few drops of blood trickled out of her nose.

"What the hell?" he thought to himself as he grabbed a tissue and wiped her nose. He shook her and she jumped up breathing heavy as if she was about to have an attack. She felt her stomach and looked at Jamal, scooting away from him as if he might harm her.

"What's wrong?" he asked.

"My dream..." she shook her head. "...it felt so real."

"What did you dream about?"

Tamera looked at Jamal confused. She opened her mouth and then closed it. She tried hard to think of her dream but like the flashes she had, it left her as quickly as it came. "Shawn... he was with me and was carrying something or he dropped something and for some reason he was trying to pull me on the ground. It's all jumbled and I can't remember. But it felt so real..." Tamera looked up at Jamal.

Jamal looked at her for a span of heartbeats. He had a dream that he was trying to find her in a hospital but no one had any information. He saw Shawn with blood on his t-shirt but when he ran after him, Shawn disappeared into a crowd. He didn't mention it to Tamera because he had no idea what the hell it meant. It scared the hell out of him, though. He pulled Tamera close to him and hugged her. He tried to shake the bad feeling that the dream left him with. But the knot in his stomach wouldn't loosen.

"It's alright babe. It was just a dream..." he told Tamera in a whisper as he rubbed the back of her neck.

A couple weeks after Dominique's funeral, Keisha was at Manny's house on his porch keeping him company. He was standing behind her with his arms around her waist, swaying side to side. He kissed her neck and Keisha closed her eyes. He then grabbed her by her hand and pulled her in the house. He started kissing her, leading her up to his bedroom and shocking Keisha all at the same time. She couldn't believe it was happening so suddenly. Just as Keisha was getting into it, Manny stopped.

"I've got an idea," Manny whispered.

"What?" Keisha asked breathlessly.

"I'll be back. Just do something to make me feel good." When he left the room, Keisha began to undress and then climbed under his covers anxiously awaiting his return. He came back a few minutes later and turned his bedroom light off. He undressed also and climbed into the bed with her. They began kissing and caressing each other again. Manny began to kiss her neck and lick around her collar bone, moving further down. Keisha felt two fingers slide inside of her and she inhaled as he moved even further down. Since it was dark, Keisha couldn't see what he was doing but she had an idea as to what was coming next and she no longer cared. When he got below her belly button, Keisha lost control. She grabbed the back of his head and moaned loudly trying to squirm away as the pleasure was far too great for her to handle. When he was done he slid inside of her and gave her a better sexual experience than she had with Dominique. When it was over, he collapsed on top of her and wrapped his arms around her. He whispered that he loved her and Keisha told him she loved him too. Before she knew it, they both had fallen asleep.

Manny woke up first. When he looked at the clock, he scrambled out of the bed. "Keisha, get up! It's almost 1:30am. Girl, get up and get dressed!"

Keisha jumped up squealing. She scrambled for her clothes. "Oh my God, I'm in trouble!" She put her clothes on in a hurry. Manny turned his light on and tied his sneakers. She grabbed his brush and smoothed her hair to the back. Manny grabbed her by her hand when she was done and rushed out of the house. He practically ran her home. When they got to her house, he gave her a brief kiss.

"Call me tomorrow if you're not in trouble," he told her.

"Okay," she replied quickly. She crept into the house and silently closed and locked the door behind her. She cautiously tip-toed up to her bedroom feeling relieved that both Maurice and their mother's doors were closed and their lights were off. She opened her door without making a sound and then closed it behind her. She turned her light on, turned around and screamed when she saw Maurice.

"You better be quiet before you wake up Mommy." Keisha had her hand on her chest, breathing heavy. "Where the hell were you at that brought your ass in here almost two o'clock in the got damn morning?" Maurice hissed.

Keisha stammered, "I…"

"Shut up, because you're about to lie," Maurice snapped, interrupting her. "What the fuck were you doing at Manny's house this time of night?" Keisha began breathing heavy as if she were about to cry. Maurice backed up and put his hands over his face. He was tired from waiting up for her all night and wanted to knock the shit out of her. "You're going to keep playing and end up like some of these fucked up girls around here. You're lucky because Mommy was looking for you. I had to tell her you were still upset about Dominique and was at Deisha's house. I'm not lying for you no more." He walked over to her door. "I'll deal with you in the morning." He closed her door and went to his room to go to bed.

That next morning, Maurice caught Keisha in her room as she was getting dressed.

"Maurice, I'm sorry. I can explain," Keisha said.

Maurice threw a bag at her. "I don't want to hear it. Keisha, you better calm your little ass down before you get caught up in something that you can't get out of. I told you I ain't want you running the streets all hours of the day and night. What, you thought I was joking? You're not grown so you better get that shit straight. Let me catch you doing one thing. The slightest slip up and I'ma turn your ass over to Mommy. I'm done because you don't listen. You're one of those people that have to learn the hard way." He looked at his sister and shook his head. "I can't stop you from having sex so you better protect yourself." Keisha looked at the bag on the floor. "Don't say I never gave you anything." He left her room and closed her door behind him.

Keisha picked up the bag and looked at it. She hid the bag of condoms in her dresser drawer.

Later on that day, Jamal was coming in from a long day at work. He was tired and annoyed and wanted to take a hot shower, check on Tamera and go to sleep. Just as he was taking his sneakers off, his phone rang.

"Hello?"

"Congratulations, Daddy," Samir said on the other end. "Word on the street is, you about to be a father, soon."

Jamal shook his head, pissed that somebody on the street not only was watching him, but was watching Tamera also. "What do you want?" he asked through clenched teeth.

"Nigga you better check your fucking tone. Don't act like you don't know who the fuck you're talking to. I got niggas out here watching your bitch-ass and will strike if I give the word so you better humble yourself," Samir threatened.

"Yo, why are you fucking with me and my girl, nigga? I said I'ma be out there. I don't give a fuck who's watching me. If they want it, they can get it, too. Fuck out of here!" Jamal snapped right back. He was not about to let his cousin make a bitch out of him.

Samir laughed, "Let me find out this nigga getting tough. Now this is the Jamal I'm used to, ain't that right, El?" Jamal heard someone laugh in the background and agree with Samir. "Remember nigga, you owe me. Now

Yani

we can do this the clean way, or we can do this shit real dirty and you know I don't have a problem with that. I'll see your ass on June 20th. Don't try no slick shit either." Samir hung the phone up and all Jamal heard was the dial tone.

Jamal hung up the phone and put his hands to his face. The flash of Shawn with a bloody t-shirt on came to mind. He shook the image from his head. He was not about to let anything happen to his brother. Nobody was going to pay for a mistake that he made. He prayed for a peaceful ending to this madness.

CHAPTER 9
THE BEGINNING TO AN END

Early June rolled around quickly and the seniors were finally in graduation practice, doing their senior class luncheon as well as their class trip. Tamera's friends were ecstatic that she was going to be one of the lead singers for their graduation song, which was *The World's Greatest* by R. Kelly. She was also singing the National Black Anthem, *Lift Ev'ry Voice and Sing* as well as *The Star Spangled Banner*.

Tamera felt a lot of pressure at practice. Their instructor was a White lady with a sharp, English accent. She claimed that Tamera put too much into the songs, yet she was the one who picked her to sing. One morning after Tamera sang, her friends cheered for her because of how good she sounded. The instructor's face began to turn red.

"Alright, alright!" she yelled to the seniors to get them to calm down. She looked at Tamera and forced a smile. "That was lovely, Ms. Harrison, but do you think you can tone it down a notch. You have a beautiful voice, just tone it down some."

"What do you mean?" Tamera asked innocently, knowing exactly what the instructor meant.

"You don't have to put so much… pizzazz into it, you know?"

"I can't help it. That's how I sing. I thought you told me to put my all into it?"

"I know, and come to think of it, I really shouldn't have said that. Just sing the song regularly," the instructor told her.

"What's wrong with the way that I'm singing it now?" Tamera asked, confused.

"You don't have the proper training and I don't want your voice to crack on graduation day. You're only singing at a graduation. This isn't American Idol where someone is looking to sign you nor is this Show Time at The Apollo. Now, I'm not going to debate with you on how to sing the song. Either sing it the way I tell you to, or you can walk," she said firmly.

Tamera gave the instructor the evil eye and then looked at Jamal. He nodded for her to walk since they previously discussed the way the instructor had changed on her. They both knew the reason for her change of heart was because she heard that Tamera was pregnant. She sat the microphone on the stage and started walking away. "Fuck it."

Jamal chuckled to himself as Tamera walked out of the auditorium.

"I talked to her nicely, there was no need for that," the instructor said furiously. "Angelica, you can take her place."

They carried on with the graduation practice. Angelica wanted to see if there were any double standards going on, so she sang the song just like Tamera did. She wasn't surprised with the instructor's reaction.

"Great, Angelica. That was wonderful." Angelica looked at the instructor as if she were stupid.

"I'm glad you liked it," she started walking off of the stage. "I'm not doing it either."

"Why not?" the instructor asked.

"Because I just sang the song just like Tammy did and it was all smiles. But when she was singing it, you had a big problem."

"Her attitude wasn't right, that is why I didn't want her singing."

"What do you mean? You're the one who picked her," Angelica argued.

"Are you trying to tell me how to conduct this graduation?" the instructor asked, feeling slighted.

"No, what I'm trying to say is, if there is no problem with the way I'm singing, then Tammy can sing it. It wasn't her attitude that you had a problem with, you have a problem with her being pregnant." Angelica hit the nail on the head and the instructor's face turned beet red.

"I think you have said enough, Angelica," the instructor said through clenched teeth.

"Look can we settle this shit so I can say my speech and go home. It's hot, I don't have to work and I'm tired of sitting here," the valedictorian shouted.

"You dig me. This cheap-ass school needs to get some AC in this bitch as much money that we paid for our class dues. We shouldn't be graduating in this damn auditorium anyway!" another senior named Dante shouted. "Shit, my nuts are starting to sweat." A few of his friends broke into a wild laughter.

"Alright!" the instructor shouted again. She looked at Angelica and sighed. "Alright, she can sing. But this is not going to be some "hood" occasion. I was serious about the American Idol comment. Do tell her that I am sorry if I offended her and I would very much like for her to sing. It's time for you all to go so I will see you tomorrow morning. Andre, make sure that you have memorized at least half of your speech so you aren't constantly looking at the paper," the instructor said.

The seniors cleared out of the auditorium and went outside. Jamal found Tamera waiting on the steps. She looked unusually happy.

"Are you alright?" he asked her.

"Hell yeah," Tamera replied with a huge grin on her face. "This guy from Philly International Records just gave me his business card. He heard me sing back in February and had been trying to locate me. Finally he came back here and heard me sing again and he wants me on a few collaborations as well as a solo album!!"

Jamal threw his arms around her and lifted her in the air before giving her a kiss. "That's what's up, babe. Are you going to call him?" he asked her.

"Damn straight I am," Tamera grinned.

"Ms. Ann apologized for how she acted and said she wants you to sing in the graduation," Jamal told her.

"What changed her mind?"

"She just knew she made a mistake and Angie came at her neck so she changed her mind," Jamal laughed out loud.

"That lady doesn't like me but who cares? In a few weeks, she can lick my boots." They laughed as they stopped at the Chinese food stand to get something to eat.

When Tamera got home, she called the guy from Philly International, whose name was Greg. They discussed the projects that he wanted her on and when he wanted to meet up with her.

"When can we meet so I can show you some of the music? I want you for a few hooks first and a young lady that I'm working with along with another friend of mine have been writing songs ever since I showed them the tape of you performing back in February. You were hot on that piano, girl!" Greg said excitedly.

Tamera laughed. "Well, there isn't any graduation practice Wednesday so will that be good for you?"

"Well, how does 1:30pm sound? Do you know where Sahara Grill is?"

"Yeah, off of Walnut and Locust," Tamera replied.

"Okay, we can meet there, have lunch and take things from there," Greg told her.

"Is it okay if my boyfriend comes because since I'm pregnant, most likely he'll want to make sure I get there and back safely?"

"Sure, that's no problem. You're pregnant?"

"Yes," she answered, shyly.

"Damn, you look so sweet. How many months are you?" Greg asked her.

"I'm three months. I'll be four months on June 12th," Tamera replied, proudly.

"Okay, well congratulations," Greg told her.

"Thank you."

"I'll see you Wednesday."

"Okay," Tamera said happily before hanging up. She jumped for joy and clapped her hands. She then rubbed her stomach and said to her unborn baby, "Do you want some ice-cream? I think we deserve some yummy cookies and cream ice-cream to celebrate." She went into the kitchen and fixed herself a bowl of ice-cream with sliced cucumbers and then went out to sit on the porch to enjoy the warm breeze. She couldn't believe that she was going to be recording an album soon.

Tamera was in a wonderful mood until she saw a black Tahoe drive past her house four times. She was starting to get nervous and was ready to get up and go back in the house. The car came back again and parked out front. Tamera tried to stay calm but every nerve in her body was shot.

"Pull off," she mumbled to herself. "Pull the fuck off."

The driver side door swung open and a guy got out. He was dressed in a New York Knicks warm up suit with a pair of Air Jordans and sun glasses. He tilted the glasses from his face and looked at Tamera for a moment. A sense of fear shot through her, putting her stomach in knots. She wanted to go in the house but her legs wouldn't move. The guy walked onto the first few steps of her porch.

"Sweetheart, is your name Tamera?" he asked sweetly.

"Why?" Tamera asked nervously.

The guy took a couple more steps towards her. "Because I want to know."

"Yes," she answered after a few moments.

The guy handed her a small package with baby booties and a hat set inside. "Tell Jamal that Sa sends his regards." He turned away from her smiling and got back into his truck, driving away as quickly as he came.

Tamera looked at the gift and then went into the house, throwing it into the garbage. She picked up the phone and called Jamal.

"Yo!" Shawn answered.

"Hey Shawn, is Jamal there?"

"He just got in. I heard about the record deal girl, congratulations."

"Thank you," Tamera managed to smile.

"Let me get him for you."

Tamera waited patiently until she heard Jamal pick the phone up.

"Yo!"

"Some guy just came here and dropped this so called gift off with some baby shit inside saying to tell you that Samir sends his regards. What the hell is going on?"

"Calm down, Tammy," Jamal told her.

"I don't want to calm down! I'm sick of this shit!" Tamera snapped.

"Does Samir know that I'm pregnant?"

"Tammy..." Jamal said.

"Does he know?!" she screamed. When Jamal didn't reply she put the phone on the counter. Tears began to spill out of her eyes as she feared the worst. A sharp pain hit her in the chest. She tried to say something but couldn't so she hung the phone up.

Jamal looked up at the ceiling and hung his phone up also. Although he was tired from work, he knew he couldn't let this little fiasco slide. He grabbed his keys and left the house before Shawn had a chance to ask him what was going on.

Jamal headed straight to Samir's house. He waited patiently for him to answer the door after he rang the doorbell.

"What the fuck are you doing here? It ain't June 20th yet," Samir said when he opened the door.

Jamal punched Samir in his mouth making him stumble back. He barged into the house and grabbed Samir by his neck, throwing him onto a table. Samir had Jamal's shirt in a grip.

"You're sending your little bitch-ass niggas to my girl's house to threaten her. Pussy, I said leave her out of this. You want me, nigga. Stop fucking playing with me, Sa," Jamal practically growled in Samir's face.

Samir chuckled and then put a gun to Jamal's neck. His facial expression changed completely. "You must've lost your damn mind. Get your punk-ass off of me." Jamal looked at Samir and then let him go. "Who the fuck do you think you are coming in my house like you're some all mighty, super muthafucking nigga? I will waste your faggot-ass if you ever disrespect me like that again. What tip are you on?"

"You talk a lot of shit when you have a gun in your hand," Jamal said calmly.

Samir looked at Jamal and then sat the gun on the table, staring at it. Out of nowhere, he punched Jamal in his mouth. "I dare you to swing back. My niggas at the corner of your girl's block, all I gotta do is say "sic-em" and that bitch is done. You come in here like you're the fuck tough after everything I did for you!" He punched Jamal in his mouth again and then put the gun back to his head. "You better hope for Shawn's sake, Tamika's sake or whatever that bitch's name is that everything goes real fucking smooth this summer." He pushed Jamal towards his front door. "Get your punk-ass up out of my house."

Jamal eyeballed Samir for a moment and then left. He used the back of his hand to wipe the blood from the corner of his mouth and then walked over to Tamera's house to make sure she was alright.

Tamera was still in the kitchen leaning onto the counter. The pain that hit her in her chest almost knocked the wind out of her. It felt like she had a bubble of air in her chest and it hurt every time she inhaled. A knock went at the door. She fixed herself a glass of ice and went to open it. She looked Jamal over.

"What happened to you?" she asked him.

"I got into a fight with Samir," Jamal told her. "Can I come in?"

Tamera hesitated. "Yeah." She opened the door wider and let him in. "Are you alright?"

"He only cut the side of my lip," Jamal replied. He felt it and then looked at his finger to see if it was still bleeding. "Are you alright?" he asked her back.

"Why is he doing this?" Tamera asked as she plopped down on the couch. She put a piece of ice in her mouth and sucked on it.

"He's trying to scare me and I seriously believe he gets some kind of kick out of this shit." He ran his fingers through her hair. She was about to put another piece of ice in her mouth but put it back in the cup instead.

"I'm sorry," he told her.

"Don't be." Tamera sighed. She swirled the ice around in her cup with her spoon and then drank the water that some of the ice melted into.

"So did you talk to the guy that wants to record with you?" Jamal asked, changing the subject.

"Yeah, I called him earlier. He wants to meet at Sahara grill next Wednesday at 1:30pm. Can you come with me?"

"Yeah, I'll come. I don't have to work anyway. Does he want you to sing?"

"I don't know." She leaned back onto the couch and leaned Jamal onto her. She took a piece of ice out of the cup and put it in Jamal's mouth. "You got my back, boo?"

"Yeah, I've got your back." Jamal laughed as he crunched on the ice.

"You better," Tamera replied after a moment.

Keisha had become sexually promiscuous with Manny. They had sex almost every day of the week, exploring different ways. Keisha was extra careful. She used birth control that Deisha took her to the clinic to get as well as the condoms that her brother gave her.

A girl that used to talk to Manny found out about him and Keisha being together. She became jealous and started plotting on Keisha. The girl, whose name was Danielle, got a few of her girlfriends together and waited for Keisha to get off of the 61 bus one day after school. She had been watching her for over a week and knew her routine. When Keisha got off the bus, she adjusted the earphones to the mp3 player that Manny bought her and started walking towards her house. The girls followed behind her but she didn't seem to notice. Danielle sped up behind her and grabbed Keisha by her ponytail before punching her in the face. Keisha reacted fast and swung back, barely catching her. She dropped the mp3 player and snatched the earphones out of her ears. She backed up and looked the four girls over. Maurice taught her that if she were to ever get caught in a situation like this, to swing on the person with the biggest mouth. She couldn't tell off hand who it was, so she swung on Danielle and began to beat her up. The other three girls jumped in it. One girl jumped on Keisha's back trying to knock her down, but Keisha swung her off of her. The other girl kicked Keisha in her ribs, knocking the wind out of her. They all began to swing on her but Keisha fought back as best as she could. People stood around watching it but didn't try to break the fight up. Had they known it was Maurice's little sister, they would've stopped the fight.

Shawn and his friends were driving back to his house when they noticed the crowd.

"What the hell is going on now?" Deisha asked as she peeped out of the window.

Chanda noticed Keisha swinging frantically on the girls and jumped out of the car.

"Where are you going?" Shawn hollered as he stopped the car.

Chanda snatched off her heels and her earrings. "They're jumping your sister, Maurice!" She took off running towards the fight with Maurice and Deisha running behind her. She wasted no time when she got over there. She hit one girl with her shoe and punched another girl in her face. Deisha followed up and they fought wildly in the street like animals until people had enough sense to stop the fight. Maurice grabbed Keisha and pulled her away.

"I'ma fuck you up when I catch you, bitch!" Keisha shrieked.

"Yo, her nose is bleeding," Jamal told Maurice. Shawn passed him a towel from out of his trunk and Maurice applied it to her face.

Deisha and Chanda came back over to the car. Chanda leaned onto Deisha as she put her shoes back on and fixed her hair. "That was some sickening shit. How they watch those girls jump you like that?"

"They probably ain't know it was me," Keisha said as she wiped her nose.

"Regardless of who it was, somebody still should've stopped that shit," Deisha said angrily.

"Who were those girls anyway?" Tamera asked.

"Danielle, Kaleesha, Brandy and Nyema," Keisha named them. She planned to get them all back one by one.

"So you knew them?" Jamal asked.

"Yeah, and I'ma get those bitches back, too. Danielle is a nut. She snuck up behind me and then hit me. That was some straight nut ass shit. She knew she had no wins if she had stepped to me one on one. That's the only reason she did that. And then she jumped me. It's on. She's only mad because Manny doesn't want her horse face looking ass no more."

"Yeah well, before you plot your little revenge, you gotta deal with Mommy first." Maurice told her.

"What?" Keisha asked.

"I told you the next thing you did I was turning you over to mommy."

"But it wasn't even my fault!" Keisha piped.

"You just said yourself that they did it because Manny doesn't want her anymore. If you weren't with him, you wouldn't have gotten jumped. So, come on. Because I am not going to explain to Mommy why your face looks like that. Plus when she finds out, she's going to make you fight them anyway." Maurice grabbed her by her arm and started walking her home.

"Go get cleaned up," he told her when they got in the house.

Keisha went upstairs to the bathroom and got her wash cloth. She wet it with warm water and washed her face. Her lip was cut and her cheek was a little swollen. It was only noticeable if she was looked at closely. She had scratches on her neck and near her eye. She was upset but refused to cry. When she finished, she went into her room to change into some sweat pants, a sports bra and a white beater. She threw on her old New Balance sneakers as well. Keisha knew her mother was going to make her fight them again, so she braided her hair to the back. She went back downstairs and grabbed a soda out of the refrigerator.

"Come here," Maurice said to her when she came out of the kitchen. Keisha took a sip of her soda and went over to her brother. He put his hand on her chin and looked her over. He shook his head in disgust. "Mommy is going to be pissed."

"I know," Keisha agreed.

Maurice looked at his watch. "She should be here any minute now," he looked at Keisha. "You're going to fuck her up, aren't you?"

"Shit, hell yeah," they laughed together just as their mother came in. Keisha's heart started to pound in her chest. She looked at Maurice and swallowed. He nodded at her. "Mom, I got jumped."

"You got what?" Ms. Brown asked as she took her suit jacket off.

"I got jumped," Keisha said again, louder.

"By who?"

"These girls that's jealous because me and Manny go together," Keisha explained.

"Do you know who one of the girls is?" her mother asked.

"Danielle was one of them."

"Come on. We're going to settle this shit right now. I don't know who the hell they think they are." Keisha sat her unfinished soda on the table and they walked around to Danielle's house.

Danielle's mother answered the door when Ms. Brown knocked. "Can I help you?" she asked with an attitude.

"Your daughter and some of her friends jumped my daughter," Ms. Brown said with her hand on her hip.

"And? What the hell do you want me to do about it?"

"Tell her to bring her ass out here. If she wants to fight my daughter, let them fight one on one," Ms. Brown replied. She was ready to whip Danielle's mother's ass since she clearly had no manners.

Danielle came behind her mother when she heard the commotion and decided to put on a show. "Oh, you want some more? You want some more?!" Her mother tried to hold her back.

"No don't hold her back. Let her ass out. She got all that mouth. If you ain't gonna beat her ass and shut her up, my daughter will be glad to do it," Ms. Brown said as she came out of her shoes as if she was ready to fight herself. Maurice watched, enjoying the scene. Danielle's mother let her out and Keisha stepped into the street willingly. "And ain't nobody jumping in this one," Ms. Brown said.

"You better kick her ass, Danny!" Danielle's mother shouted to her.

Danielle stepped in the street like she was big and bad and Keisha punched her in her face twice, cutting her with her rings. Danielle tried to grab Keisha by her hair and was sadly mistaken when she felt braids. Keisha hit her again and they fought wildly in the streets as people watched. Both of them slipped and fell on the ground.

"Get up off the ground, Keisha!" Ms. Brown shouted to her daughter.

Chanda and the others were coming around the corner when they heard the commotion.

"They're fighting again!" Chanda shouted and they ran over to get a closer look just as Danielle was about to try to stomp Keisha, but she rolled out of the way. She scrambled to her feet and threw her hands up like Maurice had showed her when they used to play fight as kids. Danielle rushed towards her and Keisha swung twice, missing with the first one but catching her in her eye with the second one. They started beating on each other as Keisha tried desperately to hit her somewhere that would drop her.

"If you don't beat her ass, Keisha I'ma beat yours!" Ms. Brown shouted from the crowd.

Keisha became so angry that she had started to cry. She grabbed Danielle by her hair and kicked her in her stomach twice making her buckle. When Danielle bent over to catch her breath, Keisha kneed her in her face twice, busting her lip and making her nose bleed. She punched Danielle in her ribs and started giving her body shots until she fell down. She was about to walk away, but her brother and his friends screamed for Keisha to stomp her.

"Stomp her, Keesh!" Maurice shouted.

"Stomp that bitch!" Jamal, Chanda and Deisha yelled at the same time.

Keisha slung around and kicked Danielle in her face. She kicked her in her stomach making her spit out blood and then stomped her some more. Maurice and his mother grabbed her thinking she had done enough when Danielle's mother came towards them like she wanted to fight also.

"I wish you would even walk up on me like you're tough and I'll splatter your ass all over this concrete next to your damn daughter," Ms. Brown threatened.

"Yeah nigga, you don't want none," Maurice added as he laughed.

Keisha was breathing heavy as she walked away. She wiped blood from her mouth as Maurice's friends gave her pounds and handshakes. She was about to walk past the crowd and go home so she could soak her sore bones but Manny's presence stopped her. Maurice decided to leave them alone. He gave Manny a handshake.

"What's up, homie?" Maurice spoke. He then went over to his friends.

Manny looked at Keisha and shook his head. "I ain't know you had it in you."

"Now you do," Keisha replied, still trying to catch her breath.

"As soon as I heard that you got jumped, I came around here because I figured you'd be back. I guess I was right." He walked her back to her house and waited for her while she took a hot shower and changed her clothes. Her hand was hurting so she put an ice pack over it while they sat on the porch talking.

Jamal and his friends were walking down the street laughing about the fight.

"I ain't know that Keisha could box," Jamal said to Maurice.

"Who do you think taught her?" Maurice asked.

Jamal sucked his teeth. "Whatever."

"You wanna box, nigga?" Maurice joked.

"We've got the whole street." Jamal played along. They slap boxed for a moment and then started laughing as Maurice almost caught Jamal with a bitch slap. Jamal threw his arm around him. "This is my nigga."

"Y'all are too violent for me," Tamera said as she ate a water ice that she bought from the stand before they saw the second fight.

"I know you ain't talking when you stomped that girl back in October," Jamal said.

"That's because that bitch was trifling. And I thought we agreed that we weren't going to talk about that anymore." Jamal smiled and kissed her on the cheek.

Deisha looked at them and smiled. "You know y'all can still have sex while she's pregnant."

Tamera put a hand to her face trying to cover her smile. Jamal grabbed her by her hand and pulled her close to him. "Oh, we know."

Chanda and Deisha looked at them with their mouths gaped open.

"Y'all are nasty," Chanda told them as she wagged her finger at them

"Hey, we're just looking out for the baby's interest and he do need to start exercising at an early age," Jamal said as he laughed.

Chanda covered her ears. "I didn't hear that."

They laughed as they continued to walk down the street.

That next Wednesday after their class picnic, Shawn dropped Tamera and Jamal off at Sahara Grill to meet with Greg. Jamal looked at her.

"You look nervous. Are you okay?" he asked her.

"I'm good," Tamera smiled as she rubbed her hands together. They felt dry so she reached in her bag and poured lotion into her hands. After rubbing them together, Jamal kissed her on the forehead and they walked into Sahara Grill. Tamera grabbed his hand. Greg waved to them to let them know what table to come to. When they got over there, he and Jamal shook hands.

"How are you?" Jamal said.

"What's up?" Greg spoke back. "How are you, Tammy?"

"I'm fine," Tamera smiled.

"Okay, well sit down and order something. It's on me of course," Greg told them.

They sat at the table and ordered their food and then got down to business after eating and getting to know one another with Greg explaining all of the details as far as publishing rights and royalties. Her first project was doing background vocals for a rapper by the name of Trinity. But he also wanted her to hear the first song for the solo album he wanted her to do. Greg took out a mini tape player and played the song for her. There was another female singing the song.

"Who's this?" Tamera asked as she listened.

"This is the girl that helped write the song. I asked her to sing it so you could have an idea as to how it goes," Greg explained.

"She's not upset that you didn't choose her, is she?"

"Oh no. Besides, it's other things that I want her to do as far as helping you with the songs to the album we're putting together for you."

"I can't believe all of this is happening," Tamera said as she shook her head in disbelief.

"Believe it, honey. You have amazing talent. Your voice is strong and it needs to be heard." He gathered up his things and paid for their meal. "Are you guys ready?"

"Where are we going?" Jamal asked.

"I want to hear how Tamera's voice sounds in the studio, though I'm sure she sounds great. But I still want to do a sound check with her," Greg explained.

Tamera and Jamal got up from the table and followed Greg to his 2002 shiny, red Expedition. They climbed in and drove to a studio just outside of Philly in Jenkintown. He gave them a tour of the studio and introduced them to everyone that they ran into. He then took them to the room that Tamera would be recording in. Tamera went inside of the booth after meeting with the young lady that originally sang the song. They practiced it until she knew she was ready to try it.

"Are you ready?" Greg asked over the microphone.

Tamera nodded her head. "Yes." She already had an idea of how she would make it her own, separate from the recording that the other girl did. Greg came into the booth and gave her a pair of earphones that covered her entire ears. Jamal watched the two of them in there, proud that Tamera was finally getting the opportunity to do what she loved.

Greg came back out of the booth and started the music and Tamera sang it perfectly, leaving both Jamal and Greg stunned. When she was done, she looked at them and started blushing.

"Was that okay?" she asked innocently.

Yani

"That was... I don't have the words. I'm glad that I recorded that. That was brilliant! And the way you added your own style to it... girl you are going to be a force to be reckoned with in the R&B genre," Greg complimented as he came back into the booth with her.

Tamera laughed at his enthusiasm and took the earphones off. She came out of the booth and they went back out to where Jamal was standing.

Greg shook her hand and then shook his hand.

"I will see you Saturday. You'll get a chance to meet Trinity along with some other guys in the industry. We can all have lunch. Jamal it would be great if you can come because it's going to be in New York. If you guys need a ride just let me know and I will be sure to have a driver bring you out there."

Tamera looked at Jamal with wide eyes completely stunned. "Oh my God, I've never been to New York before!" she squealed as she pulled on Jamal's shirt.

Greg turned to Jamal. "You are a very lucky man. She's beautiful, she can sing. Can she cook?"

"Yeah she's pretty good in the kitchen," Jamal smiled at Tamera.

"You're a lucky man. Take my word for it. I'm going to take you guys home because it's getting late. I know you have school tomorrow, so I will see you Saturday." They walked out to his truck and continued talking.

"Where do you live, Tamera?" Greg asked her.

"26th and Turner Street" she told him.

"Okay." He drove them home. When he dropped them off and drove away, Tamera started jumping up and down, screaming.

"I'm going to New York! I'm going to New York!" she screamed as she wrapped her arms around Jamal's neck.

"Damn girl, calm down before you have the baby in there tripping tonight," Jamal joked. Tamera kissed him and leaned her forehead against his.

"I'm so proud of you, babe. But you know I gotta work Saturday so I'm not going to be able to make it. I want to hear how everything goes though, okay?" he told her.

"You can't come with me?" Tamera asked with a sad face.

"Naw, I have to work. You want me to have Shawn come with you?"

"No, it's okay." Tamera smiled at him. "I'm proud of you, too."

"For what, I didn't do anything," Jamal laughed.

"You're graduating and going to college. It's not a lot of these wanna be thugs out here that can say the same thing," Tamera told him.

"Yeah, you have a point. But listen, if I wasn't trying to get us an apartment for when we have the baby, I would take off. But I need to get this money together because I want us to have our own place, okay?" Jamal told her as he looked her in her eyes.

"I understand," Tamera said.

Jamal kissed her and gave her a hug. "I'ma go home. Call me later, okay?"

"Okay," Tamera replied, still smiling.

Tamera went into the house completely excited from the day's events.

"Tamera, is that you?" Michelle called from the kitchen when she heard her come in.

"Hi Ms. Niecie. Mmm, what's that I smell?" Tamera asked as she rubbed her hands together and came into the kitchen.

"Cherry cheesecake, do you want some?"

"Yum, yum, yum!" Tamera giggled as Michelle cut her off a slice.

"So how did everything go?" Michelle asked as they ate cheesecake together.

"He signed me to a contract and he wants me to come out to New York on Saturday to meet with Trinity and some other artists," Tamera said excitedly.

"Wow, that is wonderful!" Michelle gushed.

"He took me and Jamal to this studio out in Jenkintown that was so beautiful. He showed us around and introduced us to people. It was so awesome." Tamera couldn't wipe the smile off of her face.

"I know everything is going to work out for you because you have tremendous talent."

"Thanks Ms. Niecie." Tamera fell silent as she played with a cherry on her plate. "Ms. Niecie, my God mom is getting ready to leave for New York also to locate to another firm at the end of the summer. After graduation, is it okay if I spend the summer with her until she leaves?"

"Sure, that's fine with me. Who's your God Mother?"

"My mother's best friend; she's kinda all I have left of my mom and since she died, we've been really close."

"Sure just as long as you remember to stay in touch with me," Michelle told her.

"I will. Thanks for the cheesecake. It was yummy."

"I'm glad you liked it," Michelle smiled.

Tamera went upstairs feeling bad that she lied to Deisha's aunt about where she was going to be that summer, but she saw no other way. She knocked on Deisha's door when she got upstairs.

"Yo!" Deisha answered as she watched TV.

"I'm home," Tamera told her.

"You can come in," Tamera came in the room and closed the door behind her. She took a seat at Deisha's desk. "So how did it go?"

Tamera briefed Deisha on her meeting with Greg while Deisha listened, excited. She sighed and then said, "I had to lie to your aunt, though."

"About what?" Deisha asked.

"About where I'm going to be this summer. I told her I was going to stay with my God Mother until she left for New York. She is going to New York though. I'm just not going to stay with her."

"Well, you had to do what you had to do. Just be careful," Deisha told her.

"I will," Tamera assured her. I know you're going to help me pack tomorrow, right?"

"Yeah, I'll help you."

As soon as Deisha and Tamera got back to the house after receiving their caps and gowns, they went straight to Tamera's room to start packing her things. Tamera didn't take a lot of clothes with her, as she knew that she wouldn't be able to fit much in the coming months. She did, however, take her yearbooks from middle and high-school, her photo album as well as her diary and the stuffed teddy bear that Jamal bought her for Valentine's Day.

"Damn girl, is that everything?" Deisha joked, trying to hide how sad she was feeling that Tamera was going to be leaving soon.

"I think so," Tamera said as she looked around. She sighed when she noticed the hurt expression on Deisha's face. Deisha hugged her tight as they both began to cry.

"Promise me you won't get hurt," Deisha said.

Tamera sniffed. "I won't, I promise."

"You're like a sister to me, you know that?"

"I know," Tamera said as she let her go.

"I love you, girl. And I swear to God you better be careful," Deisha told her.

"I will." Tamera wiped Deisha's face and Deisha wiped hers. She went to her room and Tamera sat on her bed looking through her photo album and her yearbook. She realized at that moment that things would never be the same.

Graduation day arrived quickly. Shawn drove his friends to the school so they could get ready. In the room where the guys were waiting, Shawn, Jamal and Maurice were acting up. They had spray bottles filled with confetti that they were going to start spraying when they were announced graduates of the Philadelphia School District.

Jamal leaped on Shawn's back. "Nigga, you're tripping," Shawn laughed.

"We're out this bitch! Yo, I ain't think I was going to make it. After we graduate, I'm getting blunted, nigga I'ma be fucked up." Jamal cracked up. The line began to move as the processional started.

Shawn clapped his hands together and shouted, "It's time to roll baby, it's time to roll!"

The graduation started off with Tamera singing the *Star Spangled Banner* and *Lift Ev'ry Voice and Sing*. She sang it better than she had during practice. Her friends and the audience cheered for her loudly. She waved at her friends but then her expression changed when she saw her father in the audience. She sat with Deisha and the rest of the Honor Society.

"You tore it up, girl," Deisha squealed quietly.

"Thank you," Tamera panted.

"What's wrong?" Deisha asked when she saw how uneasy Tamera was.

"My father is here," Tamera said.

The ceremony went on with awards being announced along with the amounts of different scholarships that were awarded. Close to the end of graduation, Tamera, Hakeem and Dante got on stage and sang *The World's Greatest*. Just as Jamal and his friends promised, they sprayed confetti on people when they were announced graduates. When they made their exit after receiving their real diplomas, Jamal started calling for Tamera. She was trying to get to him but because of the crowd as well as the people who were constantly stopping her to comment on her singing, it seemed impossible. She finally managed to get through and went over to him. He took her cap off and kissed her longingly. Tamera stopped when she felt someone tap her on her shoulder. She turned around and was startled by her father's presence.

"Hi sweetheart," he spoke.

"Hi Daddy, what are you doing here?" she asked as she hugged him.

"I came to see you walk down the aisle." He looked at Jamal and shook his hand. "Congratulations."

"Thanks," Jamal replied.

"So how have you been?" Mr. Harrison asked his daughter.

"I've been good."

"You never call or come see me anymore. I was beginning to think you dropped off the face of the Earth or something."

"I've been busy with school and stuff and trying to keep up with my doctor's appointments," Tamera replied, sneaking the last comment in.

"What doctor's appointments?" her father asked.

"I'm pregnant," Tamera said bashfully. Mr. Harrison took a step back to get a better look at her. He hugged his daughter, surprised with the news that he had just received.

"Congratulations. That was some really good singing that you did today," her father complimented.

"Thank you. I just signed a contract with a producer from Philly International Records and I'm going to be recording for Trinity. This Saturday I'm going to New York to meet with some of the guys and I'll also be recording an album this summer." Tamera was excited to share the news with her father. She wanted him to know how good she was doing.

"Wow, seems like you've been doing a lot," her father said. Tamera smiled. "I'm proud of you," he told her. Tamera's smile faded after finally hearing the words that she always wanted to hear from him. She was about to respond when Chanda and Deisha grabbed her yelling and screaming in excitement, pulling her away so they could take pictures.

"Come on girl so we can take some pictures!" Chanda yelled.

"I'll call you, Daddy!" Tamera yelled to her father.

After they finished taking pictures, Shawn dropped them all off at home so they could get dressed and go to a party that one of the guys from their school was having. They partied for the rest of the night and then returned home exhausted from the day's and night's events.

The next day, Tamera double checked to make sure she had all the things she wanted to take with her. Before she went to bed that night, she showered and dressed and wrapped her hair so when Jamal came for her, she would practically be ready.

Deisha woke her up at 1:30am and helped her carry her bags down to the living room quietly. They sat on the porch waiting for Jamal to come get her. Deisha grabbed Tamera's hand and Tamera laid her head on her shoulder. Twenty minutes later, Jamal pulled up in front of the door with Shawn. Tamera and Deisha got up. They took her bags to the car and Jamal put them in the trunk with Shawn's.

Jamal looked at her. "Are you ready?"

Tamera thought for a moment, having a feeling that she was forgetting something. "Wait a minute." She quietly snuck back up to her room and grabbed the two yearbooks, her photo album and the teddy bear that she slept with, and came back downstairs. "I'm ready now," she told Jamal.

"Are you sure?" Jamal asked her.

"Yeah." She turned to Deisha. "I guess this is it. For now that is." She hugged Deisha. They held onto each other not wanting to be separated. Deisha felt as though a piece of her was being taken away. She breathed heavy as they held each other.

"Don't forget, you promised me," Deisha reminded Tamera.

Tamera let her go. "I know, and I won't."

Deisha hugged Jamal. "Don't let anything happen to her."

Jamal looked at Deisha when she let him go. "I won't."

Deisha wiped her face and leaned into the car so she could give Shawn a hug also. "Bye Shizz. You be careful, too."

"Alright Deisha," Shawn replied. Deisha watched Jamal get into the car next to Tamera after Shawn took the driver's seat. She waved to them as they pulled off. Tamera was crying quietly to herself. Jamal put his arm around her and pulled her close to him. He stroked her hair and her face with his other hand. When they got to Shawn and Jamal's uncle's house, Jamal took Tamera's things up to the room she was going to be sleeping in.

"Are you staying here, too?" Tamera asked.

"Babe, I can't," Jamal told her.

"Why not?" Tamera asked, slightly scared.

"Because I don't want Samir or none of his niggas to be following me one night on my way back here and they find you and Shawn here. I can stay tonight, though." Jamal explained.

"I'm not going to feel comfortable here by myself, Jamal."

"Shawn will be here, too. And my uncle is cool peeps." He kissed her on the forehead. "I'm going to check on Shawn, alright?" Tamera nodded and Jamal went down the hall to Shawn's room. "Shawn, are you cool?"

"Yeah, I'm about to call Chanda to let her know that I'm here."

"Okay, well I'm getting ready to go to sleep. But while I'm gone, watch over Tamera for me."

"I will," Shawn promised.

"Alright goodnight, yo." He left Shawn's room and went back to Tamera's. She was buttoning the last few buttons to her nightshirt. Jamal hugged and kissed her. He sat on the bed and felt on her stomach which was starting to show through her clothing. "It's gonna be over before you know it," he told her.

"I hope so," Tamera said in a low, sad voice.

Jamal laid her on the bed and kissed her for a moment. He then turned the light off and wrapped his arms around her. Moments later, they fell asleep.

Jamal awoke before Tamera later that morning. After he showered and got dressed, he went downstairs to where his uncle and Shawn were talking.

"Where's your girlfriend?" his uncle asked.

"She's still asleep. Yo, thanks for letting them stay here and not telling my Mom," Jamal said as he grabbed a handful of grapes from out of the refrigerator.

"You just keep your ass out of trouble. Those streets are not for you, especially when you're dealing with an animal like Samir. You're mother has been through enough when dealing with that bastard. She doesn't need any more heartache," their uncle said to him.

Jamal was quiet for a moment. He looked at Shawn and then stared at his uncle. "Uncle Norm, do you know about Samir and our father?"

Their uncle looked at both of them. "What do you mean?"

"Kristoff…" Jamal said with his eyes slit in anger. He never told Shawn the entire story and didn't want to get into it. Shawn looked at Jamal and then looked at his uncle wondering who Kristoff was.

"Samir has a lot of friends in high places. That's what makes him so dangerous. But one day he will slip up. Soon, his day will come," Uncle Norm said as he sliced an apple.

Jamal shook his head. "I don't understand, Uncle Norm. That was your brother. It's no way in hell I would've let anybody get away with killing Shawn and not do anything!" Jamal hissed.

"And that is the very reason why you are where you are today," Uncle Norm shot back at him. "Sometimes you have to leave it to God. Don't think for one damn minute I didn't want to strangle that muthafucka with my bare hands myself. But he has too much protection. And I had a family to think of. And your mother had the two of you. So all I could do was wait. Do you know how much it pained me to see you around that fucking punk? To see him pretending to give a damn about you, grooming you for these streets knowing he was the one that killed your father, my brother?!" Uncle Norm shook his head in disgust. "Karma does not miss. And no matter how much protection a person thinks they have, no matter how well you think you may have cleaned up a mistake, God sees all. Eventually you will pay for your sins. And he will pay for his. It doesn't always come back on you directly," Uncle Norm said as he looked at both of his nephews. "But it does come back. Mistakes are hard to clean up, son, because you always lose something in the process."

Jamal and Shawn looked at each other. Shawn was confused and Jamal could tell he had questions. But Jamal was not in the position or in the mood to answer them. He was upset that so much information had been kept from them. Maybe if he had known that Samir killed his father, he never would have sought him out to help him kill Khalil. And maybe things would not be the way they were now. But it was too late to worry about the "what ifs". Jamal had a family to protect and he was not going to lose his brother or his girlfriend in the process.

"Shawn, I'll check on y'all later," Jamal said to his brother.

"Alright," Shawn said as he tossed his brother the keys to his car.

"Thanks again Uncle Norm," Jamal said as he headed out of the door.

After Jamal left, Shawn called Chanda to see how things were going in her neighborhood.

"I called Deisha's house not too long ago. Her aunt thinks that Tamera is staying with her God Mother that's going to be leaving for New York soon," Chanda told Shawn.

"Damn, that's crazy. Jamal called twice after he left. He's only been gone for two hours. And Tamera is still asleep," Shawn replied.

"Yeah, that pregnancy is going to be slowing her down now," Chanda said.

"So how are you doing?" Shawn asked.

"I'm alright. I'm just bored out of my mind. I'm trying to get used to the fact that I graduated from high-school. I found myself setting stuff on fire in here again," Chanda chuckled.

"You better cut that shit out. Didn't you set some curtains on fire before?" Shawn asked as he laughed.

Chanda laughed even harder. "You better not tell anybody about that shit."

"Do you want me to come see you?" Shawn asked out of nowhere.

"I thought Jamal had your car," Chanda replied.

"He does but I have his transpass. I'm near the 6. All I have to do is hop that to Broad and Olney, and then hop the train down to Tasker and Morris. I can probably be there in an hour."

"Are you sure?" Chanda asked.

"Yeah, what are you doing?"

"I was just painting my nails," Chanda told him.

"I'm about to leave in 15 minutes, I'm just going to check on Tamera to see if she needs anything."

"Okay," Chanda smiled. She hung the phone up.

Shawn went to the room that Tamera was sleeping in and knocked on her door.

"Yes," she answered in a sleepy voice.

"Can I come in? Are you decent?" Shawn asked.

"Yeah, come on in," Tamera said as she sat up in the bed and wiped her face. Shawn opened the door and came in. "Where's Jamal?" she asked.

"He left this morning," Shawn told her. Tamera felt slightly disappointed. "Are you alright?"

"Yeah, I just need to take a shower and get something to eat."

"Well, there's some cereal and fruit downstairs. Jamal had our Uncle buy all of your favorite foods and snacks. I'm about to go see Chanda. I just wanted to make sure that you were okay."

"You're leaving?" Tamera asked as she faced him.

"Yeah why, did you need something?" Shawn asked.

"No, I just didn't want to be in here by myself." She shrugged her shoulders as she grabbed a bathrobe and some clothes to wear for the day.

"It's alright. I'll just call Jamal."

"Are you sure?" Shawn double checked.

"Yeah, do you have the number here?"

"Sure, I'll write it down for you. My uncle went to work so if you need something, I guess the person to call would be Jamal. See you later," Shawn left her room so he could get dressed to go hang out with Chanda.

Tamera was filled with fear and edginess when Shawn left. She took her shower with the bathroom door opened and the light on. After drying her hair and getting dressed, she went to the kitchen to get something to eat. There was a list on the refrigerator letting her know what foods were in there for her to eat. When she saw the grapes and the plums, she went nuts. She sat in the dining room with her fruit and a tabloid magazine and turned on the Soap Channel so she could catch up on General Hospital. Beverly Hills 90210 was on. She shook her head. "Kelly was such a sneaky bitch.

She couldn't have been my friend. I would've knocked her ass out for sleeping with my man while I'm in Paris."

She spent the afternoon watching television but suddenly became bored and lonely. She called Jamal and left him a voicemail for him to call her back.

"What's up?" he asked when she answered the phone.

"Nothing, I'm here by myself and I wanted someone to talk to," Tamera told him.

"Where are Shawn and my uncle?" Jamal asked her.

"Your uncle went to work and Shawn went to go see Chanda."

"Did you get something to eat?"

"Yeah, I haven't stopped grubbing since I came down here," Tamera giggled. "Your uncle is going to get mad and throw my greedy ass out of here."

"Nah he's not going to do that. He bought that stuff for you," Jamal told her.

"I'm lonely here Jamal," Tamera said as she popped a grape in her mouth.

"I'll be back up there in a little while. I just had to check on some things and give some stuff to Maurice. I should be there in an hour. I have a key so don't worry about answering the door," Jamal said to her.

"Okay," Tamera hung the phone up and lay back on the couch. General Hospital was on. She had a major crush on Sonny Corinthos and Jason Morgan. She swore if she ever made it big, those were two men she had to meet. Oh and Justin Timberlake. Before she knew it, she fell asleep.

Jamal came in and saw Tamera sleeping on the couch. He knelt down next to her and watched her, thinking how lucky he was to have her. He put his hands to his face and prayed that he could get out of this with Tamera, Shawn and himself unharmed. Shawn came in rapping the lyrics to *Renegade* by Jay-Z and Eminem. Jamal shushed him.

"I thought I asked you to watch over her for me," Jamal said quietly.

"I am. I just ran down South Philly to see Chanda," Shawn explained.

"Shawn, I need you, yo. Chanda's not in the line of fire, you and Tamera are. I've got nobody on the streets watching my back except you and Maurice. I can't let anything happen to Tammy or our baby so I really need you on this." Jamal looked at his younger brother.

"I got you, yo. I got you," Shawn assured him.

"Did you eat?" Jamal asked.

"Naw, I was going to order a pizza or something," Shawn replied.

"It's some menus on the table. Order some wings and a ginger-ale for Tammy, please?"

"No problem," Shawn went into the kitchen and placed his order at a nearby pizza restaurant.

"Babe, wake up," Jamal said softly as he poked Tamera. She stirred but didn't wake. He leaned close to her face and blew in her eyes. Inadvertently, she slapped him and then woke up.

"Oh, babe I'm sorry!" she giggled. Jamal burst out laughing. She caressed his face.

"You did that shit on purpose," Jamal joked. He leaned over and kissed her.

Tamera sat up. "I'm hungry," she smiled.

Jamal smiled back at her. "I know you are. Shawn is ordering some pizza and wings and a ginger-ale for you." Tamera's smile widened. "Yeah, I knew you'd like that. Come on upstairs. We can take a shower and I'll wash your hair and then we can just chill for the rest of the night, okay?"

"Sounds like fun," Tamera replied as Jamal helped her up from the couch. He wrapped his arms around her waist and rubbed her stomach as they walked up the stairs together.

Jamal stayed with her for the entire night. He was glad that he did because he knew it would be a while before he got the chance again.

The next day, Jamal woke Tamera up before he got ready to leave.

"I'm about to leave. Do you want anything before I go?"

"No," she told him as she sat up. He gave her a hug and kissed her. "Just promise me I won't have to put 357 in your phone."

Jamal looked at her for a moment surprised that she remembered the codes they used to use if anything was wrong. He used his thumb to wipe out the corner of her mouth. "I think that can be arranged. I love you."

"Ditto," Tamera replied.

Jamal shook his head and smiled. "Here we go with that ditto shit." He knelt down and kissed her stomach. "Bye boo-boo," he said to their unborn child. Tamera stroked the back of his head. He looked up at her before getting to his feet. "I'll call you." He walked to her door and Tamera threw her stuffed animal at him playfully.

"You better," she smiled.

Jamal smiled back at her before leaving her room. He went to Shawn's room and knocked on his door. "I'm about to leave, alright? If y'all need anything or if something happens just hit my cell."

"What time is it?" Shawn asked.

"It's almost 1 o'clock," Jamal replied as he looked at his watch.

"How come you're leaving so early? I thought you didn't have to be there until close to four."

"I do. I just want to make sure that some things are taken care of," Jamal told him as he opened his door.

"Things like what?" Shawn asked him.

"Nothing really, just some little stuff. Y'all cool?"

"Yeah. Are you coming back tonight?" Shawn asked.

"I might. It depends on how things go. Why?"

"No reason, just checking. Did you tell Mommy why I'm not going to be home?"

"I told her you were here. I wasn't going to go into detail. It's a lot that Mommy knew about Daddy and Samir that she never told us. But I'm not going to get into it now because I have to go."

"Oh, alright," Shawn replied.

"I'll check on y'all later." Jamal left and went back to North Philly to get some more things done. He still didn't trust any of the guys in the neighborhood because he didn't know who was watching him. It was certain things that he needed some of his supposed to be friends besides Maurice to do that didn't get done which sent other signals that the guys were more afraid of Samir than they were of him.

He stayed at Maurice's house until three-thirty and then he went to Samir's house, making sure he wasn't late. He didn't want to start off on a bad foot.

Samir opened his door. "You're on time. Good." He let Jamal in and closed the door behind him. "Come in the den so I can tell you what you need to know in case you forgot, being as though you have such a short memory at times."

Jamal followed Samir to the den. "Yo, don't set me up, Samir. And don't try to throw no extra shit in there either."

Samir put a clip in a gun and sat it on the table. "Look nigga, I'm sick of your mouth. Just shut the fuck up and let me run this so you can get out of my face." Jamal eyeballed Samir for a moment and then sat down. "Man, get the fuck up. I ain't tell you to sit down." Jamal hesitated but then rose off of the couch. "You're starting off wrong." Samir went inside of a cabinet and pulled out a bag before tossing it to Jamal. "Alright, this is how it's going to go down. You run for me from now until the end of August." He slid a gun and two clips over to him. "Keep your shit wired at all times. It's some little young heads trying to make a name for themselves on my turf. Other than that, my corners been flowing lovely with no type of shit jumping off and I don't need nothing happening now. You're going to handle the shipments coming in with Man-Man, El and Shaheed. El and Shaheed are brothers so I advise you not to fuck with them," Samir warned.

"As long as they don't fuck with me, they don't have anything to worry about," Jamal replied.

"That's your problem, Mal. You talk too got-damn much. You swear you're hard. You just make sure those shipments come in with no problems and my corners stay flowing like I said. You know most of those crack-head muthafuckas around there, so if you see somebody you're not used to selling to..."

Jamal interrupted him. "I know, don't sell them shit."

"Yeah, or ask El and them when they leave and they'll let you know since they've been out there longer than you. I think that's it," Samir said as he rubbed the hairs on his chin. He thought for a moment. "No it's not. There are two things you don't do; Fuck with my money and fuck with the competition. Now those Columbian pigs got their shit coming in, but they're letting them niggas from 29th street push that shit for them, too. Don't let me catch you fucking with them because that's a direct slap in the face. You already know how it's going down if you cross me like that. Need I say more?"

"No," Jamal replied figuring the less he said the better off he would be. It seemed the situation with the cops had Samir a little paranoid. He hoped he wasn't about to carry this out at the start of a drug war.

Samir handed Jamal a package. "Here, and you better pray you ain't gotta use your piece. I covered for your ass not once, but twice. Three times a fucking charm, nigga." He walked Jamal to the door. "Do as I say and all this shit will be over once and for all."

Jamal left the house not commenting on what his cousin said. He went over to 26th and Cecil B. Moore where he found the other guys that worked that corner. They had a small table where they played cards so the cops wouldn't get suspicious of too many young black males being on a corner not doing anything.

Man-Man slapped Jamal a handshake. "What's up, nigga?"

"Nothing much, man," Jamal replied blandly.

"It's about time you came back out here with us," Man-Man said.

"I ain't out here permanently. This is just a favor for Sa. What are y'all niggas playing?"

"Pity Pat, $5 a hand. You want in? If so, you better count your money. The cops stay stopping us and shit. If you can't give an exact amount of how much you got, they confiscate that shit. Make a nigga stay well up on his math. I hope you got a job to explain where you get your money from," Shaheed said to Jamal.

Jamal pulled up a chair and sat down awaiting the next round.

"So, Sa got you back out here?" El asked.

"Yeah, it's just for the summer so it ain't a big thing,"

"Yeah, just make sure you stay away from the competition," El warned him as he rearranged the cards in his hand.

"Sa told me already. But just to be sure, who are those niggas?" Jamal asked.

"Them niggas that run Girard Avenue going all the way up to the Zoo. D-Ball and Kiree and 'nem. They think they're hot shit. They're cool, I just wouldn't fuck with them," El said.

Jamal thought of Kiree's little brother, Manny and Keisha. "Damn."

Tamera went to New York and met with quite a few hip-hop and R&B artist. Artists that she normally listened to on the radio like Alicia Keys, Marques Houston, Nas and Ginuwine almost made her jump out of her skin as she sat in the same room with them. She recorded hooks and did background vocals for other artists. Tamera felt a little safer being in New York and out of reach of Samir and his goons, but she worried about Jamal every day.

When Tamera received her first paycheck, it was for more than eight thousand dollars. She thought she was going to go into early labor. After returning to Philly, she opened an account with both her and Jamal's name on it and deposited the check. She was happy to be back in Philly on a Saturday morning. As soon as she got back to the house in Uptown, she took a shower and then called Deisha.

"Hello?" Deisha answered.

"Hey Deisha, what's up?" Tamera replied with a huge grin on her face.

"Hey Tammy!" Deisha replied, excited. She hadn't heard from Tamera in a couple weeks. "Where the hell have you been? Shit I know Jamal got y'all hiding, but you don't even drop a nigga a line," Deisha joked.

"No, I've just been so busy recording this music. Greg said as good as I am in the studio we might be finished my album in the next couple of weeks."

"Wow, that is freaking awesome!" Deisha exclaimed. She was so happy for her friend.

"Have you seen Jamal?" Tamera asked. It had been a week since she had seen Jamal and she was missing him like crazy even though they talked almost every day.

"Yeah, he was up near 26th and B. Moore earlier playing cards. I didn't get to talk to him because I was in a hurry. When was the last time you saw him?" Deisha asked.

"I haven't seen him in over a week. I talk to him every day, though. He calls to make sure everything is okay and to see if I need anything. I just miss him."

"Well, I'm sure that he'll show his face around there eventually. You know he can't stay away from you for too long. I know I'ma get a copy of your CD when it's finished."

"Of course you are, Deisha. I wouldn't make you buy it from the store," Tamera replied with a smile.

"And I wouldn't either. Download that shit from Kazaa," they both fell out laughing.

They talked on the phone for a little while longer before Tamera decided to go play video games with Shawn.

Shaheed and El decided to keep a close eye on Jamal. Their reason being was because they saw him too buddy-buddy with Kiree and D-Ball. Their conversations were too secretive for their liking. They didn't know that there wasn't any business involved and that they were just friends so the two of them didn't like seeing them hanging with each other. They were the competition and could rage a turf war with them if they wanted to. El and Shaheed brought the matter to Samir's attention one day when they were dropping his money off. Samir had a reason to believe El and Shaheed because Jamal rarely took the money that he made with him.

"This muthafucka better not be fucking with the competition," Samir said as he counted out his money.

"Yo Sa, if you want me to, I'll do him myself." El had never liked Jamal and would hop on any opportunity to do him in.

"Straight up, no rap," his brother Shaheed added.

"Nobody is to touch him. I'm telling y'all that now. You touch him and I'ma fucking touch you. It's just as simple as that. I'll talk to him myself."

CHAPTER 10
A PRICE TO PAY FOR THAT THUG LIFE

Jamal went to Samir's house to drop off the money he made that week after El and Shaheed had their talk with him. Jamal found an apartment for him and Tamera and made sure that he put enough to the side to cover the down payment as well as six months of rent to give them a cushion. He wanted to do everything he could to make sure Tamera and their baby could be comfortable and didn't have to struggle. But he still gave the bulk of the money he made to Samir.

"Sit down Jamal," Samir said as he closed the door behind him.

"What's up Sa?" Jamal spoke.

"Jamal, you're a money nigga right?" Samir asked him as he rubbed the hairs on his chin.

"What do you mean by that?" Jamal asked.

"I mean, you love money, don't you?"

"Who don't?" Jamal asked confused and not sure where Samir was heading with the conversation.

"Who don't?" Samir repeated with a chuckle. He shook his head. "Look, I'ma get to the muthafucking point because it's some shit that's been brought to my attention that I personally don't like. Why is it that you ain't taking all of your part of the money that you make?" Jamal was about to respond but Samir interrupted him. "What, it's not enough for you? You feel like you need to be somewhere else?"

"No. I don't want it because I'm not working for it," Jamal explained.

"What the fuck are you talking about? You be on that corner every day in the hot ass sun, risking getting snatched by the po-po." Samir stopped himself and smiled. "Oh I get it. You're supposed to be Honest Abe now or some shit?"

"Sa, it's not even like that."

"Look, I got word that you been hanging with Kiree and D-Ball on the regular. I already told you, if you fuck with the competition, I'ma end your shit. Simple as that. Now I'ma only ask you this shit once. Are you fucking with the competition?"

"No man, me, D-Ball and Kiree been cool since we went to Vaux. I see them pass through and I rap to them for a minute and that's it."

Samir waited a moment before he spoke. "That's all it better be." He counted out his money and then laughed. "Usually you gotta strong arm the shit outta niggas to get your money. You, I gotta practically shove the shit down your throat. But it's cool, though. You're just making me richer. I'ma give you the day off so you can go spend time with your little girlfriend.

When was the last time that you saw her?"

Jamal was surprised by his concern. "It's been over a week. Working for you and working at the Gallery plus trying to find us an apartment got me tied up. Plus I'm still trying to get my shit right for college and she's been back and forth in New York working on her album."

"Yeah, I know. She did some shit for Trinity and I heard it. She got a nice lil voice," Samir commented. He walked Jamal over to the door. "Just finish this shit so you don't have to worry about it no more. And I wouldn't hurt your girl. I ain't that cruel." Samir smiled at Jamal. Jamal didn't respond back. He didn't believe a word Samir said considering he was the one that murdered his father. He left the house and went straight to his uncle's house.

Deisha came home from work earlier than usual. When she got in, her aunt stopped her.

"Have you heard from Tammy?" she asked.

"Not since last Saturday," Deisha replied as she looked through the mail on the dining room table.

"Did she say when she was coming home?"

"N… no… why?" Deisha asked suspiciously.

"It's probably nothing but for the last few weeks, I've noticed that Jamal's been hanging on the corner of 26th and Cecil B. Moore Avenue on a regular. I remember hearing that he used to sell drugs, but I ain't wanna think he went back to his old ways being the fact that he has a baby on the way." She shrugged her shoulders. "He's probably just hanging out with his friends one last time before he goes off to college."

"If only you knew," Deisha mumbled under her breath.

"What did you say?" Michelle asked.

"I said I was thinking that, too." Deisha stammered.

Michelle sat down and picked up the phone to dial a number but then she put it back down. "That's strange. I was on Chestnut Street and stopped in City Blue because they had a really cute pair of Roca-Wear jeans. I was going to use Shawn's discount as usual but the guy told me Shawn quit. I haven't seen him at The Rec playing ball either. Graduation comes and everybody done disappeared. Maybe that's what the hell I need to do. Calgon take me away." She went into the kitchen to fix herself a bowl of ice-cream. Deisha gathered her things and went up to her bedroom.

Shawn was lying across his bed playing the remake of the first Resident Evil on the Nintendo Game Cube when Jamal knocked on his door.

"Yo!" Shawn answered.

Jamal opened the door and then closed it behind him when he came inside. "Did Uncle Norm get here yet?"

"Naw. What are you doing here?" Shawn asked. He wasn't used to seeing Jamal come through.

"Samir told me I ain't have to work today since I ain't seen Tamera in a while. He tried to say I was fucking with the competition." Jamal sighed and watched Shawn play the game for a moment. "Somebody is talking what they don't know. I wouldn't be surprised if it was El's bitch ass. That nigga wants to be the next Sa so bad. Young bol don't know shit about the game. Where's Tamera?"

"She's in her room. She was fine until a little while ago, but she started saying she was feeling dizzy and nauseous."

"Let me go check on her real quick." He went to her room and cracked her door opened. When he saw her sleeping, he eased onto her bed and moved her hair out of her face, waking her.

"Are you alright?" he asked her.

Tamera stretched and lay on her back. "I'm straight. Why'd you ask?"

"Shawn said you told him you were dizzy and felt nauseous. The last time that happened you almost drowned on me," Jamal told her.

"Is that why you're here?"

"No, Sa told me to take the day off and spend some time with you." Tamera sat up and rubbed her stomach which had grown massively since the last time Jamal saw her. "Damn," he piped. "You got big as shit! I mean that in a good way."

Tamera chuckled. "I can feel him moving around now. Sometimes he's in here dancing his little butt off." Jamal crawled beside her and placed his hand on top of hers. She leaned back on his chest and Jamal kissed her forehead. "I missed you."

"I missed you too, baby. Samir said he heard the cut you did with Trinity. When can I hear it?" Jamal asked her.

"Actually, Greg is bringing it over today since I couldn't pick it up myself. So you can hear it when he brings it by."

"That's what's up. When was the last time you heard from Chanda and Deisha?"

"I talked to Deisha a few days ago but I haven't heard much from Chanda. I wish they could come visit me."

"Call them and tell them to come up tonight," Jamal suggested. Tamera lay there not wanting to move. "Are you going to call them? I'll pick them up for you."

"Yeah, I just don't want to move."

"Shawn!" Jamal called out.

"Yo!" Shawn hollered back.

"Pass me the phone."

Shawn came to the room moments later with the cordless and then went back to playing his game. Tamera called Deisha first.

"Hello?" Deisha answered after the first ring.

"Hey Deisha," Tamera perked.

"Hey girl, what's up?"

"Nothing, what are you doing?"

"Actually I was just about to head out the door so I could pick up Chanda. We were going to do some school shopping for our freshman year. Girl you know I'm hype as hell."

"Oh, I was going to ask y'all to come up here. I miss y'all. Jamal said he'd pick y'all up." Tamera told her.

"I was just talking to Chanda about coming to see you. We miss you too, girl. I wanna see how big you've gotten. Let me call Chanda and tell her that the plans changed and call me in like five minutes. No, tell Jamal to pick me up at Maurice's house so my aunt doesn't get suspicious." Deisha told her.

"Okay," Tamera agreed.

"Tell Deisha to get her stuff ready now because I'm about to leave," Jamal whispered to Tamera. She repeated the message back to Deisha.

"Alright, I'll see him when he gets there."

Tamera hung up the phone. "Deisha said to pick her up around Maurice house so her aunt doesn't get suspicious about where she's going."

"Alright," Jamal replied. He got off of the bed.

"You're leaving now?" Tamera asked.

"Yeah, I want to hurry up and get them before it gets too late and nigga-itis kicks in," he grabbed Tamera by her chin and kissed her. "See you when I get back."

That night, Jamal had no idea that Shaheed and El were following him, Chanda, Deisha and Maurice, who decided to come at the last minute, back to his uncle's house. They knew who Maurice was but they couldn't tell off hand who the two girls were. They were curious as to where they were going and how long they were going to be there. Since they couldn't put the pieces together, they drove back to North Philly.

Tamera gave both of her friends a big hug. They were both surprised at how big she had gotten. They groped over her stomach, took pictures and talked until Greg came by with the CD and the single that she did with Trinity. They listened to Tamera's album and were all speechless as they looked over her album cover along with other photos that Tamera had taken with Common, Swiss Beats, Usher and Alicia Keys. Tamera looked absolutely beautiful and her album sounded awesome.

"I take it that you like what you hear?" Greg assumed once he saw the expressions on their faces.

"I can't believe that was me. Damn, y'all said I could sing but, I didn't know I sounded that good," Tamera gushed. Her eyes were teary.

"Aww don't cry, friend," Chanda said as she wiped Tamera's face and hugged her.

"So you do like it?" Greg asked.

"Yes, I love it. I'm so speechless like, wow this is my dream come true. You have no idea what this means to me," Tamera told him as she wiped her eyes.

"Well it was a privilege and a complete delight working with you. I have a feeling this album is going to do numbers and maybe even hit the top ten in the first week. We are looking at a release date of August 21 for the first single which is going to be *Stay with Me*. The label thinks it's an awesome ballad that shows off your voice. Trinity's cut is already playing with Power 99 and you're getting great reviews. Also…" Greg reached into his brief case and pulled out an envelope. "This, my dear, is yours. You deserved every penny."

Tamera took the envelope and opened it. Inside was a royalty check of $36,000. Tamera placed her hand on her chest and leaned into Jamal. Jamal took the check and looked at it.

"That was just for signing on with us and doing the Trinity cut along with the other songs you lent your voice to. You will get a quarterly check in September for whatever sales you've made on your own album. After you have the baby and get settled, we can work out concert dates and tour dates. I'm working on having you open for Usher and Alicia Keys." Greg told her.

Tamera covered her face as the tears fell. She was overwhelmed with joy from how her dream was unfolding right in front of her. Her friends were ecstatic. She was unable to form words as she thought of how proud her mother would be of her.

Jamal shook Greg's hand. "Thanks so much, she appreciates everything that you've done for her."

"Well as I said, it was a pleasure. This girl is going places. But I have to run. I'll be back on Wednesday with more copies of the CD for you, your family and friends, along with photos for you to autograph and send out."

Jamal walked Greg to the door. "Alright yo, thanks again." When Greg left, Chanda, Deisha and Tamera jumped for joy screaming and yelling.

"Girl what the hell are you going to do with all of that money and you just got a check for over $8,000?" Chanda asked.

"Me and Jamal are going to get a place together and…" Tamera was so excited she couldn't think. "Girl I don't know!!" she shrieked. They ordered food and drinks, talked and laughed for the most part of the night until everyone went to bed.

That night while everyone was sleeping, Tamera caught a sharp pain in her stomach. She sat up quietly trying not to wake Jamal. She sat on the side of the bed leaning forward, taking in slow deep breaths to see if the pain would subside so she could go back to sleep. She waited a few minutes before trying to lie back down but the pain came again. She grabbed the sheets and squealed.

"Tammy, are you alright?" Jamal asked in a deep, sleepy voice. When she didn't say anything, he clicked on the light and sat next to her. "What's wrong?" Since it hurt too much to breathe she pointed to her stomach as the tears swelled up in her eyes. The pain came again and she smacked the bed and hollered out. Jamal leapt off the bed and ran to Shawn's room to get the phone. Deisha came to their doorway when he came back.

"What's wrong with her?" she asked.

"I don't know."

"Is the baby okay? Is she okay?" Deisha asked, panicking.

"I don't know!" Jamal snapped, not meaning to. He called the hospital and asked for Dr. Jefferson, who happened to be on call that night. Jamal explained the situation to her and she told him to bring her to the E.R immediately. He hung up the phone and got a pair of sweatpants and a t-shirt for both he and Tamera. He helped her get dressed after he put his clothes on.

"Can you walk?" he asked her.

"A little," she whimpered.

Deisha ran back to their room dressed also. "I'm coming with y'all."

"Good, help me get her down the steps," Jamal said. As they were moving down the stairs, Shawn and Chanda came to their doorway.

"Where are y'all going?" Chanda asked.

"Tamera is getting cramps in her stomach and her doctor told me to bring her to the E.R." Jamal told them.

"I wanna come," Chanda said.

"I can't wait for y'all to get dressed. We'll call y'all from the hospital." They left the house and drove to Hahnemann Hospital as quickly as they could without being stopped by the cops. They went inside and sat Tamera in a chair. Jamal went over to the desk and told them what the emergency was and that Dr. Jefferson told him to bring her there. The receptionist was giving him the run around and Jamal was two seconds away from wringing her neck when Dr. Jefferson walked up behind him.

"It's okay. I told him to come," she told the receptionist.

Jamal eyeballed the receptionist and then followed behind Dr. Jefferson as she wheeled Tamera to another room.

"I wasn't expecting to see you until you came to find out the sex of the baby." She took out her stethoscope and checked Tamera's vitals. "Are you coming down with a cold?"

"Yeah, my throat was hurting earlier," Tamera replied.

Dr. Jefferson put the stethoscope around her neck and sighed. "How long have you been having these pains?"

"It comes and goes. This is the first time they've ever been this bad."

"Hmm, have you been under any stress lately?"

"Not really, I've mostly been recording my album. Other than that, everything has been fine. Do I need an ultrasound?"

"No, I can tell you now that the baby is fine." Jamal and Tamera let out a sigh of relief. "It's you that I'm worried about. You look like you're under a lot of pressure."

Tamera sat on the edge of the hospital bed and the doctor put a thermometer in her mouth. She then wrapped the blood pressure cuff around her arm to take her blood pressure and squeezed on the pump. She looked at the machine and frowned. She then tipped her glasses to her nose and looked at Tamera. She took the blood pressure cuff off Tamera's arm and wrote something on her chart.

"Jamal, I'm going to need you to leave the room for a moment while I speak with Tamera privately." Dr. Jefferson requested. Jamal looked at Tamera and then left as Dr. Jefferson asked. Dr. Jefferson closed the door behind him and took the thermometer out of Tamera's mouth. She recorded the data and then sighed.

"What's wrong?" Tamera asked with a concerned look on her face.

"Your blood pressure is extremely high. Is something going on that you're keeping in and not telling anyone? Are there any problems with Jamal?" the doctor asked.

"N... no," Tamera stammered.

"Tamera, I am your doctor. My job is to make sure that you and your baby stay safe and in good health. If there is a problem that you're dealing with on your own, I need you to tell me so I can help you," Tamera looked down at her hands folded in her lap. "Is it Jamal?"

"No," Tamera lied. "I'm just stressed over my album, wanting to make sure I do a good job." She decided not to speak on the issues with Jamal, afraid that the cops would be called.

Dr. Jefferson tapped her pen on her chin and stared at Tamera before responding. "I hope that's all. I still have to hold you over night to see what's causing these pains and to make sure your pressure goes down." Dr. Jefferson handed her a hospital gown and then left the room. Moments later, Deisha and Jamal came into the room.

"Does your stomach still hurt?" Jamal asked as he ran his fingers through her hair.

"Not as much as it did before," Tamera replied as she swung her legs back and forth.

Deisha rubbed her stomach. "Tell my God daughter to calm the hell down. It's not time for her to come into the world yet."

Dr. Jefferson came back into the room with a cup of water and two pills for Tamera. Tamera took them and drank the water down.

"When can she leave?" Jamal asked.

"If her blood pressure drops we'll release her sometime this afternoon."

"Alright," he gave Tamera a kiss. "Give me a call on my cell phone when they release you. I'm going to take Deisha back to the house."

"Okay," Tamera smiled. He kissed her again and then left with Deisha.

After Jamal got off of work later on that afternoon, he received a voicemail from Tamera letting him know that she was being released from the hospital. He went up there to get her but was held up with a bunch of release forms that took a lot of time. They talked on their way home but when he got to his uncle's house, he realized it was past four o'clock.

"Shit, I'm running late." He kissed Tamera quickly. "You know the deal, if something happens, if you need anything..."

"I know, I know, call you," Tamera said as she pushed him out the door.

"Alright y'all." Jamal waved goodbye.

"Bye Jamal," Chanda said back. Jamal left and closed the door behind him. "Damn y'all look like a married couple," Chanda told Tamera.

Tamera giggled, "It feels like it sometimes, too."

Jamal was trying to find the quickest route to get to his post without speeding and getting stopped by the cops. That was the last thing he needed. Just as he was arriving at 29th and Ridge Avenue, Samir was leaving him a message on his phone telling him to come to his house first. When Jamal got there, Samir was standing in his doorway waiting for him.

"That was quick." Samir said as Jamal got out of his car. He followed him into the house. "Where the fuck was you at?"

"My girl had to be rushed to the hospital last night," Jamal explained.

"She's in labor already?"

"No, she kept getting these pains in her stomach and her doctor told me to bring her there."

"Still, you know how a nigga gets with everything that's going on. Next time you better let somebody know because I was about to come after you. Go ahead. I just wanted to know what the deal was." Jamal left the house and went on 26th and Cecil B. Moore. Shaheed and El were sitting on Samir's couch.

"I'm telling you Sa, something is up with that nigga," El sneered.

"You better hope he ain't trying to set you up," Shaheed added.

Samir thought about it for a moment. "Naw, he knows better, because if he does, he's going down right along with me."

"It's something about him that I can't put my finger on," El mused out loud.

"Squash that shit, El. He knows better than to fuck with me. Especially if he doesn't want anything to happen to that baby he's expecting."

"Are you sure you don't want us to keep an eye on him or something?" Shaheed asked.

"Naw. Not right now at least. Y'all just make sure y'all shit don't start stinking. Watch my house. I'm about to go get some chicken wings," Samir told them before he left out.

When Samir left, El snapped, "Man, fuck that. I'm keeping an eye on that nigga. I ain't trying to have him come up in here, thinking he's going to start shit. Fuck what Sa said. I'll put him to sleep my muthafucking self. For all we know, he's probably feeding info to them bitches from Girard Avenue."

"No," his older brother Shaheed said. "What you're going to do is stay outta this shit and leave him the fuck alone like Samir said or he's going to be putting you to sleep. Don't worry about it. His punk-ass will slip up eventually."

El and Shaheed watched Jamal for the rest of the day. Jamal didn't play cards with Man-Man or the rest of the guys, he just watched. They knew he wasn't stealing from Samir but they still weren't sure if he was trying to get with the competition. They saw him with D-Ball and Kiree more than usual.

"I'm ready to waste his faggot-ass," El mumbled under his breath.

When Jamal's shift was over, he took the money he made to Samir and gave it to him. Since he promised Tamera that he would stay the night with her, he went back to his uncle's house still not knowing that Shaheed and El were following him. This time they waited outside the house to see if they would recognize anybody that came out. When no one left, they wrote the address down and went back to North Philly, unsatisfied.

That Wednesday, Greg returned with the extra photos and CDs like he promised. Tamera mailed one to her father and one to her God mother, forgetting that she was supposed to be staying there with her. She sent one to Michelle through Deisha and she sent one to Renee and Tyrone through Chanda. Tamera autographed all of the CDs that she sent out and was excited when she found out that the date had been changed for Power 99FM to start playing her first single on August 17th and her album would be available for purchase on August 28th. Tamera was ecstatic. Her dream had finally come true.

She talked with Jamal about what she wanted to do with the money. She deposited the check for $36,000 into their account so they could get them a place as soon as everything was over with Samir. Jamal wasn't comfortable with having access to the money she worked for, but she assured him that since he was a part of her life, she wanted to share everything with him. While conducting business with Greg one afternoon, she had an urge to put Jamal down as her power of attorney and did so.

A week after Tamera sent out the CDs to her family and friends, Jamal was standing on the corner having a conversation with Man-Man, one of the few guys that sold drugs for Samir that he was cool with.

"I remember when you first came on the block, the first thing you said was you're not here for good, this was just a favor. For me, I just wanna make sure I got money to help my little brother go to college and then I'm out. Cats like El and his brother Shaheed, them niggas think they're going to be the next Samir. They don't know shit about the game, but they walk around like they're tough. Them niggas gonna end up getting hurt," Man-Man was saying.

"You dig. The first time I laid eyes on El, I knew I wasn't going to like that nigga. He got this chip on his shoulder and he stays on Sa's dick. He thinks I don't know it was him and his bitch-ass brother that went to Samir and told him I was fucking with the competition, trying to start shit," Jamal replied.

"Yeah. You better watch that nigga El," Man-Man said quietly. "Every time I turn around, that nigga is watching your every move. Watch your back out here 'cause that nigga got something up his sleeve and it's only a matter of time before he pulls it out."

Jamal glanced at El and Shaheed sitting in a car and noticed that they were watching him. "I'll rock his fucking jaw if he even comes at me on some dumb shit," Jamal hissed.

D-Ball and Kiree were coming up the street and happened to hear what he said. "Who's cradle we're gonna have to shake, Jamal? Just say the word and it's done," Kiree joked. They laughed as they shook each other's hand. They talked for a moment lowering their voices as El and Shaheed tried their hardest to hear what they were saying.

"I'm trying to tell you Jamal, you should come run with us when you're finished with Samir. You can make twice the shit you make here, with us," D-Ball told Jamal.

"Naw nigga, because after I finish up here, I'm going to college and chill with my baby-mom and my son. I'm not trying to get caught up in this shit no more," Jamal told him.

"Aww, he thinks he's too good for us 'cause he's going to college," D-Ball smirked. He rubbed his chin. "Sike naw, but that's what's up, though."

"Plus I ain't here for the money anyway. I'm only doing this shit as a favor for Sa. Everything I make, I give it to him," Jamal explained.

Kiree stood close to Jamal. "We know why you're really out here, 'Mal. And trust me when I tell you, we can help you with that. Just say the word and it's done." Jamal looked at Kiree confused and Kiree nodded at him. Jamal wasn't sure how to respond so he decided to stay quiet. Kiree slapped him a handshake when he noticed El and Shaheed watching them. "I heard that cut your girl did with Trinity. That shit was like that."

"Thanks yo," Jamal replied.

"Roll with us, 'Mal. I'm telling you, it's all good on our end," D-Ball said as they began walking away.

"Yeah alright," Jamal laughed him off.

El, not catching the whole conversation, misinterpreted what Jamal said. He thought Jamal was agreeing to sell for them. He and his brother argued about it for a moment.

"How the fuck do you know what he meant?" El argued.

"Look, shut the fuck up. You swear you're tough. Samir said Jamal knows better. Obviously he knows what he's talking about. Squash it. I put everything I make on what Sa said. You better chill and worry about yourself. And don't even think about fucking with Jamal because Sa is gonna fuck with you." El quieted down to make his brother believe that he was going to obey what he said, but he had other plans.

That Friday night, Samir told Jamal to watch his house while he went out to handle some business. He let him know he would be gone for the most part of the day and to not let anyone in even if they were dropping off money because he already let his workers know he wouldn't be home. Samir wasn't to be expected until 12:30am or 1am.

El had been watching Jamal's every move despite his brother's warning. He was outside of Samir's house waiting for Jamal to come out. El didn't care what his brother said about leaving Jamal alone. He figured stupidly that taking Jamal out would be a load off Samir's shoulders and that Samir would've wanted it that way.

Jamal talked to Tamera for the most part of the night. She convinced him to come back to his uncle's house so they could be together. After agreeing and hanging up with her, he heated up some Chinese food to eat and then fell asleep on the couch while watching an old comedy.

Sometime after midnight, Samir called him on his cell-phone.

"Hello," Jamal said with the sound of sleep distorting his voice.

"You were sleep or something?" Samir asked.

"Yeah, I'm up now." He looked at his watch. "Yo, where you at? It's almost one o'clock in the morning. I got'sta roll. I promised my girl I would come see her."

"Nigga, cool your heels. It's only 12:30am. I just called to tell you I'ma be later than I said and to go ahead and do whatever it is that you were gonna do, alright?" Samir told him. "And yo, make sure you lock my shit up tight. And don't fall asleep behind the wheel."

"Alright," Jamal said and then hung up the phone. He stood up and stretched and then cleaned up whatever he messed up. He checked every window and door to make sure that the house was sealed tight. Then he grabbed his keys, set the alarm and locked the door behind him when he left.

Jamal got inside of the car and started to his uncle's house not seeing El following behind him. Half way to Ridge and Midvale Avenues near

Fairmount Park, Jamal noticed that a car had been trailing him, staying two cars behind him. He didn't know who it was but he didn't like the idea of being followed. He took his gun out and sat it next to him. He pulled into a section of Fairmount Park that no one ever went to because it was deserted and El followed behind him. Jamal got out of his car and dipped behind some trees making sure he stayed in the shadows and out of the light. He checked quietly to make sure his gun had a clip in it.

"I don't believe this shit is happening," Jamal mumbled to himself. A car pulled up next to his and the person got out. Because of how dark it was, Jamal couldn't tell who the person was. When the person stepped into a shade of light and Jamal saw that it was El, he let out a sigh of relief.

"Got-damn El," Jamal said partially coming from behind the tree. "You scared the shit outta me. What the hell are you doing here?" Jamal asked. El pointed his gun at him and he jumped back behind the tree where he was hiding just as the gun went off.

"What the fuck are you doing?!!" Jamal shrieked.

"I'm not trying to have you coming around fucking up me and Sa's operation. I know you're fucking with the competition so I'ma bang your bitch-ass," El replied.

"What the fuck are you talking about? Wait a minute, Sa set me up?!" Jamal assumed as he looked around wildly for another place to duck.

"Naw nigga, this is all me. I knew you were going to come in here trying to fuck the game up." Jamal dipped behind another tree while El was running his mouth speaking of grandeur and glory once he was out of the way. "You must ain't know who you were fucking with."

"Pussy, I don't think you know who you're fucking with," Jamal growled.

El had no idea that Jamal had a gun with him as well. He peeped behind the first tree he saw Jamal run behind. "Think of it this way, it was bound to happen eventually."

He turned around and Jamal punched him in his jaw. As soon as he staggered back, Jamal shot him in his chest, making him drop his gun. He lunged forward so Jamal shot him again. El fell into Jamal, grabbing his shirt. Shock and pain was written across his face making Jamal feel slightly remorseful. Not wanting to leave any fingerprints, he let El slide to the ground and then took a step back, trembling. He looked around and then wiped his hands on his shirt where he felt El's blood on him. He darted over to his car and drove away slowly to his uncle's house.

When Jamal arrived, he looked around to make sure no one was nearby and could see him as he crept into his uncle's house. He snuck up to Tamera's bedroom, happy that she had already gone to bed. He grabbed a towel and then looked around for his sweat pants. He couldn't see anything and ended up hitting his knee on the side of the dresser just as he was turning a lamp on. He cursed, waking up Tamera.

"Baby, is that you?" she asked sounding sleepy.

"Yeah, go back to sleep." He had his back to her so she couldn't see the blood on his shirt. He cursed himself for not taking it off before he came in her room.

"What's wrong?" she asked.

"Nothing, I'ma go take a shower," Jamal told her.

Tamera got out of the bed and started over to him. She sensed something was wrong and tried to turn him around so she could see his face, but he didn't move. She still saw the blood on his shirt and some of it got on her hands. She looked at them in horror and then looked at Jamal.

"It wasn't my fault." Jamal began to explain.

"What wasn't your fault? What happened? Tell me this ain't what I think it is on my hands, Jamal. Tell me this shit ain't blood," Tamera said sounding as though she was two seconds away from screaming.

"Calm down and let me explain. I was coming home from Samir's house and I noticed somebody was following me. Turns out that it was this nigga El that works for Samir. He tried to kill me claiming that I was messing with the competition but I'm not," Jamal explained.

"So you killed him?" Tamera assumed.

"I didn't have a choice. If I didn't put him down, you wouldn't be talking to me now."

Tamera put the back of her hands to her face and broke down in tears. Jamal put his arms around her and pulled her close to him. "Baby, I'm sorry. But I didn't have a choice."

"Well what now? What's gonna happen now? Won't they find out?" Tamera asked.

"Most likely, Samir is going to call everybody in tomorrow when he finds out that El is dead so I'ma get my uncle to clean the gun and give me one of his clips because he has the same gun. We've got less than a month and it'll all be over." He kissed her on her forehead. "Help me get cleaned up."

Tamera sniffed and nodded her head.

Jamal took his clothes off and she took them from him. "You want me to throw these in the trash?" she asked.

"No, because if the cops come and check through our garbage they'll find them. Since that's a white tee, bleach and some detergent should do. For the jeans… just put some detergent on them and scrub a little."

"Okay." Tamera left the room and went into the basement.

Jamal went into the bathroom and took a long, hot shower. He was hoping that this wouldn't cause any problems for him in the near future. He was just now getting out of debt with Samir for killing Khalil, he didn't want to be in debt with Samir for killing El nor did he want any static from the other guys.

A THUG'S REDEMPTION

When he finished in the shower, he toweled himself off, got dressed and made his way down to the basement to make sure Tamera was okay. He stood at the bottom of the steps and stared at her as she leaned into the dryer, picking her nails. He walked behind her and put his arms around her, making her jump. He shushed her and kissed the side of her mouth. He rubbed her hands and they stayed down there until his clothes were done. The blood stains were out of the t-shirt but it was a little faded in the jeans.

"Don't worry about it," he told her. They took his clothes up to his room and went to bed.

Jamal thought he wouldn't be able to sleep but as soon as his head hit the pillow he was out like a light.

Shawn woke him up the next morning and Jamal went straight to his uncle. He explained the situation to them both and his uncle agreed to help him out.

"I told you in situations like this, you always lose something. You're lucky you ain't lost your life last night," his uncle told him as he was cleaning the gun. He handed him the gun and another clip. Right after Jamal got showered and dressed, his phone went off. He wasn't surprised that it was Samir.

"Hello?" he answered in his normal voice.

"Bring your ass to my house, right now," Samir said. He hung up before Jamal could respond.

"That was Samir, wasn't it?" Tamera asked.

"Yeah," he told her. She leaned up on her elbows. "By now he knows. It didn't sound like he was too pleased either." He sat next to her and kissed her. Her eyes were still closed when he looked at her.

"Promise me I won't have to leave 357 in your phone," she said, finally looking at him.

Jamal got up and started walking to the door, "I promise."

"Stay out of trouble," she told him.

Jamal nodded and left her room. He went straight to Samir's house without making any stops. When he got there, Man-Man, Shaheed, and some other workers by the name of Christian, Omar and Derrick were already waiting. Three other guys that Jamal had never seen before were there as well.

"Sit down," Samir told him. "And don't say shit."

Jamal looked around and sat next to Man-Man.

"Gimme your piece," Samir said as he held his hand out. Jamal handed him his gun and Samir smelled it. He smiled as he nodded his head. Shaheed looked at both of them wondering what that meant. He already had it made up in his mind that Jamal was behind his brother's murder and he wanted something done about it.

Samir handed Jamal back his gun after checking the clip. Jamal tucked it back in his pants.

"Now that we're all here; except for El. It seems that he had a sudden case of death," Samir said to his workers. Shaheed eyeballed Jamal like he wanted to kill him on the spot. Jamal returned the same look figuring if he turned away or dropped his eyes that would be a sign of guilt. Samir noticed their stares when he looked at both of them.

"Yo, y'all got a fucking problem? Because if y'all do, y'all can take it up with me." They both looked at Samir waiting for him to finish what he had to say. "Now, I don't know what the fuck is going on, but from my understanding some of y'all got some animosity towards one another and y'all know I don't have that shit up in my house. El is dead, niggas is accusing niggas in here. I've heard Man-Man name come up…"

"Man-Man!" Man-Man hissed interrupting Samir.

"Shut the fuck up. You know better than to interrupt me. What tip are you on?" Man-Man shook his head. "Like I was saying, I've heard Man-Man's name come up. Jamal, I've heard your name come up a couple times." Jamal looked over at him. "Not one fucking word man I swear to God, I'll dig in your shit." Jamal sighed and Samir continued. "I heard a couple other names come up, too. All y'all know in here that the last thing you wanna do is fuck with me. If I find out that one of y'all had something to do with El getting killed, I'ma see to it that your body is never found. Now everybody get the fuck out. I know that El was y'all mans so chill, take the day off. Do whatever. Shaheed sit, Jamal sit. I want to talk to both of y'all." When everyone was out the house, Samir sat down and looked them over before he said anything. "Y'all got a problem?"

"He's cool with me as long as he don't come off the wrong way," Jamal replied.

"Pussy, I know you had something to do with my brother getting killed," Shaheed hissed.

"You better have proof of that shit before you pin my name to a muthafucking thing," Jamal said as he stood up.

Shaheed stood up also and it looked as if they were about to fight. "I'ma catch you one way or another and when I do, you better hope they don't be carrying your ass away in a fucking body bag like they did my little brother. Now watch."

Samir got in between them and got so close to Shaheed's face, he could smell his breath. "You ain't going to do shit. The last thing you wanna do is fuck with my family let alone threaten them. Because I'll knock your whole muthafucking family off before you can even think to apologize."

"You know he did it. And the only reason you taking up for that little punk-bitch is because he's your family."

"I think you better leave while you still got the chance before I do something I won't regret," Samir said coldly.

Shaheed walked over to the front door. "Man, fuck this shit," he said as he closed the door behind him.

"He better not had slammed my damn door." He looked at Jamal. "I know you did it."

"Man, I ain't do shit," Jamal replied as he looked Samir in his eye.

"Jamal, stop. Just stop. I smelled the gun. And I know that smell. It's the same cleaner I use whenever I need to clean one of my burners. You ain't slick. And the only reason I ain't blow your cover is for one, you're my family. No matter how much shit we get into, I would never throw you to the wolves like that. And for two, I know that El and Shaheed's been watching you and following you around. I warned him to stop that shit but he ain't listen. I knew this was going to happen. It was only a matter of time. I'm just glad you learned how to clean up after yourself, because I was tired of doing it." Samir said to his cousin.

"Just for the record, I didn't want to kill him. But like I told my girl last night, if I didn't, you wouldn't be talking to me now," Jamal replied.

"Nope. I'd be putting a bullet in both of their asses. Go home and chill."

"Alright, Samir."

A couple days after Shaheed buried his brother El, he was sitting in his living room with two of Samir's other drug dealers, Omar and Christian. Shaheed was plotting on taking Jamal out. Omar was going along with the plan because he didn't like Jamal either, but Christian was advising them otherwise.

"Fuck that!" Shaheed hissed. "I'm not going to let this nigga walk around freely after he killed my brother."

"I feel you, yo. And I'd feel the same way if it were my brother that he killed. But you know you can't fuck with nothing close to Sa. That nigga got too much heat and too much protection inside and outside of the law. Going to war with Samir is like bringing a knife to a gun fight. You can't win," Christian told him.

"I don't care no more. Shit, I'm at the point now where if I have to, I'll take Samir's ass out too. Fuck it."

"How do y'all know if Jamal even killed El?" Christian asked. "Y'all trying to do y'all plotting and shit and y'all not even sure if y'all going after the right dude."

"Man, shut the fuck up. I know Jamal did it for the simple fact that we found out he was trying to get with Kiree and them niggas from up Girard Avenue and we blew the whistle on his punk-ass. He was probably following my brother around and when he tried to lose him in Fairmount Park, Jamal must've caught him off guard and shot him. That's probably what happened," Shaheed assumed, getting the story twisted.

Yani

"From what the cops were saying, the gun they found by him was fired and he had gun powder on his hands," Christian said relaying information that he heard Samir speak on since he was the first one at the house the day Samir called the meeting.

"Look, fuck that shit, alright. Are you going to help us or what?" Shaheed asked.

Christian frowned as he looked at them both knowing it was a bad idea. He sighed and gave in. "But if y'all get caught, nigga I don't know nothing about nothing."

Tamera's music video with Trinity came on BET. Omar looked at Shaheed and smiled. "Ain't this Jamal's girlfriend?"

"Yeah, I heard that bitch got a record deal and she was in New York doing an album or some shit. Why?"

Omar rubbed his chin. "Ain't she pregnant by him?"

"What the fuck does that got to do with what we're talking about?" Shaheed snapped.

"Listen, everybody knows not to fuck with Samir or his family because they're just as dead as the next nigga if they do. Everybody also knows that Jamal would die before he would let something happen to his girl or his brother, Shawn. You can't touch Shawn without Samir touching you. What does Samir normally do when he needs to make somebody suffer?"

Shaheed caught on to what Omar was saying. "Knock off the one thing that he loves the most… Tamera."

"Pay back's a bitch," Omar grinned as he slapped Shaheed a handshake.

"Wait a minute," Christian said. "That's a female and she ain't got shit to do with this."

"Chris, won't you stop being a bitch for once in your life," Shaheed told him.

"Naw fuck that. You can do this shit by yourself." Christian got up and started walking to the door.

"Go ahead. But if you open your mouth to anybody about this thing right here, you better hope somebody tries to save your monkey-ass," Shaheed threatened. Christian looked at the both of them and then left the house.

Shaheed and Omar began to plot and scheme on how to get Tamera and when to get her. Shaheed realized that the reason Jamal was constantly driving to Uptown was to see Tamera. He looked in his glove box and took out the address that he wrote down one of the nights that he and El followed Jamal up there. They were going to keep an eye on that house from now on. Shaheed wanted the hit done by August 15th."

That next Tuesday, August 14th, Jamal spent the entire day with

Tamera since he didn't get to see her on her birthday because she was in New York filming the music video with Trinity as well as for her first single *Stay with me*. He tried to fix her some spaghetti for dinner since he knew that was her favorite dish, but the pot caught on fire. He put the fire out and then frowned as Tamera made fun of him.

She kissed him and then giggled. "I think we better order out," she suggested as she led him by the hand to the living room.

Jamal flipped through the menus that his uncle had lying around the house to different restaurants. "What do you want to eat?" Jamal asked her.

"Chinese is cool; the usual beef and broccoli."

"You and that damn Chinese food," Jamal teased. He made the phone call and ordered their food. While they waited, they talked about her CD, what they were going to do when the baby arrived, and what part of the city they wanted to live in. Jamal ran his fingers through her hair and rubbed her neck. Tamera closed her eyes always liking when he did that.

The delivery man came with their food and they sat down to eat, talking and laughing. Jamal cleaned up everything when they were done and they went up to her room she slept in. He lay on the bed and Tamera lay on his chest as they listened to her CD. Jamal reached into the night table draw and pulled out a black box. He opened it and then slipped the ring he gave her for her 17th birthday onto her finger.

"Remember this?" he asked. Tamera looked at her hand and smiled. "Thought I forgot about it, didn't you? I still want you to have it. But not just as my girl. I want you as my wife," Jamal asked nervously.

"Jamal…" Tamera whispered as she looked at him.

"I know we're young and no I'm not just asking you because you're carrying my baby. And even though you won't tell me, I know you love me. And I love you more than anything. I meant it when I said you were it for me. And if it's the ring, we can get another one…" Jamal rambled.

Tamera shushed him. "Yes babe. Yes I will. You're it for me too," she said softly.

"You will?" Jamal asked again. Tamera nodded her head. Jamal kissed her passionately. Tamera was the only woman for him and he knew it. Not too many women would have ridden with him throughout the madness that went on during the summer. But Tamera hung by his side and never left. No other woman could possibly fill her shoes.

They kissed and caressed each other as Jamal started to undress her. He made love to her with more passion than he ever did since they became intimate with each other.

The next morning, Jamal and Tamera took a shower together. He washed her hair and then helped her out of the shower so she wouldn't fall and hurt herself. They went back to her room and she sat on her bed with her robe on. She ran her fingers through her wet hair as she watched Jamal get dressed.

"You're still coming with me to get the ultrasound, right?" Tamera asked.

"Yeah, I'm coming," Jamal told her. He stared at her through the dresser mirror and at that moment, he realized just how beautiful she was. Not only was she going to be the mother of his child, but soon she would be his wife. "How come you're not getting dressed?" he asked her.

"Because I feel like watching you," Tamera grinned.

Jamal sat his shirt on the back of a chair and playfully pushed her on the bed. He looked at her and they began to kiss. He felt her stomach and was about to kiss it when he received a text message in his cell phone. Tamera looked at him smiling.

"Hold up," he said as he leaned up to look at his phone. It was a message from Samir telling him to meet him on 26th and Cecil B. Moore at 3:30pm. When Tamera saw his facial expression, her smile faded.

"What's wrong?" she asked.

Jamal hooked the cell-phone back to the pocket of his shorts and stood up.

"I've gotta go meet Samir down North Philly."

Tamera leaned her head back onto the pillow, disappointed. "I thought you said he gave you the day off so you could come to the doctor's with me."

"He did, but I guess something came up," Jamal told her as he pulled his white beater over his head.

"You haven't been to any of my doctor's appointments this summer, Jamal. This one is really important."

"I know baby, and I'm sorry." He tried to kiss her but she turned her face away from him. "I'll make the next one, I promise."

"That's what you said last time," Tamera moped.

"I said I was sorry," he turned her face back to his. "I'm going to make it up to you, I promise. I'll just have Shawn go with you one more time." He kissed her briefly. "Alright, Snickers."

Tamera sighed, "Alright. But don't go making promises that you can't keep."

Jamal grabbed his white t-shirt and pulled it over his head. "You know me better than that." He went into Shawn's room. "I need you to do me a favor."

"What's that?" Shawn asked.

"I need you to go with Tammy to the doctors today. I was going to go but Samir just texted me and told me to meet him down Cecil B. Moore Ave," Jamal explained.

"Alright," Shawn agreed.

"I'ma use Uncle Norm's car so you can drive yours, alright?"

"Okay," Shawn replied.

Jamal tossed him the keys. "Good looking out, yo."

After Jamal got the okay from his uncle to use his car, he went back to Tamera's room. She was writing in her diary. He sat next to her and tried to take a peek but she closed it.

"Aw, I can't see it?" Jamal asked.

"Not now. You better wait until I'm not around and then try to sneak and read it. That's the only way you'll find out what I really think of you."

"Why don't you just tell me?" Jamal asked as he kissed her ear. Tamera giggled and he got up. "I gotta go, boo." Tamera watched him walk to the door. "We're finding out what we're having today, right?"

"Yeah, Chase if it's a boy, Destiny if it's a girl," Tamera told him.

Jamal kissed his two fingers and pointed them at her. He opened the door to leave when suddenly Tamera's heart ached for him.

"Jamal," she called to him. He turned around and looked at her. "I love you."

He looked at her strangely. "You know, that's the first time you ever told me that besides that time I got shot."

"But you know I always meant it."

"I know. And it's about damn time. I love you, too," Jamal told her.

Tamera smiled and watched him leave the room. She felt a shudder and closed her eyes. A flash came to her where she briefly felt like she was being knocked back onto the ground. She jerked her eyes open and shook her head. She started to ask Jamal not to go, but figured since he only had five days left, they made it this far, they can make it to the end.

"Alright, Shawn," Jamal said as he made his way down the steps.

"Alright, Jamal," Shawn replied.

Jamal left the house and got into his uncle's car. He didn't notice Shaheed and Omar sitting in a car across the street.

Tamera got dressed a little while after Jamal left and she and Shawn drove to Hahnemann Hospital for her doctor's appointment with Shaheed and Omar following behind them.

Tamera's God Mother never opened the envelope that had Tamera's CD in it because it didn't have a return address on it. She was cleaning off her tables as she finished packing for her move to New York when she came across the envelope and decided to open it. She gasped when she saw Tamera's CD inside. She read what Tamera signed.

"To the lady that came close to being my real mother: Thank you for loving me when it felt like no one else did. You were my backbone when times were tough and I love you. I'm almost there. I love you, and I hope that you enjoy. Love, Tammy."

Tamera's God mother put the CD in her CD player and listened to it with tears in her eyes. She picked up the phone and called Deisha's house. Michelle answered the phone.

"Hello," Michelle spoke as she filed her nails.

"Hi, can I speak to Tamera?"

Yani

"Tamera isn't here, would you like to leave a message?"

"Could you tell her that her God mother Tina called? I just opened her CD. Tell her that when she isn't busy to give me a call. She sounds beautiful and I am so proud of her," Tina gushed.

"Sure thing," Michelle said, puzzled.

"Thank you," Tina said before hanging up.

Michelle hung up the phone and thought for a moment. When everything became clear, she called Deisha downstairs.

"Yes," Deisha said when she got to the bottom of the steps.

"I just got a phone call from Tamera's God mother wanting to speak to Tammy. Now unless she has more than one God mother, somebody better tell me what the hell is going on right now." Deisha knew they were caught and was at a loss for words. "Where the hell is she?!" Michelle yelled.

"Jamal got into some trouble with his cousin and he came and got Tamera in the middle of the night and took her to his uncle's because he didn't want anything to happen to her or Shawn. We didn't tell you because we didn't want you to call the cops and make things worse," Deisha rambled.

"So, Jamal is selling drugs again. You mean to tell me that y'all done got so grown that when trouble stirs up, y'all can just run my house? She's pregnant and you let her walk out of here?! Suppose something happens to her, Deisha? What the hell were you thinking?" Deisha sniffed and wiped her face. "Where is she?" Michelle asked again.

"She's in Uptown," Deisha told her.

"And all this time the both of you were lying to me. You knew damn well she wasn't at her God mother's house and every time I asked about her, the lies just kept running out. Do you have the phone number?"

"It's upstairs," Deisha replied.

"Go give it to me." Deisha went up to her room, knowing that they were caught but praying that nothing would happen since Jamal only had five days left to work for Samir.

Jamal was on the corner of 26th and Cecil B. Moore sitting in the car, listening to some music and waiting for Samir. He looked at his watch and saw it was 3:38PM. He tapped the wheel and sighed as he nodded his head to the beat of a song that was on the radio. He began to get tired of waiting for Samir so he decided to drive around the block to kill time, hoping that he would be there when he got back. He saw Man-Man when he got back to his original parking spot.

"Yo Man-Man," Jamal spoke.

"What's up, Mal?" Man-Man spoke back.

"Nothing man, yo did you see Samir around?"

"Naw," Man-Man shook his head.

"Well if you do, tell him I'm out here waiting for him."

"Alright, I'll keep an eye out for him." Man-Man told him as he walked away. Jamal looked at his watch. It was 3:52PM. He sighed and waited some more. He told himself that if Samir wasn't out there by 4PM, he was going to drive to his house.

Tamera was getting her ultra-sound done and was very excited. She couldn't wait to find out what she and Jamal were having. Dr. Jefferson adjusted the screen so they could see the sex.

"Well Tamera, it looks like you are having a girl," Dr. Jefferson told her. "Congratulations."

"Destiny," Tamera said as she smiled and then chuckled to herself.

"What was that?" Dr. Jefferson asked.

"Oh, Jamal and I picked out names and we said that if we had a girl, we would name her Destiny," Tamera explained.

"Oh, that's sweet. Let me print these for you. I'll be right back."

Tamera fixed her clothes after she wiped the jelly from her stomach. Shawn looked at the screen more closely. "No offense, but y'all baby got a big ass head," he joked.

Tamera smacked his arm. "You block head, that's her body. And don't be talking about my baby, punk." They laughed together.

"My bad," Shawn laughed. Dr. Jefferson came back with the pictures from Tamera's ultrasound and they looked at them for a moment before putting them in the envelope.

"Okay Tammy, your next appointment is the second Tuesday in September. Do you have any questions or is there anything that you need?"

"No, but thanks a lot, Dr. Jefferson," Tamera smiled. She and Shawn left the hospital. They were walking down the street to his car still looking at the pictures and talking, not noticing that Omar and Shaheed were in a car slowly driving up behind them.

Jamal was getting pissed off. It was ten minutes after four and there was still no sign of Samir. He drove over to his house and knocked on the door.

Samir opened the door angrily. "Nigga don't be banging on my got-damn door like you're the fucking law. What do you want?"

"I was on 26th and Cecil B. Moore waiting for you for over a half hour. Why did you leave me out there?" Jamal asked as he came inside.

"What are you talking about? If you wanted to see me, why you ain't let me know you were going to be up there? Better yet, you should've just came by the house. I thought you were with your girl today anyway," Samir replied.

"Wait a minute; you ain't leave a text message in my phone?" Jamal asked, puzzled.

"What the fuck am I going to leave you a text message for when I told you to go with your girl to the doctor's?"

"I got a text message in my phone telling me to meet you on 26th and Cecil B. Moore at 3:30PM," Jamal explained.

"I didn't text you, Jamal…"

While Jamal was on his way to Samir's house, Tamera felt a shudder. A flash came to her, and then another flash but she couldn't make them out.

"What's wrong?" Shawn asked her.

"I just had a sudden case of déjà vu." She shrugged her shoulders. "Oh well." She dropped her ultra-sound pictures accidentally. "Could you pass me that?" she asked Shawn.

Shawn bent over and past her the ultra sound pictures. He then dropped his keys. Just as he was getting ready to bend over and pick them up, Tamera made eye contact with Omar and Shaheed. The expression on their faces let her know that they were bad news. Her heart began to race wildly and everything seemed to move in slow motion as an odd sound of children playing began to get louder and louder by the second. By the time the memory of her dream and the flashes she periodically had, came back to her to warn her, Shaheed fired the first bullet but missed. Shawn jumped and grabbed Tamera's shirt, trying to pull her to the ground but his hand slipped twice. The second time his hand slipped, Shaheed shot her in the chest. Tamera staggered back and he shot her in the stomach. Blood splattered on Shawn's face. She doubled over and then dropped to the ground.

The only thing Shawn heard were tires screeching as a car sped off and a few bystanders screaming. He scrambled over to Tamera and turned her over. There was blood everywhere. She was breathing heavy, crying and wheezing. She placed a hand on her stomach and looked at it, looking as if she was going to scream.

"Hold on, Tammy. Just hold on! Somebody call the fucking ambulance!!" Shawn screamed.

"Call… Jamal…" Tamera struggled to say the words as blood spilled from her mouth.

"Shhh!" Shawn said. "He's going to be here just hold on, please," Shawn begged with tears in his eyes.

"Don't let me die like this, Shawn… please…" Tamera begged as she squeezed his hand and struggled to breathe. "Oh God, my baby… Destiny…" The tears spilled from her eyes as she tried to look.

"You're not, Tammy. You're not. You just gotta hold on. SOMEBODY PLEASE!! SOMEBODY HELP ME!!!" Shawn screamed. He buried his face in her hand as she squeezed it. "Please hold on, Tammy."

Tamera mumbled again and again for him not to let her die. Each time her words became softer and softer. Shawn cried harder when he felt her grip weaken.

"Don't go, Tammy! Please don't go. You can't go, you can't!" Shawn begged and cried.

With the hospital nearby, the ambulance got there in record time.

"She's shot in her chest and in her stomach and she's pregnant. You gotta do something fast man, she can't die yo… she…" Shawn felt weak and helpless. He promised his brother that he would protect Tamera and he didn't want to fail. He didn't want to break that promise.

"Son, we're gonna have to ask you to step back so we can do our job. We promise we'll do everything that we can." They loaded Tamera into the ambulance and started working on her. Shawn tried to climb in with her but the paramedic stopped him. "Son, I'm sorry but only family can ride back here."

"That's my brother's girlfriend and she's carrying his baby!" Shawn yelled.

"I'm sorry, but that's policy." They closed the doors in his face. Shawn looked inside to see what he could see. He saw Tamera's arm slide over the side of the stretcher. He closed his eyes and sighed deeply. He then picked up her ultra sound pictures from off of the ground. He started sobbing as he wiped the blood from them. He picked up Tamera's purse and took her phone out. He didn't have the heart to tell his brother that he failed. He texted Jamal, telling him to get to Hahnemann Hospital as soon as possible with 357 on the end. Then he walked back over to the hospital before the cops had a chance to question him.

Jamal was still at Samir's house trying to sort out who left him the message.

"I want to know who the fuck left me the message. I don't have time for this shit. I had plans," Jamal ranted.

"Look, calm down. It's probably a mix up," Samir told him just as Jamal's phone went off. Jamal looked at it.

"Fuck!" he yelled. He ran out of the house and jumped into the car before Samir could ask him what the problem was.

Jamal drove to the hospital praying that things weren't as bad as he was thinking. When he got to the ER, he saw Shawn sitting in a chair with his hands folded to his face, leaning on his knees.

"Shawn!" Jamal called to him as he started walking his way. Shawn looked up at him. His eyes were blood shot red almost matching the stains on his shirt. Jamal too felt a moment of déjà vu as his dream came back to him as well. He didn't want to believe what he was seeing. "Where's… where's Tammy?" he asked.

Shawn became choked up again as he tried to get the words out. "I tried to protect her, Jamal. I swear to God I did."

"What are you talking about, Shawn? Where's my girl?! Where's my baby?!" he asked frantically.

"She's... they killed her, Jamal. We were on our way to the car... and they shot her."

Jamal broke down in uncontrollable sobs almost falling onto the floor. Shawn grabbed onto him and held him up as Jamal cried like a baby in his arms. When he partially had himself together, he went over to a nearby doctor.

"They just brought my fiancée in here. She was shot and my brother just told me that she's dead. Is there any way I can see her? I just want to be sure," Jamal said as the tears spilled from his eyes.

"What's her name?" the doctor asked him.

"Tamera Harrison." Jamal told him.

"Right this way," the doctor led him to the room and Jamal went in. He immediately fell to his knees when he got over to her and pulled the sheet from over her face. He grabbed her hand and put his face there after he slid the ring from off of her finger, apologizing over and over for breaking his promise of protecting her and prayed that she could hear him.

Shawn called Maurice from the waiting room. He answered on the second ring.

"Yo!" Maurice spoke into the phone.

"Maurice," Shawn said softly.

"Yeah, who's this?"

"It's Shawn, man."

"What's up, nigga? Why do you sound like that?" Maurice asked.

Shawn took a deep breath as the tears started to come again.

"Tammy... she's dead, man. They killed her right in front of me, Mar. They killed her right in front of me." Shawn started sobbing again.

"You're lying, man! You're fucking lying, yo! Tell me you're lying," Maurice said as his heart raced.

"She begged me not to let her die and it wasn't nothing I could do. I know Samir did this shit, man. I know he did. Fuck family. He's gonna feel this shit, I swear to God. Jamal only had five more days, man, he ain't had to do this shit, man," Shawn ranted.

"Calm down, man. Does Jamal know?" Maurice asked him.

"I just told him," Shawn replied.

"Where is he?"

"He's in the room they put her in after they pronounced her dead. Can you tell Deisha and Chanda? I just told Jamal and I don't think I can handle them, too."

"I got you, homie. Don't worry about it. Go take care of your brother. Keep an eye on him. Make sure he don't do anything stupid. Both of y'all just chill for a minute." Shawn didn't respond. "I'm serious, man. Don't do shit." Maurice said firmly.

"I hear you," Shawn replied.

Maurice hung up the phone but waited a few minutes before he called Deisha.

"Hello," Deisha answered when Maurice finally got the courage to dial the number.

"What are you doing?" Maurice asked without saying hello.

"I'm panicking like a muthafucka. My aunt knows Tamera is staying with Jamal and his uncle and that Jamal is selling again. She don't know he killed Khalil but she's been calling over there all day and ain't nobody answering. Why? What's up?" Deisha said quickly.

"I need you to sit down for me, Deisha."

"Why?" Deisha asked. Maurice didn't answer her so she sat on the side of her bed. "I'm sitting."

"Shawn just called me and told me that somebody killed Tamera not too long ago when they were coming from her ultrasound."

Before Maurice could finish what he was saying Deisha began screaming.

"Deisha, calm down... Deisha." Maurice was saying. Somehow they got disconnected. Maurice hung up the phone and put his hands to his face, crying. He always knew in the back of his mind that this was going to end badly. But he prayed like hell that he was wrong. Maurice had a bad feeling that this was going to send Jamal over the edge.

Jamal was pissed. Three nights after Tamera was killed, he grabbed his gun and went to Samir's house. When Samir opened the door, Jamal pushed him inside and pushed him on top of a table. He put the gun under his chin.

"Pussy, you set me up!" Jamal said, practically growling in Samir's face.

"What the...?" Samir said as he was caught off guard.

"Shut the fuck up!" Jamal said, cutting him off. "You set me up. You distracted me to get to my girl. You killed her and my fucking daughter. Not to mention you killed my muthafucking father. I should waste your faggot-ass right now."

"Jamal, I ain't kill your girl. I ain't had anything to do with it. Somebody ordered a hit in here without my permission. If you want to know who, I suggest you get that gun out of my face." Jamal looked at Samir breathing heavily. It was tempting as all hell to blow Samir away. He slowly pulled the gun from him instead and stood up. "You put another gun to my fucking face and your girl will be meeting you at the gates. Put that shit away," Samir ordered.

"Somebody put a hit out on my girl and I want to know who and I want to know why!" Jamal said angrily.

"Yeah and they're fucking with the wrong one because now they got me to deal with. Not only did they set you up, but they tried to make it look like I had something to do with it."

"Who was it?" Jamal asked.

"I ain't going to tell you. Why? So you can go out and plot your revenge like with Khalil? No, you're going to go to college and make something out of yourself. Give this street life up because it ain't doing you any good. I'll handle this one. I feel like I owe you anyway."

"You don't owe me Sa," Jamal said sadly.

"That might be true. But this one, I'ma do for you. Go home and get some sleep."

Jamal rubbed his hands across his tired and sad face. He felt empty inside like a piece of him died with Tamera and their daughter. He turned and walked to the door.

"Mal, I'm sorry about your girl and I'm sorry about your daughter." Jamal didn't say anything. "You're not going to go after anyone, are you?" Samir asked.

Jamal looked at Samir as he hugged himself. "I thought I'd let you handle it." He left Samir's house and closed the door behind him.

The next day, Deisha was in Tamera's room. Jamal dropped off the stuff that she left at his uncle's house. Everything except the ring that he retrieved and her diary was there. Deisha cried as she packed away Tamera's things so they could go to the Good Will. She started to strip the wall of Tamera's posters but decided not to, wanting to leave things just the way she had left them the last time she slept in that room. She sat down on Tamera's bed and covered her face as she sobbed loudly. She thought back to all of the times they shared together in that room, the tears they shed together and the arguments they had. Tamera had a trophy on her dresser from a singing contest that she won back in the 9th grade. She also had the extra pictures that Greg took of her. Just as Deisha began to look through the pictures, Power 99FM began playing her first single *Stay with me*. Deisha broke down and started crying harder.

One of the DJs started talking when the song went off. "That was Philly's own Tammy aka Tamera Harrison. She was discovered by Greg Townsend from Philly International Records. Sadly, she was shot and killed a few days ago. She had just turned 18 and if I remember correctly, she was six months pregnant at the time. You know, the violence needs to stop. It has to. Stop the violence people. Coming up, we have new music from Nelly, Aaliyah and more. Don't touch that dial."

Deisha wiped her face and stood up. She began packing up more of Tamera's belongings when she came across a photo album. She flipped through it as she reminisced on their school years at University City High School.

Tamera's memorial service as well as the funeral made the news. After they spoke on it, Shaheed's and Omar's pictures appeared. Apparently they had been missing for the past 36 hours. Some reporters stated that unidentified witnessed alleged they were the ones who gunned down Tamera. Samir came through for Jamal just as he said he would because their bodies were never found.

A week after Tamera's funeral, Jamal quit his job in the Gallery and packed up his things to go to college, which had changed from Cheyney to West Chester University. He used part of the money Tamera left in their account to expunge his record. He made a last minute change to his major from business to criminal justice. He made up in his mind that it would be a long time before he came back to that neighborhood.

Shawn had already packed up his things to move to Georgetown's Campus. He was going to be a Hoya and was hell bent on realizing his dream of making it to the NBA. Jamal was zipping his duffle bag when Shawn knocked on his door.

"Yo," Jamal answered solemnly.

"What's up, Jamal?" Shawn said as he came into the room. Jamal didn't say anything. Shawn looked around. Just about everything in his room was gone. His dresser was cleared as well as his closet. The room was completely empty besides his bed and dresser. Shawn looked in the trashcan and saw that there were torn pictures of Jamal and Tamera in there. "Don't you want to keep some memories?" he asked.

Jamal looked at a picture he had blown up of him and his friends on graduation day and then looked at one of Tamera's ultrasound photos. "That's one hundred and some odd memories that I don't want or need." He put his other pictures in his bag. "This is enough."

"Pretending y'all never existed ain't gonna help none," Shawn told him.

"Remembering is only making it worse." He looked at Tamera's diary that he kept. "I had just asked her to marry me and she said yes. Everything was so right with her in my life." Jamal sniffed and shook his head. "I read her diary. She must've known she was about to die because she left a note in the back for me to always keep this with me. All she wrote about was us. Even when we broke up, all she wrote about was how much she loved me and how she could never love another person the way she loved me. She made me promise that she wouldn't have to leave 357 in my phone. All she asked me for was that, my time, my attention and my love and I couldn't even give her that much. I never even understood why she stayed with me."

"You just answered your own question," Shawn told him.

Jamal coughed and wiped his face. He put Tamera's diary in his book bag and then put it on. He grabbed one of his duffle bags and a box. "Carry that down for me?" he asked Shawn as he nodded to another duffle bag and box.

Shawn grabbed them and they started downstairs. "Mommy's probably crying her eyes out like, 'Aw, my babies are leaving me'." Jamal chuckled at his brother's imitation of their mother. Shawn hadn't heard him laugh or seen him smile since before Tamera had been killed.

They sat Jamal's things in the back of the car Jamal bought. He used another part of the money Tamera left along with the money he saved up from working at the Gallery and with Samir to get an apartment. When they came back in, their mother hugged the both of them.

"Even though I don't want you to go, I'm proud of both of you." Her and Shawn walked Jamal to his car. "You be careful."

"I will," Jamal told her.

"And don't let things get you so down that you can barely get back up. God'll take care of everything," Ms. Keyona said speaking of Tamera's death. Jamal nodded his head and she hugged him. "It's a reason why you changed your major to criminal justice. You know what you need to do."

Jamal blinked back his tears and then hugged his younger brother.

"Alright, Jamal," Shawn said as he patted his brother on the back.

"Alright, Shawn." Jamal got into his car and drove away. Ms. Keyona waved as her son's car disappeared down the street. She went in the house. Shawn stayed out a little longer.

Jamal stopped off at Maurice's house to say goodbye. Maurice was headed to Immaculata University to study Engineering. After visiting him, for some strange reason, Jamal stopped at Deisha's house.

"Hey!" Deisha said, shocked to see Jamal pull up. She was sitting on the porch enjoying her last night in Philly before she headed to Immaculata also, to study Child Psychology. "I didn't expect to see you again." She stood up to give him a hug when he came onto the porch.

"I'm not going to stay long. I just came to say goodbye," Jamal told her. Deisha didn't respond. She put her hands in her back pocket and leaned into the gate. "I know you uh, you probably still blame me for Raheem getting killed and you probably hate me because of Tamera..." he stopped himself as he fought off the tears. "Look, I just came by to say that I'm so sorry about Raheem and I'm sorry about Tamera."

Deisha stopped him. "Jamal, I don't hate you. Back then I was being stupid. I thought Raheem was all I had when all along you guys were with me through so much. I know you loved Tamera with all your heart. You were supposed to be together even if it wasn't for as long as you both wanted. Look at how she changed your life." She hugged Jamal again and rubbed his back. "Good luck in college. If you need to talk, just holla at me. I'm here for you," Deisha told him.

"Thanks," Jamal said as he hugged her back. He let her go and got back into his car, driving over to Penn's Landing. He went over to a spot where hardly anyone was standing and pulled out the gun that Samir gave to him. He looked down at it and something that his uncle told him came back to him. *"Eventually you will pay for your sins. Karma doesn't miss. It doesn't always hit you directly… Mistakes are hard to clean up because you always lose something in the process".* Jamal shook his head and then furiously threw the gun a few yards into the water. He looked on for a little while and then got into his car and drove away to his new apartment, hoping to start a new life.

EPILOGUE
TAMERA'S LAST ENTRY

August 15, 2002 Wednesday 1:25pm

Today is the big day! I finally find out what Jamal and I are having. I'm so excited. Too bad Jamal can't be there, once again. His cousin wants him to meet him on 26th and Cecil B. Moore Avenue, so he's sending Shawn to go with me. Shawn has been such a big help since all of this started and I'm grateful for that. I really am. But it's not the same. I really wanted Jamal to be there so he could see the baby... our baby. I love how that sounds. I love that man so much it's hard to imagine sometimes. I never knew I could love a person the way that I love him. Here he come's now...

(A little while later) Punk. He tried to read you. (Giggle) I just told him to wait until I'm not around and then he can sneak and read you and find out what I really think of him. (Ha ha!) He suggested I tell him. Well, when he was on his way to go out to meet his cousin, I felt this urge to tell him that I loved him. I don't think I told him before except that time he got shot but I think that was just because of the heat of the moment. I write about it all the time but I don't think I said it directly to him. I'm glad I said it today. I should've said it last night when he asked me to marry him. Of course I said yes!! I love that man with all my heart. Hmm, I just had this hunch to leave him a little love note...

Jamal, I love you and since I never told you I hope you read this one day and realize I do. Words can't express what you mean to me. And even though I never said it, I meant it and felt it every day. If something were to happen to me, I just have one request: keep this by your side and never forget the love I have for you... always.

I'm out... Peace

www.ingramcontent.com/pod-product-compliance
Lightning Source LLC
Chambersburg PA
CBHW020300010526
44108CB00037B/233